The Cosmopolitan Cook and Recipe Book

You are holding a reproduction of an original work that is in the public domain in the United States of America, and possibly other countries. You may freely copy and distribute this work as no entity (individual or corporate) has a copyright on the body of the work. This book may contain prior copyright references, and library stamps (as most of these works were scanned from library copies). These have been scanned and retained as part of the historical artifact.

This book may have occasional imperfections such as missing or blurred pages, poor pictures, errant marks, etc. that were either part of the original artifact, or were introduced by the scanning process. We believe this work is culturally important, and despite the imperfections, have elected to bring it back into print as part of our continuing commitment to the preservation of printed works worldwide. We appreciate your understanding of the imperfections in the preservation process, and hope you enjoy this valuable book.

THE
COSMOPOLITAN
COOK AND RECIPE BOOK.

CONTAINING RECIPES FOR THE PREPARATION OF

American, French, German, English, Irish

AND OTHER NATIONAL DISHES,

BOTH COSTLY AND ECONOMICAL.

ALSO

HOUSEHOLD RECIPES,
MEDICAL RECIPES,

Rules of Health, Tables of Distances, Measures, Weights, Statistics, Etc., Etc.

———o———

COMPILED, EDITED AND PUBLISHED BY

DINGENS BROTHERS,

BUFFALO, N. Y.

———

1882.

PRINTING HOUSE OF E. H. HUTCHINSON,
12 TO 16 EAGLE STREET.

Entered according to Act of Congress, in the year 1882, by
DINGENS BROS, Buffalo, N. Y.

PREFACE.

The object of the Cosmopolitan Cook and Recipe Book is to provide the Public with a cheap but honest and practical Cook Book, containing Recipes for the preparation of dishes to suit all tastes and purses.

The compilers of this work have examined a large number of Cook Books varying in price from one to five dollars, and while they all contained *some good Recipes*, still they seemed to a great extent to be copies of each other, most generally lacked the details required to successfully produce the dish required, and frequently seemed to be intended for persons of large means only—that is, there was no attempt at economy.

The Recipes contained in this work are *practical*, Economical, *and have been tested;* many were received from families right here at home in response to an invitation, issued to the Public by the Publishers, to kindly send us recipes that were both practical and economical. How few servants possess good Cook Books, owing principally to the large price demanded for them, and yet it is in such hands that a good Cook Book would be most serviceable. No excuse now. Not only will this Book be sold at a price within the reach of all, but anyone lacking the means to purchase one will be presented with a copy upon application to the Publishers.

The Publishers do not realize the cost of this Book at the price it is sold, but the difference is made up by the sums received from the few advertisements found in the work, advertisements of Houses and articles of known merit, none other would be permitted. In addition to cooking recipes we have added many valuable ones for domestic use as well as information on subjects and questions arising daily in every household. May this Book serve the purpose for which it is issued, is the earnest wish of the Publishers,

DINGENS BROS.,
Buffalo, N. Y.

TABLE OF CONTENTS.

(For General Index see page 395.)

PART I.

	PAGE
Calendars .... Inside Front Cover	
Travelers' Guide .. Ins. Back "	
Preface	3
List of Leading Business Houses and Specialties	4 & 5
Classification	6
The Table	7
The Breakfast Table	9
The Dinner Table	10
The Tea Table	11
Duties Maid of all Work	12
The Mistress of the House	17
Widow Prudence's Story	18
Our Recipes	20
Our Guarantee	21
Milk	22
Rice	27
Farina	29
Cocoanuts	30
Jellies	33
Ice Creams, Water Ices, etc.	35
To color same	37
Maizena	41
Corn Starch	43
Eggs	49
Tomatoes	52
Cheese	54
Salt Fish	57
Hominy	61
Potatoes	62
Beans and Peas	66
Sauces for Meats	71
Sauces for Puddings, etc.	73
Meats	76
Beeves' Hearts	76
Beeves' Tripe	78
Beef Palates	79
Sheeps' Trotters	81
Hogs' Head and Feet	82
Ox Heads	84
Animals' Brains	85
Lights and Lungs	89
Kidneys	90
Haslets	92
Ox Heels	93
Pigs' Feet	94
Calves' Heads and Feet	97
Liver	100
Hams, Shoulders and Bacon	102
Tongues	104
Recipes for cooking Meats	107
Vegetables	110
Baked and boiled Puddings	115
Making and baking Cakes	121
Pastry and Pies	126
Indian Meal, Mush, Bread, Biscuits, Cakes, Puddings	132
Flour, Bread, Wheat, Rye, Barley, Corn and Oat Flour	144
Yeast Bread, etc.	145
Oysters	158
Lobsters	168
Fried Pastry, Doughnuts, etc	177
Fancy Dishes for Dessert	189
Preserves	195
Pickling Vegetables, etc.	200
Manioca	205
Jelly Ice Creams	207
Rich Ice Creams	212
Apples	217
The Sick Room	225
Household Remedies	234
Nursery Recipes	236
Various Household Recipes	237
Rates of Postage	238
Value of Foreign Money	238
Business Laws	239
Weights and Measures	240
Distances from Buffalo to the principal points of Globe	246

TABLE OF CONTENTS. (Concluded.)

PART II.

	PAGE		PAGE
Soups	260	Sauces for Meats	316
Soups from Stock	262	Vegetables	320
Soups not made from Stock	266	Omelets	323
Fish	279	Salads	324
Shell Fish, Oysters	291	Combinations	327
" Clams	293	Puddings, Custards, etc.	333
" Crabs, Lobsters	294	Sauces for Puddings	343
Terrapins, Turtles, etc.	296	Cakes for Dessert, Tea, etc.	344
Carving	297	Fancy Beverages	368
Poultry	297	To prepare Company Dinners	379
Chickens	300	Bills of Fare or Menus	381
Ducks, Geese and Game	302	Serving of Wines	383
Venison	306	Proper temperature at which	
Rabbits	307	Wines should be served	385
Meats	308	Suitable combin't'n of Dishes	386
Veal	310	Additional Recipes	390
Mutton	313	General Index	395
Lamb	316	Blank pages for Recipes	416

WHERE AND WHAT TO BUY!

THE BEST HOUSES
AND
THE BEST ARTICLES.

Excellence was our aim in this work, in all its details. This idea has been maintained in seeking advertisers. We sought and have obtained **only houses and articles of the highest standing in the community,** and our readers can rely upon having their wants filled in the various lines represented, not only at the lowest market prices, but they will there find the largest and most varied stocks to be found in the city of Buffalo, to select from, while the specialties advertised can be relied upon as to quality and merit. The different lines of business ARE ALPHABETICALLY ARRANGED.

		OPPOSITE PAGE
Art Store,	Hoddick & Co.	14
Ales,	English Bottling Co.	15
Baggage Express, Livery, etc.,	C. W. Miller	384
Baking Powder,	Royal	47
Binding, Books, etc.,	W. H. Bork	385
Books, Stationery, etc.,	Peter Paul & Bro	46
Boots and Shoes,	H. H. Koch	110

Carpets, Drapery, etc.,	D. E. Morgan & Son...... 142
Carpet Beating, Bedding, etc.,	Allan & Barnard.......... 352
Champagne,	G. H. Mumm & Co........ 143
Chocolate,	Menier.................... 95
Clothiers,	Riegel & Robinson........ 174
Coal,	D. J. Stickney............ 206
Cocoanut, Prepared,	Maltby's.................. 31
Confectionery & Ladies' Rest'nt	Mayer's................... 111
Crockery, etc.,	G. E. Newman............ 191
Druggists,	Geo. I. Thurstone & Co.. 79
Dry Goods,	Flint & Kent 78
Flavoring Extracts, etc.,	Burnett's 63
Flour,	Schoellkopf & Mathews.. 273
Furniture,	Schlund & Doll 127
Furnishing Goods, Men's, etc.,	Humburch & Hodge...... 368
Gelatine,	J. Chalmers' Sons......... 369
Ginger Ale,	Ross's 223
Grocers,	Dingens Bros.............. 256
Hardware, Stoves, etc.,	C. E. Walbridge........... 190
Hats, Caps and Furs,	C. & F. Georger........... 222
Meats,	Augustus F. Weppner.... 304
Newspaper,	The News 336
Painting and Artists' Materials,	C. F. Chretien & Bro..... 30
Plumbing, Gas Fitting, etc.,	Irlbacker & Davis......... 126
Printing, Advertising, etc.,	E. H. Hutchinson.......... 62
Sapolio,	Enoch Morgan's Sons..... 94
Sauces,	Lime Juice................. 321
Sewing Machines,	N. O. Tiffany 175
Soaps, Toilet,	Indexical 207
Soups,	Huckins'.................. 337
Spices,	Pinckney's................ 353
Starch,	Kingsford's 305
Variety Store,	Barnum's 272
Wall Paper, Oil-cloths, etc.,	A. Neupert & Co.......... 158
Watches, Jewelry, etc.,	T. V. Dickinson 289
Wines,	Cruse Fils and Freres..... 159
Whiskey,	Hermitage, etc............ 288
Yeast,	Gaff, Fleischmann & Co.. 320

WE HAVE DIVIDED OUR WORK

INTO TWO PARTS.

PART I

WILL CONSIST OF

ECONOMICAL RECIPES.

PART II

WILL CONSIST OF

MORE COSTLY & FANCY RECIPES

IN BOTH PARTS, HOWEVER, WILL BE FOUND

NUMEROUS HOUSEHOLD RECIPES,

TABLES, Etc., Etc.,

The Index to which being very complete, should be carefully noted, in order that the reader may become acquainted with the contents of the Book for future reference. To simplify the finding of the recipe desired, we have numbered each one, and so indicated them in the Index, which will be found in the latter part of this work.

THE TABLE.

BY MRS. E. S. MILLER.

No silent educator in the household has higher rank than the table. Summoned three times a day by the family, who gather from their various duties and callings, eager for refreshment of body and spirit, its impressions sink deep, and its influences for good or ill form no small mean part of the warp and woof of our lives. Its fresh damask, bright silver, glass and china give beautiful lessons in neatness, order and taste; its damask soiled, its silver dingy, its glass cloudy and china nicked, annoy and vex at first, and then instil their lessons of carelessness and disorder.

An attractive, well-ordered table is an incentive to good manners, and being a place where one is inclined to linger, it tends to control the BAD HABIT OF FAST EATING. An uninviting disorderly table gives license to vulgar manners, and encourages the haste which has proved so deleterious to the health of Americans. Should it not, therefore, be one of our highest aims to bring our table to perfection in every particular?

To this end, cleanliness, order and taste must be carefully observed. Beautiful damask has no charm if soiled; but, be it ever so old, worn and darned, if white and well ironed it commands our respect. Even when no table cloth can be afforded, the well-scoured pine table is most welcome, and so beautiful in its whiteness that we almost persuade ourselves it is better than damask.

Silver has no attraction if dull and tarnished; sticky pitcher and tea-pot handles, streaked china, murky glass, the molasses pitcher dotted with hints of its contents, cruets with necks and stoppers dingy and thick with dried condiments, stray crumbs of bread, and spatters of gravy in the lumpy salt of the smeared salt cellars, are almost repugnant. And if, moreover, one knows that a similar *regime* controls the *cooking* for such a table, though the rolls be ambrosia, and the coffee nectar, they cannot tempt the appetite. But the most thorough cleanliness will not atone for a lack of order. The table-cloth may be clean and white, but unless well ironed and laid straight, it is very unsatisfactory. Knives, forks and spoons must be in a line, and plates must have strict reference to their *vis-a-vis*. The china must be of one kind, and neither nicked nor cracked.

Then taste must come in for its share.

The selection of silver and china, glass and damask, gives fine scope for its exercise. Let all be of beautiful design, the damask particularly, and of as choice a quality as can be afforded. Extravagant, "say you?" Then can you not dress more simply; and as you purchase a fine engraving or painting for the refinement and cultivation of yourself or your children, so furnish your table with this beautiful fabric, which is a study in its delicate tracery and artistic groupings?

In the appointments of the table, very much depends upon refined taste. Without it, there may be a stiff bouquet in the centre, with flowers fitted together like stones in a mosaic; with it there would be a loose, graceful arrangement of flowers, with drooping ferns, leaves and tendrils. Evidences of taste in the table are particularly acceptable to us, most deservedly so, and always worthy of cultivation, as they take from the grossness of indulgence in mere animal appetite.

Let us give then, to these three graces of the table, cleanliness, order and taste, the importance which so justly belongs to them, let us provide an abundant supply of wholesome food, well cooked and well served, and the hours spent at the table shall aid in our highest development.

THE BREAKFAST TABLE.

First see that it stands in the centre of the room, and perfectly straight, for no matter how well arranged, if it stands but little out of line, everything looks awry. Then put on the cover of canton flannel; this preserves the table-cloth, gives it a whiter shade, and deadens sound.

Have an eyelet hole in each corner to fasten over corresponding knobs under the ledge of the table; by this means it is held in position and cannot be displaced by the table-cloth, which comes next in order. In laying the table-cloth be careful to have the point where the folds cross in the centre, lie exactly on the centre of the table. Then arrange the mats; they are disliked by the most fastidious, and where the canton flannel cover is used, there is less necessity for them.

Then place the tumblers and napkins at the right hand of the places intended for the plates. Then arrange the silver and knives, making this square for every plate, viz.: dessert spoon for fruit or oatmeal at the right hand, fork at the left, and knife with the back of the blade towards the plate, across the top. Every large spoon should lie with the handle towards the right hand of the person sitting before it. Always place the silver right side up; the inside of a spoon is much more beautiful than the outside, and the fork gains nothing by being turned over. Then arrange the cups and saucers, sugar, etc., on a waiter or not, as you please, but by all means at the end of the table in preference to the side. The head and foot of the table are for the lady and gentleman of the house. This old established rule is sometimes waived for convenience sake but the change detracts greatly from the elegant appearance of the table.

THE DINNER TABLE.

In changing the table-cloth during the week, contrive to let the fresh one be for the dinner table. Place a large napkin over each end of the table to protect the table-cloth during the carving; these must be removed when the crumbs are brushed. For company dinner, many families prefer using two table-cloths, having the upper one removed after the first courses, thereby dispensing with brushing the crumbs, and generally securing a clean cloth for the dessert. Put on the mats and glasses, and as for breakfast, make a square for every plate with the knife, fork and soup spoon. If raw oysters are to be a part of the dinner, they should be the first course; select a small kind, serve them on the half shell, five or six on a plate, with a bit of fresh lemon in the centre.

The soup is helped by the lady. The rule is one ladleful and but one helping; at the end of this course, the soup plates are first removed, then the tureen. In handing plates, the waiter should always go to the left side of the guest; plates should be removed from the right side.

The waiting on the table should be as noiseless as possible, and the voice of the waiter should never be heard; if necessary, a low tone to the lady is admissible. No reproof should be given a servant at table, and no instructions that can possibly be avoided. Full directions before every meal should be given to an inexperienced servant. The foreign mode of serving a dinner is beautiful, and has great advantages over our way. The table is handsomely set with glass and silver, fruit and flowers. The first course is soup, then comes fish, already carved, that you may help yourself with ease. Then there is a *Filet de Bœuf*, part of which is carved, and the whole garnished with sliced potatoes, browned; then a cauliflower or macaroni; after that roast fowl and sweet-meats; then a pudding, followed by ices and coffee, fruit being the last course.

The wines being first, a small glass of sherry before the fish; then claret: next a fine Sauterne, followed by champagne with the fruit.

The little delay between the courses gives time for pleasant conversation, and would be admirable here in preventing our fast eating. This custom also saves the cook that last severe pressure of serving from four to eight hot dishes at the same time.

No well-ordered house has noisy servants. The housekeeping in every department should move like perfect, well-oiled machinery, with invisible wheels. Shrieks of laughter from the kitchen, singing and calling through the halls, stamp a house at once as belonging to the vulgar and uncultivated. Let the comforts and luxuries provided for your family and guests come to them as by magic; let them hear no preparatory sounds, and see no sights, that shall take from them the freshness of the entertainment.

———:o:———

THE TEA TABLE.

Set the table without a cover. This is a privilege that neither the breakfast nor dinner table can claim, and should therefore be cherished as particularly distinguishing the tea table. Of a summer's evening the effect is cool and refreshing, and in the winter its polished surface is rich with the reflection of lights and silver. On some tea tables we find a delicately crocheted mat for every plate, the tongue, biscuit, etc., placed on white mats of heavier make, and the tea service arranged on one large oval mat. Arrange the knife, fork and spoon as for breakfast, using a smaller sized plate. Use fringed napkins, one lying on each plate. Let the cups be of thin china and placed before the lady of the house, the relish of fish or cold meat before the gentleman, flowers in the centre, fruit and biscuit each side, the cake basket between the flowers and "tea things," and the butter on the other side of the flowers.

The gathering at the tea table is perhaps one of the most social of the day, there being none of the hurry of the breakfast table; and the rest, so charming when contrasted with the anxieties, formality and etiquette of the dinner table, comes, to the mother especially, as a sweet benediction.

No soup tureen looms up before her, or heavy, smoking joints. These have given way to fragrant tea or delicious chocolate, cold tongue, or meats thinly sliced and garnished with curled parsley, light and snowy biscuit, sweet golden butter, and honey in the comb, etc.

Physicians tell us that the heaviest meal of the day should come at noon, when the digestive organs have more vigor than at night. We think their counsel good, and a light repast at night will make our slumbers more peaceful, our rest more profound, and leave our heads clear for our next day's duties.

―――― o ――――

DUTIES OF THE MAID OF ALL WORK.

The general servant must be an early riser. Her first duty, of course, is to open the shutters, and in summer, the windows of all the lower part of the house.

Then she must clean the kitchen range or stove, sift the cinders, remove the ashes, brush the stove, and rub the bright parts with a leather or woolen cloth kept for that purpose.

She must light the fire, fill the kettle, and as soon as the fire burns, set it on to boil

She must then clean the room in which the family breakfasts, first pinning up the curtains out of the dust. She should let the dust settle for a few minutes, running meantime to the kitchen to get the breakfast things ready to bring in. In five minutes or so, she must return and thoroughly dust all the furniture, the ledges about the room, the mantel-piece, and all ornaments. Not a speck of dust should be left on any object in the room. Then she lays the breakfast cloth ready for breakfast, and shuts the dining or breakfast room door.

Her next duty is to sweep the hall or passage, shake the door mat and clean the door step, and if necessary, polish the door plate and door knobs. Then she cleans the boots, washes her hands and face, puts on a clean apron, and prepares the toast, eggs, bacon, coffee, or whatever is required for breakfast, if the family is ready for breakfast, she brings it on the table; if the family do not require her to wait on the table, she may then go up to the bed rooms, open the windows, strip the bed-clothes off, and leave the mattresses or beds open; by this time probably the bell will ring for her to take her breakfast and remove the breakfast things, which she should do quickly and carefully; sweep up the crumbs in a dust pan, put back the chairs and clean the room. The china is then washed and put away, and the kitchen tidied a little.

Her mistress will then give her orders for dinner.

As soon as these are settled, she will put on a large clean apron in which to make the beds, that she may not soil the bed clothes with her working dress. The mistress of the house generally assists a maid of all work in making the beds, but this is by no means a right of the maid, and very frequently she has this work to do alone.

In making the beds she should turn the mattresses frequently, the sheets being always placed with the *marked* end towards the pillow.

When the beds are made and the slops emptied, the rooms should be carefully dusted. Then she sweeps down the stairs and dusts the banisters. She sweeps the dust from each stair into a dust pan and is careful that no dust lies about the passage or hall which she has already dusted. She next proceeds to the sitting room, dusts the furniture, (dusting the ornaments is frequently done by the mistress, but cannot always be expected.) In winter when stoves are used, they must always be first attended to. It is scarcely necessary to mention that great care should be exercised in dusting ornaments and to evade breaking little keepsakes which are highly prized by the owner and which no money can replace.

The maid then returns to the kitchen, puts on a large canvas apron, which will tie all round her and which has a bib, and proceeds to cook the dinner. While the meat is roasting or boiling, any little kitchen work which will not take her away from the neighborhood of the fireplace, may be done.

Half an hour before taking up the dinner she will set the table, following explicitly the directions given by her mistress, and serve the various dishes during the meal as her mistress may direct; after she has had her own dinner she sweeps, folds up the table-cloth, sweeps up the crumbs under the table, and if the room is left vacant, opens the windows; then washes up the dishes and plates, cleans the knives, (washing off the grease carefully before she rubs them on the knife-board,) washes the silver spoons and forks, and just rubs them over with the leather, cleans any boots and shoes required, and then cleans up her kitchen and goes to wash and dress herself.

Her next duty is to bring in the tea, make the toast, etc.

After tea she turns down the beds, sees that there is water in the rooms, shuts the windows and closes the blinds.

These are the ordinary daily duties, but in order that the house may be well cleaned, every bed-room should be swept once a week, and the tins and silver must have weekly attention beyond that of the daily washing. A tidy girl will generally wash up the glasses and plates after supper and not leave them for the morning; she should also carefully fasten up the house. She should ask her mistress for housemaid's gloves,

ART STORE

285 MAIN STREET.

PAINTINGS,
   ENGRAVINGS,
      CHROMOS,
         WATER COLORS,
            PHOTOGRAPHS,
               ETCHINGS,
VELVET FRAMES,
   MIRRORS,
      GILT FRAMES,
         EASELS,
           FANCY FRAMES,
              CORNICES, Etc.

MIRRORS AND FRAMES REGILT EQUAL TO NEW, AT

HODDICK & CO.'S

285 Main Street, - BUFFALO, N. Y.

We make a Specialty of
ODD STYLES OF FRAMES IN VELVET, GOLD AND BRONZE.

THE ENGLISH BOTTLING COMPANY'S

SELECTED BREWINGS OF ROBERT SMITHS,

PHILADELPHIA.

INDIA PALE ALE,

Acknowledged to be

SUPERIOR TO ANY IMPORTED ALE,

And Especially Recommended for its Purity and Medicinal Properties.

English Bottling Company,

Wholesale Dealers in

EXPORT BEERS AND CARBONATED GOODS,

1509 & 1511 Stillman Street, Philadelphia, Pa.

T. M. CLARE & CO., Prop's.

———o———

DINGENS BROS.,

Sole Agents for Buffalo and vicinity.

and endeavor as much as possible to keep her hands clean, so as never to leave smutty marks of fingers on anything she touches; her hair should be banded carefully back and be kept smooth and her face clean; and as she has to answer the door, she should wear her coarse apron as much as possible, and at a knock or ring, exchange it for a clean white one kept within reach.

Recollect, my little general servant, that if your place is a hard one, it is also the best possible one for training you for a better one. After all, too, you have not more to do, nor, in fact, so much as you would have as the mistress of your own home when married, when you would probably have to clean house, work for your family's support, and take care of children, besides enduring anxiety and the many cares of the mother and wife. In your place you have no care for daily bread or clothes, your food and raiment are sure and you have every comfort.

If you rise early, bustle about and waste no spare moments, you will get through your work very well, only do THINK ABOUT IT. A little arrangement and thought will give you *method and habit*—two fairies that will make the work disappear before a ready pair of hands If, when you put your head on your pillow, you would just plan how best to get through next day's work you would find it a great help.

TRY NOT TO FORGET ORDERS. Do everything as well as possible at once. Remember, "Once well done is twice done." "A place for everything and everything in its place."

Be sure to always wash china, that is, cups, saucers, plates, etc., in very hot water, and wipe them dry with a very *clean, dry cloth;* a wet, dirty cloth will make them smeary and sticky. Find time for your own work of an evening, and take care to leave no holes in your stockings or rents unmended. "A stitch in time saves nine," and if every Saturday night you mend all fractures, both in the clothes that return and those that are going to the wash, you will keep your needlework nicely under.

Be personally clean, it is the great charm of ladies; and a good wash every night before going to bed will refresh you, make you healthy, prettier, and more cheerful than if you fell asleep, still dirty from your daily toil. Be active, cheerful, good tempered and obliging, and you will find work easy and employers kind.

THE MISTRESS OF THE HOUSE

The Mistress of the House commands daily a small realm of which she is queen. Let her rule with justice, meekness and quietness. The most self-governed person will always govern best, and we should have fewer bad servants if they were all under the firm and patient training of an employer who understood what their duties really were, and who required the best fulfillment of them compatible with the frailty of human nature.

GOOD TEMPER, PATIENCE, and a knowledge of domestic affairs, come first therefore, in the list of requirements for a model housewife.

A FREQUENT VISIT TO THE KITCHEN IS VERY ESSENTIAL, for there, usually the greatest waste takes place, this may be attributed, not so much to the carelessness and indifference of the servants, as to the fact that they do not realize the amount expended for that department of the household. The writer had in his employ a servant-girl who was thought quite economical, a year after her marriage she stated, that while in our employ she did not realize how wasteful she was, but now that she had a home of her own to provide for, she realized how much food cost, and saw where she might have been much more economical.

How and Where to Buy.—Buy of first-class establishments only. Prices are no higher (quality and quantity considered) and frequently lower than establishments that seek a cheap trade, while the goods are sound, unadulterated, healthy, first-class, the variety larger, and the goods fresh. Beware of establishments who profess to sell cheap and give you prizes besides.

PART I.

WIDOW PRUDENCE'S ECONOMICAL NEW ENGLAND RECIPES.

HER STORY.

Having been left a widow with six children to support, I had to study economy. My husband had been in the wholesale fruit business, but the failures of 1857 were the cause of the loss of both his life and fortune. Following his death I was attacked by a severe illness, during which my family were scattered among relatives. After my recovery I again gathered them together, resolved that they should not leave me, except of their own desire; each one that was able now put all their earnings in the household purse. With seven to feed and clothe, and rent to pay, it became a duty how to buy the cheapest, yet good articles. I bought for cash and invariably of first-class houses; the advantages of purchasing from such houses, are these: you are sure of full weight, you are sure of pure, fresh, sound and uniform goods, while prices are, as a rule, lower than at small establishments. In meats the fine cuts are generally very expensive, (BUT THE HEAD, FEET, HEART, LIVER, TRIPE AND COARSER PARTS ARE GENERALLY AS GOOD IF COOKED PROPERLY,) AND GIVE A GREATER VARIETY. Many of those now dependent upon the corner grocer and butcher who give a very limited credit at exorbitant profits, and whose customers are forced to buy just what they have, if they would begin to save enough to buy but a few articles for cash, they would soon buy all. Why should the poor man labor hard all the week, that when Saturday night comes he must give one-third of his earnings as profit to such small dealers who lead an easy life and get rich off his trade? I give you many recipes for each article, and if you have nothing in the house but meal you can make a comfortable repast, at least you need not hunger.

IN THE SELECTION OF GOODS at large establishments you will have but little trouble, for you will deal with men of honor and principle as a general thing, who do a large business and are above misrepresentation; there are certain brands that are the best and you will soon find them out and will use no other.

SUGAR.—Use only granulated, for it is the cheapest in the end, no drying up, no waste and it is impossible to adulterate it.

FRUITS AND VEGETABLES.—Always buy them fresh, clean looking, and free from decay, as they vary in quality very much. Good judgment is better than advice.

FISH.—Fish should always be perfectly fresh when cooked. To select fresh ones observe the eyes, if they have a bright life-like appearance, the fish is fresh; if on the contrary, the eyes are sunken and dark colored, and have lost their brilliancy, they are certainly stale. Some judge by the redness of the gills, but they are sometimes colored to deceive customers. Do not buy any more fresh fish than you want to use for the day (except in winter, when they will keep) but the fresher the better.

MEATS, POULTRY, GAME, ETC., ETC.—The finest grained beef is the best. The flesh is of a fine red, and the fat a light cream color, but not yellow, the fat, too, is solid and firm. The lean of mutton should be of a red color, and the fat white. The skin of pork should be of a light color, and if young, it is tender; the fat should appear firm. A tender goose is known by taking hold of the wing and raising it; if the skin tears easily, the goose is tender, or if you can readily insert the head of a pin in the flesh it is young. The same remarks will hold good with regard to ducks. Young chickens may be known by pressing the lower end of the breast bone, if it yields readily to the pressure they are not old, for in all animals the bones are cartilaginous when young. The breast should be broad and plump in all kinds of poultry, the feet pliable, and the toes easily broken when bent back.

———:o———

OUR RECIPES.

All persons who have used Cook Book recipes know, that as a rule, they give information to cook only fine rich dishes. They dishearten a prudent housekeeper. How can it be otherwise when some recipes of a single small dish call for eight to ten eggs (at four to five cents a piece, as they are in winter) and ounces of dear spices and outlandish herbs and costly fruits. Mrs. Prudence having for forty years cooked for a large family of her own, and kept a fashionable boarding house, now getting old, gives to the world the benefit of NEW ENGLAND COOKING, with *French*, *English*, *German*, *Scotch*, *Irish* and other national recipes, that have been used by her and improved and cheapened. Her struggle through life to support her children caused her to use many of the cheaper foods, and her great love for her offspring caused the old lady to make them good and palatable, but at the same time healthy. It is well known that many, very many families, have nothing but dry bread the most of the time, others have but little meat, others are tired of beef, pork, mutton and lamb. They want something new; all parties will find their wants supplied here, many of her cheap dishes are as good as the much more costly ones of the modern cook books.

We Will Guarantee

THAT ANY FAMILY

Will Reduce their Table Expenses One-Half

BY THESE RECIPES,

And have Healthier and Better Dishes, besides Many New Ones

THAT

NEVER HAVE BEEN KNOWN TO THE PUBLIC.

THE GREAT ADVANTAGE OF THESE RECIPES IS

CLASSIFICATION.

---o---

We classify the dishes by the name of the principal food of which it is made, and keep them all together, so that one can see at a glance which one of that kind they prefer, and if they have only Indian corn meal in the house with the few things required, they can select from fifty dishes to suit their palate; thus bread, porridge, pudding, cakes, etc.

TIME.—The time is also seen at once, the time it takes, without reading the whole recipe, so that if the cook has not time to prepare it one way she can another, so with meat of any kind, it can be cooked to suit the time at one's disposal.

ARTICLES AND QUANTITY.—The name of each article, and its quantity, are given separate, so that the cook, after having read the recipe, knows if she has the necessary ingredients, or can get them. If so she has but to read the DIRECTIONS, to go on, and then, if she desires to, can reduce the amount so as to make less, or increase and make more.

OUR REMARKS upon dishes are to give information as to their excellence, and for whom they are best adapted, sick or well.

MILK.

Is a very common article of food, enters into a great many dishes; bread, cake, puddings, pies and drinks; it gives like eggs, a rich flavor without being unhealthy. In large cities it is apt to be adulterated with water, etc.; to avoid which, many use condensed milk, which can be bought of grocers anywhere, and has many advantages over common milk.

REMARKS —In the following recipes we have given the time required for boiling, based upon the use of a double kettle or boiler (no well-appointed kitchen should be without one); many articles of food are easily burnt or scorched in cooking when cooked in open pans, and require close attention. This difficulty is obviated by the use of the double boiler, by some called, oatmeal or farina kettle; be careful and have the outer kettle always filled with water.

1. Boiled Milk. [TIME.—TWENTY MINUTES.]

ARTICLE.—Milk, two quarts.

DIRECTIONS.—Pour two quarts of milk into your double boiler, have the water in the outer kettle boiling, let the milk remain twenty minutes or longer; it will not burn.

REMARKS.—Boiled is much richer, better, and healthier, than without boiling; the chemical action of heat upon milk condenses and solidifies it. In too many cases milk sold to families is watered or impure; boiling it will correct this in a measure, as all physicians and chemists say that water boiled is made purer. The component parts of milk are about eighty-seven parts of water; sugar, five; caseine, five; butter, three; all perishable. When boiled it will keep twice as long. In all recipes for cooking, boiled milk should be used where milk is required; although fresh milk may be used, the cook will find that the use of boiled milk produces richer results.

2. To Preserve Milk.

Boil it in a double boiler, add a quarter of a teaspoonful of soda to two quarts.

3. Cocoa Milk. [TIME.—FIFTEEN MINUTES.]

ARTICLES.—Quarter of a pound of cocoa; a quart of milk.

DIRECTIONS.—Put the milk in a double boiler, let it boil, then pour in the cocoa, first powdered and made to a paste. Chocolate may be made the same way.

REMARKS.—Cocoa or chocolate is very healthy and nutritious, and for children excellent.

4. Cocoa or Chocolate. [TIME.—FIFTEEN MINUTES.]

ARTICLES.—Quarter pound of cocoa or chocolate; half a pint of milk; water one quart.

DIRECTIONS.—Make your cocoa or chocolate into a paste by adding a little hot water to the grated material, then pour your boiling water into the double boiler, add the cocoa or chocolate and milk, and boil as above.

5. French Chocolate. [TIME.—FIFTEEN MINUTES.]

ARTICLES.—Three ounces plain chocolate, grated, three pints milk, one pint water.

DIRECTIONS.—Make your chocolate into a thin and smooth paste with a small quantity of hot water, let your milk and water come to a boil, then add your chocolate paste, stirring well; let boil up once, sweeten to taste.

6. Rice Milk. [TIME.—FIFTEEN MINUTES.]

ARTICLES.—Rice, ground, a tablespoonful, milk, a pint.

DIRECTIONS.—Boil the milk in your double boiler, then add the rice, sweeten and flavor to taste.

REMARKS —Rice, flour, corn-starch or arrow-root, made in the same proportions is as good. Half a teaspoonful of magnesia added will correct acidity of the stomach; there is no better food for the sick, feeble, children, and infants.

7. Coffee Milk. [TIME.—TWELVE MINUTES.]

ARTICLES.—Two tablespoonfuls of ground pure coffee; a pint of milk, water, half a teacup.

DIRECTIONS.—Pour the milk into the double boiler, after it boils add the coffee, first soaked in boiling water; let it stand covered two minutes, sweeten to taste.

REMARKS.—This coffee is perfectly delicious.

8. Improved French Coffee. [TIME.—FIVE MINUTES.]

ARTICLES.—A tea cupful of finely ground coffee; three pints boiling water.

DIRECTIONS.—Keep your coffee in a tight tin can; grind it only as you need it; procure a French coffee pot, put your coffee in the upper part, pour the boiling water on it, and let it percolate through the coffee; pour it over a second time, and the liquid coffee will run through clear and strong; use boiling milk.

REMARKS.—We give no other recipe for preparing coffee, for the wretched way of boiling it is not cooking, it is spoiling the aroma of coffee, which is all there is of it to drink. A proper combination of Mocha and Java, the secret of which some grocers possess, makes the finest beverage, some use half of each, one-third Mocha and two-thirds Java makes a nice combination. Coffee is very stimulating and good for those it agrees with. The best is the cheapest, but buy it of first-class establishments, especially when buying it roasted or ground.

9. Tea Milk. [TIME.—FIFTEEN MINUTES.]

ARTICLES.—Milk, one pint; tea, a tablespoonful.

DIRECTIONS.—Pour the milk in your double boiler, let it boil; then pour in the tea, let it remain five minutes; then strain and serve.

REMARKS.—This is good for the well and sick, especially for those who are feeble. Tea is stimulating and refreshing.

10. Tea. [TIME.—TEN MINUTES.]

ARTICLE.—Half a teaspoonful for each person.

DIRECTIONS.—Scald the teapot; put in the tea; add a little water; then add the rest of the water in five minutes.

REMARKS.—Black tea is the best and healthiest, needless to say buy tea only of first-class grocers, and beware of teas sold where prizes are given with each purchase.

11. Suet Milk. [TIME.—ONE HOUR.]

ARTICLES.—Mutton suet, two ounces; milk, one pint; flour, one ounce.

DIRECTIONS.—Boil the above in your double boiler one hour. Good for dysentery and diarrhœa.

12. Bread and Milk. [TIME.—TEN MINUTES.]

ARTICLES.—Old bread, six slices; milk, a pint.

DIRECTIONS.—Boil the milk in your double boiler; when hot pour it over the bread.

13. Real Cream. [TIME.—TWENTY MINUTES.]

ARTICLES.—Two quarts of milk.

DIRECTIONS.—Heat the milk slowly in the double boiler; as the cream arises take it off.

REMARKS.—Cream is often required, but not easily procured; this recipe will show how to get it at once.

14. Cream Toast. [TIME.—TWENTY MINUTES.]

ARTICLES.—Milk, one quart; flour, three tablespoonfuls; butter, two tablespoonfuls.

DIRECTIONS.—Boil the milk in the double boiler; when hot mix the flour in cold milk, strain through a sieve, and stir in rapidly, add the butter and salt to taste, let it boil five minutes. Toast any bread, pour the cream over it, and serve.

REMARKS —This is far preferable to plain milk, as is most commonly used Any old bread toasted will answer. All who have eaten this, like it very much

15. Mock Cream. [TIME.—TWENTY MINUTES.]

ARTICLES.—Milk, one quart, an egg, a tablespoonful of maizena; and butter, the same quantity.

DIRECTIONS.—Boil the milk in the double boiler, stir up the egg, maizena, and butter, together, add to the milk when hot.

16. Milk Porridge. [TIME.—HALF AN HOUR.]

ARTICLES.—Milk, one pint; water, one pint, oat, graham, rye, or cornmeal, grits, farina, or hominy—either of these a large tablespoonful; a little sugar, salt, and butter to taste.

DIRECTIONS.—Put the hot water into the double boiler, mix the meal in a little cold water, add this, and seasoning (add more meal if it is preferred thicker), then add the milk.

REMARKS —These porridges are good for the sick and well, very easy of digestion, yet nutritious.

17. Wheys. [TIME.—ABOUT HALF AN HOUR.]

ARTICLES.—Milk, a pint, or either one of the following added to it: rennet, or vinegar, or mustard, or alum, or cream of tartar, a teaspoonful, or an orange or lemon; tamarinds, two ounces; wine, a tumblerful.

DIRECTIONS.—Pour one pint of milk in the double boiler; when boiling hot add either one of the above articles, stir it in rapidly for a few minutes, separate the curd, drink cold or warm. The curd can be eaten by well persons.

REMARKS.—Wheys are made with anything that will coagulate the milk, and derive their name from that used; for the sick and feeble they are very nourishing.

18. Curds. [TIME.—HALF AN HOUR.]

ARTICLE.—Milk, a pint.

DIRECTIONS.—Make a curd as above directed for wheys,— as whey is the watery part of the dish used for the sick, so the curd is for the well,—turn the curd after it is separated, into a mold or dish, or make into cakes; they can be eaten with sauce or plain.

19. Plain Custard. [TIME.—ABOUT HALF AN HOUR.]

ARTICLES.—Milk, one quart; eggs, four; sugar, a quarter of a pound; flavor to taste.

DIRECTIONS.—Pour a quart of sweet milk into the double boiler, stir in the sugar; beat the eggs well, and stir until thick; pour it into a dish or custard cups.

20. English Custard. [TIME.—ONE HOUR AND A HALF.]

ARTICLES.—Milk, two quarts, sugar, quarter of a pound; eggs, six.

DIRECTIONS.—Beat the yolks of the eggs; pour the milk into the double boiler, keep the cover off; boil it down to one-half; pour the milk when reduced on the eggs, stir it until nearly cold, then pour back into the boiler, and boil for one hour; then pour into a buttered mold; let it cool, then turn out; serve with sauce or jellies.

21. French Custard. [TIME.—HALF AN HOUR.]

ARTICLES.—Milk, a quart; eggs, four; lemon peel; quarter of a pound of sugar.

DIRECTIONS.—Pour a quart of milk into the double boiler; add one lemon peel, beat the yolks of the eggs, add to the milk, add the sugar, boil all till it is thick.

22. Condensed Milk Custard. [TIME.—HALF AN HOUR.]

ARTICLES.—Condensed milk, one pint, water, one pint, sugar, quarter of a pound six eggs.

DIRECTIONS.—Pour the milk and water into the double boiler, beat and add the eggs and sugar; boil until it thickens; pour it into cups; grate some nutmeg over each cup; let them get cold, and serve.

23. Fruit Custard. [TIME.—HALF AN HOUR.]

ARTICLES.—Custard and fruit.

DIRECTIONS.—Place any preserved fruits or jellies in a deep dish about one inch thick; pour over them any of the above custards when hot, and serve them very cold.

REMARKS.—More or less eggs, sugar, or milk, can be used in any custard; flavor of any kind to suit the taste. Custards may be thickened with maizena, corn starch, or gelatine.

24. Chocolate Custard. [TIME.—TWENTY-FIVE MINUTES.]

ARTICLES.—Four ounces sweet chocolate, eight eggs, three tablespoonfuls sugar, one quart of boiling milk, half pint boiling water.

DIRECTIONS.—Scrape the chocolate, pour the water on it, stir it until dissolved; pour this by degrees into the boiled milk, stirring all the time, add the eggs previously beaten, leaving out two of the whites, stirring continually, then add the sugar, pour the mixture into cups and bake ten minutes; serve cold with sweetened cream, or the white of an egg beaten to a stiff froth and heaped on top.

RICE

Supports millions of people in the eastern countries, and is a very nutritious food, easy of digestion, never does any harm, good for the sick and well. It can be made into many dishes. At present we give only the plain ones, but will hereafter give some thirty others. In boiling, use the double boiler, or it will be very liable to burn. Rice, when boiled, may be used in custards, bread batter, cakes, muffins, stuffing, fried, etc

25. Rice Water.

To one quart of water add two tablespoonfuls of rice and boil two hours.

26. Rice Gruel.

Ground rice, a heaping tablespoonful, ground cinnamon, a teaspoonful, water, a quart, boil half an hour.

27. Rice Boiled.

Wash it in pure water, boil it in salted water in the double boiler. Keep it from boiling to a jelly.

28. Rice for Children.

Boil in water until half done, then add a little butter, some sweet milk, sweeten; add eggs if desired.

29. Rice Pudding.

Wash the rice; soak it an hour, mix as many raisins in weight as rice; boil it to a hard jelly. It will come out of the boiler all in one piece. Eat with sauce, or turn hot into cups; it will come out solid when cold.

30. Rice Boiled Whole.

Soak a pound of rice, more or less, six hours, in cold water, to which a little salt has been added; pour boiling hot water in the double boiler; pour in the rice; boil twenty minutes; drain it in a colander. It will be very nice.

31. Rice and Apples. [TIME.—TWO HOURS.]

ARTICLES.—Rice, a pound, butter, an ounce; sugar, a tablespoonful; apples, six, or dried apples the same.

DIRECTIONS.—Boil the rice until soft, add the butter and sugar; stew six green or dried apples, sweeten; pour the apples in a dish and cover with the rice, and serve.

32. Rice Fritters. [Time to Fry.—Ten minutes.]

Articles.—Rice, four ounces; eggs, four; milk, one quart.

Directions.—Boil rice in the milk; when the rice is soft, remove it; when cold add four eggs well beaten, as much flour as will make a batter; drop a spoonful into hot fat, and fry brown. Eat with sugar and sauce.

FARINA,

One of the products of wheat. It is delicate, yet nourishing; good for the sick and well, especially so for dyspeptics. This and wheaten grits to eat, when costive, are two indispensable articles for them, and no household should be without them.

33. Boiled Farina, Plain. [Time.—One hour.]

Articles.—Water, a quart; farina, a quarter of a pound.

Directions.—Have boiling hot water in the double boiler, sprinkle and stir in the farina slowly, boil it an hour, sweeten, salt and flavor to taste. Eat warm or cold. Fried in slices, it is excellent.

34. Ice Farina Pudding. [Time.—Two hours.]

Articles.—Milk, three pints, or water, a quart; farina, one-quarter of a pound; eggs, two.

Directions.—Boil the milk in the double boiler, when hot add the farina, sprinkle and stir it in slowly, sweeten to taste, then boil an hour or so until thick; beat the eggs, add, let it boil a little longer, flavor and remove; pour into molds to cool. Eat with milk or sauce. The eggs can be omitted, if desired.

35. Boiled Plum Farina Pudding. [Time.—Three hours.]

Articles.—Farina, quarter of a pound; milk, three pints, or water, a quart; currants or raisins, a pound.

Directions.—Boil the milk, or pour the hot water into the double boiler, then stir in the farina and fruit; boil all together in the boiler three hours, or tie it in a pudding cloth, and boil until done, in a pot.

36. Baked Farina Pudding. [TIME.—TWO HOURS.]

ARTICLES.—Farina, four ounces; milk, three pints, or water, one quart; three eggs; half a pound of sugar.

DIRECTIONS.—Boil the farina in the milk or water, in the double boiler for an hour; beat the eggs well, add the sugar; let the farina cook, then add the above, with lemon or vanilla to taste, and bake in a dish.

37. Wheaten Grits

Is broken wheat. Wash it well until all the bran is separated. Boil it in the double boiler, using plenty of water. Salt to taste. After it is done, use syrup. A good dish for anyone, especially for those costive.

COCOANUTS

Are at times very cheap, and very little is required to make a rich flavored pudding. A new desiccated cocoanut answers the same purpose.

38. Cocoanut Bread Pudding. [TIME.—THREE HOURS.]

ARTICLES.—Milk, one quart; cocoanut, one teacupful; bread, two cups; sugar, half cup; eggs, two.

DIRECTIONS.—Boil the milk in the double boiler; when hot add the cocoanut, boil two hours, then add the bread, the eggs well-beaten, and the sugar; boil an hour. Eat it cold; currants or raisins can be added.

39. Plain Cocoanut Pudding and Pies. [TIME.—FOUR HOURS.]

ARTICLES.—Cocoanut, half a pound; milk, three pints; eggs, three; sugar, a cupful.

DIRECTIONS.—Boil the cocoanut in the milk in the double boiler, three hours, then add three eggs, well-beaten with the sugar boiled until thick; pour into a mold, or bake for pies.

PAINTING AND ARTISTS' MATERIALS.

[ESTABLISHED 1838.]

C. F. CHRETIEN & BRO.,

—— DEALERS IN ——

ARTISTS' MATERIALS

—{ AND }—

PAINTERS' SUPPLIES.

GENERAL PAINTING, GLAZING, GRAINING

AND FRESCOING

ATTENDED TO PROMPTLY.

We will submit designs and make estimates on work of any kind in our line, and with our facilities and years of experience, we can guarantee satisfaction.

Our line of Artists' Materials is as complete as can be found the city, and the prices as low as the lowest.

We invite an inspection of the same.

601 MAIN STREET 603

BUFFALO, N. Y.

THE ONLY GENUINE

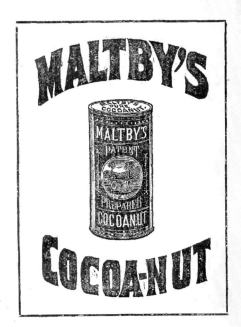

FOR PIES, PUDDINGS, &c.

40. Cocoanut and Corn Starch Pudding. [Time.—Two hours and a quarter.]

Articles.—Milk, a quart; cocoanut, corn starch, sugar, each a teacup; eggs, two.

Directions.—Boil the cocoanut in the milk in the double boiler two hours, then wet the corn starch in cold milk, beat two eggs, add both to the milk, also the sugar when desired, the liquids can be used for pies.

41. A Very Rich Pudding. [Time.—Three hours.]

Articles.—Cocoanut, one pound, milk, one pint, sugar, half a pound; eggs, four, rosewater, one gill.

Directions.—Boil the cocoanut in the milk two hours (with the cover on) in the double boiler, beat the eggs well, add the sugar, stir all together. Bake in a pudding dish lined with paste, and boil until thick, and eat cold.

42. Rich Cocoanut Custard. [Time.—Three hours.]

Articles.—Milk, a quart, sugar a quarter of a pound; cocoanut same; eggs, two, maizena, two tablespoonfuls.

Directions.—Boil the milk with the cocoanut in the double boiler two hours, then add the sugar, beat the eggs well, add also the maizena, boil until thick, and pour hot over sliced peaches, oranges, pears, or preserved fruits. Eaten cold it is delicious.

43. Cocoanut Pie. [Time.—Two hours.]

Articles.—Cocoanut, one cup; milk, two cups; sugar, half a cup; soda crackers, three eggs.

Directions.—Soak the cocoanut in the milk half an hour, roll the crackers fine, beat three eggs well, stir all together, bake without upper crust in a slow oven.

44. Rich Cocoanut Pie. [Time.—Two hours and a half.]

Articles.—Cocoanut, half a pound; sugar, a quarter of a

pound; lemon rind, one-half; eggs, three; milk, a cup; water, a cup.

DIRECTIONS.—Boil the cocoanut and sugar in the water and milk, in the double boiler, two hours; let it cool, add the eggs well-beaten, then the lemon peel well-grated, and bake as before.

45. Cocoanut Gingerbread. [TIME.—THREE-QUARTERS OF AN HOUR.]

ARTICLES.—Cocoanut, four ounces; flour, four ounces; maizena, four ounces; sugar, four ounces; butter, four ounces; peel of a small lemon; a coffeecup of molasses or syrup; half an ounce of ground ginger.

DIRECTIONS.—Put the syrup into a saucepan with the butter when hot, pour it into the flour and maizena, previously mixed with the sugar, ginger, and grated lemon peel. Beat the mixture well together, set it to become cold, stir into it the prepared cocoanut, beat it for a few minutes, then drop the mixture from a tablespoon, on a buttered tin, any size you prefer the cakes to be, and bake them in a slow oven.

46. Cocoanut Pound Cake. [TIME.—HALF AN HOUR.]

ARTICLES.—Sugar, one pound; butter, a quarter of a pound; milk, a teacupful; essence of lemon, a teaspoonful; soda, a teaspoonful; eggs, three; cocoanut, half a pound.

DIRECTIONS.—Mix the white sugar with the butter beaten to a cream, add the lemon and the milk, beat the eggs separately, then add the soda; beat all thoroughly together with the flour, as much as will make it as thick as pound cake; then lightly stir in the grated cocoanut. If the prepared cocoanut is used, soak it first in milk. Bake it in a quick oven in one or many tins.

47. Cocoanut Cake. [TIME.—HALF AN HOUR.]

ARTICLES.—Sugar, half a pound; cocoanut half a pound; butter, quarter of a pound; eggs, two.

Directions.—Beat the sugar and butter up well together, beat the eggs, mix all well together, roll out, cut into cakes, and bake in a moderate oven.

JELLIES.
Gelatine and Isinglass.

Animal Jellies are nutritious and very cheap, if made according to our directions, and are very pleasant to the taste. They have been considered very expensive and not hearty. This is a mistake Jellies are the very strength of meat and the vital juices, so to speak Fruit and farina jellies are the same; try them by our directions, if you do not wish the trouble, prepared gelatine can be easily purchased at the stores. Animal jelly can be made of calf's head and feet, pig's head and feet, or cattle's feet. In making jellies the head and feet are good for the table, and make a good meal (see recipes for cooking for the table), so that the jelly is a clear gain, only a little trouble a trifling expense, and you have a delicacy for well and sick. Use the double boiler in preparing them.

48. Plain Jelly Stock. [Time.—To clean, half an hour; to boil, six hours, to clarify, ten minutes.]

Articles —Calves' feet, four, or a calf's head, or a hog's head, or four ox heels, pig's feet for either; four quarts of water; sugar, two ounces; one egg.

Directions.—Take either of the above (not all), scald and clean them in boiling hot water, knock off the hoofs or horned part of feet, take out the eyes and brains if it is the head. Split the feet or head, put them into the pot, add a gallon of cold water, boil six hours, or until very tender; then remove with a skimmer, use no salt or spice in the water (the meat can be used for food as directed hereafter). When it is cold, skim off every grain of fat; a gallon of water generally makes a quart of jelly, which, after it is cold, must be clarified.

49. To Clarify Plain Jelly Stock. [Time.—Twenty minutes.]

ARTICLES.—Stock, a quart; one egg; sugar, two ounces; flavor.

DIRECTIONS.—Pour a quart of stock into a double boiler, add the white of an egg, with the shell well beaten together, two ounces of sugar, and any flavor preferred; let it boil six minutes; then skim, pour all into a jelly bag, or through a piece of cotton cloth, run it into a bowl or mold. More eggs can be added if desired.

REMARKS.—If you wish to make it any flavor, do so while the stock is hot. Jellies take their names from the flavor; lemon, orange, cinnamon, etc. The cost of a quart of jelly is but the labor and ten cents at the most; for the meat is worth all that is paid for it.

50. Lemon Jelly. [Time.—Altogether, one hour.]

ARTICLES.—Peel of four lemons and juice; three glasses of sherry; three-quarters of a pound of loaf sugar; one ounce and a half of gelatine or stock; one pint of water.

DIRECTIONS.—Steep the thin peel of four lemons in half a pint of boiling water until strongly flavored with the peel. Put the sugar pounded with the stock into the double boiler, and boil it slowly for about a quarter of an hour or twenty minutes; then add the strained lemon juice and the water from the peel. Let it just boil up; skim it well, add the wine, and strain it until quite clear.

51. Orange Jelly. [Time.—About an hour.]

ARTICLES.—Peel of four oranges and two lemons and juice; a quarter of a pound of loaf sugar; a quarter of a pint of water; two ounces of gelatine.

DIRECTIONS.—Grate the rinds of the oranges and lemons, squeeze the juice of each, strain it, and add the juice to the sugar and the water, and boil it until it almost candies. Have ready a quart of jelly, put to it the syrup, and boil it once up. Strain off the jelly, and let it stand to settle before it is put into the mold.

52. French Jelly.

ARTICLES.—One quart of calves' foot or clear gelatine or stock, some ripe fruit, or any preserved or brandy cherries.

DIRECTIONS.—Have ready one quart of very clear jelly, select ripe and nice looking fruit, and pick off the stalks; commence by putting some jelly at the bottom of the mold, and let it remain about two hours to harden, then arrange some fruit according to taste round the edge of the mold, if currants, lay them in as they come from the tree, on their stalks, and pour in more jelly to make the fruit adhere, and let that layer also harden, then add more fruit and jelly, until the mold is full. If peaches, apples, apricots, etc., are used, they are better boiled first in a small quantity of syrup; but strawberries, grapes, cherries, or currants may be put in uncooked. An extremely pretty jelly may be made from preserved fruits, or brandy cherries. It may be garnished with any fruit, or an open jelly may have some strawberries piled in the center, or a whipped cream piled up, with strawberries stuck in it, which has a very good effect.

53. To Make Twenty Kinds of Jelly.

Take a quart of jelly stock, or make it out of gelatine, then make and add any of the recipes to make ice cream.

ICE CREAMS,
Water Ices, Frozen Custards.

Many families think because ice cream and water ices are sold so high in the confectioneries that they must be expensive to make. It is a mistake, it is not so. A variety of food is essential to the maintenance of human life.

Cheap luxuries are also, in moderation, necessary to pleasure and enjoyment after a hard day's work. We know of nothing more delightful and refreshing than ice cream, for milk, sugar, eggs, and fruits are all healthy and very nutritious, so it is not money wasted that you spend for ice cream or water ices Ices are cheaper, but of course not so substantial. In eating them DO NOT GOBBLE THEM DOWN IN A HURRY, BUT LET THEM MELT IN YOUR MOUTH. That is the way to eat them, and we will guarantee no one will ever be hurt by eating ice creams or water ices. The swallowing of masses of ice cream upon a heated stomach is enough to make anyone sick, but when it is melted in your mouth it can not.

Condensed milk used alone, or in proportion of one part water to one part condensed milk, will be found an excellent substitute for cream, and much richer. Two or three parts water to one of condensed milk, will make good cream. If you live where you cannot get it at the door, use the canned milk, which does not require sugar. Try it and you will prefer it to cream, or common milk.

LEMON JUICE makes the flavor taste richer. Sometimes it is not to be put in. It will be stated when.

54. How to Make Ice Cream. [TIME.—FROM TEN TO TWENTY MINUTES.]

ARTICLES.—Sweet milk, a pint; a tablespoonful of sweet butter; white sugar, half a pound; juice of one lemon; two well-beaten eggs (or not); essence, half a teaspoonful, or fresh fruit a pint, or syrup of fruit, half a teacupful; a tablespoonful of maizena, or flour, or pure corn starch.

DIRECTIONS.—Boil the milk in the double boiler; add the butter, a spoonful of corn starch, maizena or flour, first stirred up in a little cold milk; add to the milk then two well-beaten eggs; let it get cool, then stir in the essence or juice of fruit or syrup as directed below; freeze. Cream is richer than milk, but cannot be got readily, and is expensive. Those who use cream need no butter or flour.

55. Frozen Custards

Are made as above, except using two tablespoonfuls of maizena, and boiling all until thick. Flavor and freezing are the same as ice creams. If you desire, these custards can be made without freezing.

56. Water Ices

Are made in the same manner, using ice water instead of milk, without eggs, and no boiling.

57. Fruit Creams, Ices, and Custards.

Juices direct from fresh fruit are the best and the cheapest, where parties raise it. Jam your berries or fruit; sprinkle half a pound of white sugar over it; squeeze a lemon over the sugar, let it stand one hour, then sift it through a fine sieve, or better, squeeze it through a piece of cotton cloth; then stir it well into the cold milk, as prepared for creams and custards, or water for ices, and freeze at once.

58. Spice Creams, etc.

Steep whole spice in a gill of hot water. Use this instead of fruit. Coffee, tea, and chocolate come under this class. If whole spice is not to be had, tie up ground in a cloth.

59. Essence Creams, etc.

Where essences can be bought they are the handiest, half a teaspoonful to a pint of milk. Custards can be made of any of the recipes. We generally use the essences, as they are no trouble.

TO COLOR.

Ice creams, water ices, jellies, and custards can be made of different colors.

60. Red.

One ounce of cochineal, one ounce of salts of wormwood, one pint of water boiled five minutes; take it off the fire, add three ounces of cream of tartar, one ounce of rock alum, put them in slowly or it will boil over; add, if to keep, sugar syrup, instead of water.

61. Purple.

Infuse a pound of mallow flowers in a quart of water six

hours; add a little salt of tartar and strain; it gives a deep purple; or boil an hour and add a little huckleberry juice, or use huckleberries or blackberries.

62. Yellow.

Use the yolks of eggs, or, for a bright yellow, soak a half pound of turmeric root in a pint of alcohol until it is yellow enough. Color to suit.

63. White.

Use milk, white of eggs, white sugar, and white essence.

64. Pink.

Use currants, raspberries, or strawberries, or a little red coloring.

65. Brown.

Coffee and chocolate creams are brown.

The different kinds of ICE CREAMS, WATER ICES and CUSTARDS are made as follows:

66. Strawberry.

Take a pint of fresh strawberries, jam them with a spoon; sprinkle half a pound of sugar over them; then squeeze a good sized lemon over it; add coloring if desired; let it stand an hour; sift it through a fine sieve, or press the juice through a cloth; if the sugar has not all melted, stir it up in the fruit, add half a teacupful of water, then stir this juice into the cold prepared cream and freeze at once. If you have no fresh strawberries, use the canned ones, or essence, or syrup, as above directed.

67. Raspberry.

Made same as strawberry. A delicate dish, and pink.

68. Blackberry.

Made same as strawberry. As healthy a cream as made.

69. Whortleberry.

Made same as strawberry. A novel cream ice or custard made a fine purple.

70. Gooseberry.

Same as strawberry—no lemon. Makes a fine green.

71. Red Currant.

Made same as strawberry—no lemon. A fine pink.

72. Pine Apple.

Made same as strawberry.

73. Apple.

Boil in enough of water to make a pint of solid stewed apples. Strain through a fine sieve or cloth. Then make as above.

74. Pear.

Made same as apple.

75. Quince.

Made same as apple.

76. Peach.

Peel a dozen large peaches, mash them through a colander, and make same as apple.

77. Cherry.

One pint of cherries, mashed, strained, and made as above.

78. Grape.

A pint of grapes, mashed, sugared, strained, and made as above.

79. Orange.

Juice of four oranges, if desired, boil the peel in the milk and make as above.

80. Lemon.

Juice of two lemons, boil the peel in the milk, then make as above.

81. Ginger.

Boil the ginger in the milk or water, or use essence to taste.

82. Nutmeg.

Same as ginger.

83. Cinnamon.

Same as ginger.

84. Vanilla.

Same as ginger.

85. Clove and Allspice.

Same as ginger.

86. Ice Cream Freezers.

There are now in the market many ice cream freezers that will freeze ice cream inside of five minutes, and sold so low that any family can buy one. They rarely get out of order, and last for many years. By the use of one of these the process of freezing is rendered so much more expeditious and satisfactory as to more than compensate for the trifling expense involved in its purchase. They all have the wooden tubs to hold the salt and ice.

87. Directions for Freezing

Always accompany them, but we give the following directions so that you will always have them, and if you do not have a freezer, you can do so by using a tin pail and a bucket. A quart of ice cream can be frozen, taking care that there are no holes in the freezer to let in the water and spoil the cream. Set the freezer, containing the cream, in a wooden tub or bucket several inches larger, and pack closely around its sides a mixture of pounded ice and salt (mixed in the proportion of six pounds of ice to one of salt), extending to within two inches of the top of the freezer, cover the freezer and keep it in constant motion, removing the cover frequently (if it does not clean itself as some do) to scrape the congealed cream or ice from the sides with a silver spoon or wooden paddle, taking care to keep the sides clear, and stirring it well to the bottom. Keep the tub well filled with salt and ice outside the freezer, and take care that none of the salt water gets in to spoil the cream. The outside tub or bucket should have a hole in or near the bottom, from which the bung can be removed to allow the water to pass out as the ice melts. After the cream is well frozen, it may be packed in molds, and set in salt and pounded ice. When you wish to serve it, wrap the mold with a hot cloth a minute, so as to loosen it, turn out the cream on a dish and serve immediately.

MAIZENA.

It is the farinaceous product of corn. It affords many delicate, nourishing, attractive, and palatable dishes, suitable for the use of invalids and children, and family use. In custards for thickening it is preferable to wheat flour. It is the best pudding any cook can make. With a paper of this in the house, and some milk and sugar, and an egg or two, a pudding or cake can be had in a few minutes, easy of digestion, a luxury, and very nutritious. It must always be boiled in the double boiler, to prevent burning, as it is very liable to scorch, and, as the flavor is delicate, be spoiled. In adding the maizena to the milk, it must be first wet in cold milk, this prevents its being lumpy; powdered sugar is best to use with it.

88. Maizena Custard   [TIME.—HALF AN HOUR.]

ARTICLES.—Maizena, two tablespoonfuls, milk, one quart, egg, one; sugar, a cupful.

DIRECTIONS.—Heat the milk in the double boiler hot, mix the maizena in a little cold milk, beat the egg with the sugar, add all, let it boil three minutes, salt and flavor to taste.

89. Maizena Blanc Mange.   [TIME.—HALF AN HOUR.]

ARTICLES.—Maizena, five tablespoonfuls; milk, a quart, eggs, two.

DIRECTIONS.—Cook as for custards, flavor and salt to taste, let it run into molds, eat with sugar and milk or sauce

90. Maizena Lemon Pudding. [TIME.—HALF AN HOUR.]

ARTICLES.—Maizena, three ounces, sugar, six ounces, lemon, one; milk, three pints, eggs, three.

DIRECTIONS.—Heat the milk in a double boiler, grate the

rind of one lemon, add the juice and the rind to the sugar and the maizena, stir this in a little cold water to make it smooth; when the milk is hot, stir it all in; stir until it thickens, beat the eggs well, and add with a little butter; as soon as thick pour it into cups or molds, first wet in cold water; when cold eat with sugar and milk or sauce.

91. Maizena Plain Pudding. [TIME.—HALF AN HOUR.]

ARTICLES.—Maizena, five tablespoonfuls; of sugar, same; milk, a quart.

DIRECTIONS.—Heat the milk and sugar in the double boiler; when hot, add the maizena, let it boil five minutes, flavor to taste, pour into a dish, eat with fruits, preserves or jellies, or plain.

92. Maizena Baked Pudding. [TIME.—ONE HOUR.]

ARTICLES.—Maizena, four tablespoonfuls; sugar, same quantity; eggs, two; milk, a quart.

DIRECTIONS.—Heat the milk in the double boiler; when hot add the maizena and sugar; salt and flavor to taste; let it cool a little, add the eggs well beaten, pour into a buttered dish, and bake half an hour.

93. Floating Island. [TIME.—HALF AN HOUR.]

ARTICLES.—Maizena, two tablespoonfuls; sugar, four; milk, three pints; eggs, four.

DIRECTIONS.—Beat the yolks of the eggs and sugar together, mix the maizena with a little of the cold milk, put the remainder in the double boiler to boil; when it boils add the eggs and maizena, stir well until it thickens, put it in an earthen dish, beat the whites of the eggs with a spoon to a stiff froth place it on the custards; heat the custard in the oven until it is of a light brown, or eat without baking.

94. Cream Cake. TO MAKE THE CREAM. [TIME.—FIFTEEN MINUTES.]

ARTICLES.—Milk, a cup; sugar, half a cup; maizena, a tablespoonful, butter, a teaspoonful, flavor to taste.

DIRECTIONS.—Boil half the milk and sugar together in the double boiler, mix the maizena in half of the cold milk, and stir in the maizena, boil five minutes.

95. TO MAKE THE CAKE. [TIME.—HALF AN HOUR.]

ARTICLES.—Maizena, half a cup, same of wheat flour, sugar, a cup, eggs, three, half a tablespoonful of butter, half a teaspoonful of soda, one of cream of tartar, flavor with lemon.

DIRECTIONS.—To be baked in round tin pans, about three-quarters of an inch thick, bake two or four, spread the cream on one, cover over with the other and put them together. Jellies can be used instead of cream if desired.

96. **Sponge Cake.** [TIME.—FORTY MINUTES.]

ARTICLES.—Sugar, half a pound, eggs, four, maizena, three-quarters of a pound; cream of tartar, a teaspoonful; soda, half a teaspoonful.

DIRECTIONS.—Beat the eggs and sugar well together, stir the dry tartar well into the maizena, add the soda dissolved in a little hot water; stir all well together and bake in a quick oven.

CORN STARCH,

Like the maizena, is the product of Indian corn, and deservedly ranks high as an article of luxurious yet cheap food It is all nutriment, and differs from maizena in the manufacture, both are good, try both, same recipes for both.

Corn starch has a peculiar thickening property in itself, and owing to being cheap and hearty, should be extensively used for custards, blanc mange, creams, jellies, gravies, omelets, soups for children and invalids, and the well.

The preparation of maizena and corn starch is very simple, when the double boiler is used, giving no care or trouble about burning or spoiling.

CORN STARCH must be first mixed in a little water or milk

before being stirred into the double boiler, as it prevents its being lumpy.

97. Thin Corn Starch Custard. [TIME.—TWENTY MINUTES.]

ARTICLES.—Starch, a tablespoonful, sugar, four, milk, a quart, eggs, three.

DIRECTIONS.—Boil the milk and sugar in the double boiler, beat the yolks of three eggs, mix the starch in cold milk; then add all to the hot milk, stir and take off; pour this in a deep dish, beat the whites of the eggs to a froth, put on top of the custard, flavor to taste.

98. Muffled Cake.

Pour the above over a sponge cake and serve cold.

99. Apple Souffle.

Boil a dozen apples, sweeten, and strain through a sieve, pour the above custard over it, eat cold. Dried apples will do as well.

100. Cup Pudding. [TIME.—BAKE HALF AN HOUR.]

ARTICLES.—Four tablespoonfuls of corn starch, four eggs, a quart of milk, candied citron or lemon peel, and wine sauce

DIRECTIONS.—Make a smooth batter of the corn starch, eggs and milk, fill little buttered cups and stick in little chips of the candied citron or lemon peel. Bake and serve with sauce.

101. Corn Starch Fruit Blanc Manges. [TIME.—HALF AN HOUR.]

ARTICLES.—Starch, a quarter of a pound; sugar, same; any fruit, water, a quart.

DIRECTIONS.—Have a quart of boiling water in the double boiler, add the sugar; then add the starch first wet, let it boil until thick; then take any berries, sliced peeled peaches or oranges, mellow pears, or preserved fruit, and lay in a mold or dish, pour the starch over it. Let it cool.

102. Coffee Corn Starch. [TIME.--HALF AN HOUR.]

ARTICLES.—Starch, five tablespoonfuls, same of sugar, two of coffee, milk, a quart.

DIRECTIONS.—Boil a quart of milk and the sugar in the double boiler, make a cup of very strong coffee, and add to the milk hot, then add the starch, let it thicken for a few minutes and pour into cups or molds.

103. Corn Starch and Cocoanut Jelly. [TIME.—THREE HOURS.]

ARTICLES.—Starch, three tablespoonfuls; cocoanut, the same, sugar, two, milk, a quart; one egg

DIRECTIONS.—Boil the cocoanut in half the milk for nearly three hours in the double boiler, to make it tender, then add the starch and sugar and egg, let it boil five minutes, pour into molds, and eat cold.

104. Corn Starch Omelets. [TIME.—TEN MINUTES TO COOK.]

ARTICLES.—Four heaping tablespoonfuls of corn starch; a teacupful of milk and three eggs, pepper, salt, and a teaspoonful of butter, quarter of a teaspoonful of soda, half a teaspoonful of cream of tartar.

DIRECTIONS —Beat the eggs, cream of tartar, and corn starch together,, add the milk with the soda dissolved in it, pepper, salt, and butter. Fry brown, turn them over when done, place upon the table hot.

REMARKS —Eggs are generally dear in price, nothing has ever taken the place of them; but corn starch in its composition is partly a substitute, and that is one of the reasons why it is so good in making omelets. Herbs, ham, or meat can be used to give a flavor, and add to the quantity

105. Cake of Corn Starch. [TIME.—HALF AN HOUR.]

ARTICLES.—Starch, eight ounces; sugar, same; butter, four ounces; eggs, two; baking powder, a teaspoonful.

DIRECTIONS.—Beat the butter and sugar well together, beat the eggs, add with the starch and powder, flavor to taste. Bake.

106. General Recipe for Making Creams of Corn Starch.

ARTICLES.—Corn starch, a tablespoonful, more or less; sugar, four tablespoonfuls, or more if desired; milk, a quart; butter, a teaspoonful; yolks of eggs, from one to ten, as may be preferred; juice of lemons and juice of fruits, essences, or other flavoring that may be preferred.

DIRECTIONS.—Heat the milk and sugar in a double boiler, mix the corn starch in a little cold milk, add the yolks of the eggs well beaten, the butter and juice of lemon and fruit juice or essences, etc.

REMARKS.—Creams are eaten cold, and if desired thin use less corn starch; if thick, more. The thin is generally whipped to a froth, and poured into glasses to eat, or poured over fruits, preserves, jams, etc. The combination is delicious. If thick, pour into molds.

107. General Recipe for Making Corn Starch Jellies.
[TIME.—TO MAKE, ABOUT TEN MINUTES.]

ARTICLES.—Three to four tablespoonfuls of corn starch, or maizena, one quart of sweet milk, or a half a pint of condensed milk, and three half pints of water, or a quart of water, sweeten to taste with sugar, less than a teacupful will do; half a pint of wine improves the jelly. Fruits, essences, spices, juices of lemons, oranges, etc., can be used to flavor, same as for ice creams and frozen custards.

DIRECTIONS.—Boil the milk or water and sugar in a double boiler, mix the corn starch in a little cold water, pour into the boiler and let it boil five minutes. Stir it up, flavor with any fruit, essence, etc., to suit the taste; color with any color, same as for ice creams; two or more colors can be made by dividing the jelly, and coloring one part; turn it into the mold. *Let it cool;* then pour in another part with a different color.

REMARKS.—These jellies are very cheap, easily made with a double boiler and nutritious and healthy for invalids, children, and well persons. A little practice will enable the cook to make them perfect. Molds of crockery and metals can be bought cheap.

THE ENGRAVING
AND
FASHIONABLE STATIONERY
DEPARTMENT,
OF
PETER PAUL & BROTHER

Publishers, Booksellers and Stationers,

363 MAIN STREET,

YOUNG MEN'S LIBRARY BUILDING

BUFFALO, N. Y.,

Embraces the Latest Styles produced in the Markets of New York, Boston and Philadelphia.

Wedding Invitations, Reception Cards,
CALLING AND MENU CARDS,

Engraved and Executed in the Highest Style of Art, and on our own premises.

We Submit Sketches for any Work desired in our Line, Free of Charge.

108. General Recipe for Making Corn Starch Custards. [TIME.—TO MAKE, ABOUT TEN MINUTES.]

ARTICLES.—Corn starch, two or three tablespoonfuls, milk, one quart, or condensed milk, half a pint, and three half pints of water, half a teaspoonful of salt; one to three eggs, teaspoonful of butter, juices of fruits, essences, or spices, or any thing to flavor that suits the taste, sugar, four tablespoonfuls or more, according to taste.

DIRECTIONS.—Heat the milk to nearly boiling in a double boiler, and add the corn starch previously dissolved in a little milk, then add the eggs well beaten with the sugar, and let it boil five minutes, stirring it, then add the flavor.

109. General Recipe for Making Corn Starch Puddings. [TIME.—ABOUT TEN MINUTES.]

ARTICLES —Corn starch, five tablespoonfuls; same of sugar (more or less to taste), eggs or not, as desired; fruit of any kind or not; milk, a quart; sweet butter, a tablespoonful; and flavor of fruit juices, the same as for ice creams.

DIRECTIONS.—Heat the milk in a double boiler until hot, add the butter, then the corn starch first mixed in a little cold milk to prevent any lumps, then add the eggs well beaten, if any are used, the flavoring to taste.

110. To Color Corn Starch Creams, Custards, Jellies, Puddings, and Sauces.

For variety and ornament it is sometimes desirable to color them, if any color is desired, use the recipes for coloring ice creams.

111. Corn Starch Sauces.

ARTICLES.—Milk, one cup, sugar, one cup; corn starch, three tablespoonfuls, same of wine or brandy; one of butter; juice of half a lemon.

DIRECTIONS.—Heat the milk and sugar in a double boiler, mix the corn starch with the wine or brandy, butter, and juice of lemon; add to the corn starch, and boil ten minutes with the cover on.

REMARKS.—Corn starch sauces can be made of every variety by using the ice cream recipes for flavors, and following the above. Water can be used if no milk is in the house.

112. Corn Starch and Cocoanut Pies. [TIME.—THREE HOURS AND A HALF.]

Make the above recipe of jelly, line a deep plate with paste, bake it in a quick oven; when done, fill with the jelly and again bake. This is richer than all cocoanut, and will be preferred.

113. Milk or Cream in Corn Starch.

It is almost useless to put cream in recipes, as it can not be had without trouble To obviate that, *mock cream* can be used; or, if our recipes are followed, the expense and trouble to get cream is avoided, except it is made from

114. Condensed Milk,

which is now in use, and can be used in all our recipes instead of ordinary milk; we use it as follows:

DIRECTIONS FOR USING CONDENSED MILK.

—For CREAM, add one part cold water to one of milk; for rich milk, add three; for ordinary milk, add four; for infants, six to nine parts.

115. Corn Starch Snow. [TIME.—TEN MINUTES.]

ARTICLES.—Tablespoonful of corn starch; water, half a pint; four tablespoonfuls of white sugar; one lemon; whites of two eggs.

DIRECTIONS.—Dissolve the corn starch in a little water, add the rest of the water, then the sugar, then the juice of the lemon, then the whites of the eggs well beaten; whisk it all together until it becomes thick and white.

116. Corn Starch Charlotte Russe Cake.

ARTICLES.—Half a pound of corn starch; half a pound of

powdered white sugar, quarter of a pound of butter, three eggs; essence of lemon to flavor.

DIRECTIONS.—Beat the eggs well with the butter, add the sugar and beat them in, then the corn starch, then the essence of lemon. Bake in a moderate oven and let it get cold; then cut it up in strips half an inch thick.

THE INSIDE OF THE RUSSE.—Make a cream or custard of any kind, wipe a mold well and see that it is dry, then line the bottom and sides with the cake cut up so as to cover it all over, fill with the cream or custard, and place it on ice. When cold, turn it upside down on a dish and remove the mold, the cake only is seen.

EGGS.

We have fifty good recipes to cook eggs. We give some of the plain ones, and shall in Part II. give the rest. Eggs in summer are very cheap, especially in the country, and we know of no better dish than well-cooked eggs. They can be cooked for the invalid to digest in an hour, and the hearty man to digest in five hours, they contain a great deal of nutriment, and strengthen the sick and well. In cooking eggs the best way is to break them separately in a cup, for one bad one will spoil all that have been broken before. Always serve hot. As they are cheap and plentiful in summer, and scarce and dear in winter, it is best to save them for the time when they are expensive.

117. To Preserve Eggs.

There are several ways to preserve eggs, but they must in all cases be prepared fresh or new laid, otherwise they will not keep, no matter how they are prepared. The principle of preserving is to keep them fresh, cool, and in the dark.

118. To Preserve with Mucilage.

Dissolve the gum arabic in water to any ordinary thin paste, and dip the eggs in it twice, when dry, which is in a few minutes, lay them away in charcoal dust or bran, or dry sawdust; put the box in a cool, dry closet or cellar, small end downward.

119. To Preserve with Mutton Fat.

Melt the suet, dip them in it twice—do not have the suet too hot—and follow the above directions.

120. To Preserve with Lime.

To ten quarts of water, add two pounds of salt and two ounces of saltpeter; boil together for twenty minutes; when nearly cold, add eight ounces of quick lime; let it stand three days, stirring it every day; place the small end downward in layers in a jar; when filled pour in the mixture. They will keep for months; the water should cover them two inches.

Do not remove the eggs, when packed for preservation, until you wish to use them, as eggs are of a delicate nature, and easily spoiled after being kept some time.

121. Poached Eggs. [TIME.—THREE MINUTES.]

ARTICLES.—Eggs; butter; water, a pint; vinegar, a tablespoonful; a little salt.

DIRECTIONS.—Put the vinegar and salt in the water in the double boiler; let it boil, break and pour the eggs in, boil three minutes and take out. Butter them and serve on toast, or heat some cream, or mock cream, and pour over them.

122. To Bake Eggs. [TIME.—FIVE MINUTES.]

Butter a dish, break the eggs, pour in pepper, salt, and butter; bake in a slow oven until well set. Serve hot.

123. To Boil Eggs.

TIME.—To boil MEALY, fifteen minutes; VERY HARD, ten minutes; HARD, seven minutes; SOFT, four minutes; VERY SOFT, two minutes.

DIRECTIONS.—Have the water boiling; place the eggs in with a spoon, or in a wire-basket; keep them boiling, as above directed. Boiling water, poured on eggs in a bowl, will cook them soft by keeping them in it from six to ten minutes.

124. Dropped Eggs. [TIME —THREE MINUTES.]

Break the eggs so as not to break the yolk, drop them separately in hot water in a flat dish, let them stay three minutes, or until the white coagulates. Serve on toast. Good for the sick and well.

125. To Fry Eggs. [TIME —THREE MINUTES.]

Melt any ham fat, lard, or butter, in a frying pan and break the eggs in a cup one at a time and pour into the pan, sprinkle with pepper and salt, turn them over or not, as desired, fry until brown on one or both sides, and serve hot.

126. Scrambled Eggs. [TIME.—FIVE MINUTES.]

ARTICLES.—Six eggs, milk, a coffeecupful, flour, a teaspoonful, butter, a tablespoonful, salt.

DIRECTIONS.—Pour the milk into the double boiler, rub the flour into the butter, add this to the milk, salt to taste, beat six eggs light and stir them into the milk when hot, when the whites are well set, serve hot or pour over toast.

127. Fricassee Eggs. [TIME.—TWENTY MINUTES.]

ARTICLES.—Six eggs, butter, a cupful of mock cream or milk.

DIRECTIONS.—Boil the eggs hard, cut them in quarters, take out the yolks, mix them up with hot mock cream, pour this over the whites of the eggs and serve. Salt to taste.

128. Plain Omelet. [TIME.—FIVE MINUTES.]

Beat six eggs very light, have a pan of hot fat or butter ready, pour the eggs in and fry till it is a fine brown on one side, sprinkle a little pepper and salt on the top, then lap it over showing the brown side out. Serve hot.

129. Herb, or Ham, or Meat Omelet.

Made same as above, but mincing up any meat, herbs, rice, or other articles, and mix with the eggs before frying.

TOMATOES.

There is no vegetable that grows that can be raised so easy, and that is sold so cheap. Any yard or garden that has a few feet in it to spare, can raise all a family wants; they are very healthy, and are an agreeable addition to any meal. Gather them ripe, but firm to the touch. For pickling or making preserves, gather young and green.

130. Raw Tomatoes.

Select the fairest ripe ones, put them on ice; when cold slice, use vinegar, pepper, and salt to taste.

131. To Stew Tomatoes. [Time.—An hour.]

ARTICLES.—Tomatoes, a dozen; salt, a teaspoonful; pepper to taste; butter, a tablespoonful; grated bread crumbs, two tablespoonfuls.

DIRECTIONS.—Scald the tomatoes with boiling water, then peel the skins off, put them in the double boiler, with the butter, salt, and bread crumbs and pepper, and cover them over; stew an hour, stir up two or three times; serve hot.

132. Baked Whole Tomatoes. [Time.—One hour.]

ARTICLES.—Tomatoes, a dozen; salt, pepper, and butter.

DIRECTIONS.—Wash, cut off a small piece from the stem end, put a little pepper, salt, and butter in each one, place them in a dish, and bake them in a moderate oven; serve hot.

133. Baked Tomatoes. [Time.—To bake, two hours.]

ARTICLES.—Tomatoes, a dozen; an ounce of bread crumbs; butter.

DIRECTIONS.—Scald, peel, and slice the tomatoes, put a layer of bread crumbs, then a layer of tomatoes, then bread crumbs, then onions with pepper, salt, butter a little, sugar, and last bread crumbs; bake in a moderate oven two hours.

134. Tomato Fritters. [Time.—Twenty minutes.]

ARTICLES.—Tomatoes, green corn, each a pint; eggs, two;

milk, a cupful; flour.

DIRECTIONS.—Take a pint of peeled and mashed tomatoes strained from their liquor, same of green corn cut from the cob in summer (or boiled samp in winter), season with pepper, salt, and sugar; add two well-beaten eggs, one tumbler of sweet milk, and enough of flour to hold it together. Fry in cakes in boiling lard. Serve hot.

135. Boiled Tomatoes. [TIME.—TWO HOURS.]

DIRECTIONS.—Scald a dozen or more tomatoes, put them in the double boiler and boil two hours; season to taste.

136. Tomato Paste. [TIME.—TO STEW, THREE HOURS.]

ARTICLES.—Two quarts of tomatoes; sugar; pepper; nutmeg; vinegar, half a pint.

DIRECTIONS.—Skin and cut up the tomatoes, let them stand twelve hours, strain out the liquor, put the pulp in the double boiler; then season with sugar and spice, add the vinegar, stew three hours or more, with the cover off, or until it is a thick paste; dry upon dishes, and pack in and cork well in open-mouth bottles; keep dry. A small piece will make a gallon of soup.

137. Tomato Leather. [TIME.—AN HOUR.]

ARTICLES.—Scald, mash fine through a sieve, add a little sugar; grease panes of glass or tins, spread over the mixture and dry. This can be used in soup, sauce, or stews.

138. Tomato Sauce.

DIRECTIONS.—Peel, mash, and boil until tender, rub through a colander six tomatoes, a tablespoonful of sweet oil and vinegar; mustard, pepper, and salt to taste. Mix all together; excellent for meats. Serve the paste or leather same way for winter use.

139. Preserved Tomatoes. [TIME.—FOUR HOURS.]

ARTICLES.—Tomatoes, six pounds; white sugar, four pounds; six lemons; water, a quart.

DIRECTIONS.—Take the small yellow, or red, or green ones. (I prefer the green), prick their skins with a fork, cut the lemons in thin slices. Boil the sugar in a quart of water in the double boiler or preserving kettle; when the syrup is clear, and boiling hot, add the lemons and tomatoes and let it boil until the fruit is clear; then skim out the tomatoes, set them to become cold; then pour over them the syrup. Many use a pound of sugar to a pound of fruit. The above is the general way to preserve all fruits with sugar.

140. Tomato Figs. [TIME.—FOUR HOURS.]

ARTICLES.—Tomatoes, four pounds; white sugar, one pound; two lemons.

DIRECTIONS.—Do them as above directed; then take them out to become cold, keep the syrup boiling; when the tomatoes are cold, put them back, and repeat this twice; then take them out, flatten them and dry in a warm oven. When dry place them in glass jars; dry the lemon at the same time.

CHEESE.

Cheese is another cheap food, cheap for the amount of nutriment in it; it is not the quantity as much as the quality that gives nutriment. It is a fact, the poorer a cheese, the more muscle-making power it has; chemical analysis giving it the greatest amount of all food, especially skim milk cheese. Dyspeptics or those confined to the house, or costive persons must not use cheese as it is very binding; for those whose digestive organs are strong, and work hard, it is good, or for those who do not feel any bad effects after eating it. Persons should eat nothing that disagrees with them.

141. Improved Welsh Rarebit. [TIME.—TWENTY MINUTES.]

ARTICLES.—Cheese, a cupful; milk, a cupful; an egg, pepper, salt.

DIRECTIONS.—Cut or grate the cheese, put it with the milk

in a double boiler, after the cheese has melted, add pepper and salt to taste, and one egg well-beaten; pour over dry toast.

142. Stewed Cheese. [TIME.—HALF AN HOUR.]

ARTICLES.—Cheese, a teacupful, milk, two; bread crumbs, two; mustard, a teaspoonful; pepper and salt.

DIRECTIONS.—Heat the milk and the cheese in the double boiler; when it melts mix in the mustard, salt, and pepper to taste, when all is well mixed, serve.

143. Cheese Sandwich.

Spread the stewed cheese (when cold) thick between two slices of bread.

144. French Macaroni. [TIME.—TO BOIL, HALF AN HOUR; TO BROWN IT, SIX MINUTES.]

ARTICLES.—Half a pound of pipe macaroni; seven ounces of cheese, four ounces of butter, one pint of new milk, one quart of water, a pinch of salt.

DIRECTIONS —Flavor the milk and water with a pinch of salt, put into a double boiler when boiling, drop in the macaroni, let boil half an hour, drain in a colander, then place a layer of macaroni in the bottom of the dish in which it is to be served, next a few small pieces of butter, then a layer of cheese, either grated or cut in very small pieces, next another layer of macaroni, then cheese and butter, and so on till the dish is filled, finish the top with cheese and butter, then place in the oven to brown six minutes, serve immediately.

145. Cheese Custard and Macaroni.

Boil half a pound macaroni, and a quarter pound of cheese together, when cooked and cold pour over it any custard, and serve cold.

146. Cheese Fingers. [TIME.—QUARTER OF AN HOUR.]

ARTICLES.—A quarter of a pound of puff paste, a pinch of salt; two ounces cheese, a quarter teaspoonful cayenne pepper.

DIRECTIONS.—Take the puff paste, and roll it out thin; then take the grated cheese, cayenne, and salt; mix these, and strew the cheese over half the paste, turn the other half over, and cut it with a sharp knife half an inch wide, and any length you like. Bake in a quick oven, and serve them quite hot, shaking a little grated cheese over them. Pile them in a dish crossing each other at right angles.

147. Pastry Remakins. [TIME.—A QUARTER OF AN HOUR.]

ARTICLES.—Some good cheese; puff paste; yolk of one egg.

DIRECTIONS.—Take some puff paste, and roll it out rather thin, strew over it some good grated cheese, and fold it over; repeat this three times, rolling it out each time. Then cut the remakins with a paste cutter in any form you please. Brush them over with the yolk of a well-beaten egg, and bake them in a quick oven for about a quarter of an hour. When done serve them quickly on a hot napkin.

148. Macaroni. [TIME.—HALF AN HOUR; TO BOIL, FIVE MINUTES WITH CREAM.]

ARTICLES.—Four ounces of macaroni, two tablespoonfuls of good cream; one ounce and a half of butter rolled in flour; some toasted cheese.

DIRECTIONS.—Boil the macaroni until quite tender, and lay it on a sieve to drain; then put it into a pan with the cream, and the butter rolled in flour; boil it five minutes, pour it on a dish, spread toasted cheese all over it, and serve it up very hot.

149. Macaroni and Fish. [TIME.—TO BOIL MACARONI, HALF AN HOUR; TO BROWN IT, FIVE MINUTES.]

ARTICLES.—Some cold cod; twice its weight in macaroni; six ounces of cheese; a large piece of butter.

DIRECTIONS.—Chop any quantity of cold cod very fine, mix with it the macaroni boiled tender, and the cheese; mix the whole well together and put it on a dish, with a few pieces of butter on the top. Grate cheese thickly over it, and brown it before a fire in an oven.

150. Mock Crab—Sailor Fashion.

ARTICLES.—A large slice of cheese, a teaspoonful of mustard; the same of vinegar, pepper and salt to taste.

DIRECTIONS.—Cut a slice of cheese rather thin, mash it up with a fork to a paste, mix it with vinegar, mustard, and pepper. It has a great flavor of crab.

SALT FISH.

There is much nourishment in fish—almost as much as in meat, pound for pound—also, medicinal properties, such as iodine, in them, which have a beneficial effect upon the health. In no class do we see so large families, handsome women, and robust, active men, or greater exemption from maladies than among fishermen and their families. As salt fish are easily procured in any part of the country, and generally at a low price, we give many good and practical recipes, how to prepare them. Any dry, salt, pickled, or fresh fish will answer to cook. Codfish, however, is the best. Dry or pickled fish can be kept almost any length of time in a cool place.

151. The Best way to Soak Salt Fish.

Soak that intended for use in plenty of tepid water, adding to each gallon of water a teacupful of vinegar, if the fish is very dry and hard; use a tablespoonful of saleratus or soda to a gallon of water, taste one of the flakes to ascertain when it is sufficiently fresh, too much soaking will render the fish too insipid. Pickled fish must be soaked over night, flesh side down.

152. To Cook Fish. [TIME.—AN HOUR OR TWO, ACCORDING TO SIZE.]

Nothing is better to cook salt fish in than a double boiler, as it must be heated gradually, and simmer very gently; boiling will make the fish hard and tough. It is generally to be picked in flakes free from bones and skin.

153. Fish Sauce. [TIME.—TWENTY MINUTES.]

Mix a little flour in cold water, add it to hot milk in the double boiler; a little butter and salt; add an egg or two if desired; let it boil five minutes; then serve.

154. A Down-East Fish Dinner. [TIME.—TO PREPARE, ONE HOUR AND A HALF.]

ARTICLES.—A fish, potatoes, beets, and pork.

DIRECTIONS.—Take more salt fish than you want to eat for this meal, soak, boil until tender in as large pieces as possible; boil more potatoes and beets than you want; cut some fat salt pork in small square pieces and fry brown; peel the beets and slice them into vinegar, or eat without. Serve all separately. This recipe makes a cheap dinner; the balance can be made into that desirable dish called

155. Fish Balls.

Take one-third fish, and two-thirds potatoes chopped fine, and fried into balls; brown, and serve with the beets or pickles.

156. Croquettes of Fish. [TIME.—TEN MINUTES, TO PREPARE.]

ARTICLES.—Fish, eggs, bread crumbs, tablespoonful of flour, and one of milk.

DIRECTIONS.—Take any fish, separate the skin and bones, mince it with seasoning to taste; an egg well beaten with the flour and milk; roll it into balls; brush the outside with egg; dredge it with bread crumbs; fry brown.

157. Fish Fritters. [TIME.—TEN MINUTES, TO PREPARE.]

ARTICLES.—Fish, bread crumbs, mashed potatoes, equal parts; an egg; half a teacupful of milk; pepper, and any sauce.

DIRECTIONS.—Take the above articles, mix all together to a proper consistency; then cut into small cakes and fry brown.

158. Spiced Soused Fish. [TIME.—TWELVE HOURS.]

ARTICLES.—Any boiled fish, vinegar, pepper, allspice, cloves and mace.

DIRECTIONS.—Put any cold boiled fish into a dish, boil enough vinegar to cover, put in the spices to taste; then pour on the hot vinegar. Let it stand twelve hours, it is then fit for use.

159. Lobster Fish. [TIME.—AN HOUR]

ARTICLES.—Salt fish, vinegar, pepper, and sweet oil.

DIRECTIONS.—Pick some salt fish into shreds into the double boiler, pour boiling hot water over it; let it cook half an hour, pour off the water; add vinegar, sweet oil, and pepper to taste. Cold fresh fish can be prepared at once without soaking.

160. Oyster Fish. [TIME.—TWENTY MINUTES.]

ARTICLES.—Fish, oysters, butter, bread crumbs, pepper and milk.

DIRECTIONS.—Take any cold boiled salt, or fresh fish and separate from it the bones and skin; take as much in quantity of oysters, a cup of milk; boil them slowly in their own liquor in the double boiler for four minutes, then add a little butter, as many bread crumbs as fish, then the fish with spices to suit the taste. This can now be eaten, or it can be poured into a dish and baked.

161. Stewed Fish. [TIME.—TWENTY MINUTES]

ARTICLES.—Any cold boiled fish, milk, flour, salt, butter.

DIRECTIONS.—Prepare the milk, flour, butter and salt to taste, as for fish sauce, in the double boiler; pick the fish free from bones and the skin; put it into a dish, pour over it the hot sauce, and serve with boiled or baked potatoes.

162. Fricasseed Fish. [TIME.—ONE HOUR AND A QUARTER]

ARTICLES.—Any cooked fish, parsnips, milk, butter, flour, eggs.

DIRECTIONS.—Break the fish into flakes on a dish; boil enough parsnips, mash them, pour enough milk into the double boiler, a piece of butter, little flour wet first in water, two hard boiled eggs minced fine; add the mashed parsnips; when all is boiling hot add the fish ; serve with mashed potatoes.

163. English Baked Fish. [Time.—Twenty minutes.]

ARTICLES.—Any cooked fish, same quantity of mashed potatoes, parsnips, and a quarter of a pound of butter.

DIRECTIONS.—Pick the fish, butter a pie dish, place in it alternate layers of the parsnips, potatoes and fish ; season and bake for twenty minutes ; pour over it melted butter or fish sauce.

164. French Stew of Fish. [Time.—Half an hour.]

ARTICLES.—Fish, cup of milk, two ounces of butter, sprig of parsley, sweet herbs, pepper and salt.

DIRECTIONS.—Any cooked fish ; make a sauce of the milk, butter and flour, pepper and salt, parsley and sweet herbs chopped fine ; pour in the fish ; stew all half an hour.

165. Parisian Style. [Time.—Half an hour.]

ARTICLES.—Fish, butter, flour, sugar, onions, and vinegar.

DIRECTIONS.—Any boiled fish picked into flakes ; brown some butter, dredge in a little flour and sugar ; in this, fry some slices of onion ; throw in a little vinegar ; boil it up, pour it over the fish, and serve.

166. East India Style. [Time.—Half an hour.]

ARTICLES.—Fish, butter, peppers, nutmeg, parsley, onions, lemons, sweet oil.

DIRECTIONS.—Any cooked fish in flakes ; brown some butter, add to it some whole peppers, grated nutmegs, parsley, onions chopped fine, spoonful salad oil ; mince and shake this seasoning well. Serve the fish with the sauce and squeeze the juice of a lemon over it.

167. Italian Style. [Time.—Twenty minutes.]

ARTICLES.—Fish, flour, milk, pepper, salt, cheese.

DIRECTIONS.—Flakes of any fish ; thicken the milk with the flour stirred very smooth ; two tablespoonfuls grated cheese ;

stir in the fish, pepper and salt, pour into a dish; strew bread crumbs over it, and brown in an oven.

HOMINY

Is a coarse preparation of corn. It is cheaper than maizena or starch, and answers for many purposes. It is, however, liable to burn in boiling, and care must be taken to prevent it. With the double boiler there is no danger or trouble.

Hominy is used very much south and west, for children or persons who wish to grow fat. This, with farina, will fatten them very fast.

168. Hominy Plain Boiled.

Soak a quart, boil it in the double boiler until soft, eat with syrup, milk, sugar, or butter. Salt to taste.

169. Hominy Fried.

Boil as above and pour into a dish; when cold, slice, and fry it brown.

170. Hominy Cakes. [TIME.—HALF AN HOUR.]

ARTICLES.—Cold boiled hominy, a pint, flour, half a pint, one egg, lard, a tablespoonful, milk; yeast powder, a teaspoonful.

DIRECTIONS.—Beat the eggs, mix all together, make a thin batter, fry in cakes brown.

171. Hominy Bread. [TIME.—AN HOUR.]

ARTICLES.—Hominy, cold boiled, three cups; cornmeal, a cup, melted lard, a tablespoonful. eggs, two, milk.

DIRECTIONS.—Beat the eggs well; stir the hominy and meal together, add the eggs, salt and make a thin batter and bake.

172. Hominy Muffins. [TIME.—HALF AN HOUR.]

ARTICLES.—Hominy, corn meal, flour, each two tablespoonfuls, lard, one tablespoonful, egg, one; water.

DIRECTIONS.—Make a thin batter, add the egg and salt, and bake in rings or pans.

173. Samp Boiled

Is large hominy, corn cracked, or whole with the hulls off; it is very palatable boiled in boiler until soft. Eat with milk; salt to taste.

174. Hominy Gruel. [TIME.—TO BOIL, AN HOUR.]

ARTICLES.—Half a pound of hominy; one pint of milk; salt.

DIRECTIONS.—Mix the hominy in the milk; boil in the double boiler, salt to taste. Good for invalids and children.

175. Hominy Cakes.

A cup of boiled hominy; two eggs; half a cup of sugar; tablespoonful of butter; spice to taste.

POTATOES.

Plain and sweet potatoes are roots, and are extensively used among all classes. They are, when mealy, light, nourishing, palatable, and healthy; but two-thirds of the potatoes are watery, and require different methods of cooking them from the ordinary way of boiling. When bought, if over FIFTY CENTS A BUSHEL is paid, they are not profitable as compared with meal and flour; yet for a change it is well to have some once or twice a week; but potatoes at a dollar a bushel are dear food, at two dollars they are extravagant. Many families never save their cold potatoes; it is a mistake, for many of the best recipes require cold cooked potatoes. Potatoes are improved by soaking in cold water over night, or for an hour or two before cooking.

176. Steam Potatoes. [TIME.—FORTY MINUTES.]

DIRECTIONS.—This is a good way; pare or not, wash in cold water, put them in a steamer, steam until a fork goes through them easily, and serve hot.

177. To Boil Old Potatoes. [TIME.—NEARLY AN HOUR.]

DIRECTIONS.—Pare or not, wash in cold water, and put them in cold water in the pot with a little salt; boil slowly, the

ADVERTISING AND FINE PRINTING.

ESTABLISHED 1875.

E. H. HUTCHINSON,

NEWSPAPER ADVERTISING AGENCY

AND DEALER IN PRINTERS' MATERIALS,

Nos. 12, 14, 16 & 18 EAGLE STREET.

In connection with the Advertising Agency, Mr. Hutchinson, in 1877, established his

Book and Job Printing Department

Under the management of MR. H. C. SPENDELOW. In this department every description of printing for

Societies, Manufacturers, Merchants, Bankers, Insurance and Business Men Generally,
is executed with neatness, promptness and despatch. Printing of Mercantile Blanks or Forms in various colors of Transfer or Copying Ink a specialty. Particular attention paid to the reading of proofs, and every care taken to avoid mistakes and insure accuracy in the work. In this department Eight Presses are in operation, and power is furnished by a Seven-horse *Otto Silent Gas Engine.* The latest styles in Job and Display Type are being constantly added, and with the Two-Revolution Campbell Press, anything in the printing line from a VISITING CARD to a FULL SHEET POSTER, may be turned out with facility and despatch. Call for estimates and prices and inspect samples of work done, before ordering elsewhere. Our motto is:—" Good Work at Reasonable Rates."

With constantly increasing facilities, and a determination to execute promptly all orders confided to me through the Advertising Agency, to turn out only first-class work in my Printing Department, and to deal only in the best of Printers' Materials, I respectfully solicit a continuance of the liberal patronage bestowed upon me in the past, and shall welcome new customers, endeavoring to please all and merit the patronage with which I may be favored.

E. H. HUTCHINSON,
Nos. 12, 14, 16 and 18 EAGLE STREET, - BUFFALO. N. Y.

FLAVORING EXTRACTS AND PERFUMERY.

BURNETT'S
COLOGNE WATER.

THIS COLOGNE IS

UNRIVALLED IN RICHNESS AND DELICACY OF PERFUME.

In Quarter and Half Pints, Pints and Quarts.

In Basket style, or plain with cork or glass stoppers.

Without effort on our part, it has, in a brief time, attained a large and constantly increasing sale, confirming the opinion of the best judges, that it is SUPERIOR to any foreign or domestic.

Highest Awards at the Centennial Exposition,

At Louisville, St. Louis, Cincinnati, Chicago, Boston, and New York.

For Sale by First-class Grocers, Druggists and Fancy Goods Men.

Burnett's Flavoring Extracts,

FOR FLAVORING

ICE CREAMS, CUSTARDS, PIES, BLANC MANGE, JELLIES, SAUCES,

Soups, Gravies, etc.

"*Pre-eminently Superior.*"—Parker House, Boston.
"*The best in the world,*"—Fifth Avenue Hotel, New York.
"*Used exclusively for years.*"—Continental Hotel, Phila.
"*We use them exclusively.*"—Sherman House, Chicago.
"*We find them the best.*"—Southern Hotel, St. Louis.
"*We find them excellent.*"—Occidental Hotel, San Francisco.

BURNETT'S FLAVORING EXTRACTS. The superiority consists in their perfect purity and great strength. They are warranted free from the poisonous oils and acids which enter into the composition of many of the fictitious fruit flavors now in the market. They are not only true to their names, but are prepared from fruits of the best quality, and are so highly concentrated that a comparatively small quantity only need be used.

A full line of Burnett's goods for sale by

DINGENS BROTHERS.

slower the better, if the water boils too fast, set it further off from the fire. Try with a fork, when done, pour off the water, put the pot on the stove, the cover off to dry the potatoes; serve hot as soon as dry. Never let the water stop boiling, as it makes them watery.

178. To Boil New Potatoes.

Scrape off the skins, and lay them in cold water for an hour or two; boil as above.

179. To Bake Potatoes. [TIME.—ONE HOUR.]

DIRECTIONS.—Wash, wipe dry, put in a hot oven, and bake an hour, or until done; many prefer them this way. IN COOKING *the four ways above,* if not peeled cut off a thin slice from each end, it lets the water out from them.

180. Mashed Potatoes.

Boil the potatoes, peel and mash, season with milk, pepper, salt, and butter to taste.

181. Browned Mashed Potatoes.

Prepare as above, turn them into a pudding dish or pan, and set in an oven to brown; this is an excellent way to cook poor watery potatoes.

182. Potato Cakes.

Take seasoned mashed potatoes and make them into cakes nearly an inch thick. Bake or fry them.

183. Stewed Potatoes.

Cut cold boiled potatoes into slices, cover with hot mock cream. Stew slowly until hot in a double boiler.

184. Baked Chopped Potatoes.

Chop cold boiled potatoes in a chopping tray till very fine, turn them into a pudding dish, cover with mock cream, and bake half an hour.

185. Fried Cold Potatoes.

Slice cold boiled potatoes, or chop fine, fry brown with pork fat, or any grease or lard; pepper and salt to taste.

186. Fried Raw Potatoes. [TIME.—TWENTY MINUTES.]

DIRECTIONS.—Peel some good potatoes, throw them into cold water, and heat pure lard so as to have the frying pan have an inch or more in it. Slice the potatoes very thin; when the fat is boiling hot, put them in; when of a delicate brown and crispy, remove. This is a quick cheap way, for they do not soak fat, and well done are a delicacy. Sprinkle a little salt on while hot.

187. Potato Ribbons.

Prepare and cook in the same manner as fried raw potatoes, except they are pared round and round into ribbons.

188. To Fry Them Light or Swelled.

When fried, turn into a colander, and have the fat over a brisk fire; leave the potatoes in the colander only about half a minute, then put them back in the very hot fat, stir about one minute and put them again in the colander; salt them and serve hot. If the fat is very hot when dropped into it for the second time, they will certainly swell. There is no other way known to do it. It is as easily done as it is simple.

189. To Broil Potatoes.

Cut some cold boiled potatoes up lengthwise, a quarter of an inch thick, dip each piece in flour, lay them on a gridiron over a clear fire; when both sides are browned, put them on a hot dish, butter, pepper, and salt them. Serve hot.

190. Potato Rissoles. [TIME.—TO FRY, TEN OR TWELVE MINUTES.]

ARTICLES.—Some boiled potatoes; bread crumbs; egg; pepper and salt; a piece of butter.

DIRECTIONS.—Boil some potatoes; when done, drain the water from them, and set them by the side of the fire to dry;

then peel and mash them with a fork in a clean stew pan, with a seasoning of pepper and salt, and a piece of fresh butter; stir the mash over the fire for a few minutes, and then turn it out on a dish. When cool roll it into small balls, cover them with a beaten egg and bread, and fry them in hot lard or beef-drippings. When a light brown let them drain before the fire, and serve.

191   Potato Puffs.

ARTICLES.—Three ounces of flour; three ounces of sugar; three well-boiled potatoes, a piece of butter the size of a nutmeg, two eggs; a little grated nutmeg.

DIRECTIONS.—Boil and mash the potatoes, mix them with sugar, flour, nutmeg, butter and beaten eggs. Make them into cakes, fry a nice brown, and serve them with white sauce.

192.   Potatoes a la Maitre d'Hotel.

ARTICLES.—Some boiled potatoes, a little melted butter; pepper, salt, and the juice of half a lemon.

DIRECTIONS.—Take some potatoes boiled and peeled; when nearly cold, cut them into rather thick slices, and put them into a stew pan, with a little melted butter, seasoned with pepper, salt, and the lemon. When very hot, put them in a dish, and serve with the sauce over them.

193. Stuffed Potatoes.   [TIME.—TO ROAST, ONE HOUR.]

ARTICLES.—Some of the largest potatoes, one tablespoonful of cheese; pepper and salt; a little flour; two ounces of fresh butter.

DIRECTIONS.—Take some potatoes, boil them well, cut off the tops, and scoop out the inside completely. Rub this quite fine through a sieve, and add a tablespoonful of grated cheese, pepper, and salt, melt the butter in a stew pan; put in the potato flour, and make it hot, fill the skins of the potatoes with it, put them into the oven, and serve them up quite hot.

194. To Brown Potatoes and Meat.

DIRECTIONS.—Boil some fine, large, mealy potatoes, take off the skins carefully, and about an hour before the meat is cooked, put them into the dripping pan, having well dredged them with flour. Before serving them, drain them from any grease, and serve them up hot.

195. Hashed Potatoes.

Any cold boiled, baked, fried, or cooked in any way, left over, and minced with cold meat or fish of any kind, and seasoned well, make a palatable and healthy dish of food.

196. Potato Souffles.

Steam a quart of potatoes, then peel and mash them in a double boiler, and mix an ounce of butter with them; set on the fire, pour into it, little by little, stirring the while, about half a pint of milk; stir a little longer after the milk is in, and until they are turning rather thick; dish the potatoes, smooth or scollop them with the back of a knife, and put them in a quick oven till of a proper color, and serve.

197. Potatoes a la Parisienne.

Chop an onion fine and partly fry it with butter, then put with it some potatoes cut in dice, add a little water, salt and pepper; boil gently until done; take from the fire, add chopped parsley, and serve.

BEANS AND PEAS

Are among the best and most nutritious of foods, and for the amount of nourishment and strength they give, to the actual cost of them, are among the cheapest of foods. A quart swells to over two quarts; if old, they require more soaking. Add a little salt to the water in which they are soaked. These recipes answer for dry and fresh beans and peas.

They are too hearty for dyspeptics, and should not be eaten by those of weak stomachs.

The New England people eat them often, and especially every Sunday morning, and for dinner that day or the next. The founders of the six New England States almost lived upon them and corn. We give all the known methods of cooking them.

198. How to Improve Beans.

Soak dry beans for sixty hours before cooking them; it takes out the strong taste and bilious nature in them.

199. New England Baked Beans. [TIME.—ALL DAY OR NIGHT.]

ARTICLES.—Dry beans, a quart, lean pork, half a pound; two tablespoonfuls of molasses; water.

DIRECTIONS.—Wash and soak the beans in double as much water from two to six hours; put the beans into a boiler with the pork, scored fine on the skin, add double as much water, boil until the skin cracks (not mashed), pour the water away, then skim the beans into an earthen pot, add the pork last; pour in hot water—not that in which they were boiled—so as to cover them; add two tablespoonfuls of molasses. set them in the oven to bake, cover over the pot, make a good coal fire, shut up the stove, let them cook all night. In the morning you have a good hot breakfast. If preferred dry, use less water in baking them.

200. New York Baked Beans. [TIME.—TO BAKE, TWO HOURS.]

ARTICLES.—Dry beans, a quart, lean pork, two pounds, water.

DIRECTIONS.—With the pork, first scored, boil the beans until the skins break, pour away the water, then put the pork into a shallow pan, then the beans, then boiling water until it covers them, bake, and eat with vinegar and pepper. Not so good as the New England style. The pork should be covered with the beans, except the top of it.

201. Dry Beans Boiled Pudding. [Time.—To boil second time, an hour.]

Articles.—Dry beans, one quart; pork, half a pound, seasoning.

Directions.—Wash and soak the beans over night; boil them with the pork until very soft; mash the beans through a colander, cut the pork fine, put all into a pudding cloth, boil an hour and season to taste.

202. Dry Beans Baked Pudding

Is made as above, but baked in a pan instead of boiling.

203. Dry Beans Whole, French Style. [Time.—To boil, about one hour.]

Articles.—Dry beans, a quart; two tablespoonfuls of butter.

Directions.—Wash, soak, and boil the beans until tender, but keep them whole; put them in a double boiler with the butter, a pint of hot milk, pepper and salt; boil them all for five minutes and serve hot.

204. Beans Stewed. [Time.—Two hours.]

Articles.—Dry beans, a quart; pork, half a pound.

Directions.—Wash, soak and boil to a thin mash; boil the pork with them in small pieces; serve hot, with pepper to taste.

205. Beans and Bacon, English Style. [Time.—To cook, about two hours.]

Articles.—Dry beans, a quart; bacon, half a pound; six small onions, flour, butter, salt and pepper.

Directions.—Wash and soak them about an hour; put at the same time into the stew pan, the bacon; in an hour, add the beans with the onions whole; boil gently until cooked (whole); drain; then put into the double boiler a tablespoonful each of flour and butter, a half pint of milk, a half pint of the water the beans were cooked in; boil ten minutes, then pour it over the beans, etc. Eat hot.

206. Beans and Meat.

Boiled beans, prepared in the French style, are a very good addition to a dinner.

207. Beans a la Creme. [Time.—Two hours.]

Articles.—Dry beans, a pint ; two eggs ; two tablespoonfuls of cream, same of butter, one of vinegar.

Directions.—Wash, soak an hour, boil until tender in salted water ; beat up two eggs with the cream and butter ; put it into the double boiler ; when hot put in the vinegar and then the beans ; let them boil ten minutes ; serve hot.

208. Bean Soup. [Time.—Four hours.]

Articles.—Beans, a pint ; pork, half a pound.

Directions.—Wash the beans, boil in two quarts of water in the double boiler until they are mixed with the water ; strain the soup through a sieve, and serve hot.

209. Succotash in Winter. [Time.—To boil, four hours.]

Articles.—A pint of Lima beans, a pint of sweet corn, half a pound of bacon or pork, a pint of milk, and the same quantity of water.

Directions.—Soak the beans and corn all night, cut up the bacon in small pieces ; put into the double boiler, pour in the beans and corn, and boiling milk and water ; cook about four hours. Excellent.

210. Succotash in Summer.

Use green corn and beans and cook as above.

211. Green Peas in Winter.

Take green marrowfat peas just before they are ripe ; shell and dry.

212. Boiled Peas.

Soak all night, boil them until soft, not mashed ; add a little butter and salt when done. As good as canned peas.

213. Green Peas in Summer.
Cook same way without soaking.

214. Boiled Pea Pudding. [Time.—To boil second time, an hour.]
Articles.—Dry peas, one quart; pork, half a pound, with pepper and salt.

Directions.—Wash and boil the peas, until very soft, with the pork, mash the peas through the colander; cut the pork fine; put all into a pudding cloth, boil an hour, season to taste.

215. Baked Peas. [Time.—To bake, an hour.]
Articles.—A quart of peas, half a pound of lean pork.

Directions.—Soak the peas an hour, boil in the double boiler with the pork until quite soft; pour all into a deep dish and bake an hour, or until quite stiff; be careful not to burn them while baking.

216. Pea Pudding. [Time.—To boil, two hours.]
Articles.—One pint of peas, butter, salt, and pepper.

Directions.—Soak the peas several hours in plenty of water, pour them into the double boiler; when tender turn them out, mash them, season with pepper, salt, and butter; strain through a sieve, turn them back into the boiler to get hot, then serve.

217. Pea Soup. [Time.—To boil, three hours.]
Articles.—Peas, a pint; pork, a quarter of a pound.

Directions.—Boil the peas and pork in the double boiler with three pints of water until they are dissolved; strain through a sieve, serve hot, season to taste.

218. Winter Pea Soup. [Time.—To boil, four hours.]
Articles.—Split peas, a pint; three quarts of water; a pound of lean beef; a quarter of a pound of pork and seasoning.

Directions.—Boil the peas in the double boiler, in the water with the beef and pork cut up, until all is soft; serve hot; season to taste; fried bread, cut small, improves it.

SAUCES FOR MEATS.

Well-made sauces are the best proof of the skill of a good cook, and the very essential part of a dinner. They often give a zest to poor meat, or cheap pudding. It is economical to use good sauces, and we regret to say that many families use but one or two during the whole year, because they have no practical recipes for others. Most of ours are made in the double boiler; it prevents burning, and waste of material and time.

219. Mint Sauce. [TIME.—TO MAKE, THREE MINUTES.]

ARTICLES.—Green mint, two tablespoonfuls; sugar, same quantity; vinegar, half a teacupful. Good for any meat.

DIRECTIONS.—Mix the sugar in the vinegar, add the mint, first chopped fine; let it stand ten minutes, and it is fit for use.

220. Onion Sauce. [TIME.—HALF AN HOUR.]

ARTICLES.—Onions, four; milk, a pint; butter, a teaspoonful; pepper and salt.

DIRECTIONS.—Heat a pint of milk in the double boiler, peel and chop fine the onions, put them into the milk, boil until soft, add the butter and seasoning, serve hot or boil the onions in water; then add to the hot milk. Add flour to thicken if desired.

221. Butter Sauce. [TIME.—FIVE MINUTES TO BOIL.]

ARTICLES.—Flour, two teaspoonfuls; butter, four teaspoonfuls; half a pint of milk or water, and a little salt.

DIRECTIONS.—Put the flour and salt into the bowl, mix them smooth with the milk; then pour it into a double boiler, add the butter, and boil ten minutes.

222. Tomato Sauce. [TIME.—FIVE MINUTES TO PREPARE.]

ARTICLES.—Six large tomatoes, or a pint of canned ones; a tablespoonful of sweet oil; same of vinegar, half a teaspoonful mixed mustard, pepper, and salt to taste.

DIRECTIONS.—Mix the above together, and eat cold, or heat up for warm meats in the double boiler.

223. Potato Sauce. [TIME.—FORTY MINUTES.]

ARTICLES.—Equal quantities of potatoes and onions; piece of butter; pepper, and salt; and a cup of milk.

DIRECTIONS.—Boil until done; mash together, heat a cup of milk, add the mash and seasoning, boil two minutes, and serve with the seasoning.

224. New England Egg Sauce

Is made the same way, using eggs instead of potatoes.

225. Celery Sauce. [TIME.—ONE HOUR TO BOIL.]

ARTICLES.—Six stalks of celery; a pint of fresh milk; a tablespoonful of flour; same of butter.

DIRECTIONS.—Boil the milk in the double boiler, add the celery cut up in small pieces, boil until tender, add the flour mixed with the butter, and salt to taste. Extracts or the seeds bruised can be used.

226. Egg Sauce. [TIME.—TWENTY MINUTES.]

ARTICLES.—Two eggs; a cup of butter; a little salt; a cup of milk.

DIRECTIONS.—Boil the eggs hard, shell them, cut them up into small square pieces; melt the butter with milk into the double boiler, heat it very hot, add the salt, put the chopped eggs into a sauce bowl, and pour the butter over the eggs.

227. Oyster Sauce.. [TIME.—HALF AN HOUR.]

ARTICLES.—A tumblerful of oysters; tumblerful of milk; tablespoonful of butter; teaspoonful of flour.

DIRECTIONS.—Heat the milk and the liquor in the double boiler, chop the oysters fine, add to the milk; add the flour and butter first rubbed together. Boil well.

228. Caper Sauce. [TIME.—TO BOIL FIVE MINUTES.]

ARTICLES.—A cup of butter; flour, a tablespoonful; pint of

sweet milk ; four tablespoonfuls of capers.

DIRECTIONS.—Heat the milk in the double boiler, add the butter and flour mixed together ; add the capers.

229. Maitre d'Hotel Sauce. [TIME.—TEN MINUTES.]

ARTICLES.—Three ounces of butter ; juice of one lemon ; a teacupful of milk ; same of gravy ; a sprig of parsley.

DIRECTIONS.—Mix the butter smoothly with the juice of the lemon ; then mix the boiling milk with any gravy from the meat in the double boiler and heat it hot ; then stir in the butter until it is melted, and mix the parsley leaves in the sauce.

230. Salad Sauce. [TIME.—THREE MINUTES.]

ARTICLES.—Yolks of two hard boiled eggs ; a teaspoonful of sweet oil; tablespoonful of finely grated horse-radish ; a tablespoonful of strong vinegar; a teaspoonful of mustard ; salt and pepper to taste ; a tablespoonful of white sugar.

DIRECTIONS.—Mix all together using more or less of each article, according to taste ; it can be made thick or thin by using more or less vinegar.

SAUCES FOR PUDDINGS, PIES, AND CAKE.

231. Custard Sauce for Tarts or Puddings. [TIME.—TEN MINUTES.]

ARTICLES.—One pint of milk ; two eggs ; half a wine-glass of brandy ; sugar to your taste.

DIRECTIONS.—Stir two well-beaten eggs into hot milk and pounded sugar, quantity to your taste ; add half a glass of brandy, and pour it all into a double boiler, and stir it the same way till it is of the consistency of thick cream ; serve it over pudding, or in a tureen.

232. Egg Sauce for Pudding. [TIME.—TEN MINUTES TO BOIL.]

ARTICLES.—Yolks of four eggs ; a glass of sherry wine ; a lemon ; sugar to your taste.

DIRECTIONS.—Put the yolks of the eggs into a double boiler, and whisk them for two minutes; then add the wine and lemon juice strained, and the rind grated, and boil. Then pour it over the pudding.

233. Fruit Sauce. [TIME.—FIFTEEN MINUTES.]

ARTICLES.—A quart of any berries; six ounces of sugar, and five tablespoonfuls of water.

DIRECTIONS.—Put the berries, sugar, and water into a double boiler, letting it simmer fifteen minutes; then strain it through a sieve, and serve with any pudding that you think the flavor will improve. Berries or jams boiled and strained will be quite as good in the winter when fresh fruit cannot be obtained.

234. Wine Sauce. [TIME.—TEN MINUTES.]

ARTICLES.—Half a pint of melted butter; four tablespoonfuls of sherry wine; the peel of half a lemon; sugar to your taste.

DIRECTIONS.—Add to the butter, the wine, and the grated rind of half a lemon, and the sugar pounded and sifted; let it boil in the double boiler, and serve with any pudding, etc.

235. Dried Apple Sauce (French Style). TIME.—FIFTY HOURS, TO STEW.]

ARTICLES.—Dried apples, lemon, sugar.

DIRECTIONS.—Wash as many apples as you wish to stew, soak them in water all night, the next morning put them on to stew in the same water in a porcelain kettle. Stew all the next day after, add the sugar to taste, then strain through a sieve.

REMARKS.—This is a fine sauce; by cooking so long it loses the dried-apple taste. If you prefer the old style, cook four hours as above directed.

236. Cold Brandy Sauce for Puddings.

ARTICLES.—A quarter of a pound of loaf sugar; a quarter of a pound of fresh butter; one wine-glass of brandy.

DIRECTIONS.—Beat the butter with the sugar to a froth; then beat in gradually the brandy.

237. Cold Butter Sauce. [TIME.—THREE MINUTES TO MAKE.]

ARTICLES.—Butter, half a cupful; sugar, two cupfuls; two eggs; flavoring.

DIRECTIONS.—Beat all together, flavor with any essence, lemon, orange, or spice, to taste.

238. Orange Hard Sauce.

The juice of three oranges, and powdered sugar enough to make the hard sauce.

239. Banana Sauce.

Peel and mash three ripe mellow bananas; the juice of half a lemon; enough sugar to make a hard sauce.

240. Condensed Milk Hard Sauce. [TIME.—TWO MINUTES.]

ARTICLES.—A teacupful of condensed milk; a grated nutmeg; powdered sugar; a wine-glassful of sherry wine.

DIRECTIONS.—Mix all together, using sugar enough to make a hard sauce.

241. Transparent Sauce. [TIME.—HALF AN HOUR.]

ARTICLES.—A coffeecupful of water; a tablespoonful of butter; a coffeecupful of white sugar; the whites of two eggs; essence of lemon or vanilla.

DIRECTIONS.—Put the sugar, water, and butter into a double boiler, let it heat ten minutes, stirring it well; let it cool, and then beat the whites of the eggs into the cool sauce.

242. Hot Milk Sauce. [TIME.—TO BOIL, FIVE MINUTES.]

ARTICLES.—Milk, a pint; two eggs; a cup of sugar.

DIRECTIONS.—Heat a pint of milk hot in a double boiler, beat up the eggs and sugar, flavor to taste, add to the milk and boil.

243. Water Sauce.

Made as above, using water instead of milk, and adding juice of a lemon.

244. Dried Fruit Sauce of any Kind.

Wash the fruit, soak, stew, and sweeten to taste. Can be made thick or thin, by adding more or less water.

MEATS.

As all know, most meats are expensive, but many parts of animals are as good when cooked properly, or even better than the more costly and fashionable parts. In Europe, all parts of the animals are used, nothing is wasted, and it will be so here as soon as people understand how to cook them. This is most important, and when the wife or cook can make a wholesome, palatable dish at a saving of from one-half to three-quarters in price, it is her duty to do it, and save money.

Beef's Hearts

Are sold very low, and when cooked by any of these recipes, are very nourishing and good. They require to be well cooked. These recipes answer for hogs', sheeps', or calves' hearts. Soak them two hours in salt or warm water, and trim them of every waste, which is quite small.

245. Roast Heart. [TIME.—TWO HOURS TO ROAST.]

ARTICLE.—One heart.

DIRECTIONS.—Wash and soak, then bake or roast it well, and baste same as for beef.

246. Baked Stuffed Heart. [TIME.—TWO HOURS AND A HALF.]

ARTICLES.—One heart; loaf of bread; sage, salt, and pepper.

DIRECTIONS.—Wash and soak, cut out the lobes or strings, trim it; then fill it with bread stuffing, season with sage, etc., cover over the large end with strong paper. Bake two hours and a half.

247. Boiled Stuffed Heart. [TIME.—THREE HOURS.]

DIRECTIONS.—Prepare as above, tying the heart up in cloth; then boil.

248. Stewed Heart Whole. [Time.—Two to three hours.]

ARTICLES.—Heart, bread, seasoning, one egg, a carrot, three onions, cloves, allspice, and half a lemon.

DIRECTIONS.—Prepare as for boiling, make stuffing, fill it, then place it in a stew pan with water, let it stew two hours, then add a sliced carrot, three onions, twenty cloves, and same of allspice, and let it stew an hour longer. Take out the heart, add a tablespoonful of flour, juice of half a lemon, let it boil up once, pour over the heart, and serve.

249. Sliced Stewed Heart. [Time.—Two to three hours.]

Cook as above, slicing the heart in pieces.

250. Broiled Heart.

ARTICLES.—Heart, pepper, salt, and butter.

DIRECTIONS.—Prepare the heart, then cut it lengthwise in slices half an inch thick, broil over a clear fire. Pepper, salt, and butter to taste.

251. Fried Heart.

Prepare as for broiling, fry with hot fat, pepper, and salt.

252. Heart Soup. [Time.—Three hours.]

ARTICLES.—Half a heart, six turnips, six onions, two carrots, eighteen potatoes; salt and pepper.

DIRECTIONS.—Prepare as for stewing; then boil nearly two hours, add the vegetables and seasoning.

253. Corned Beef's Heart.

Put a heart in a bucket of strong salt water for two days; then boil with vegetables. It is equal to any corn beef.

254. Beef's-Heart Hash.

When any heart is left from the above dishes, cut the fat off, as it is not good in hash, then cut it up fine with as much cold potatoes (and onions to taste), cook it in a frying-pan; salt and pepper to taste; an onion chopped fine, and added will give it a good flavor.

255. Beef's-Heart Pie Meat.

To make mince pies nothing is better or so cheap as beef's hearts. Wash, but do not soak them; boil until tender.

Beef's Tripe,

One of the healthiest and cheapest of animal foods, and will give as much nutriment as the meat. Plain boiled and tender it is good for weak stomachs and dyspeptics. As it is always cheaper in price than beef, veal, mutton, or pork, it is very economical. It should be boiled tender; the thick parts are the best. In the recipes the tripe is first boiled tender.

256. Tripe Fried Plain. [TIME.—TEN MINUTES.]

DIRECTIONS.—Cut up the tripe in convenient pieces, and fry brown in any fat; season to taste.

257. Tripe Fried in Butter. [TIME.—HALF AN HOUR.]

ARTICLES.—Tripe, two pounds; flour, eight ounces; tablespoonful of butter; one egg; water, half a pint.

DIRECTIONS.—Make a batter of the last four (as for recipe for batter), dip the pieces of tripe in, and fry brown.

258. Tripe Broiled. [TIME.—TEN MINUTES.]

DIRECTIONS.—Broil the tripe plain over a bright coal fire. Butter, pepper, and salt; eat hot.

259. Tripe Baked. [TIME.—ONE HOUR.]

ARTICLES.—Tripe, butter, and bread crumbs.

DIRECTIONS.—Spread butter and a thick layer of bread crumbs on one side of a piece of tripe, roll it up, the bread, etc., inside. Tie it around tight with a cord. Bake one hour. Serve with onion sauce. Cut across the roll to serve.

260. Tripe Soused.

After it is boiled tender, put it in weak vinegar, add whole

FLINT & KENT

DRY GOODS

251 Main and 268 Washington Sts.

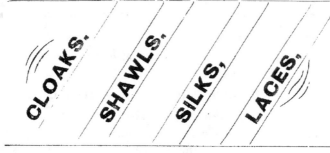
CLOAKS, SHAWLS, SILKS, LACES,

WHITE GOODS, LINENS,
Foreien and American Dress Goods,
Woolens, Flannels,
HOSIERY, GLOVES, UNDERWEAR,

 DOMESTIC COTTON GOODS,

LADIES' AND CHILDRENS'
COTTON UNDERWEAR,
UMBRELLAS AND PARASOLS,
WITH A FULL ASSORTMENT OF SMALL WARES.

ADULTERATION IN FOOD AND DRUGS.

ADULTERATION IN FOOD AND DRUGS has become so alarmingly prevalent that the only real safety to the consumer lies in the determination to patronize only houses of well-known reputation and reliability, avoiding all the **cheap** places, for where you find a business man advertising to sell at UNREASONABLY CHEAP prices you may rest assured there is a reason for his action which he does not care to disclose. In food and medicines the **best is the cheapest.** A FAIR PRICE for an HONEST ARTICLE is all any house of reputable standing will ask, and what is the saving of a few cents as compared with the preservation of health and strength? In drugs and medicines it is doubly important that **absolute purity** should be the standard of the dealer, for life itself often depends upon the virtue and efficacy of the medicines prescribed by the physician. In view of this fact MESSRS. GEORGE I. THURSTONE & CO., the well-known Druggists of 416 Main street, Buffalo, N. Y., have always kept in mind the maxim that "Quality in medicine is of the first importance." While they do not charge their customers FANCY PRICES they believe that the public is willing to pay a REASONABLE PRICE for a PERFECTLY PURE ARTICLE, and their success and popularity is no doubt attributable in a large measure to this fact. In addition to the purity of the medicines sold by them, the care and attention given by their corps of competent clerks in the prescription department to the compounding of Physicians' Prescriptions, is reassuring to the patron, as all possibility of a mistake is precluded, so systematic are the arrangements of this department in all its details. MESSRS. THURSTONE & CO. also have a full stock of the latest styles and most improved patterns in Trusses, Shoulder Braces and Supporters, as well as a large line of Toilet Articles, including Brushes, Combs, Face Powders, Handkerchief Extracts, Colognes, Sponges, Chamois, Pungents, Atomizers, etc., and in fact everything usually kept in a first-class drug store. Upon all these articles, as in the case of drugs and medicines, they adopt the principle of QUALITY and a **fair, reasonable price for first-class reliable goods.**

cloves, allspice, mace, pepper, to the vinegar. It is good eaten cold. (Can be cooked in any of these recipes same as if fresh.)

261. Tripe Stewed Plain. [Time.—Half an hour.]

Articles.—Tripe, a pound; water, a pint; flour, two tablespoonfuls.

Directions.—Pour a pint of boiling water into a double boiler, mix the flour in a little cold water, strain into the water, stir; then cut the tripe in small pieces, add pepper and salt to taste. Boil all nearly half an hour.

262. Tripe Stewed With Onions. [Time.—One hour.]

Articles.—Tripe, two pounds; onions, three; milk, a quart; flour, two tablespoonfuls.

Directions.—Cut three onions up, cook them in a frying-pan with a little water until soft; while doing this have a quart of milk on heating in the double boiler; when the milk is hot add the onions, and the tripe cut up in small pieces; then add the flour, as before, salt and pepper to taste; boil half an hour and serve hot.

263. Tripe Fricasseed. [Time.—Half an hour.]

Articles.—Tripe, a pound; mace, a blade; egg, one; water, a pint; one lemon; spice to taste; butter.

Directions.—Cut the tripe up in pieces, two inches square, put it into a stewing pan with the water hot, slice in a lemon, a great spoonful of butter, the mace, and let it stew; add pepper, salt, and spice to taste. Boil an egg hard; when done, pour out the tripe, and ornament the dish with slices of the egg.

Beef Palate

Is another part of the ox, scarcely if ever eaten in this country, but they are in Europe, and make a fine addition to the bill of fare. Butchers will gladly furnish them, upon being called for, at a low price.

264. To Prepare Beef Palates. [TIME.—TO BOIL, FOUR HOURS.]

Soak them for five hours in lukewarm water, then put them into a pot, scald them whole—they are hard—scrape off the skin if it does not come off easily; scald again until they look white and clean; boil them until they are tender.

265. To Stew Beef Palates. [TIME.—HALF AN HOUR.]

ARTICLES.—Three palates, three onions, a quart of milk, a dozen cloves and some allspice.

DIRECTIONS.—Prepare and boil as above, then cut them in small pieces with the onion and cloves; stew in a double boiler until all is done, then serve.

266. To Broil Beef Palates. [TIME.—TO BROIL, FIVE MINUTES.]

ARTICLES.—Three palates, pepper and salt, bread crumbs and egg sauce.

DIRECTIONS.—Prepare, boil as directed above until tender, press them flat; dip them in egg, then bread crumbs or meal and broil brown; serve with Worcestershire sauce.

267. Fry of Beef Palates. [TIME.—TO FRY, TEN MINUTES.]

ARTICLES.—Three palates, some bacon or pork, flour, butter, pepper, salt, horse-radish.

DIRECTIONS.—Prepare and boil the palates, cut them in square pieces and fry brown with pork or bacon; make some rich gravy, thicken with flour and butter, seasoned with the pepper, salt, and horse-radish; serve hot.

268. Palates au Friture. [TIME.—TO FRY, TEN MINUTES.]

ARTICLES.—Three palates, two eggs, flour, butter, salt, and pepper.

DIRECTIONS.—Prepare and boil; cut them in two; make a thick batter, dip the palates into the batter; fry brown, and serve hot.

REMARKS.—Any person desiring more spices can add them to these dishes.

269. Boiled Sheep's Trotters. [TIME.—THREE HOURS.]

ARTICLES.—Four trotters ; a tablespoonful of flour ; a saltspoonful of salt.

DIRECTIONS.—Perfectly clean and blanch the trotters, taking care to remove the little tuft of hair which is found in the *fourche* of the foot ; beat up a spoonful of flour and a little salt in the water you use for cooking them in, and let them stew till the bones come out easily.

270. Sheep's Trotters. [TIME.—THREE HOURS AND A HALF.]

ARTICLES.—Sheep's trotters, some force meat, pepper and salt, a spoonful of sauce.

DIRECTIONS.—Stew the sheep's trotters for about three hours; then take out the bones without injury to the skin, and fill the part from which the bones have been removed with force meat; put them into the double boiler, with a sufficient quantity of the liquor in which they were boiled to cover them, adding a teaspoonful of sauce and a little pepper and salt ; let them stew for about half an hour ; take them out, strain the gravy and boil it down to a glaze, with which glaze the trotters ; serve.

271. Sheep's Head (French). [TIME.—TWO HOURS TO BOIL.]

ARTICLES.—One head, two onions, two carrots, two turnips, a piece of celery, five cloves, a sprig or two of thyme, two tablespoonfuls of salt, a quarter of an ounce of pepper, two quarts of water.

DIRECTIONS.—Put the head into a gallon of water, and let it soak for two hours or more ; wash it thoroughly ; saw it in two from the top ; take out the brains ; cut away part of the uncovered part of the skull and the ends of the jaws ; wash it well ; put in a double boiler the onions, carrots, celery, cloves, thyme, a bay leaf, salt, pepper, and water ; let it simmer very gently, take out the vegetables and herbs; skim off the fat; lay the head on a dish; have the brains ready boiled—it will take ten minutes to do—chop it up fine, warm it in parsley and butter; put it in under the head and serve; any of the spices may be left out.

Hogs' Heads and Feet

Are the cheapest parts of the hogs, and full as good as any; in fact, many delicacies may be made of them.

272. Hog's-Head Cheese. [TIME.—FIVE HOURS.]

ARTICLES.—One hog's head, ears, feet, and tongue; salt, pepper, and sage.

DIRECTIONS.—Let the butcher split the head open, and remove the eyes, and cut off the nostrils; cut off the ears, clean them and the head well; also, the feet and tongue (do not boil the brains); boil all together until tender; while warm remove all the bones, cut it up coarsely, then season with salt, pepper, and sage; pour it into a pan or dish; eat cold, or fry.

273. Improved Hog's-Head Cheese. [TIME.—FIVE HOURS.]

ARTICLES.—Three quarts of liquor, salt, Indian meal.

DIRECTIONS.—Cook as above for cheese, strain the liquor, wipe out the pot; first strain off the fat; have about three quarts of liquor to use (if you have not as much, add water enough to make three quarts), strain it, return into the pot, stir in Indian meal until it becomes almost thick, let it cook, stirring constantly, to prevent burning, about ten minutes; salt, then stir in the meat; it must be well seasoned so as to season the meal; pour into pans; when cool, cut in slices, roll in meal, and fry brown. This will make a good dish.

274. Hog's Head Soused.

Prepare as for cheese, without meal, adding a little vinegar to the mass to suit the taste; pack in jars; keep a cloth wet with vinegar over it; eat cold, or fry.

275. Hog's Head Stuffed. [Time.—To cook, four hours.]

ARTICLES.—A hog's head, heart, liver, bread, pepper, salt.

DIRECTIONS.—Split open the head at the top, leaving the under part whole, remove the eyes, brains, and all the bones; strew the inside with salt, let it drain, make a stuffing of the haslet by chopping up the heart and liver, adding bread; season with pepper and salt, sew up the head where it is split open, now stuff it with the stuffing, sew over the back part a piece of white cloth, if to bake, it is ready, if to boil, wrap it in a towel, either way will take four hours (if a large one) to cook, serve hot or cold.

276. Hog's Head Baked. [Time.—Three hours.]

ARTICLES.—A head, one egg; sage, pepper, salt and butter.

DIRECTIONS.—Divide the head, take out the eyes, save the brains in a dish. Thoroughly clean the head and bake it two hours. Scald the brains, beat them up with an egg, sage, pepper, and salt, and a little butter, fry them brown. Serve with the head.

277. Stew, Hog's Head, Haslet, and Kidneys. [Time.—Four hours]

ARTICLES.—One head, haslet, kidneys, onions, potatoes, and flour.

DIRECTIONS.—Clean the head, and boil as before described, taking the upper part only, adding the kidneys and haslet, boil until tender, remove, cut up with a knife coarsely. Mix and add to the meat sliced onions and potatoes. When the meat is removed stir flour in the broth to thicken it. Serve hot.

278. Pig's Cheek. [Time.—Three hours.]

ARTICLES.—Pig's cheek, one ounce of bread crumbs.

DIRECTIONS.—Boil and trim in the shape of ham.

279. Boiled Corned Hog's Head.

Boil a hog's head with vegetables, it makes a cheap good dish. Boil the head four hours.

OX HEADS

Are used only by our foreign-born citizens, who understand the value and use of them; they contain a great deal of nutriment, and can be bought very cheap.

280. Ox Cheek Cheese (American Style). [TIME.—FOUR HOURS.]

ARTICLES.—Half an ox head, one teaspoonful of fine salt, half a teaspoonful of pepper, one tablespoonful of powdered thyme, enough water to cover the head.

DIRECTIONS.—Split an ox head in two, take out the eyes, crack the side bones, and lay in water one hour; then put it in a saucepan, with sufficient water to cover it, let it boil very gently, skimming it carefully; when the meat loosens from the bones, take it from the water with a skimmer, and put it into a bowl; take out every particle of bone, chop the meat very fine and season it with thyme and pepper; tie it in a cloth and press it with a weight; when cold, it may be cut in slices for dinner or supper; the gravy remaining will make a rich broth if a few vegetables be stewed in it.

281. Ox Cheek Stewed (German Style). [TIME.—SEVEN HOURS, ALTOGETHER.]

ARTICLES.—Half an ox head, one head of celery, some pepper and salt, four small onions, six cloves, two quarts and a half of water.

DIRECTIONS.—Well wash part of an ox head, and let it soak in cold water several hours; then put it into a stew-pan with a little pepper and salt, onions, celery cut into slices, cloves; pour in the water and set it over a gentle fire to simmer slowly; when tender, take out the head, and cut the meat from it in rather small pieces, strain the gravy and put about a third part of it in a stew-pan, with some force meat balls and pieces of head; make all very hot and serve.

282. Stew of Ox Cheek (French Style). [Time.— Four hours.]

ARTICLES.—An ox cheek, a little salt, and a few cloves, three onions, six carrots, four or five turnips, a head of celery.

DIRECTIONS.—Clean and wash the cheek well, cut off the fleshiest parts and break the bones into an available size, then put it into a pot with enough water to cover it, and season with pepper and salt, then with a few cloves, the onions and carrots, celery cut into pieces, and turnips of tolerable size, stew it slowly; before serving, the meat may be removed and the gravy thickened and browned; serve it very hot with the meat in the gravy. A shin of beef is excellent, dressed in this fashion.

283. Ox Cheek Corned.

Cut them off and salt; boil with vegetables; serve as for corned beef.

284. Ox Cheek Hash.

Boil, corned or fresh, and use for hash. See hash recipes.

285. Ox Cheek Pies.

Boiled, it is first rate for mince pies, in place of costly meat.

Animals' Brains

Are cheap, palatable, eatable, and a good many persons are fond of them. Believing nothing in this world should ever be wasted, we give these recipes, hoping the people will try them. Although they are generally thrown away, butchers will save them if purchasers can be obtained.

286. To Prepare Ox Brains.

Soak the brains in lukewarm water and clean them well from blood and fibers, and skin them; soak them ten hours in cold water in winter, and five hours in summer.

287. To Prepare Calves', Hogs,' and Sheeps' Brains.

Put the brains in cold water, with a tablespoonful of vinegar for each brain; soak them from one to five hours; remove the skin, fibers, etc.

An ox brain is as large as three or four of those of the smaller animals, but all are good to eat—there is no perceptible difference.

288. Brains Boiled (French Style). [Time.—To boil, one hour.]

ARTICLES.—An ox brain, or three other brains; two ounces of bacon, one carrot, four small onions, salt and pepper, a lemon, water.

DIRECTIONS.—Slice all the articles except the brains; put all into the double boiler, boil until the vegetables are done, then strain the sauce, boil all again fifteen minutes; serve with potatoes.

289. Brains and Tongue. [Time.—To boil, ten or fifteen minutes.]

ARTICLES.—A little parsley, thyme, pepper and salt; two tablespoonfuls of melted butter or cream; juice of a quarter of lemon, a pinch of cayenne.

DIRECTIONS.—Clean the brains, boil them in a little water fifteen minutes in the double boiler; take them up, drain and chop them, and put them to warm in the boiler, with the herbs chopped, the melted butter or cream, and the seasoning; squeeze a little lemon juice over them; stir them well together; boil the tongue, skin it, take off the roots, lay it in the middle of the dish, and serve the brains round it.

290. Mock Oysters (Made of Brains). [Time.—To boil, twenty minutes.]

ARTICLES.—Brains, milk, vinegar, whole cloves, allspice, cinnamon, pepper, salt.

DIRECTIONS.—Take brains from the heads as whole as possible, remove the skin and throw them into salt and water; let them remain in this two hours, then boil them until done in sweet milk in the double boiler, take them up in an earthen bowl or dish, and pour over weak vinegar to cover them; prepare sufficient vinegar to cover them by adding to it whole cloves, allspice and cinnamon to taste, season well with pepper, using part red pepper, scald the vinegar; pour off the weak vinegar and cover with the spiced vinegar. Eat cold, or stewed with crackers, as oysters.

291. Brains Fried (French Style).

ARTICLES.—Brains, pepper, salt, sage, flour, and bread crumbs.

DIRECTIONS.—Wash the brains, parboil them, remove all the skin, season them with pepper, salt, and sage, dust flour, meal, or bread crumbs over them, and fry a delicate brown.

292. Brains Baked. [TIME.—ONE HOUR TO BAKE.]

ARTICLES.—One ox or three hogs', calves', or sheeps' brains; two eggs, four tablespoonfuls of milk or cream, two of corn starch, one-third as much bread crumbs as brains, pepper, salt, and sage to taste.

DIRECTIONS.—Soak and clean the brains as directed parboil ten minutes, beat the eggs up with the corn starch, then beat all the articles together, season to taste. If too moist, add more bread crumbs, grease a dish well with butter, pour in the mixture, cover it over with bread crumbs.

293. Au Beurre Noir.

When prepared and boiled as above directed, put two ounces of butter in a frying pan, and when melted, turn into it two tablespoonfuls of vinegar, boil two or three minutes; then throw into it half a dozen stalks of parsley, take them off immediately with a skimmer, turn the butter and vinegar over the brains, spread the parsley around, and serve.

294. Brains Boiled.

ARTICLES.—Brains of one ox, or more of the others; four

tablespoonfuls of vinegar; two onions; ten cloves; same of allspice; salt and pepper to taste.

DIRECTIONS.—When prepared put the brain in a double boiler, cover it with cold water, add the vinegar, onions sliced, parsley, cloves, allspice, salt and pepper; boil about five minutes, and take off the fire; cut each half of the brain in two from side to side; place the four pieces on a dish, the cut part upward.

295. Brains Stewed in Wine.

When prepared as directed, put into a double boiler, and cover it with claret wine, add half an onion sliced, one clove of garlic, one clove, two sprigs of parsley, one of thyme, salt, six pepper corns, and boil. Cut and dish it as directed above, turn the broth over it through a strainer, and serve.

296. Brains en Matelote. [TIME.—TWENTY MINUTES.]

ARTICLES.—The brains; a spoonful of vinegar; one of salt; three small onions; half a glass of white wine; half a pint of milk, and two ounces of butter; pepper and sage.

DIRECTIONS.—Clean and soak the brains; then put them into a pot of boiling water, with the vinegar and salt, and let them scald for ten minutes; take them out and pass them through cold water. Fry the onions in butter and flour; then pour them in the milk and white wine, stir all well together. Put in the brains, mix them with the sauce, and stew them until done; season to taste.

297. Croquettes of Brains. [TIME.—TEN MINUTES.]

ARTICLES.—Brains; one spoonful of sage leaves; one egg; some bread crumbs; pepper and salt; a little milk.

DIRECTIONS.—Blanch the calf's brains, and beat them well together with a spoonful of sage leaves chopped very fine, seasoned with pepper and salt; mix them with bread crumbs soaked in a little milk and a well-beaten egg. Make them into balls, and fry them in butter. Serve them piled upon a dish.

298. Brains a la Worcestershire. [Time.—A quarter of an hour.]

Articles.—The brains; a spoonful of salt; one tablespoonful of vinegar; three ounces of butter; some Worcestershire sauce.

Directions.—Prepare the brains; then boil them in salt water and vinegar. Cut some thin slices of bread in the shape of scallop shells, and fry them in butter, lay these on a dish, divide the brains in two, and place on the fried bread, pour the sauce over them, and serve.

Lights or Lungs

Of sheep, calves, and hogs, if sound, are good and healthy eating. Like all the vitals and extremities, in this country they have not been used for food as commonly as in Europe; yet they are better eaten than wasted. If any part of an animal is diseased, none of it is fit to be eaten; this may easily be ascertained upon examination.

299. To Prepare Lights.

Trim and cut them up in slices, soak in cool water three hours, wash them well in lukewarm water twice, and squeeze the blood out of them.

300. To Fry Lights.

Prepare as above, slice and fry brown with pork fat.

301. To Stew Lights.

Articles.—Lights, butter, flour, onions, yolks of three eggs; salt and pepper, any other spice to taste.

Directions.—Prepare as above, parboil them three minutes, throw the slices of lights into cold water, drain them, cut into dice, fry them five minutes with butter, sprinkle them with flour, add six sliced onions, a pint of hot milk, salt, pepper, spice to taste; cook all in the double boiler until tender. Beat the yolks of the eggs with a tablespoonful of vinegar, mix with the whole, and turn on a dish and serve hot.

Lights may be cooked otherwise by any of the haslet recipes.

Kidneys.

Beeves', calves', lambs', and hogs' kidneys are all good, cheap, and hearty for the strong and well, but not fit for the weak and feeble. They make many excellent dishes. All butchers keep them; but buy only fresh ones.

302. To Prepare.

Wash, soak them in warm water half an hour, and trim. Beef kidneys three hours.

303. Kidney Stews. [TIME —TWO HOURS.]

ARTICLES.—Kidneys, onions, salt pork, flour, milk, and pepper.

DIRECTIONS.—Wash, trim, and cut up in thin slices any kidneys, put them into the double boiler, with onions sliced to taste, and two slices of salt pork. Cover with boiling hot water. Stew two hours. Make a cup of gravy of flour in cold milk, pour into the boiler; then add salt and pepper to taste, let it boil five minutes, serve hot.

304. Stewed Beef Kidneys. [TIME.—HALF AN HOUR.]

ARTICLES.—A beef kidney, pepper, and salt.

DIRECTIONS.—Cut the kidney into slices, and season it highly with pepper and salt, and fry it a light brown; then pour a little warm water into the pan, dredge in some flour, put in the slices of kidney, and let it stew very gently. Serve hot.

305. Rissoles of Kidneys. [TIME.—HALF AN HOUR.]

ARTICLES.—Some slices of cold kidneys; the same quantity of ham or bacon; yolks of two eggs; one ounce of butter; pepper and salt, and some bread crumbs.

DIRECTIONS.—Cut some neat slices from a cold beef kidney, with about the like quantity of ham or bacon cut into the same sized slices, and two hard-boiled eggs; lay the bacon over the kidney, then the slices of eggs, season with pepper and salt, and bind them together with a little melted butter and the yolk of a beaten egg. Dip them into beaten bread crumbs, fry them lightly and serve, with a little gravy in the dish.

306. Kidneys Fried. [TIME.—TEN MINUTES.]

ARTICLES.—Kidneys, flour, salt, pepper, butter and vinegar.

DIRECTIONS.—Trim, parboil, cut in thin slices, dredge them well with flour, fry on both sides, season with salt and pepper, make a gravy of butter and flour, add a little vinegar, and serve hot.

307. Broiled Kidneys. [TIME.—EIGHT MINUTES.]

ARTICLES.—Kidneys, pepper, salt, bread crumbs, and butter.

DIRECTIONS.—Cut each kidney through without dividing it, take off the skin, and season highly with pepper and salt; dip each kidney into melted butter, and strew bread crumbs over them, pass a small skewer through the white part of them to keep them flat, and broil them over a clear fire, serve them with hollow part uppermost, filling each hollow with the sauce. Use small kidneys.

308. Baked Kidneys. [TIME.—ONE HOUR TO BAKE.]

ARTICLES.—Kidneys, salt-pork, and pepper.

DIRECTIONS.—Prepare and slice the kidneys, place alternate layers of slices of salt-pork and kidney on a skewer, put these in a pan, a little cold water under the pan grate, and bake until done.

309. Kidneys Sautes au Vin. [TIME.—TEN MINUTES.]

ARTICLES.—Kidneys, a tablespoonful of butter; same of chopped onions and parsley; one saltspoonful of salt, and one of pepper; brown sauce; a teacupful of any wine.

DIRECTIONS.—Cut the kidneys into rather thin slices and put them into a pan with a little butter. When they are nearly done, add the chopped onion and parsley, with pepper and salt to taste. Pour in a little good sauce, and any wine. Boil it up and serve. This is a nice dish.

310. Kidney Gravy. [TIME.—ONE HOUR AND THREE-QUARTERS.]

ARTICLES.—Four kidneys; two ounces and a half of butter; a few sweet herbs; a little salt and cayenne; one teaspoonful of catsup; half an onion; one pint of water.

DIRECTIONS.—Slice four kidneys, cut them into pieces, and dredge them with flour; put them into a double boiler, with the butter, a few sweet herbs, and half an onion. Shake these over the fire for eight minutes, and then add the water. Let it simmer for two hours, skimming it carefully, strain the gravy, and set it by for use.

This gravy can be made from one beef kidney, instead of four sheep's kidneys which are about equal.

311. Roast Kidneys.

Prepare as above, and roast.

Haslets.

Sheeps', lambs', calves', and hogs' haslets.

312. To Fry Haslets.

Cut the heart and liver in slices, and fry with salt-pork fat and pepper to taste. Haslets should be well-cooked.

313. To Broil Haslets.

Cut them up in slices and broil until well-done; butter, salt, and pepper to taste.

314. To Stew Haslets.

Cut up in small pieces a haslet and two onions, put all into a double boiler, add boiling water, and stew until tender; season with pepper, salt, and butter to taste, and serve hot. It can be thickened with flour if desired.

315. Haslet and Milk. [TIME.—HALF AN HOUR.]

ARTICLES.—Milk, liver, pepper, salt, butter, flour, vinegar.

DIRECTIONS.—To a quart of boiling hot milk add the liver only from a haslet; boil half an hour in the double boiler. Pepper, salt, and butter to taste; add a little flour to thicken, wet first in cold milk, then boil a few minutes, add three tablespoonfuls of vinegar, stir it in briskly, and serve at once.

Ox Heels

Are not generally used as food, except by a few who know how good they are.

They make nutritive, agreeable, economical, and healthy dishes. Any butcher will furnish them cheap. A set of four will make a meal for twenty persons. Try these recipes.

316. To Clean and Prepare Ox Heels.

Dip them in boiling water, let them remain sufficient time to loosen the horny parts and hair, scrape, put the knife under the horn, and pry it off; wash until white and clean.

317. Ox Heels Boiled. [TIME.—ABOUT FOUR HOURS TO BOIL.]

ARTICLES.—Two or more heels; potatoes and other vegetables; pepper and salt.

DIRECTIONS.—Put two or more in a pot with plenty of water, boil until the bones can be taken out easily, season with pepper, salt, etc., and eat with potatoes and other vegetables.

318. Ox Heels Stewed. [TIME.—FOUR HOURS.]

Prepare and cook the heels as above, with less water, add onions, potatoes, and seasoning to taste, with a little flour.

319. Ox Heels Fried. [TIME.—TEN MINUTES TO FRY.]

ARTICLES.—Cow heels; yolk of an egg; bread crumbs; a sprig of parsley; cayenne pepper and salt; a piece of butter.

DIRECTIONS.—Having boiled, cut the heels into pieces about two inches long, and one inch wide, dip them into the yolk of a beaten egg, cover them with fine bread crumbs mixed with chopped parsley, cayenne, and a little pepper and salt; fry them in boiling fat, and arrange them neatly on a hot dish.

Ox heels can be cooked the same as pigs' feet, in any of the pigs' feet recipes.

320. Ox Heel Soup. [TIME.—SIX HOURS.]

ARTICLES.—Two feet; six carrots; six turnips; three small onions; ten potatoes, and a spoonful of black pepper; two heads of celery.

DIRECTIONS.—Cut up the feet; then put them into a double boiler; cut the carrots and turnips in slices; three small onions; add the black whole pepper, and about five quarts of water. Let it boil, and then simmer slowly till reduced to a pulp, and serve with vegetables.

Pigs' Feet.

Buy them before they are boiled, as they are much cheaper, and you can clean and boil them better, than is usually done at the markets.

321. Pigs' Feet Stewed. [TIME.—FORTY MINUTES.]

ARTICLES.—Pigs' feet, onions, pepper, allspice, salt, flour, vinegar.

DIRECTIONS.—After they are boiled tender cut them up, put them into the double boiler, with enough hot water to cover them, add an onion or two sliced at the bottom. Pepper, allspice, and salt to taste. Stew half an hour, turn off the gravy, thicken with flour and butter, add vinegar to taste, and pour it back on the feet. Boil ten minutes and serve hot.

322. Pigs' Feet Fried.

Take split boiled pigs' feet, rub them in meal, bread crumbs, or batter; fry until brown.

323. Picked Pigs' Feet.

ARTICLES.—Feet, meal, pepper, salt, vinegar, egg and flour.

DIRECTIONS.—Boil the feet until tender; while hot pick off the meat, season with pepper, salt, and vinegar to taste, put

CHOCOLAT MENIER,

PARIS, LONDON, NEW YORK, BOSTON.

THE BEST & PUREST CHOCOLATE MADE.

—{SOLD BY ALL}—

Grocers, Confectioners, Etc.

FOR FURTHER PARTICULARS APPLY TO

Menier, 54 Wall Street, N. Y.

Menier, 134 State St., Boston, Mass.

A FULL LINE OF

MENIER'S CHOCOLATES

CAN BE HAD AT

DINGENS BROTHERS,

333 Main Street, - - BUFFALO, N. Y.

the meat in pans and press it down. When cold cut in slices, dip them in meal, fry until slightly brown ; to prevent them falling to pieces dip the slices in egg, or fry in flour batter.

324. Pigs' Feet Broiled.

Take split boiled pigs' feet, broil until brown. Spread sweet butter on them and eat with mustard.

325. Pigs' Feet Fried in Batter. [TIME.—TWENTY MINUTES.]

ARTICLES.—Pigs' feet ; one egg ; one tablespoonful of flour ; one and a half gills of milk, a pinch of salt, a little lard for the pan.

DIRECTIONS.—Make a nice batter of an egg, a tablespoonful of flour, a gill and a half of milk, and a pinch of salt. Split the feet in halves, and dip them into the batter. Fry them a nice brown, and serve.

326. Pigs' Feet Fricasseed. [TIME.—ONE HOUR.]

ARTICLES.—One pint of milk ; one small onion, half a lemon peel, a small piece (size of a nut) of butter rolled in flour, one saltspoonful of salt ; pigs' feet.

DIRECTIONS.—Cut the feet in neat little pieces, and boil them in a little milk in the double boiler with a small onion and some lemon peel. Before you serve them, add a little butter, flour, and salt.

327. Pickled Pigs' Feet. [TIME.—ONE DAY.]

ARTICLES.—Vinegar, whole cloves, mace, allspice, pepper.

DIRECTIONS.—After they are boiled tender, put them in plain weak vinegar (add with whole cloves, mace, allspice, and pepper if desired in the vinegar), and scald the vinegar every week or two to keep it.

328. To Cook Pigs' Feet Thirty Other Ways.

They can be cooked in every style that heads, tripe, and calves' heads are. See those recipes.

329. Mock Brawn. [Time.—Four hours.]

ARTICLES.—Two hocks, feet, and ears.

DIRECTIONS.—Take two hocks, feet, and ears, boil them so tender that you may run a quill through them. Then pick the meat off the bones, have an oval pan, and lay the skin at the bottom and round the sides of it, put the meat in the middle, fill it as full as you can, and lay a heavy weight on it for a couple of days. Then take it out of the pan quite whole, bind it round with a broad piece of coarse tape, and put it into a pan with salt and water, changing the water every two or three days. It will keep for a fortnight or three weeks.

330. Pigs' Pettitoes. [Time.—Forty minutes.]

ARTICLES.—Feet, heart, and liver of a pig; a small piece of butter (size of a walnut); half a teaspoonful of pepper; a little salt; one pound of toasted bread.

DIRECTIONS.—Put them in just sufficient water to cover them, add the heart and liver, boil them ten minutes; then take out the liver and heart, and mince them small, return them to the feet, and stew until quite tender; thicken with flour and butter, season with pepper and salt, and serve up with sippets of plain or toasted bread, make a pyramid of the minced heart and liver, and lay the feet around them. When pettitoes are fried they should be first boiled, then dipped in butter, and fried a light brown.

331. Pigs' Feet With Onions. [Time.—To boil, one hour and a half; to broil, ten minutes.]

ARTICLES.—Four boiled pigs' feet; two onions; one teaspoonful of made mustard; two ounces of butter; one teaspoonful of flour.

DIRECTIONS.—Split the feet in halves; egg and bread; crumb them and broil them; cut the ears into fillets; put them into a double boiler, with two sliced onions, the butter, and the flour. When they are browned, take them up, add the mustard, and lay them on a hot dish. Put the feet on the top of them, and serve.

Calves' Heads and Feet

Are generally sold cheap. They are healthy, nutritious, and palatable when cooked properly. If you buy them uncleaned, dip the head and feet into scalding water, with a little rosin added to it; remove the hair and scrape well. After the head is cleaned, cut it open, take out the brains and eyes, let it soak all night in cold water, and cook as per recipes.

332. Mock Turtle of Calf's Head. [TIME.—ONE HOUR.]

ARTICLES.—Calf's head and feet, mace, cloves, nutmeg, red pepper, sweet herbs, a large onion, salt, butter and flour.

DIRECTIONS.—Take a calf's head, split it open, and lay it for two or three hours in cold water, then put it on to boil in as much water as will cover it; when it is done enough to take the meat off the bones, cut the meat into square pieces, and put them into the double boiler with some mace, cloves, nutmeg, red pepper, some sweet herbs and a large onion; salt to taste; put in as much of the liquor as will cover it, and let it stew gently one hour; then take one-quarter of a pound of butter, rolled in flour, and some browned butter, mix it with the stew, and let it boil half an hour; when done, fry the liver and lay it round the dish. Use as much spice as desired.

333. Calf's-Head Cheese.

Made precisely like hog's-head cheese; very good.

334. Boiled Calf's Head. [TIME.—ABOUT THREE HOURS.]

DIRECTIONS.—Clean, keep the skin on, remove the eyes, jaws, and nose; also the brains; put the head and tongue, with enough warm water to cover them, into a pot, tie the brains in a cloth, boil all together until tender; any vegetables can be added. Serve plain, or with brain sauce.

335. Calf's Head Stewed.

Cook same as for boiling, using less water, stirring in flour to thicken; when thoroughly done, season to taste and serve.

336. Calf's Head a la Maitre d'Hotel. [TIME.—ONE HOUR AND THREE-QUARTERS.]

ARTICLES.—Remains of a cold calf's head, three-quarters of a pint of maitre d'hotel sauce.

DIRECTIONS.—Remove the bones from the head and cut it into thin slices. When the sauce is sufficiently thick to cover the meat nicely, lay the slices in it, warm gradually, and as soon as it boils up place it on one side to simmer for a few minutes.

337. Collar'd Calf's Head. [TIME. — SIX HOURS, ALTOGETHER.]

ARTICLES.—A calf's head, a few thick slices of ham, three tablespoonfuls of minced parsley, three blades of pounded mace, half a teaspoonful of white pepper, six eggs.

DIRECTIONS.—Scald the head and scrape off the hair, clean it nicely, divide it and take out the brains, boil it for two hours, or until the meat leaves the bones, which must be taken out; then flatten the head on the table, cover it with a thick layer of parsley, a layer of slices of ham, the yolks of the eggs boiled hard, and cut into thin rings; between each layer put a seasoning of the pepper and spices; roll the head in a cloth very tightly, boil it for four hours, at least, then take it up and put it under a heavy weight; let it remain until cold; remove the cloth, etc., and serve.

338. Fricassee of Calf's Head. [TIME.—ONE HOUR AND A HALF.]

ARTICLES.—The remains of a boiled calf's head, a bunch of savory herbs, two dessertspoonfuls of lemon juice, one onion, one blade of mace, pepper and salt, two eggs, a piece of butter, flour, and a quart of the liquor in which the head was boiled.

DIRECTIONS.—Cut the meat from the head into nice thin pieces, and put the bones into a double boiler, with nearly a quart of the water in which the head was boiled, a bunch of savory herbs, a blade of mace, the onion browned, and a little pepper and salt; let it simmer for nearly an hour, then strain it into a double boiler, put in the slices of head, thicken the gravy with a little butter and flour, and bring it nearly to a boil, when done, take out the meat, and stir gradually in two dessertspoonfuls of lemon juice, and the yolks of two well-beaten eggs, but do not let it boil or it will curdle; pour it over the meat, and serve it up very hot.

339. Hashed Calf's Head. [TIME.—ONE HOUR AND A HALF.]

ARTICLES.—Half a calf's head, a bunch of savory herbs, a little cayenne pepper, salt, one lemon, one onion, one carrot, one quart of broth, or the liquor in which it was boiled.

DIRECTIONS.—Cut the meat from the remains of a boiled calf's head into small pieces of about two inches across, put a quart of broth, or the liquor in which the head was boiled, into a double boiler with a carrot, and one small onion, boil it until reduced to nearly half the quantity, then strain it through a hair sieve and add the wine, the juice of a lemon, two dessertspoonfuls of mushroom catsup, and a piece of butter rolled in flour; lay in the slices of head, and when gradually well heated, let it just boil up; then serve it on a hot dish, with rolled bacon, and forcemeat balls as a garnish.

340. Lamb's Head and Pluck. [TIME —ONE HOUR AND A QUARTER TO BOIL.]

ARTICLES.—A lamb's head, egg, bread crumbs, a cup of milk, a piece of lemon peel, pepper, salt, and nutmeg.

DIRECTIONS.—Soak the head in water for two hours, then boil it until nearly done, take it out and brush it over with the yolk of a well beaten egg, cover it thick with bread crumbs; again add the eggs and repeat the bread crumbs, season it with pepper and put it into a moderate oven until sufficiently brown, in the meantime, after scalding the pluck and setting to cool, mince it up fine, mix in the brains and season them with pepper, salt, and grated nutmeg; put them in a double boiler, with a piece of lemon peel cut thin; put the mince into a dish, and serve the lamb's head on it.

Liver.

The livers of all domestic animals that are eaten, are cheap, good, and healthy, and are generally sold for about one-third to one-quarter the price of other parts of the whole carcass.

341. To Prepare Liver.

When to be roasted whole soak them three hours in cold water; when to be boiled, wash only; when to be cooked in slices, have water with a little salt, on the fire; as soon as it boils throw the liver in for about five minutes, then take it out and drain it.

342. To Broil Liver.

Cut the liver in slices about a quarter of an inch thick, sprinkle on them salt and pepper, place them on a gridiron over a sharp fire, turn over only once, and serve with butter spread on the slices; a few drops of lemon juice may be added.

343. To Fry Liver.

Cut in slices as above; slice fat salt pork, fry the pork brown, and take it out when done, leaving the fat in, then put in the liver, cook until done, with salt, pepper and vinegar.

344. Liver and Bacon. [TIME.—QUARTER OF AN HOUR.]

ARTICLES.—Two pounds and a half of liver, one pound of bacon, juice of one lemon; two ounces of butter, a little flour, pepper and salt.

DIRECTIONS.—Soak the liver in cold water for half an hour, then dry it in a cloth and cut it into thin, narrow slices; take about a pound of bacon, or as much as you may require, and cut an equal number of thin slices as you have of liver, fry the bacon lightly, take it out and keep it hot; then fry the liver in the same pan, seasoning it with pepper and salt, dredging over it a little flour. When it is a nice brown, arrange it round the dish with a roll of bacon between each slice; pour off the pan, put in about two ounces of butter well rubbed in flour to thicken the gravy, squeeze in the juice of a lemon, and add a cupful of hot water; boil it and pour it into the center of the dish.

345. To Bake Liver. [TIME.—FROM THIRTY TO NINETY MINUTES, ACCORDING TO SIZE.]

DIRECTIONS.—Envelop the liver with buttered paper, place it in an oven and baste often; a few minutes before it is done, take the paper off, and baste continually; serve with the gravy or sauce.

346. To Saute Liver. [TIME.—ABOUT TEN MINUTES.]

ARTICLES.—Two ounces of butter, an onion, liver, flour, a wine-glass of warm milk, same of claret wine, salt, pepper and allspice.

DIRECTIONS.—Put two ounces of butter in a frying-pan, and set on a sharp fire; when melted, add an onion, then the liver cut in slices (after having been prepared as above); sprinkle on a saltspoonful of flour, then half a wine-glass of warm milk, same of claret wine, salt, pepper, and a pinch of allspice; serve when done.

347. To Stew Liver.

Prepare the liver as directed above, and when drained and cold, lard it well; have butter in a frying-pan on a brisk fire; when hot, put the liver in for about five minutes, turning it over on every side; have in a double boiler four ounces of bacon, cut in dice, set it on a good fire, and when hot, lay the liver in, then add pepper and salt, a sprig of thyme, two cloves, and a small carrot cut in two, cover the double boiler, subdue the fire, and let it simmer three hours, stirring now and then; place the liver on a dish, strain the sauce on it, and serve.

348. Liver a la Mode (French). [TIME.—TWO HOURS AND A QUARTER.]

ARTICLES.—A liver, or part of one; seven ounces of bacon, two ounces and a half of butter, a bunch of sweet herbs, two onions, six cloves, one clove of garlic, three carrots, two turnips, one wine-glass of brandy, one of wine, one tablespoonful of sauce.

DIRECTIONS.—After well washing the liver, soak it a short time in cold water, then wipe it dry and insert lardoons of bacon at equal distances in the interior part of the liver; put it into a stew-pan with about two ounces and a half of butter, a small bunch of herbs tied together, half a blade of mace, and a small onion stuck with six cloves, and fry it a nice brown; then add three carrots, two turnips, an onion cut, and a wine-glass of brandy, with sufficient water to just cover the whole; baste it frequently with its own gravy, and let it simmer slowly for two hours; when done take out the liver and put it on a dish, garnished with the cut vegetables; strain and skim the gravy, and the sauce, and glass of wine; boil it to the quantity required, pour it over the liver, and serve it up hot.

Hams, Shoulders, and Bacon.
HOW POOR ONES ARE MADE GOOD BY COOKING.

Hams, shoulders, bacon, and pickled pork are very economical and handy dishes, but they are so hearty that a person can not eat much; properly cooked, however, they are a luxury. By our mode of cooking, a common ham or shoulder is made as good as the best sugar-cured ones. Never buy them unless warranted sweet.

349. To Prepare Smoked and Salt Hams, Shoulders, and Bacon for Cooking.

Soak from twenty to fifty hours, according to the size, in three pails of water; trim neatly, removing any rusty parts—this soaking opens and fills the pores of the meat, which salting, smoking, and drying has hardened, and which cooking, with-

HAMS, ETC.

out long soaking, does not fill. By this process much waste is prevented. Try it, and this one recipe will pay for the book.

350. To Steam Ham, Shoulders, and Bacon. [TIME.—ABOUT SIX HOURS.]

DIRECTIONS.—After preparing as above, put over some boiling water in a pot, in which you have put an ounce of whole cloves, an ounce of allspice, an ounce of pepper; then put the meat in a steamer, cover tight and steam until tender; eat hot or cold.

351. To Boil Hams, etc. [TIME.—FIVE OR SIX HOURS.]

DIRECTIONS.—Prepare the ham as above, pour in enough water in a pot to cover the ham, add half an ounce each of whole cloves, allspice, mace, and nutmeg, half a pound of sugar; boil until the skin peels and it is tender; as the scum rises skim it off carefully; take off the pot and let it cool in the liquid until cold; remove the skin whole. If to eat hot, of course take it out before cooling.

352. To Bake a Ham, etc. [TIME.—FIVE HOURS.]

DIRECTIONS.—Prepare it as above; cover it over with a quite thick paste, then put it in a pan, bake it in a moderate oven until done, basting it frequently; the flour prevents its drying up; when done, remove the crust and skin; serve hot or cold.

353. To Bake, Boil, etc., a Ham.

Prepare and boil a ham as above directed for boiling three hours, no longer; then put it in a moderate hot oven from the pot, and bake it two hours more. This gives a fine flavor to the ham.

REMARKS.—Any family once using the above recipes to cook hams, shoulders, bacon, and pickled pork, will use no other. We have repeatedly tried the most inferior hams this way, and then tried the old way with the best cured hams, costing much more, and found the common hams the best.

354. Ox Tail Soup. [TIME.—TWO HOURS.]

ARTICLES.—One ox tail, white or Russia turnips, onions, potatoes, carrots, salt, pepper, and flour.

DIRECTIONS.—Ox tail makes a rich soup, rich in strength and nutriment. Cut up an ox tail in three-inch pieces, wash it, put it in the soup pot, cover with cold water and heat it slowly; as the scum rises to the top skim it off until all is removed; when boiled two hours to a gallon of soup, peel and slice six white or two Russia turnips, six large onions or more small ones, also a dozen Irish potatoes; and two carrots; add salt and pepper to taste; when almost done add flour, beaten up in water, strain, boil up, then remove and serve.

REMARKS.—Rice and barley can be added to soups, if preferred to flour. Any meat can be used—beef, mutton, pork, or veal.

355. Tongues

Are good corned, or smoked, boiled tender.

356. Rolled Beef to Eat Like Hare. [TIME.—A QUARTER OF AN HOUR TO EACH POUND.]

ARTICLES.—The inside of a sirloin of beef; half a pound of bacon; some rich gravy; two glasses of port wine; two of vinegar; twenty pounded allspice; currant jelly, and melted butter.

DIRECTIONS.—Soak the beef for a day and night in a glass of port wine, and the same of vinegar; lay some good forcemeat over it, lard it with shreds of bacon, and bake it. Baste it frequently with port wine and vinegar, in the same proportion that you used for soaking it, and season it with some pounded allspice. Serve it up with a rich gravy poured round it, with currant jelly in a tureen.

357. Potted Ox Tongue.

ARTICLES.—One pound and a half of boiled tongue; six ounces of butter; a little cayenne; a small spoonful of pounded mace; nutmeg and cloves.

DIRECTIONS.—Remove the rind of the tongue, cut and pound it in a mortar as fine as possible with the butter, and the spices beaten fine. When perfectly pounded, and the spice well blended with the meat, press it into small potted pans, and pour clarified butter over the top. A little roast veal added to the potted tongue is an improvement.

358. Potted Beef Like Venison. [TIME.—TO BAKE, TWO HOURS TO TWO HOURS AND A HALF.]

ARTICLES.—Four pounds of buttock of beef; two ounces of saltpeter; two ounces of bay salt; a quarter of a pound of common salt; half an ounce of salprunella; half an ounce of cloves and mace, a quarter of an ounce of pepper; half a nutmeg.

DIRECTIONS.—Take four pounds of buttock of beef, and cut the lean into four pieces; beat the saltpeter, bay salt, common salt, and salprunella very fine, mix them well together, and rub them into the beef. Let it remain in the pan four days, turning it night and morning; after that put it into a pan, cover it with water and a little of the brine. Send it to the oven, and bake it until very tender; then drain it from the gravy, and take out all the skin and sinews; pound the beef in a mortar, put it on a broad dish, and strew over it the mace, cloves, and pepper, all beaten very fine, and grate in half a nutmeg, mix the whole well with the pounded meat, and add a little fresh butter clarified to moisten it. Then press it down into pots, set them at the mouth of the oven just to settle, and then cover them two inches deep with clarified butter. When quite cold, cover them with white paper tied over, and set them in a dry place. The beef will keep good a considerable time.

359. Pressed Beef. [TIME.—FIVE HOURS.]

ARTICLES.—Ten or eleven pounds of the flank; two pounds of salt; half a pound of moist sugar; a quarter of an ounce of saltpeter.

DIRECTIONS.—Take about ten or eleven pounds of the thin flank, and rub well into every part two pounds of salt, and half a pound of moist sugar, mixed with the saltpeter dissolved;

repeat the rubbing with the pickle every day for a week; then roll it round, and bind it with a wide piece of tape. Have ready a stew pan of scalding water, put in the beef, and when it simmers allow five hours for ten pounds of meat. When sufficiently done, drain off the water in which it was boiled, and pour cold water over it for six or eight minutes, drain it on a sieve reversed, and then place it on a board with a weight on it to press the meat well. Then remove the tapes, trim it neatly, and serve it when required.

360. Boiled Marrow Bones.—Served on Toast. [TIME.—TWO HOURS.]

ARTICLES.—Flour, bread, pepper, and salt.

DIRECTIONS.—Saw the bones any size you may prefer, cover the ends with a common paste of flour and water, tie a cloth over them, and place them in a small stew pan, with sufficient boiling water to cover them. When sufficiently boiled, serve them upright; or when boiled, take out the marrow, and spread it on toasted bread cut into small square slices; season it with pepper and salt, and send it to the table quickly.

361. Loin of Mutton to Eat Like Venison. [TIME.—THREE HOURS.]

ARTICLES.—A large fat loin of mutton; one onion; a sprig of thyme and parsley; a little whole pepper and salt; one pint of port wine.

DIRECTIONS.—Bone a large and fat loin of mutton, take the skin off the fat, and put the bones and mutton into a stew pan wtth an onion, a sprig of thyme and parsely, and a little whole pepper and salt; add a pint of port wine, cover the pan close, and set it over a very slow fire to stew. Then skim off the fat from the gravy, and serve it very hot with sweet sauce in a tureen.

362. Shoulder of Mutton Spiced. [TIME.—FOUR HOURS.]

ARTICLES.—Two ounces of coarse sugar to one pound of

meat; one saltspoonful of cloves to the same; mace and pepper mixed, one teaspoonful; ginger, a pinch; half an ounce of salt; beef gravy to a whole joint, one pint and a half.

DIRECTIONS.—A shoulder of mutton, boned, may be rubbed with the seasoning above given, increased in proportion to its weight. The salt to be added the day after the sugar, cloves, mace, ginger, and pepper have been rubbed into the meat. Turn and rub the meat with this pickle every day for a week or a little longer.

Roll it up tightly, bind it with a string, and stew it gently in beef broth. Serve it in its own gravy with good piquante sauce.

General Recipes for Cooking Meats, etc.

We give some general rules for soups, stews, roasting, baking, boiling, and frying neats.

363. Soups

Are a compound of meats and vegetables, or meats and vegetables separately. Soups are called by the name of the principal meat or vegetables of which they are made. Meats should always be put into cold water for soups, heated gradually, and boiled gently. This converts nearly all the goodness of the meat into the soup. Soups are cheap, healthy, and nutritious, can be made out of the liquors that meats are boiled in, or shins and coarse pieces of meat, and are just as good. All kinds of vegetables, also rice and barley, are used to suit the taste.

364. Stews

Are similar to soup, but much thicker and richer; less water makes a stew.

365. Roasting

Is simply turning the meats before a fire until cooked. As it is very seldom done, we will only say that it is a good method, but we do not think it worth so much trouble, if you have a good oven, which will roast as well, and is more convenient.

366. Baking is more Economical.

All cooking in range, stove, or any oven, is baking; therefore meats cooked in an oven is baking. Meats should be put on a grate in a pan to raise them an inch from the bottom of the pan, pouring in a pint of salted water to keep the oven moist; bake slowly and steadily and baste frequently with the gravy; the gravy is good plain, or mixed with flour, and can be seasoned to taste.

367. Boiling

Either salt or fresh meats, is a good way to cook them; boil them tender, if fresh; to be cooked whole, drop them in hot water; if corned, drop it in warm water. The first closes the pores of the meat, the second draws out the salt. Corned beef is a healthy dish.

368. To Broil Beef Steak, Veal Cutlets, Pork and Mutton Chops, Liver, Fowl and Game.

Grease the bars of your gridiron (use the kind that turns over instead of turning the meat), place the meats on it, and broil over a hot coal fire; cut the meats one-half an inch thick; do not stick a fork in them while cooking, as it allows the juice to run to waste. The meats should not have too much fat on them. After they are done lay in a hot dish (if not done return to the gridiron at once). Salt and pepper to taste. Spread on good sweet butter; recollect, serve and eat hot. This is the plain way of broiling any kind of meat, fowl, or game. Before broiling or frying livers or hearts, soak in salt and water a few minutes if preferred.

369. To Fry Steaks, Chops, Cutlets, Fowl, Game, etc.

A large deep wrought-iron frying-pan is best. Always let the fat be hot before putting in the meat (I prefer salt pork fat fried out of clear salt pork to any other); lard, oil, or butter can be used. Have enough to cover the meat. All meats except beef should be well cooked.

Watch the meat carefully, and turn often, so that it does not burn. Salt and pepper to taste ; but do not salt until the meats are done ; salt hardens meats. Spread sweet butter over the meats hot. Put on a hot dish. Persons who like onions can cut up one or more, fry and cook in the gravy.

370. Semi-Frying, or Broiling in the Frying-Pan.

Heat the pan very hot, grease it, lay in it the meat, turning it frequently until done ; finish as above.

371. Frying Covered Meats.

Roll the meats in flour, meal, or bread crumbs, shaking off what will not adhere, and cook as above. Tomatoes, mustard, vinegar, wine, or any seasoning may be used.

372. Cutlets, Steaks, Chops, Beef's Heart, Liver, Tripe, etc., With Tomatoes.

A pint of canned or whole tomatoes, an onion, a tablespoonful of sugar, salt and pepper to taste, a tablespoonful of butter, and three of fine bread crumbs and a tumbler of hot water. Let these simmer gently together, while the meat is being fried or broiled; take them out when done; pour the tomatoes over them.

373. Hashes, Entrees of Cold Meats.

All meats left over, also potatoes, will make good entrees, hashes, etc.

374. To Make Good Hashes,

Take out all the bones, and leave only one-quarter of fat to three-quarters of lean meat. Onions, parsley, pepper and salt to taste ; chop all fine, heat up well and serve hot.

375. Cold Meats

Are often as good as hot eaten with a salad, or maitre d'hotel sauce.

376. Entrees of Cold Meats, etc.,

Are made in almost any style to suit the taste, by slicing and warming them in sauces or gravies, spiced and seasoned highly.

377. Forcemeats,

Or stuffings for poultry, and game, meats or vegetables, can be made of ham or bacon suet, veal, oysters, bread crumbs, soaked bread, or eggs; any spice or sweet herbs to taste.

A selection can be made from any of the above list and flavor as desired. Sometimes milk, butter, wine, and brandy, are used. Onions are used with bread to stuff geese, ducks, or strong game.

Any meat or vegetables can be stuffed; and, by using good taste, can be improved.

VEGETABLES

Are healthy, but not very nutritious. The various ways of preparing them given below will repay a trial of them.

Turnips

Are cheap, hardy, and plenty, and will keep all winter.

378. Plain Boiled Turnips.

Peel, and boil them until soft, with any corned meats.

379. Mashed Turnips with Onions.

Mash the boiled turnips with a few boiled onions; salt, pepper, and butter to taste

380. Fried Turnips.

Cut cold boiled turnips lengthwise in slices half an inch thick; fry brown and eat hot.

381. Puree of Turnips. [TIME.—TO PREPARE, TEN MINUTES.]

ARTICLES.—Six turnips, three tablespoonfuls of butter, same of milk, pepper and salt to taste.

DIRECTIONS.—Wash, peel and slice six turnips; when tender, press them through a sieve, mix in the butter, milk, and seasoning; put the mass into the double boiler, and cook half an hour.

BOOTS AND SHOES.

FOR GOOD AND RELIABLE

BOOTS AND SHOES

AT PRICES TO MEET THE MASSES,

——{ GO TO }——

HARRY H. KOCH'S,

No. 480,   -   Ladies' Department.

No. 482,   -   Gents' Department.

MAIN ST.,   -   BUFFALO, N. Y.

Hand-Made Work at Prices of Machine-Made Goods a Specialty.

MAYER'S CONFECTIONERY
—⟨ AND ⟩—
LADIES' RESTAURANT,
386 MAIN STREET.

Parties and Families supplied promptly and on short notice with

CHOICE CAKES and PASTRY
SALADS, ICE CREAMS, WATER ICES,

AND EVERYTHING REQUIRED FOR

PUBLIC and PRIVATE ENTERTAINMENTS

OYSTERS IN SEASON.

—⟨ OUR ⟩—

Chocolate and Coffee Cannot be Surpassed.

WE MAKE OUR OWN CANDIES OF

PURE CANE SUGARS.

OUR PRODUCTIONS AND GOODS ARE ALL FIRST-CLASS AND OUR PRICES REASONABLE.

Carrots.

382. To Fry Carrots.

Boil, slice, and fry brown.

383. Carrots (Flemish Way). [TIME.—FORTY MINUTES TO BOIL.]

ARTICLES.—Six or eight good-sized carrots, five small onions, a sprig of parsley, salt and pepper, a pint of milk, and a quarter of a pound of butter.

DIRECTIONS.—Boil the carrots forty minutes, or until they are tender; cut them into dice, then stew them in a double boiler with the small onions, chopped parsley, a little pepper and salt, a pint of milk, and melted butter; serve very hot.

384. To Stew Carrots. [TIME.—TO PARBOIL THEM, FIFTY MINUTES; NEARLY TWENTY MINUTES TO SIMMER.]

ARTICLES.—Some carrots, a piece of butter rolled in flour, and cream.

DIRECTIONS.—Cut into large slices five carrots scraped and washed, parboil them, and then simmer until tender in about a quarter of a pint of milk, and five large spoonfuls of cream, in a double boiler. Add a seasoning of pepper and salt, and a piece of butter rolled in flour; when done serve on a hot dish.

385. Mashed Carrots. [TIME.—TO BOIL THE CARROTS, ONE HOUR AND A HALF TO ONE HOUR AND THREE-QUARTERS.]

ARTICLES.—Some carrots, butter, pepper and salt.

DIRECTIONS.—Scrape off all the skin, wash them well and boil them tender in a stew-pan of boiling water. Then take them up with a skimmer, mash them smooth, add a piece of butter, and salt; place them in the center of a dish piled up and marked over with a knife; serve with boiled or roast meat.

Onions.

386. To Stew Onions Brown. [TIME.—TWO HOURS.]

ARTICLES.—Some onions and good beef gravy.

DIRECTIONS.—Strip off the skin and trim the ends neatly, taking care not to cut the onions; place them in a double boiler, cover them with some very good beef gravy, and let them stew very slowly for two hours, or until they are perfectly tender without breaking. The onions may be dredged lightly with flour and fried a light color, before they are stewed, if preferred.

387. Baked Onions.

Wash and bake them with the skins on same as potatoes; peel when done, and eat with sauce.

388. Onions a la Creme. [TIME.—TWO HOURS.]

ARTICLES.—Four or five onions, three ounces of butter, a little flour, pepper, salt, and a cupful of milk.

DIRECTIONS.—Boil the onions in two or three waters to take off the strong taste, then put them into a double boiler, with the butter, a little flour rubbed smooth, pepper, salt, and milk; stir them frequently until sufficiently done; serve them with the sauce poured over them.

389. To Stuff Onions. [TIME.—TO FRY, TEN MINUTES; TO STEW, TWO HOURS.]

ARTICLES.—Some large onions, a little fat bacon, a little lean beef, bread crumbs, a sprig of parsley, lemon peel, pepper, salt, and mace, one or two eggs, a piece of butter and some brown gravy.

DIRECTIONS.—Peel some onions, parboil and drain them, then take out the inside, but be careful to keep the onions whole; chop up the inside of the onion, a little beef and a little fat bacon; add some bread crumbs, a sprig of parsley, a lemon peel minced up, and a seasoning of pepper, salt and mace; beat it all up with a well-beaten egg or two, into a paste, and stuff the onions with it; dredge them all over with flour, and fry them a nice brown; then put them into a double boiler with sufficient brown gravy to cover them, and stew them gently for two hours. If stewed in water, add flour and butter.

Celery.

390. Celery with Milk. [TIME.—TO BOIL THE CELERY, THREE-QUARTERS OF AN HOUR.]

ARTICLES.—Six heads of celery, a pint of milk, a piece of butter rolled in flour, nutmeg and salt.

DIRECTIONS.—Take celery, cut them about three or four inches long, wash them very clean, and boil them in water until they are tender, put in the milk, mix the butter and flour, and a little salt and grated nutmeg, boil it up till it is thick and smooth, put in the celery, warm it up, and serve with the sauce poured over it.

391. Celery with Cream. [TIME.—TO BOIL THE CELERY, THREE-QUARTERS OF AN HOUR ; TO THICKEN THE SAUCE, SIX OR EIGHT MINUTES.]

ARTICLES.—Three or four heads of celery, yolks of four eggs, half a pint of cream, a little salt and grated nutmeg.

DIRECTIONS.—Cut the white part of three or four heads of celery into lengths of three or four inches long, boil it until tender and strain it from the water, beat the yolks of four eggs and strain them into the cream, season with a little salt and grated nutmeg, put it into a double boiler with the celery until it boils and is of a proper thickness, and then send it to the table on toasted bread.

392. Celery Fried. [TIME.—TWENTY MINUTES.]

ARTICLES.—Three stalks of celery, two eggs, salt, nutmeg, two ounces of butter, four spoonfuls of white wine, two ounces of flour and two ounces of lard.

DIRECTIONS.—Make a batter with the yolks of two eggs well beaten, the white wine, salt and nutmeg, and stir the flour in thoroughly ; dip each head of the celery into the batter and fry in lard, when done, serve quite hot with melted butter poured over them.

Cucumbers.

393. To Stew Cucumbers. [TIME.—TO FRY, FIVE OR SIX MINUTES; TO STEW, SIX OR SEVEN MINUTES.]

ARTICLES.—An equal quantity of cucumbers and onions, two ounces of butter, six tablespoonfuls of wine, and a half a blade of mace, a little salt, cayenne, and a piece of butter rolled in flour.

DIRECTIONS.—Cut into slices an equal quantity of cucumbers and onions, and fry them in the butter, strain them from the butter and put them into a double boiler with the milk, wine, and mace; stew for about six or seven minutes in the boiler; stir in a bit of butter rolled in flour, a seasoning of salt and a very little cayenne; boil the sauce, thicken, and then serve it up hot.

394. To Stuff and Boil Cucumbers. [TIME.—ONE HOUR AND FIVE MINUTES.]

ARTICLES.—Two large cucumbers, a little forcemeat, a pint of milk, two ounces of butter and seasoning to taste.

DIRECTIONS.—Peel two large cucumbers, cut a piece of the large end, and scoop out the seeds, fill them with forcemeat, replace the pieces from the end, and secure it with a very small skewer; put the milk into a double boiler, with two ounces of good butter and seasoning, put in the cucumbers and let them boil very slowly for one hour; then take them out and boil down the sauce for a few minutes, pour it over the cucumbers and serve hot.

395. To Roast Cucumbers. [TIME.—TWENTY MINUTES, OR HALF AN HOUR.]

ARTICLES.—Two large cucumbers, some forcemeat, a little butter and half a pint of gravy.

DIRECTIONS.—Boil the cucumbers ten minutes, then cut them down and take out all the inside; fill them with forcemeat and tie them together, dredge over them a little flour, and place them in an oven to become brown, basting them frequently with fresh butter; when done put them on a hot dish.

396. To Dress Cucumbers.

ARTICLES.—Five tablespoonfuls of vinegar, three of sweet oil, pepper, and salt.

DIRECTIONS.—Pare the cucumbers and commence cutting them at the thick end with a sharp knife, shred them as thin as possible on a dish, sprinkle them with pepper and salt, and pour over them the above proportion of oil and vinegar.

397. Cucumbers, a la Poulette. [TIME.—TWENTY-FIVE MINUTES.]

ARTICLES.—Three large cucumbers, a little salt, two tablespoonfuls of vinegar, yolks of two eggs, a piece of butter, a little flour, two spoonfuls of cream, and half a pint of broth.

DIRECTIONS.—Take the cucumbers, pare off the rind and cut them into slices of an equal thickness, pick out the seeds and boil them tender in boiling water, with salt and vinegar, when done take them carefully out with a slice, and when drained, put them into a double boiler with half a pint of milk, butter, flour and cream, skim off any fat which may rise, and boil it gently for a quarter of an hour, taking care that the slices of cucumbers are not broken; when ready to serve, stir in the eggs, beaten with a spoonful of vinegar.

BAKED AND BOILED PUDDINGS.

Puddings are generally cheap, and a healthy food, nutritious and agreeable to the taste.

For boiled puddings you will require either a mold or a pudding-cloth, the former should have a close-fitting cover, and be rubbed over the inside with butter before putting the pudding in it, that it may not stick to the sides. A pudding-cloth must be kept very clean, and in a dry place. Bread, flour, and meal puddings should be tied very loosely as they swell very much in boiling.

The water must be boiling when the pudding is put in, and continue to boil until it is done. If a pudding is boiled in a cloth, there must always be water enough to cover the pudding; but if boiled in a tin mold it is best not to let the water quite reach the top. When the pudding is done, take it out from the water, plunge whatever it is boiling in, whether cloth or mold, suddenly into cold water; then turn it out immediately; this will prevent its sticking. If there is any delay in serving the pudding, cover it with a napkin, or the cloth in which it was boiled; but it is better to serve it as soon as removed from the cloth, basin or mold.

Bread or rice puddings require a moderate heat for baking; batter or custard require a quick oven. The time needed for cooking each particular pudding is given with the recipe.

Eggs for puddings are beaten enough when a spoonful can be taken up clear from strings.

Souffles require a quick oven. These should be made so as to be done the moment they are required for serving, otherwise they will fall in and flatten.

398. Boiled Arrow-Root Pudding. [TIME.—ONE HOUR TO BOIL.]

ARTICLES.—Three tablespoonfuls of arrow-root; one pint of milk; two eggs; sugar and flavoring to taste.

DIRECTIONS.—First mix the arrow-root smooth in a few spoonfuls of cold milk, stir into it the remainder, add two well-beaten eggs, and sugar and flavoring to your taste, put it into a double boiler, and boil it for one hour with the lid close on.

399. Baked Arrow-Root Pudding. [TIME.—HALF AN HOUR TO BAKE.]

ARTICLES.—Three dessertspoonfuls of arrow-root; a pint and a half of milk; peel of half a lemon; a piece of butter, the size of a walnut; half a cupful of sugar; three eggs; a little nutmeg, and puff paste.

DIRECTIONS.—Mix into a rather thick smooth batter the arrow-root, with a little cold milk. Put the remainder of the milk into a double boiler, with the lemon peel and sugar. When it boils strain it gradually into the batter, stirring it all the time and adding the butter. When nearly cold stir in three well-beaten eggs, and pour the whole into a pie dish, round which has been placed a border of puff paste. Grate a little nutmeg over the top, and bake it in a moderate oven.

400. Boiled Sago Pudding. [TIME.—THREE-QUARTERS OF AN HOUR.]

ARTICLES.—Two ounces of sago, one pint of milk; two eggs; two biscuits; one glass of brandy, and sugar to your taste.

DIRECTIONS.—Boil the sago in a double boiler in the milk until it is quite tender. When cold add the eggs, biscuits, brandy, and sugar, beat all together, and put it into a buttered basin. Boil it three-quarters of an hour, and serve with wine sauce.

401. Baked Sago Pudding. [TIME.—ONE HOUR TO BAKE.]

ARTICLES.—One quart of milk, four tablespoonfuls of sago; rind of one lemon, three eggs, two ounces of butter, two ounces and a half of sugar, and puff paste.

DIRECTIONS.—Boil the milk in a double boiler with the lemon peel, then strain it through muslin, and stir in the sugar and sago, set it over a slow fire, and let it simmer for twenty minutes. Then put it into a bowl to cool. Add the butter and the eggs well-beaten, put it into a pudding dish with some puff paste round the edge, and bake it for an hour in a moderate oven.

402. Boiled Macaroni Pudding. [TIME.—ONE HOUR AND A QUARTER.]

ARTICLES.—Two ounces and a half of macaroni; one quart of milk, three eggs; a wine-glass of brandy or wine, and the peel of one small lemon.

DIRECTIONS.—Simmer the macaroni in the milk and the peel

of a lemon for about an hour, or until it is tender, and take out the lemon peel. Beat the eggs well, add sugar to taste, the brandy or wine, and stir all into the milk; when cool then boil again ten minutes.

403. Boiled Vermicelli Pudding. [TIME.—TO BOIL THE VERMICELLI, ONE HOUR.]

ARTICLES.—Three ounces of vermicelli; three teacupfuls of milk; two ounces of butter; three eggs, and three tablespoonfuls of sugar.

DIRECTIONS.—Wash the vermicelli, and put it into a double boiler with the milk; boil it for an hour; then add the butter. Beat three eggs well with the sugar, and when the vermicelli is cool, stir in the eggs and sugar. Boil it one hour, and serve with sauce.

404. Baked Macaroni Pudding. [TIME.—ONE HOUR; THREE-QUARTERS OF AN HOUR TO SIMMER THE MACARONI.]

ARTICLES.—A quarter of a pound of pipe macaroni; three pints of milk; a piece of butter the size of an egg; a quarter of a pound of sugar; four eggs, and a little nutmeg.

DIRECTIONS.—Break a quarter of a pound of pipe macaroni into small pieces; then simmer in the milk until tender in a double boiler. Then mix the eggs, butter and sugar, add them to the macaroni and milk, beat all well together, and pour into a buttered dish; grate a little nutmeg and lemon peel over the top, and bake it for one hour in a moderate oven.

405. Baked Vermicelli Pudding. [TIME.—ONE HOUR.]

ARTICLES.—Three ounces of vermicelli; three teacupfuls of milk; two ounces of butter; three eggs, and three tablespoonfuls of powdered sugar.

DIRECTIONS.—Wash the vermicelli, and put it into a saucepan with milk, bake it for a quarter of an hour; then add the butter. Beat the eggs with the sugar, and when the vermicelli is quite cold, stir in the eggs and sugar; bake it one hour, and serve with sauce to taste.

406. Boiled Tapioca Pudding. [TIME.—ONE HOUR.]

ARTICLES.—One quart of new milk ; three ounces of tapioca ; an ounce and a half of butter ; four eggs ; grated lemon peel or any other flavoring, and three ounces of sugar.

DIRECTIONS.—Put the tapioca into a double boiler with the milk, and let it boil ; turn it out to cool, and then stir into it the sugar, the flavoring, and the eggs well-beaten ; return it to the boiler, and boil ten minutes. Serve hot with sauce.

407. Baked Tapioca Pudding. [TIME.—ONE HOUR.]

ARTICLES.—One ounce and a half of tapioca ; a pint of milk ; two eggs ; sugar to taste, and grated lemon peel.

DIRECTIONS.—Soak the tapioca in cold water until soft, stirring it now and then ; well-beat the eggs with sugar to taste, and mix them with the milk, stir the tapioca into it, and pour the whole into a buttered dish. Grate the peel of a lemon on the top, and bake it in a moderate oven.

408. Boiled Condensed Milk. [TIME.—THREE-QUARTERS OF AN HOUR.]

ARTICLES.—Half a pint of condensed milk ; half a pint of water ; two eggs ; three ounces of sugar, and a little cinnamon.

DIRECTIONS.—Boil some cinnamon with the sugar, milk, and water in a double boiler. When cold add the eggs well-beaten, and stir it over the fire until it thickens ; then set it aside to get quite cold. Butter and flour a cloth, and tie the custard in it, put it into the boiler, and boil it three-quarters of an hour.

409. Baked Condensed Milk. [TIME.—THREE-QUARTERS OF AN HOUR.]

ARTICLES.—Four eggs ; one pint of condensed milk ; half a nutmeg ; sugar to your taste ; a teaspoonful of vanilla, and one pint of water.

DIRECTIONS.—Beat the eggs very light, stir them into the cream, sweeten it to your taste, and add the nutmeg and the vanilla. Bake it one hour in a quick oven, in a dish with or without a bottom crust.

410. Farina Pudding. [TIME.—TEN MINUTES.]

ARTICLES.—A quart of milk, and half a teacupful of farina; some orange marmalade, or any kind of jam.

DIRECTIONS.—Put the milk into a double boiler, and when boiling, stir in the farina, and continue to stir it over the fire for ten minutes; then put it into a mold to cool, turn it out, and serve with jam or marmalade round it. It is delicious iced.

411. Spanish Pudding. [TIME.—TEN OR TWELVE MINUTES TO FRY.]

ARTICLES.—Half a pint of milk; one ounce of butter; some flour, and the yolks of three eggs.

DIRECTIONS.—Put the milk and butter into a double boiler, and just before it boils, dredge in sufficient flour to make a thick dough, stirring it all the time with one hand as you add the flour; then take it off the fire, and stir in, one at a time, the yolks of three well-beaten eggs, mixing each well in before adding the other. Fry it in small round pieces in boiling butter until a light brown. When done drain them from the fat, and serve on a folded napkin, with sifted sugar over them.

412. Pork Pudding. [TIME.—BOIL FROM THREE TO SIX HOURS.]

ARTICLES.—A cup of chopped pork; two cups of chopped raisins; a teaspoonful of soda; five cups of flour; three cups of milk; one coffeecup of molasses, and one cup of dried apples.

DIRECTIONS.—Chop up the pork, raisins, and dried apples together, mix the flour with the milk and the molasses, dissolve the soda in a little water, and add; then mix all together, put into a cloth, and boil, the longer the better, up to six hours. Serve with rich sauce.

MAKING AND BAKING CAKES.

Cakes are luxuries not necessities, and, where fat, butter and spices are used are generally expensive, indigestible, and unhealthy; yet civilized life seems to demand them and pay the penalty for eating them by sickness, loss of health, time, and money. We give the best known general directions for cooking that can be followed with confidence.

An oven to bake well should have a regular heat throughout, but particularly at the bottom, without which bread or cakes will not rise or bake well.

An earthen basin is best for beating eggs or cake mixture.

Cakes should be beaten with a wooden spoon or patent cake beaters. Butter may be beaten with the same.

Eggs should be beaten with a broad fork; or use the patent egg beaters; they cost but little, and are the best. Eggs should be clean and fresh for a cake. It is well, as a general rule in cake making, to beat the butter and sugar (which must be made fine) to a light cream; indeed, in the making of pound cake, the lightness of the cake depends as much upon this as upon the eggs being well-beaten; then beat the eggs and put them with the butter, and gradually add the flour and other ingredients, beating it all the time.

In common cakes, where only a few eggs are used, beat them until you can take up a spoonful clear from strings.

In recipes in which milk is used as one ingredient, either sweet or sour may be used, but not a mixture of both.

Sour milk makes a spongy, light cake; sweet milk makes a cake which cuts like pound cake.

In making cakes, if you wish them to be pleasing to the palate, use double-refined sugar, although light brown sugar makes a very good cake.

To ascertain whether a cake is baked enough, if a small one, take a very fine broom straw and run it through the thickest part; if not done enough, some of the dough, or unbaked dough, will be found sticking to it; if done, it will come out clear. Cakes to be kept fresh, should be placed in a tin box tightly covered, in a cool dark place.

Other recipes for cake will be found in the corn starch, maizena, and cocoanut recipes.

413. Rock Cakes. [Time.—Half an hour to bake.]

Articles.—Half a pound of butter; one pound of flour; half a pound of sugar; forty drops of essence of lemon; two eggs, and half a glassful of brandy or wine.

Directions.—Rub the butter into the flour and sugar, mix the whole with the eggs and half a glass of brandy or wine. Drop them on a baking-sheet and bake.

414. Strawberry Shortcake.

Articles.—One large tablespoonful of butter; two of loaf sugar; one well-beaten egg; two even teaspoonfuls of cream of tartar; three cupfuls of flour; one small teaspoonful of soda; one cupful of milk, and strawberries and sugar.

Directions.—Beat the butter with sugar to a cream, add the beaten egg, rub the tartar in the flour, dissolve the soda in the milk, add it last; bake in a flat pan in a quick oven; when done let it get cold, cut it into three layers, or in half, cover one layer with strawberries and sugar, lay on the top layer, and dust sugar over it.

415. Snow Cake (Corn Starch). [Time.—One hour and a quarter to one hour and a half.]

Articles.—One pound of corn starch; eight ounces of sugar; eight ounces of fresh butter; whites of seven eggs, and flavoring of essence of lemon.

Directions.—Beat the butter to a cream before the fire, and add the sugar, and the starch, beating the mixture all the time. When well mixed stir in the whites of the eggs, whisked to a stiff froth, and the essence of lemon to your taste. Again whisk the mixture for nearly half an hour, pour it into a buttered tin, and bake in a moderately heated oven.

416. Chocolate Cakes.

ARTICLES.—One pound of flour, one pound of sugar; one pound of butter, eight eggs, two tablespoonfuls of brandy; a pinch of salt, and chocolate glazing.

DIRECTIONS.—Mix the above ingredients well together with a wooden spoon, putting the butter (melted before the fire) in last Spread a baking-sheet with butter, put over it the mixture half an inch thick and bake it. Cut the cake into oblong pieces and glaze them thickly with chocolate.

417. Ginger Snaps. [TIME.—TWENTY MINUTES TO BAKE.]

ARTICLES.—Half a pint of syrup, quarter of a pound of brown sugar, one pound of flour; one tablespoonful of ground ginger, and one of caraway seed.

DIRECTIONS.—Work the butter into the flour, then mix it with the syrup, brown sugar, ginger, and caraway seed. Work it all well together, and form it into cakes; place them on a baking-tin in a moderate oven, when they will be dry and crisp.

418. Hunting-Nuts. [TIME.—FIFTEEN TO THIRTY-SIX MINUTES.]

ARTICLES.—One pound of flour, half a pint of molasses; half a pound of brown sugar, and six ounces of butter and ginger.

DIRECTIONS.—Mix the above ingredients well together, make them into small nuts, and bake them on a baking-sheet.

419. Sponge Cake. [TIME.—THREE-QUARTERS OF AN HOUR TO ONE HOUR.]

ARTICLES.—Four eggs, half a pound of powdered sugar; the weight of two eggs and a half of flour, and one lemon.

DIRECTIONS.—Take the sugar, break the eggs over it, and beat all together for full half an hour. After you have beaten the eggs and sugar together for the time specified, grate into them the peel of a lemon, and add the juice if approved. Stir the flour into the mixture and pour it into a tin. Put it instantly into a cool oven.

420. A Rich Pound Cake. [Time.—One hour.]

ARTICLES.—One pound and a half of flour; four and one-half teaspoonfuls of baking powder; one pound of butter; one pound of white sugar; six eggs; a wine-glassful of brandy; half a nutmeg, and a teaspoonful of vanilla or essence of lemon.

DIRECTIONS.—Beat the butter and pounded sugar to a cream; whisk the eggs to a high froth; sift the flour and mix well with the baking powder; then put all the ingredients together and beat until light and creamy. Put it into a tin lined with buttered paper, and bake it in a moderate oven for one hour. When done, turn it gently out, reverse the tin, and set the cake on the bottom until cold. Let the paper remain on until the cake is to be cut; use more eggs if desired.

421. Lemon Cake. [Time.—One hour.]

ARTICLES.—Four eggs; half a pound of sugar; seven ounces of flour; one and one-half teaspoonfuls baking powder, and the peel of one large or two small lemons.

DIRECTIONS.—Beat the sugar with the yolks of the eggs until it is smooth; whisk the whites to a froth stiff enough to bear the weight of an egg, and add to the beaten yolks; then stir in gradually the flour, in which the baking powder has been well mixed, and the grated peel of the lemon; line a tin with buttered paper, pour in the cake mixture and bake it.

422. A Rich Plum Cake. [Time.—Two hours or more.]

ARTICLES.—One pound of fresh butter; twelve eggs; one quart of flour; two teaspoonfuls of baking powder; one pound of sugar; half a pound of mixed spice; three pounds of currants; one pound of raisins; half a pound of almonds; half a pound of candied peel, and half a pound of citron.

DIRECTIONS.—Beat the butter to a cream, and stir into it the yolks of the eggs well beaten with the sugar, then add the spice and the almonds chopped fine. Stir in the flour in which the baking powder has been well mixed, add the currants washed and dried; the raisins and citron peel chopped. As each ingredient is added, the mixture must be beaten by the hand; then butter a piece of paper, place it round a tin, put in the cake; and bake it for two hours, or more if required. Slice the citron.

423. A Delicate Cake. [TIME.—ABOUT ONE HOUR.]

ARTICLES.—One pound of sugar; one pound of flour; three teaspoonfuls of baking powder; seven ounces of butter; whites of six eggs; half a nutmeg grated, and a little lemon extract.

DIRECTIONS.—Beat the butter to a cream and stir into it the sugar and flour, in which the baking powder has been well mixed; then add the whites of the eggs beaten to a froth; the nutmeg grated and the lemon extract. Beat all well together, and put it into a tin lined with buttered paper. Five or six ounces of pounded almonds may be added to this cake, according to your taste.

424. Common Gingerbread.

ARTICLES.—Half a pound of butter; half a teacupful of ginger; one pint of molasses; two pounds of flour, and six teaspoonfuls of baking powder.

DIRECTIONS.—Rub the flour, in which the baking powder has been well mixed, and butter together, and add the other ingredients. Knead the dough well, roll it out, cut it in cakes, wash them over with molasses and water, and bake them in a moderate oven.

425. Jelly Cake.

ARTICLES.—Half a pound of white sugar; one-fourth of a pound of butter; six eggs; one pound of flour, juice and grated rind of one lemon; three teaspoonfuls of baking powder, and jelly or marmalade in proportion to suit the quantity.

DIRECTIONS.—Beat and mix well, and bake very thin on tins. While hot spread each layer with nice jelly or marmalade, placing one layer upon another. Ice the top or sift loaf sugar very thickly upon it.

426. Silver or Bride's Cake.

ARTICLES.—The whites of ten eggs; one pound of pulverized sugar; three-quarters of a pound of butter, and one pound of sifted flour; three teaspoonfuls of baking powder, and lemon, vanilla, rose, or almond flavoring.

DIRECTIONS.—Beat the eggs to a froth; cream together the butter and the sugar; add one-half of the flour, next half of the eggs, then the rest of the flour and then the eggs; flavor with lemon, vanilla, or rose. Almonds blanched and pounded are an improvement. Use rose water with the almonds to prevent them from oiling. Use no spices.

427. White Cup Cake.

Four teacupfuls of sifted flour, two of sugar, one of butter, one of sour cream or rich milk, a small teaspoonful of soda, the whites of four eggs well beaten. Flavor with lemon or other flavor.

PASTRY AND PIES.

We could all exist without pastry or pies, and no doubt live longer, healthier, and become wealthier, and we do not advise their indiscriminate use, yet plain pastry (for the mischief is caused by rich paste) in pies would do no particular harm.

First, the cook should have smooth, cold hands, very clean, for making paste or crust. She should wash them well, and plunge them in cold water for a minute or two, in hot weather, before beginning her paste, first drying them well.

The pastry slab, if possible, should be made of marble; but a wooden paste-board will do. They should be kept scrupulously clean.

FINE SANITARY PLUMBING GOODS,

—⟨ SUCH AS ⟩—

ROYAL PORCELAIN

BATHS AND SINKS

PORCELAIN WASH TRAYS,

Hartford Glass-Lined Water Closets.

—⟨ ALSO THE ⟩—

HELLYER, ALEXANDER, DEMAREST HYGEIA, JENNINGS, TIDAL WAVE, BOSTON, SANITARY, and other approved WATER CLOSETS.

CUDELL, BOWERS, DUBOIS

— AND —

ADEE PATENT TRAPS,

As well as all other Goods in their Line constantly on hand at the now Famous Establishment of

IRLBACKER & DAVIS,

Nos. 529 to 533 Main Street, - BUFFALO, N. Y.

Where you can also find an elegant assortment of

CHANDELIERS AND GAS FIXTURES

We are also Sole Agents for the justly celebrated GOLD PATENT Steam and Hot Water, Heating and Ventilating Apparatus for STORES, DWELLINGS AND PUBLIC BUILDINGS.

PLUMBING, GAS and STEAM FITTING in all its various branches.

FURNITURE!

We have placed on sale in our Show Rooms the largest and most attractive

STOCK OF FURNITURE

Ever shown in this City.

Our assortment is so large that we can furnish any home from the humblest to the most elegant mansion with a line of

NEW GOODS

and Latest Designs. We are prepared to show a stock of Goods unsurpassed anywhere, at prices that will compare with any in the city.

Our stock of Dining Room, Office and Hall Furniture is complete. Our line of Book Cases needs only to be seen to be appreciated. In Parlor Goods we cannot be equalled, and our stock of

CHAMBER SUITES

Surpasses anything ever shown before.

A general inspection of the Goods is all that is required to corroborate these statements, and a cordial invitation is extended to all to call and make the same.

SCHLUND & DOLL,

472 MAIN STREET,

(OPPOSITE TIFFT HOUSE.)

The crust used for common pies may be made of clarified beef dripping, or lard, instead of butter.

Be careful about the proper heat of the oven for baking pies, as, if it be too cold, the paste will be heavy and have a dull look; if too hot, the crust will burn before the pie is done.

Try if the oven is hot enough by holding your hand inside of it for a few seconds; if you can do so without snatching it out again quickly, it is too cold. It is best, however, to try it by baking a little piece of the crust in it first.

Always make a hole with a knife at the top of the pie to allow the gases, generated in it by cooking, to escape. This aperture is also useful for pouring gravy into meat pies when done, if more is required. The hand of a pastry cook should be light, and the paste should not be worked more than is absolutely required for mixing it.

We give first a plain recipe for pie crust, such as people of small means can use and will find good. A puff paste, and one which will be found good enough for all ordinary purposes, of butter, flour, and eggs made stiff, will also suit raised pies. Use spices to suit the taste.

We begin by giving instructions for clarifying house fat so as to render it fit for use.

428. To Clarify House Fat.

Put the fat in a pan, fry it out, then peel some raw potatoes, slice them in it, fry them brown, pour boiling hot water in the fat, let it all boil half an hour, then strain fat and water, and all the small impurities drop down into the water.

This fat is good for anything, except cake. Mix all kinds, mutton, beef, pork, or ham fat, all together; only it must be sweet.

429. To Make Hygienic Pie Crust. [TIME.—FIFTEEN MINUTES.]

Equal quantities of flour, graham flour, and cornmeal, rub

evenly together, and wet with sweet cream or milk; use same as other paste. This is excellent for the dyspeptic and feeble; as a change, good for all.

430. Plain Pie Crust or Paste. [TIME.—TEN MINUTES.]

ARTICLES.—Flour, a pound; fat, four ounces, and water.

DIRECTIONS.—Put the flour into a bowl and work it into a smooth paste with water; divide the fat into four parts; roll out the paste; put over it in rows one portion of the fat in pieces the size of a bean; flour it, fold over the edges, and again roll it; repeat the whole again three times, dredging a very little flour over the paste, and rolling thin each time; do not touch with your hands any more than you can help; use a large knife or spoon; use ice water; do this in as cool a place as possible.

431. A French Puff-Paste. [TIME.—TEN MINUTES.]

ARTICLES.—Flour, a pint; butter, a pound; two eggs; one lemon, and a pinch of salt.

DIRECTIONS.—Pour the flour into a bowl; make a hole in the center of it, in which put the yolks of two eggs, the juice of the lemon, salt, and ice-water, and a quarter of the butter into a paste, dredge the board and rolling-pin with flour; roll out the paste very thin; put little pieces of butter on the paste; fold over three times, still buttering (as the butter separates the paste and forms the flakes); do so three times; this forms nine flakes; keep it cool, and at each turning let it cool, if convenient in a refrigerator, a few minutes.

432. To Make Other Pastes.

The above is the way to make paste. Any amount of butter or fat, not to exceed pound for pound, may be used; lemon juice and eggs may be omitted.

433. Sweet Apple Pie.

Pare mellow sweet apples, and grate them upon a grater (a

very large grater is necessary for this purpose). Then proceed as for pumpkin pie.

434. Sour Apple Pie.

Take nice tart apples, slice them; add cinnamon. Fill the under crust an inch thick; sprinkle sugar over them; add a spoonful or two of water. Cover with a thin crust, and bake three-quarters of an hour, in a moderate oven.

435. Mock Green Apple Pie.

To five soda-crackers add five cups of boiling water; cover in a dish, let them soak; add three full cups of sugar, two lemons—grate the rind, and add both rind and juice. Bake with two crusts.

436. Mock Apple Pie.

One large grated lemon, three large soda crackers, two even tablespoonfuls of butter, two teacupfuls of sugar, one egg, a wine-glassful of water, poured over the crackers. These will make two pies. Bake with two crusts.

437. Apple and Pie-Plant Pie.

Equal quantities of apple and pie-plant made in the same manner as all pie-plant, make excellent pie.

438. Pie-Plant Pie.

Remove the skin from the stalks; cut them into small pieces; fill the pie dish evenly full; put in plenty of sugar, a teaspoonful of water; dredge a trifle of flour evenly over the top, cover with a thin crust, and bake the same as apple pie.

439. Pumpkin Pie.

Select a pumpkin which has a deep rich color, and firm, close texture. Stew and sift it. Boil some milk in the double boiler, and add enough to make it thin. Sweeten with equal quantities of sugar and molasses, and bake about one hour in a hot oven; add ginger or nutmeg to taste.

440. Squash Pie.

This is superior to pumpkin, as it has a richer and sweeter flavor. It is made in precisely the same manner as pumpkin pie. Eggs and nutmeg can be added.

441. Sweet Potato Pie.

Boil and sift through a colander any sweet potatoes, add milk boiled in the double boiler, and make the same as pumpkin pie; or bake, or boil and slice, same as for sour apple pie.

442. Custard Pie.

ARTICLES.—Corn starch, one tablespoonful; sugar, two; one egg; milk, a quart.

DIRECTIONS.—Boil the milk in the double boiler, add the starch and sugar; when it is all boiled five minutes let it cool, then add the egg well beaten, nutmeg, and a little butter; line some plates with pie crust, pour in the custard and bake.

443. Cherry Pie.

Choose fair ripe cherries, the large black English being the best for this purpose; wash and look them over carefully; fill the pie plate evenly full; strew sugar over the top; dredge in plenty of flour; cover with a moderately thick upper crust, and bake one hour.

444. Raspberry Pie.

Take nice ripe berries, (either red or black are about equally good); wash and pick them carefully; place them an inch or more thick on the under crust; strew a small quantity of sugar, and a trifle of flour over them; put on the upper crust and bake half an hour.

445. Blackberry Pie.

This is made in the same manner as the preceding. All berries for pies should be ripe or nearly so, and as fresh as possible.

446. Whortleberry Pie.

Whortleberries make excellent pies, and are in market

usually longer than any of the summer fruits. It is made in the same manner as raspberry.

447. Cranberry Pie.

Wash the berries in a pan of water, rejecting all the bad ones; simmer them until they become soft and burst open, strain through a fine wire sieve, removing all the hulls, add sugar to taste, bake on a thick under crust in a moderate oven.

448. Peach Pie.

Select rich juicy peaches, of a rather small and nearly uniform size. They should be very ripe, peel and slice them, fill the pie dish with them, sprinkle sugar and a little flour over them, add a tablespoonful of water, cover and bake one hour.

449. Plum Pie

Is made in the same manner as the peach pie. It requires much more sugar to make it at all palatable.

450. Currant Pie.

Currants are made into pies by stewing them and sweetening according to the degree of acidity, and baking between two crusts in the ordinary manner. Or better still, merely fill the pie with them without any previous cooking, sprinkle sugar over, dredge in a little flour, and bake the same as apple pie.

451. Gooseberry Pie.

This is made in precisely the same manner as currant pie, it is very palatable.

452. Minced Meats for Pies.

One pound of currants, four pounds of peeled and chopped apples, one pound of suet chopped fine, one beef's heart boiled tender and chopped fine, pull the strings from the suet and add one pound of raisins stoned and cut in two, the juice of four oranges and two lemons, with the chopped peel of one, add of ground mace and allspice each a spoonful, and a tumblerful of brandy. Mix all well together, and boil the liquor down, and when done cover the mince meat over with the liquor and keep it closely covered in a cool place, until wanted for use. When you want to use the mince meat add cider to your taste.

453. Imitation of Mince Pie.

An excellent imitation of mince pie may be made by placing between the layers of raisins, currants and chopped apples; season precisely as for a mince pie.

INDIAN MEAL, MUSH, BREAD, BISCUIT, CAKES, PUDDINGS, ETC.

Indian meal is Indian corn ground coarse. In many parts of our country it is eaten in every variety of form, not only on account of its cheapness, but of its health and strength-giving qualities; it agrees with almost every one. Perhaps less of this is used in cities than in the country; yet it is not because the city folks do not like it. No, it is because their wives and cooks do not know how to cook meal.

The estimate of the cost to support a man on Indian meal is about ten dollars a year. Of course, no one would live on cornmeal alone; but where is the food that will compare with it? No one, not one. If families would or have to economize, they should bear in mind that a pound of meal swells to more than double in cooking; that it is nearly all nutriment; that it takes four pounds of meat or potatoes to equal one pound of meal; in reality, one pound of flour does not go as far as a pound of meal.

We give *more recipes* for cooking Indian meal, and in *greater variety* than ever were given before by any and all the cook books combined; try them.

And recollect that every pound o meal used where flour would have been, saves you a least four cents, and any of the very palatable dishes are cheaper than any others. Many families use fried mush in place of potatoes; of children, ninety-nine in a hundred prefer it.

In all cases buy yellow meal; it is sweeter and stronger than the white. It comes to the market sifted; but in using our recipes always sift it again. Buy meal made from old corn; it costs more, but keeps longer. Keep meal in a cool, dry place, uncovered.

454. Indian Meal and Hog's-Head Cheese. [TIME.—FIVE HOURS.]

ARTICLES.—Meal, hog's head, and seasoning.

DIRECTIONS.—Clean and boil a hog's head; when tender remove the bones, chop the meat fine, put the meat back into the broth (first skim and strain off the fat), season and salt well, stir into the broth as much meal as will make a thick mush; let this simmer half an hour, taking care not to let it burn; pour into pans, let it cool, then cut into slices, and fry.

For a hearty strong meal, nothing can excel it.

455. Meal and Broth Mush. [TIME.—THREE HOURS.]

ARTICLES.—Meal, bones, broth, and salt.

DIRECTIONS.—Take the broth of any boiled meat or poultry, or get some beef bones, boil them in water without salt, two hours and a half; then skim out the bones, salt to taste, sift in the meal until thick, boil twenty minutes, eat hot, or pour into pans, and fry in slices when boiled.

456. Cornmeal Mush.

ARTICLES.—Indian meal, a quart, and salt to taste

DIRECTIONS.—Take a quart of Indian meal, sift it, wet it up in water, then pour into the double boiler, pouring in boiling hot water until thin, cook an hour and salt to taste. (We say an hour, but it can be eaten before that, if in a hurry.) Eat with milk, butter, syrup, or sugar. This can be cooked in any boiler with care, in any amount.

457. Fried Mush.

Any of the above mushes left over can be poured into a pan; when cold cut in thin slices, and fry brown. You will like it.

458. Mrs. Prudence's Corn Bread. [TIME.—FORTY MINUTES.]

ARTICLES.—Sour milk, a quart; two eggs; soda, two teaspoonfuls; molasses, four tablespoonfuls; salt, and meal.

DIRECTIONS.—Into the milk mix the meal and molasses to a thin batter, beat the eggs, dissolve the soda in water, add a little salt, stir all into thin batter, bake it in pans, in a hot oven, forty minutes.

459. Mrs. Prudence's Brown Bread. [TIME.—TO BAKE, TWO HOURS; TO STEAM, TWO HOURS.]

ARTICLES.—Sour milk, two quarts; Indian and rye meal; soda, three teaspoonfuls; molasses, six tablespoonfuls, and salt.

DIRECTIONS.—To the milk add one-third rye and two-thirds cornmeal. Dissolve the soda in warm water, add with the salt and molasses, bake in a deep pot, tin, or stone, two hours; then steam from two to ten hours, the longer the better, or place the pot in a boiler, but prevent the water from boiling over.

460. New England Brown Bread. [TIME.—FIVE HOURS OR LONGER TO BAKE.]

ARTICLES.—Cornmeal, six cups; rye meal, three cups; yeast, one cup; molasses, one cup, and salt.

DIRECTIONS.—Scald the cornmeal; when lukewarm add the rye meal and the yeast, molasses and salt. Bake in a stone or iron pot.

REMARKS.—This is the justly celebrated New England Brown Bread, made and used by every New England family, cheap, wholesome, and good. Put it in an earthen or iron pot, cover it over, and bake it all night; it is then hot for breakfast. Thousands of these loaves are eaten every morning, and especially Sunday morning, with baked beans.

461. Soda Brown Bread. [TIME.—THREE HOURS TO BAKE.]

ARTICLES.—Cornmeal, two large cups; rye flour, one large

cup ; molasses, half a small cup ; vinegar, two tablespoonfuls ; same of fat ; soda, half a teaspoonful ; salt, and water.

DIRECTIONS.—Scald the meal, add a little cold water and the rye flour and salt ; add the vinegar and molasses ; stir all together, dissolve the soda in a little warm water, add, and make it a thick batter, pour into a deep dish or pan, and bake three hours. Eat hot.

462. Washington's Bread.

DIRECTIONS.—Mix Indian meal with a little salt, wet with cold water, and make a thick batter ; put into tin pans, and bake well ; to be eaten with butter. This is preferred to wheat bread at the South and West, and was the only bread used by General Washington.

463. Mrs. Smith's Yeast Corn-Bread. [TIME.—To BAKE, FIFTY MINUTES.]

ARTICLES.—Meal, a quart ; two tablespoonfuls of lard; and a teacupful of yeast.

DIRECTIONS.—Put a quart of meal in a pan, pour boiling water on it, add the butter and yeast, make it into a batter, beat well, set it to rise. When light, grease your pans, pour in the batter, about half an inch thick, and bake in a moderate oven.

464. Togus Cornmeal Bread. [TIME.—TO STEAM, FOUR HOURS OR LONGER.]

ARTICLES.—Cornmeal, three cups ; flour, one cup ; milk, three cups ; molasses, half a cup ; soda, a teaspoonful, and salt.

DIRECTIONS.—Mix all together, first dissolving the soda in warm water, mixing it with the milk ; pour in a double boiler, or other cone-shaped pot ; steam it in an iron pot, four hours or longer—the longer the better ; very fine.

465. Mrs. Prudence's Suet and Meal Bread. [TIME.—TO STEAM, FIVE HOURS.]

ARTICLES.—Milk, one quart ; suet, a teacupful ; molasses,

same; soda, a teaspoonful, and cream of tartar, two.

DIRECTIONS.—Boil a quart of milk, stir in some meal to a batter, and the suet chopped fine, add the soda and tartar, bake an hour, or steam five hours.

466. Mush Bread. [TIME.—TO BAKE, ONE TO TWO HOURS.]

ARTICLES.—Cornmeal mush, three quarts; flour, and half a pint of yeast.

DIRECTIONS.—Boil meal enough to make three quarts, add a little salt and the yeast, and enough wheat flour to form a soft dough; let it rise; when light, add only enough flour to prevent it adhering to the board or pan; make it into loaves, put them in pans, let them rise again, and bake. It makes fine cheap bread.

467. Indian Meal and Wheat Flour Bread. [TIME.—TO BAKE, TWO HOURS.]

ARTICLES.—Indian meal, two quarts; wheat flour, one quart; yeast, half a pint; molasses, half a teacupful, and a teaspoonful of salt.

DIRECTIONS.—Scald the meal with boiling water; when cooled add the salt, molasses, and yeast; stir in some flour, set it to rise, knead well with flour, make it into loaves, put it in pans, let it rise a second time, and bake.

468. Wheat and Indian Bread.

Make as for the above recipe, except use only one quart of meal, and no molasses, using two quarts of flour.

469. Meal Johnny Bread. [TIME.—TO BAKE, HALF AN HOUR.]

ARTICLES.—Indian meal, three cups; flour, a cup; molasses, one-third of a cup; salt; sour or butter milk, and a teaspoonful of soda.

DIRECTIONS.—Mix the meal, flour, molasses, and salt, dissolve the soda in the milk, make a batter, and bake in a quick oven.

470. Grandmother's Meal Bread. [Time.—Half an hour.

Articles.—Meal, a pint; lard, a teaspoonful, and salt.

Directions.—Mix the meal, lard, and salt in boiling water, stir it up to a dough, spread it on a tin pan, and bake before a fire, or in an oven.

471. Cornmeal Pone or Biscuit. [Time.—Bake forty minutes.]

Articles.—Indian meal, a quart; wheat flour, a pint; milk; cream of tartar, two teaspoonfuls; soda, one; eggs, two; sugar, three tablespoonfuls, and the same of lard.

Directions.—Beat the eggs with the sugar, rub the tartar into the meal and flour, add the eggs and sugar, and the soda first dissolved; thin down to a batter, with milk or water. Eat all biscuits hot, with sweet butter.

472. Blot's Meal Batter Biscuit. [Time.—To bake, forty minutes.]

Articles.—Cornmeal, a pint; eggs, two; butter, two ounces, and salt and sugar to taste.

Directions.—Beat the eggs, melt the butter, mix with the meal, sugar, and salt; then pour in hot milk till it makes a thick dough, and put in a pan and bake.

473. Mother's Meal and Rye Biscuit. [Time.—Forty minutes to bake.]

Articles.—Meal, three cups; rye meal, one cupful; lard, a tablespoonful; molasses, three; soda, half a teaspoonful, and vinegar, a tablespoonful.

Directions.—Scald the meal, add the lard, vinegar, and molasses, dissolve the soda in water, stir in briskly, make into flat biscuits an inch thick, and bake in a moderate oven. Bake these cakes well. Eat hot.

474. Egg Meal Biscuit. [Time.—To bake, half an hour.]

Articles.—Meal, a pint; butter or sour milk, a pint; one

egg; lard, a tablespoonful; salt, a teaspoonful, and soda, a teaspoonful.

DIRECTIONS.—Work the lard into the meal and salt; beat the egg, stir into the milk, add to the meal; then add the soda; if the milk is sweet, use two teaspoonfuls of tartar. Bake in a moderate oven.

475. **Indian Biscuit.** [TIME.—TO BAKE, ABOUT FORTY MINUTES.]

ARTICLES.—Meal, a pint; butter, two ounces; two eggs, and milk.

DIRECTIONS.—Wet the meal well with boiling hot water, put in the butter and a little salt, beat two eggs very light, and add when cool; stir in enough milk to make a batter, beat well, and bake in a hot oven.

476. **Mrs. Prudence's Meal Muffins.** [TIME.—FIFTEEN MINUTES TO BAKE.]

ARTICLES.—Cornmeal, a pint; lard, two tablespoonfuls; two eggs; soda, a teaspoonful; cream of tartar, two, and milk.

DIRECTIONS.—Melt the lard, beat the eggs well, dissolve the soda, mix the tartar in the meal, stir in all, and as much sweet milk as will make a batter. Bake in tins or muffin rings in a moderate hot oven. Use half flour, if desired.

477. **Indian Meal Wafers.** [TIME.—TEN MINUTES.]

ARTICLES.—Meal, six tablespoonfuls; flour, two; lard, two; milk, and salt.

DIRECTIONS.—Mix all, using enough milk to thin it to a batter, fry a light brown, and always have the pans hot before frying.

478. **Wheat and Corn Crumpets.** [TIME.—TO FRY, ABOUT FIFTEEN MINUTES.]

ARTICLES.—Half a gill of yeast; a quart of warm milk; a teaspoonful of salt; a teacupful of melted butter, and yellow cornmeal.

DIRECTIONS.—Put the yeast into a quart of warm milk, with a teaspoonful of salt; stir in sufficient wheat flour to make a good batter, set it in a warm place to rise; in the morning add the melted butter, and a handful of yellow cornmeal. Fry them on a hot griddle previously rubbed over with butter before putting on the cakes. A spoonful of butter will be sufficient for one.

479. Meal Fadge. [TIME.—ONE HOUR.]

ARTICLES.—Four ounces of meal; two ounces of butter; a saltspoonful of salt, and a quarter of a pint of milk.

DIRECTIONS.—Take four ounces of meal, two ounces of butter, and a little salt; make it into a stiff paste with milk, and bake it for one hour on a griddle over the fire, turning it often. It will not do to bake it in an oven. If baked too long it becomes like pie crust.

480. Meal Griddle Cakes. [TIME.—TO FRY, A FEW MINUTES.]

ARTICLES.—Meal, a pint, and salt.

DIRECTIONS.—Scald at night half a pint of meal, mix the rest in cold water, add the salt and set it to rise. In the morning fry slowly. Eat with butter and syrup.

481. All Kinds of Griddle Cakes. [TIME.—TO FRY, A FEW MINUTES.]

ARTICLES.—Eggs, two; sour milk, a tumblerful; soda, a teaspoonful; or use sweet milk, and yeast-powders, and eggs; or one teaspoonful of soda, and two of cream of tartar, with water and eggs. Indian meal, or rye meal, or graham meal, or wheat meal, or buckwheat meal, or wheat flour, can be used, and in any proportions. Crumbs of bread can be mixed with the batter.

482. Meal Drop-Nuts. [TIME.—TO BAKE, HALF AN HOUR.]

ARTICLES.—Meal, one pint; rye flour, same; syrup, three tablespoonfuls; soda, a teaspoonful; tartar, two, and milk.

DIRECTIONS.—Make as above, drop the batter into greased pans, bake in a moderate oven, and eat with butter and syrup.

483. Meal Omelets.

Scald a cup of meal, beat up six eggs, add to the meal and fry brown. Very good for breakfast. One-half flour can be added if desired.

484. Meal Pound-Cake, Rich. [TIME.—TO BAKE, ABOUT ONE HOUR.]

ARTICLES.—Cornmeal, a pound; sugar, the same; wheat flour, half a pound; butter, the same; baking powder, four teaspoonfuls; nutmeg grated; cinnamon, a teaspoonful, and six eggs.

DIRECTIONS.—Stir the butter and sugar to a cream, beat the eggs very light, and add to them the meal and flour first mixed with the baking powder, then the spices; line your pan with paper well buttered, pour in the mixture, and bake it in a moderate oven.

485. Molasses Meal Pound Cake.

Made the same as above, with exception of molasses instead of sugar.

486. Cornmeal Pudding Without Eggs. [TIME.—TO BAKE, ABOUT TWO HOURS.]

ARTICLES.—Cornmeal; four cups very strong coffee; a cup of sugar; molasses, a cup; butter, a cup; raisins, a cup; soda, a teaspoonful, and spices.

DIRECTIONS.—Make four coffeecups of very strong coffee, scald two cups of meal, with the coffee; chop the raisins, and add the molasses, sugar, butter, and the currants, dissolve the soda in a little warm water, and add. Stir all well together, and if too thin, stiffen it with flour. Use very little spice.

487. Meal, Fruit, and Coffee Cake. [TIME.—HALF AN HOUR TO BAKE.]

ARTICLES.—Seven heaped tablespoonfuls of sifted cornmeal;

two dessertspoonfuls of lard or butter, heaped; a tumblerful of molasses; two teaspoonfuls of powdered ginger, and a quart of hot boiled sweet milk.

DIRECTIONS.—Mix well, and pour into a buttered dish, and just as it is put into the oven, stir in not quite a tumblerful of cold water, and bake half an hour. Serve with a rich sauce.

488. Indian Suet Pudding. [TIME.—TO BAKE, TWO HOURS.]

ARTICLES.—Half a pint of Indian (yellow) cornmeal; one quart of milk; half a teacupful of suet; one teaspoonful of ground ginger; two ounces of sugar; half a teacupful of butter; one egg, and a little salt.

DIRECTIONS.—Stir the cornmeal very gradually to a quart of boiling milk; when it has cooled, add a little salt and half a teacupful of suet chopped very fine, or the same quantity of butter; add to it half a nutmeg grated, a teaspoonful of ground ginger, one well-beaten egg, and two ounces of sugar; put it into a buttered dish and bake.

489. Baked Pudding.

To a quart of mush, add two well-beaten eggs, quarter of a pound of butter, sugar, and spice to taste; add a little milk, and bake in an earthen dish.

490. English Baked Meal Pudding. [TIME.—ONE HOUR.]

ARTICLES.—Cornmeal, seven heaped tablespoonfuls; lard, two; ginger, half a tablespoonful; milk, a quart; molasses, a cup; water, a large cupful, and a grated lemon peel.

DIRECTIONS.—Mix the meal in hot milk, then add the rest; pour it into a greased dish, pouring on top a cup of water or milk, and bake in a moderate oven.

491. New England Pudding. [TIME.—TO BAKE, FOUR HOURS.]

ARTICLES.—Cornmeal, one large cupful; molasses, half a cupful, and one quart of milk.

DIRECTIONS.—Scald a little over half of the milk, stir the meal into the hot milk, then the molasses with a little salt; let cool; pour into a dish, and then pour on top the rest of the cold milk as you set it in the oven to bake.

REMARKS.—The New Englanders have this pudding for their Sunday dinners generally. They make it, as per recipe, more or less in quantity, on Saturday, set it away in a cool place, and four hours before dinner, in winter, pour on the milk, put it into the oven, and have it hot without any labor on Sunday. In summer it is generally cooked on Saturday, and eaten cold on Sunday.

492. French Baked Indian Pudding. [TIME.—TWO HOURS.]

ARTICLES.—Meal, a coffeecupful; milk, two quarts; molasses, one-third of a cup, and same of sugar.

DIRECTIONS.—Boil the milk in the double boiler; when boiling pour out one-half, and into the remainder stir the meal in slowly, leaving no lumps in it; pour it into a pudding dish; add the rest of the milk, the sugar, and the molasses, and bake two hours; stir once, the first half hour, but not afterward.

493. Steamed Plum Pudding.

One quart Indian meal; one cup molasses; one cup raisins; one quart boiling water; stir all together, and steam three hours.

494. Boiled Corn Meal and Cheese Pudding. [TIME.—TWO HOURS.]

ARTICLES.—Meal, a pound; cheese, half a pound; milk, a quart; hot water, and salt.

DIRECTIONS.—Boil a quart of milk in the double boiler; scald a pound of meal with hot water; grate or cut in thin slices, the cheese; stir all into the hot milk, then into a pan, and bake or boil an hour.

495. Boiled Corn Meal and Pork Pudding. [TIME.—TO BAKE, TWO HOURS.]

ARTICLES.—Salt pork, one cupful chopped fine; one egg; milk, a pint; soda, a teaspoonful; cream of tartar, two teaspoonfuls; salt to taste, and meal.

CARPETS AND DRAPERY.

D. E. MORGAN & SON,

EXCLUSIVE DEALERS IN

Carpets,

Oil Cloths,

Mattings,

DRAPERY AND UPHOLSTERY,

INTERIOR DECORATIONS,

PORTIERE AND LACE CURTAINS,

SHADES,

BEDDING,

FEATHERS,

LINOLEUMS, &c.

OPPOSITE THE OLD FIRST CHURCH.

331 MAIN STREET,

BUFFALO, N. Y.

G. H. MUMM & CO.'S
CHAMPAGNE.

IMPORTATION IN 1881

81,355 CASES.

THE LARGEST IMPORTATION TO THE UNITED STATES

G. H. MUMM & CO.'S CHAMPAGNE,
The Most Popular Wine in the United States.

UNSURPASSED in Quality

AND

NATURALLY DRY.

DIRECTIONS.—Mix all together, using meal enough for thickening; boil in a cloth or bake. Flour can be used instead of meal, if prepared.

496. Boiled Meal, Fruit, and Pork Pudding. [TIME.—TWO HOURS.]

ARTICLES.—Meal, four cups; pork, chopped, one cup; raisins, chopped, one cup; milk, hot, three cups; molasses, one cup; soda, a teaspoonful, and salt to taste.

DIRECTIONS.—Mix all the above together, first scalding the meal with the milk; tie in a cloth and boil two hours; use half, or all flour for a change, instead of meal.

497. Boiled Meal and Dried Apple Pudding.

Scald a quart of Indian meal, add a little salt, molasses, and a little fat; a few hours previous, set half a pound of dried apples to soak, chop them up and add; mix together, adding a tablespoonful of soda; boil two hours in a cloth, and eat with sauce.

498. Meal and Apple Dowdy. [TIME.—FIVE HOURS.]

ARTICLES.—Meal a quart; flour, a pint; apples, green, half a peck, or dried apples; molasses, two cups; soda, a teaspoonful, and cream of tartar, two teaspoonfuls.

DIRECTIONS.—Scald the meal, mix the tartar with the flour and a little lard; then stir in the soda in water; mix all with the meal, and make a paste; line an earthen dish, put the apples in first peeled and sliced, add the molasses and cinnamon, cover with the top crust and bake five hours in a slow oven. A very fine dish.

499. Freedman's Hoe-Cake. [TIME.—TO BAKE, HALF AN HOUR.]

ARTICLES.—A quart of Indian meal; a spoonful of fat, a little salt and boiling water.

DIRECTIONS.—Pour hot water on the meal, add butter and

salt, make a stiff dough, knead, or work it for ten minutes, and bake on a board or tin before the fire slowly.

FLOUR, BREAD, Etc.
Wheat, Rye, Barley, Corn, and Oat Flour.

Flour is made from all the above grains, especially from wheat and rye, for general use ; one contains about as much nutriment as the other, but general use and taste have selected wheat flour, although foreigners use much rye flour. Well made of good rye, it can hardly be told from wheat. The writer has made a dinner from rye bread and cheese, on many occasions, and at one time a party of which he was one, called at a house in the country. The German woman said all she had was some bread and cheese. Not one of the party knew what kind of bread they were eating until the writer told them. She said it cost her five dollars and a half a barrel ; good wheat flour was worth nine dollars and fifty cents at the time. I mention this fact to show that a poor German wife could make as good bread from rye as wheat flour, saving four dollars a barrel. Flours are ground too fine ; the whiter and finer the flour the more starch, and the less nutriment and health-giving properties there are in it, and the more costly it is.

Most people are unaware how unhealthy fine flour is. In experiments made on healthy dogs with fine flour bread alone, with water, two years ago, it killed them all within forty days ; most of them died within thirty days. On graham flour bread, which is wheat ground coarse, with the hulls or chaff in, they grew fat and healthy, and did not die. When fed on corn meal bread they were healthy and fat, and we assert that any one who should eat fine flour bread of any kind alone, without medicine, would not live sixty days. The reason of it is that its starchy nature is like a paste, clogs up the stomach and intestines ; the liver refuses to act ; the result is sickness and

Let all enjoy nature and art, but not to excess. In many things fine flour is excellent—for cakes, pastry, and once a day for bread, biscuit or rolls.

In making bread by our recipes, we give a variety of methods for making flour bread and biscuit. Wheat, rye, corn, graham and barley flours can be used in any quantity to suit the palate, or a little meal of either of the above can be put in. A pound of fine wheat flour costs as much as two pounds of rye or graham flour, or three of cornmeal, giving no more nutriment. Try a variety, for it is the spice of life. You will not regret it. You will thereby SAVE HEALTH AND ACQUIRE WEALTH.

YEAST BREAD, Etc.

500. How to make Excellent Yeast Bread, Rolls, Biscuit, Twists, Etc.

Yeast is made from hops, flour, potatoes, etc. We give three of the best ways to make it. Yeast acts by fermentation, which produces gases in the dough, and is held by it, in consequence making the dough light; heat causes the fermentation, cold prevents it. As the heat of the oven holds the dough just as the gases make it,—the more kneading the better, as it makes it fine. It is necessary, in order to make good bread, to understand the reasons fully why yeast makes the bread rise; therefore, to make nice bread, etc., follow these rules :

1. FLOUR should be kept in a dry closet—if at all damp it will make the bread heavy. When about to make bread put the quantity of flour you are to use in a pan near the fire, in order to have it warm and dry for use. Seven pounds of flour or meal make a good batch of bread.

2. YEAST.—Use fresh liquid yeast, or if your own, keep it well corked in a bottle ; or use the yeast cakes now for sale in the stores. The better the yeast the less you require. Too much yeast makes the bread taste of yeast and has a bad effect

on the bread; it dries quick and is not so sweet as if risen slowly. Too little yeast will make it heavy. Seven pounds of flour or meal require a gill of yeast.

3. SALT.—Sift it with the flour. To seven pounds of flour or meal, add a large tablespoonful.

4. FAT.—Three tablespoonfuls of any fat kneaded into the dough after it has risen the first time, makes it flaky, rich and short.

5. CLEANLINESS is all important; have the pans, hands and arms clean.

6. DOUGH.—Never have it half made, nor allow it to get cold before it is finished; if you do, it will be heavy. After making it, cover the pan with a thick cloth.

7. KNEADING.—Fold the fingers over the thumbs, beat and pommel the dough until it ceases to stick to your hands. Do this on making, and after it has risen. Much kneading makes it whiter and finer. Bread can scarcely be kneaded too much; the reason is plain—the fermented yeast forms very small globules, making a dense yet light bread.

8. SOURING.—If the dough sours, dissolve a teaspoonful of soda in as much hot water; work it into the dough—some prefer it after this is in; it gives a different taste to it, and the bread is whiter and more tender.

9. HEAT.—Dough should be made in cold weather in a warm room and kept there. If it is too slow in rising, set it over a pan of hot water and keep it warm.

10. CONSISTENCY.—If too thin, add more flour; it should not run or spread; if too thick, let it rise a little longer, or add a little warm water.

11. TO KEEP DOUGH GOOD.—Keep in winter in the cellar, or any cool place; in summer, in the refrigerator. Thus you can have bread or biscuit at any time. If it sours, use soda.

12. BAKING.—Bake in a moderately hot oven for bread; biscuit should have a hotter oven.

13. TO KNOW WHEN BREAD IS BAKED.—When bread is brown and firm to the touch all over, it is done. We give the time of baking as near as possible, but the heat of the ovens varies very much; therefore care must be taken not to overdo or underdo the bread or biscuit.

501. How to make Yeast Cakes.

Put a large handful of hops into two quarts of boiling water. Boil three large potatoes until they are tender. Mash them and add to them two pounds of flour; pour the boiling hop water over the flour through a sieve or colander, and beat it until it is quite smooth. While it is warm add two tablespoonfuls of salt, and half a teacupful of sugar. Before it is quite cold stir in a pint of good yeast. After the yeast has become quite light, stir in as much Indian meal as it will take to roll it out in cakes, and place them on a cloth in a dry place, taking care to turn them every day. At the end of a week, or ten days, they may be put into a bag, and should be kept in a dry place. When used, take one of these cakes, soak it in some milk-warm water, mash it up smooth, and use it as you would any other kind of yeast.

502. To make Baker's Yeast. [TIME.—TWO HOURS.]

ARTICLES.—Three tablespoonfuls of flour, two quarts of water, a quarter of a pound of brown sugar, a quarter of a pound of yeast.

DIRECTIONS.—Make three spoonfuls of flour into a smooth batter with a little cold water; then add to it nearly two quarts more water, and a quarter of a pound of brown sugar; put it over the fire; stir it occasionally, and then set it to cool; when it is only lukewarm, add two tablespoonfuls of good yeast; set it in a warm place, or near the fire, for a day to ferment; then pour off the thin liquor from the top, shake up the remainder and put it in a bottle for use, or keep it in a covered stone jar. A gill of this yeast will be sufficient for seven pounds of flour.

503. Potato Yeast.

Boil a quarter of a peck of potatoes, mash them fine, and thin them a little with the water in which they have been boiled; add some salt and a tablespoonful of brown sugar; when lukewarm, stir in about half a pint or more of old yeast, let it rise, then cover it closely and put it in a cool place,—it is fit for use then.

504. Hop Yeast.

Tie a large handful of hops in a thin bag and boil them in three quarts of water; moisten with cold water a sufficient quantity of flour, and stir in the hop yeast while boiling hot; add a handful of salt; let it stand until it is about lukewarm, and then add about a pint of old yeast; when it is light, cover it and stand it in a cool place, for use.

505. How to make Nice and Good Cream of Tartar and Soda Bread.

It is very important to have light, sweet bread. It is not always convenient to have yeast bread, and a change is agreeable. To have the above chemicals pure and uniform is all-important; they will keep in tin cans any length of time, therefore we recommend that cream of tartar, saleratus, or soda, be bought of first-class dealers, and buy the best.

Cream of tartar is made from the settlings of wine; saleratus and soda are made from potash.

THE WAY THEY WORK.

Cream of tartar is an acid; soda and saleratus are anti-acids.

When the dissolved soda is worked into the dough, it meets the acid, and they form into gases, which, trying to escape, cause the dough to rise into little minute bubbles; the heat of the oven causes them still more to ferment, and then baking the dough forms a crust which confines the gases, and that causes the bread or biscuit to be light.

1. CREAM OF TARTAR.—Two heaping teaspoonfuls to two quarts of flour or meal; sift it with the flour or meal. Too much tartar makes the bread sour, and is unhealthy.

2. SALERATUS.—An even teaspoonful, or soda a teaspoonful, to two quarts of flour or meal; dissolve first in half a teacupful of water; when dissolved, put it into the water or milk; that is to be used as soda; unless prepared in this way it is apt to discolor the bread. Too much soda makes the bread yellow and unhealthy.

3. SALT.—A heaping teaspoonful to two quarts of flour or meal; sift it with the flour or meal, and cream of tartar.

4. FAT.—A tablespoonful of any kind of fat to two quarts of flour or meal; after it is sifted, work it into the dry flour or meal, that is if shortening is desired.

5. MILK OR WATER.—A pint; milk is much the best, and adds all it costs to the goodness of the bread.

6. SOUR OR BUTTER MILK.—A pint. If you have or can get either, it is best, as it saves the cream of tartar, the acid of the milk doing as well; use the soda, however, but no tartar.

7. DOUGH.—The dough must be as thin in consistency as possible, so as to pat it out on a board half an inch thick, and cut it with a round cake-cutter.

8. THE OVEN.—Always have that ready and hot, for this bread must be baked as soon as made, in a quick oven.

9. HEALTH.—Hot bread is not as healthy as cold bread, still a little will kill no one, As these biscuits are very good warm, the healthy can eat them. The dyspeptic and invalid had better not eat them.

506. Yeast (or Baking) Powder,

(not yeast cakes, nor hop cakes), is made of one-third soda, or one-quarter improved saleratus, or two-thirds of cream of tartar, well mixed. I prefer to use the soda and tartar separately.

507. To make Good Corn Meal Yeast Bread or Biscuit.

The above rules apply to cornmeal, or graham flour, or rye meal, or brown bread, biscuit, etc., except:

1. They must be made thinner in a thick batter, and all the work can be done with a strong spoon; no lard is needed; they are not so much trouble to make.

2. They generally require molasses to sweeten them.

3. They require longer baking.

4. Cornmeal soda-biscuit and bread do not require so hot an oven as flour.

5. Except these five things, the yeast and soda rules apply to the corn-meal recipes for bread, biscuit, etc.

508. Rye or Wheat Flour Yeast Bread. [TIME.—ONE HOUR TO BAKE LOAVES OF TWO POUNDS WEIGHT EACH.]

ARTICLES.—Seven pounds of flour; two quarts of warm water; a large tablespoonful of salt; half a pint of yeast, and two large tablespoonfuls of fat.

DIRECTIONS.—Put the flour into a deep pan, heap it round the sides, leaving a hollow in the center, put into it a quart of warm water, the salt and yeast; have ready three pints more of warm water, and with as much of it as may be necessary, make the whole into a rather soft dough, kneading it well with both hands. When it is smooth and shining, strew a little flour on it, lay a thickly folded cloth over the pan, and set it in a warm place by the fire, for four or five hours in cold weather, or all night; then knead it again for a quarter of an hour, at the same time kneading in the fat; cover it over, and set it to rise again. Divide it into two or three loaves, and bake it in a quick oven. It will take one hour to bake it, if divided into loaves weighing two pounds each; and two hours, if the loaves weigh four pounds each. This bread can be made of rye, or wheat, or graham flour, or any kind that may suit. Cornmeal can be added.

509. Graham Flour Bread. [TIME.—BAKE A LITTLE LONGER THAN YEAST BREAD.]

Made same as yeast bread, adding a cup of molasses, and baking longer. This bread is made from graham flour. If you wish it coarse, do not sift it; if, on using it, it is found to be too coarse or opening for the bowels, the bran can be sifted out. More molasses can be added, or none, as preferred. It is better for costive persons than any medicine.

510. Graham and Flour Bread.

Made same as yeast bread, sifting the graham flour, and adding one-half wheat flour. Add a cup of molasses.

511. Potato Bread. [TIME.—TO BAKE, ONE AND A HALF TO TWO HOURS.]

ARTICLES.—Two and a half pounds of mealy potatoes; seven pounds of flour; a gill of yeast, and two ounces of salt.

DIRECTIONS.—Boil two pounds and a half of nice mealy potatoes, till floury; rub and mash them smooth; then mix them with sufficient cold water to let them pass through a coarse sieve, and any lumps that remain must be again mashed and pressed through. Mix this paste with the yeast, and then add it to the flour. Set it to rise, knead it well, and make it into a stiff, tough dough and bake.

512. Rice Bread. [TIME.—ONE AND A HALF TO TWO HOURS.]

ARTICLES.—Half a pound of rice; three pints of water, and six pounds of flour.

DIRECTIONS.—Boil half a pound of rice in three pints of water, till the whole is quite thick; with this, and yeast, and six pounds of flour, make the dough.

513. Bread without Yeast or Soda. [Time.—Five hours to rise.]

Articles.—Milk or water, a quart; salt; flour, and two tablespoonfuls of lard.

Directions.—Make the milk or water lukewarm; stir in the salt, as much as will do for the bread; stir in flour to make a paste; do this in a kettle; set it in a pot of warm water; keep the water or milk warm. In five hours it will foam like yeast; then knead in flour and lard, put into pans, let them rise again, and bake in a quick oven.

514. French Rolls. [Time.—Half an hour.]

Articles —One pound of flour; one egg; one ounce of butter, one spoonful of yeast; a little salt, and some milk.

Directions.—Beat well the butter into the flour, adding a little salt; beat an egg, and stir it into the flour with the yeast, and a sufficient quantity of milk, to make the dough rather stiff. Beat it well without kneading it; set it to rise, and bake it on tins. This quantity will make about six rolls.

515. Irish Rolls. [Time.—Fifteen to twenty minutes.]

Articles.—Two pounds of fine flour; one teaspoonful of fine salt; one dessertspoonful of powdered sugar; half a teaspoonful of best carbonate of soda; whites of eggs, and some sour buttermilk.

Directions.—Mix with the flour, the salt, sugar, and carbonate of soda. Then beat the whites of two eggs into a strong froth, with a sufficient quantity of sour buttermilk, and mix them up the same as rolls made with yeast. Make them up at once into whatever shape you like. Wash them over with the white of an egg, and bake them in a rather quick oven, of a light brown, for about a quarter of an hour, or according to the size of your rolls. They are very light and white. The sourer the buttermilk, the lighter the rolls will be. A basin of buttermilk will keep for a week, or very sour milk will answer as well.

516. English Rolls. [TIME.—TWENTY MINUTES TO BAKE.]

ARTICLES.—Two pounds of flour; two ounces of butter; three spoonfuls of good yeast, and one pint of warm milk.

DIRECTIONS.—Take the flour and rub the butter into it; add the yeast strained, and mix all well together with a pint of warm milk. Set it before the fire to rise, make it into twelve rolls, and bake them in a moderate oven.

517. Baker's Rolls. [TIME.—TWENTY MINUTES TO BAKE.]

ARTICLES.—Three pounds of flour; two tablespoonfuls of yeast; one teaspoonful of salt, and half a teaspoonful of soda.

DIRECTIONS.—Put the flour into a pan, make a hollow in the center, and put in the salt, soda, and yeast. Make it into a soft dough with some warm milk; work or knead it until it is smooth and shining, then cover it and set it in a warm place, for two hours. Work it again very smooth, let it rise, and again knead and divide it in pieces twice the size of a hen's egg; roll it between your hands to the length of your finger; lay them so as to touch each other, on baking tins, brush them over with milk, and set them in a quick oven, for fifteen or twenty minutes, until they are a delicate brown. Break one open to see if it is done, and serve them hot for breakfast, broken open, as cutting them when hot soddens them. To make a roll egg-shaped in form do not quite half lap it over, or cut round and lap over one-third.

518. Baker's Twists. [TIME.—NEARLY ONE HOUR.]

DIRECTIONS.—Let the bread be made as directed for baker's rolls; then take three pieces as large as a half-pint bowl; strew a little flour over the paste-board; roll each piece under your hands to twelve inches in length, making it smaller in circumference at the ends than in the middle. Having rolled each piece in this way, take a baking tin, lay one part on it, join one end of each to the other two, and braid them together the length of the roll. Join the ends by pressing them together;

dip a brush in milk, and pass it over the top of your twists. After ten minutes, set them in a quick oven, and bake them for nearly an hour. They can be made smaller if desired.

519. Velvet Biscuit. [Time.—Fifteen minutes.]

ARTICLES.—One pint of warm milk; two eggs; half a gill of yeast; a teaspoonful of soft butter; a teaspoonful of salt, and sufficient flour to make a soft dough.

DIRECTIONS.—In the milk and two well-beaten eggs put the yeast, soft butter, and salt. Stir into it sufficient flour to make a soft dough; strew some flour over it; lay a warm towel over the pan, and set it in a warm place to rise (three hours in the summer, or until light in the winter). Dip your hands in flour, and work the dough down; make it into small flat cakes; lay them on a buttered tin pan, quite near each other, and bake them in a quick oven for fifteen minutes, or until done.

These cakes may be mixed at night, and baked for breakfast. Keep the dough cool for supper, if required.

520. Sponge Flour Biscuit. [Time.—About ten minutes.]

ARTICLES.—Flour, a quart; sweet milk, a pint; lard, a tablespoonful; salt, a teaspoonful, and a teacupful of yeast.

DIRECTIONS.—Sift the flour and salt into a pan; heat the milk and lard together; pour the yeast and milk into the flour; make a stiff dough when risen; grease a pan and drop the batter on in large tablespoonfuls; let them set where they will be merely warm (no more), then bake in a quick oven, and eat at once. They may be baked in cups.

521. Rye and Flour Tea Biscuit. [Time.—To make and bake, half an hour.]

ARTICLES.—Rye flour, one tumblerful; wheat flour, two tumblers or large cupfuls; cream of tartar, a teaspoonful; soda, half a teaspoonful; fat, a tablespoonful, and milk.

DIRECTIONS.—Sift the flours and tartar together; rub in the fat and salt; add the soda and milk, or water enough to make a soft dough; roll an inch thick; cut them out, prick, and bake in a hot oven. Use all, or parts of, any flour.

522. Breakfast Biscuit. [TIME.—TWENTY MINUTES.]

ARTICLES.—A piece of risen bread dough the size of a small loaf; one egg; one tablespoonful of butter or lard, and a little milk.

DIRECTIONS.—Take a piece of risen bread dough, and work into it one beaten egg and a tablespoonful of butter or lard; when it is thoroughly amalgamated, flour your hands and make it into balls the size of an egg; rub a tin over with milk, and set them in a quick oven for twenty minutes, and serve them hot for breakfast. When eaten, break them open; to cut would make them heavy.

523. Milk Biscuit. [TIME.—HALF AN HOUR.]

ARTICLES.—Six handfuls of flour; half a pint of milk; a small piece of butter; half a teacupful of yeast, and one egg.

DIRECTIONS.—Put the flour in a basin, with half a pint of milk and a small piece of butter; warm the milk—in the winter increase its temperature. Mix the yeast in a little cold water; add it to the milk and batter; make a hole in the flour, and pour the mixed milk and yeast into it, stirring it around until it is a thick batter; add to it one beaten egg; cover it over, and set it before the fire, keeping it warm. When it has risen a little, mix it into a dough; knead it well and put it again to rise; and when it is risen a great deal, form your biscuit. They will take nearly half an hour to bake, or according to the size you make them. Rub them once, while hot, with a paste brush dipped in milk.

524. Sour Milk Biscuit. [TIME.—TO MAKE AND BAKE, FORTY MINUTES.]

ARTICLES.—One pint of rye flour; one pint of wheat flour; half a teaspoonful of soda; sour milk; fat, a tablespoonful, and salt.

DIRECTIONS.—Rub the fat in the flour; dissolve the soda in hot water; add salt to taste; wet the flour with sour milk until a soft dough is formed; make into thin biscuit; bake in a quick oven; use all of one kind of flour, if preferred.

525. **Rye or Wheat Flour Crackers.** [TIME.—HALF AN HOUR, TO MAKE AND BAKE.]

ARTICLES.—Rye or wheat flour, one quart; butter or fat, four ounces; soda, half a teaspoonful; salt, same, and milk.

DIRECTIONS.—Take the flour and salt, and rub the fat well into it; dissolve the soda; then add sweet milk to make a stiff dough; knead well; cut the crackers round, half an inch thick, and bake in a quick oven.

526. **Rye or Wheat Flour Drop Cakes.** [TIME.—TO MAKE AND BAKE, HALF AN HOUR.]

ARTICLES.—A pint of rye or wheat flour; two eggs; salt; sugar, a teaspoonful; milk; soda, a third of a teaspoonful, and cream of tartar, two-thirds.

DIRECTIONS.—Sift a pint of either, or parts of the flours, and tartar, salt and sugar; add the eggs well beaten, and the dissolved soda; lastly, drop the batter in balls on a greased pan or small pans, and bake in a quick oven.

527. **Graham Flour Mush.**

This is an excellent article for infants and young children. It will do for a change for adults, but it is not equal to the coarser preparation of the grain. It is cooked like Indian mush.

528. **Unleavened Bread.**

This bread is made by the water-cure, and hygienic believers who are opposed to the use of yeast, soda, saleratus, salt and cream of tartar. Persons with very weak stomachs will derive benefit from the use of this bread. As a change any one can use it, if they desire to. This bread requires a hot oven.

529. Graham Gems.

Into cold water stir graham flour sufficient to make a batter a trifle thicker than that used for ordinary griddle cakes. Bake from one-half to three-quarters of an hour in a hot oven, in small tins or a tin pan. The flour should be stirred in slowly. Use soft water or part milk.

530. Graham Diamonds.

Pour boiling water on graham flour, stirring rapidly till all the flour is wet. Too much stirring makes it tough. It should be about as thick as can be stirred easily with a strong iron spoon. Place the dough with plenty of flour upon the moulding board, and knead it for two or three minutes. Roll out half an inch thick, and cut in small cakes or rolls. If a large quantity is required, roll about three-fourths of an inch thick, and cut with a knife in diamond shape. Bake, in a very hot oven, forty-five minutes.

531. Graham Biscuit.

Make graham mush as for the table; when cool, mix with it graham flour sufficient to roll well. Knead for a few minutes, roll three-fourths of an inch thick, cut with a common biscuit cutter, and bake in a hot oven, from thirty to forty-five minutes.

532. Wheat Meal Crisps.

Make a very stiff dough of graham flour and cold water; knead thoroughly, roll as thin as possible, and bake for twenty minutes in a hot oven.

533. Oat Meal Mush.

This, in Scotland, is called stirabout. It is a favorite with many persons, and makes a pleasant change of dishes. It is cooked precisely like Indian meal mush.

534. Uses for Stale Bread.

Stale bread may be cut into slices and softened by pouring a small quantity of boiling water over them. Cover the pan containing the bread, to prevent the escape of the steam. As soon as it is soft, season the slices with pepper and salt, have some hot lard, ham fat, or sausages, dripped in a pan, dust a little flour or Indian meal on each slice, and fry them a delicate brown. Boiling milk, if you have it, is better than water to soften the bread.

OYSTERS.

As a healthy, nutritious, and cheap article of food we recommend oysters; many dishes can be made from them. In cases of debility, raw oysters and the soup made from them are very strengthening.

The American oysters are unquestionably the best that can be found. They vary in taste according to how they are treated, either after being dredged or while imbedded, and also according to the nature of the soil and water in which they have lived. It is very wrong to wash oysters; we mean by washing oysters, the abominable habit of throwing them in cold water as soon as opened, then to be sold by the measure. It is more than a pity to thus spoil such an excellent and delicate article of food.

Oysters, like lobsters, are not good when dead. To ascertain if they are alive, as soon as opened, and when one of the shells is removed, touch gently the edge of the oyster, and if alive it will contract.

535. To Feed Oysters.

Wash them perfectly clean with water, then lay them bottom downwards in a deep pan, and pour over them salt water; the salt should be previously dissolved in the water, allowing about five or six ounces to each gallon of water. Change the water every day. You may fatten them by putting oatmeal into the water every day.

536. To Keep Oysters Alive and Good.

Put them in a clean pan, cover them with pure water

A. NEUPERT & CO.,

361 MAIN ST., - 360 WASHINGTON ST.,

YOUNG MEN'S ASSOCIATION BUILDING,

—— DEALERS IN ——

Paper Hangings, Oil Cloths & Linoleum,

WINDOW SHADES AND FIXTURES IN ALL SIZES.

THE BEST PATENT EXTENSION CORNICE

Brass and Walnut Poles.

———o———

We make a specialty of

INTERIOR WALL AND CEILING DECORATIONS

and are prepared to submit designs and estimates.

———o———

Our Stock of

PAPER HANGINGS

Is so large and varied that any taste and means can be suited.

We invite an inspection of our Stock and will guarantee satisfaction both in prices and work.

CHAS. F. SCHMIDT & PETERS,

24 Beaver Street, - NEW YORK.

Sole Agents in the United States and Canada for the Celebrated

CLARET AND SAUTERNE WINES OF CRUSE AND FILS FRERES,

BORDEAUX, FRANCE.

CRUSE'S Fac-Simile of Style of Bottling.

All Bottled Wines sent out by Cruse and Fils Freres have a ☞ **PATENT WIRE NETTING** around each bottle, which netting cannot be removed without breaking. This is a protection against counterfeiting and guarantees the genuineness of their Wines.

These Wines are acknowledged by connoisseurs to be of the finest quality and always give satisfaction.

For Sale by the Trade generally.

———o———

A Full Line can always be had at

DINGENS BROTHERS,
GROCERS,

No. 333 Main Street, - - BUFFALO, N. Y.

(SEE CATALOGUE.)

moderately salted, and changed every day. Keep them in a cool place.

537. To Open Oysters.

In opening them, try and avoid cutting them by keeping the point of the knife close to the shell. In New York they crack the point of the oyster to open them, but they can be opened without that, and it avoids the fine pieces of shell getting into the meat of the oyster.

538. Raw Oysters.

When well-washed open them, detaching the upper shell, then detach them from the under shell, but leave them on it; place on a dish and serve.

To eat them, sprinkle with salt, pepper, and lemon juice. They are excellent eaten with thin slices of brown bread and butter.

539. Steamed Oysters (Washington Style). [Time — About Ten Minutes.]

Put a peck of oysters in a steamer, steam them until they open their shells, open them while hot, eat with vinegar and pepper or sauce, on the half shell or on a plate.

REMARKS.—We have eaten them in this style, and consider it one of the best modes of cooking them known; in Washington it is very popular.

540. Roast Oysters (in the shell). [Time.—A few minutes.]

Wash some oysters, lay them on a gridiron over a bright coal fire, roast until the shells open, lift off the upper shell, put the lower half, with the oyster in it, on a plate, and eat them with butter and any sauce.

541. Baked Oysters. [Time.—A few minutes.]

DIRECTIONS.—Wash some oysters, put them in a pan, then in a hot oven, and let them bake until the shells open, and then serve and eat same as roast oysters.

542. Boiled Oysters. [TIME.—A FEW MINUTES.]

Let the shells be nicely cleaned, boil the oysters in them as you do lobsters, and serve them in their shells with plain melted butter.

543. Broiled Oysters. [TIME.—SIX OR EIGHT MINUTES.]

ARTICLES.—As many oysters as you require; one or two eggs; bread crumbs; a little pepper, and a small piece of butter.

DIRECTIONS.—Take the largest oysters from their own liquor, lay them on a folded napkin to dry off the moisture, then dip them into beaten egg, and then into grated bread; place a gridiron made of coarse wire, over a bright, but not a fierce fire, lay the oysters carefully on it, and when one side is done turn them. Serve them on a folded napkin, or put a piece of butter on a hot dish, sprinkle a little pepper over it, lay the oysters on, and serve plain or on toast.

544. Fried Oysters. [TIME.—FIFTEEN MINUTES.]

ARTICLES.—Oysters, crackers, cayenne pepper, salt, eggs, cream, and butter or lard.

DIRECTIONS.—Select the largest oysters for frying; dry them; have ready some grated crackers seasoned with cayenne pepper and salt; beat the yolks only of some eggs, and to each egg add half a tablespoonful of thick cream; dip the oysters one at a time, first in the egg, then in the cracker crumbs, and fry them in plenty of hot pork fat or butter, till they are of a light brown on both sides. Serve them hot.

545. Stewed Oysters Plain. [TIME.—TWENTY MINUTES.]

ARTICLES.—Oysters, butter, pepper.

DIRECTIONS.—Stew as many oysters as desired in their own liquor, add a little butter and pepper to taste. Eat hot.

546. Stewed Oysters with Milk. [TIME.—HALF AN HOUR.]

ARTICLES.—One quart of oysters, four ounces of butter,

a small tablespoonful of flour, a teaspoonful of parsley, pepper, salt, and a pint of milk.

DIRECTIONS.—Procure good and fresh oysters, set them on a fire with their liquor and a little water, and boil twenty minutes.

Put the butter in a double boiler, set on the fire, and when melted stir into it a small tablespoonful of flour, as soon as mixed, add also the parsley chopped fine, and about a pint of milk, boil gently about ten minutes, then add the oysters, salt and pepper, boil again about one minute. dish the whole, sprinkle lemon juice on, and serve A less quantity may be used if desired.

547. Stewed Oysters with Cream. [TIME.—TO BOIL TEN MINUTES.]

ARTICLES.—A dozen oysters, salt, cayenne pepper, and a very little mace, some butter, grated cracker, a little cream.

DIRECTIONS —Rinse the oysters, and put them in a double boiler with the water which adheres to them, season them with salt, cayenne pepper, and mace As soon as they begin to boil pour in the cream, and stir in the butter rolled in a little grated cracker. Let them boil and serve hot.

548. Stewed Oysters with Eggs. [TIME.—TWENTY MINUTES]

ARTICLES.—Oysters, butter, salt, pepper, eggs, bread crumbs.

DIRECTIONS.—Place a chafing-dish upon the table, with the lamp burning, pour in the oyster liquor, season with butter, salt and pepper, when hot add the oysters, cover with the chafing-dish cover, and stew twenty minutes, beat the eggs in a bowl, remove the dish cover and pour the eggs in, stirring rapidly. Serve from the chafing-dish immediately

549 Stewed Oysters with Wine, (French Style).
[TIME.—THREE QUARTERS OF AN HOUR.]

ARTICLES.—Oysters, sweet milk, a teacupful of bread crumbs,

salt, pepper, and a tablespoonful of butter.

DIRECTIONS.—Strain the liquor so as to remove every fragment of shell; mix in equal proportions the sweet milk and the oyster liquor; add to a quart of the liquor a teacupful of finely pulverized bread or cracker crumbs; season with salt and pepper, and a tablespoonful of butter; boil gently in a double boiler, stirring frequently, a quarter of an hour, then add the oysters; stew half an hour, or less time if preferred, and serve hot. Use wine and spice as seasoning. Use sherry or champagne wine and mace.

550. Boiled Oyster Chowder.

Use recipe for fish chowder, using one quart of oysters instead of fish. Made properly it is cheap and good.

551. Baked Oyster Chowder. [TIME.—THREE-QUARTERS OF AN HOUR.]

ARTICLES.—Sweet milk, crackers, oysters, butter, pepper, salt and celery.

DIRECTIONS.—Butter a deep earthen dish; soak in sweet milk as many crackers or slices of bread as will be needed; cover the bottom of the dish with these (soda crackers are best); strew over these bits of butter; then put in a thick layer of oysters; season with pepper and salt, a little chopped celery or parsley, if liked; then crackers, butter, oysters, and seasoning until the dish is full, always having the crackers on top with bits of butter over. Pour in enough hot oyster liquor and hot sweet milk, mixed in equal proportions, to half fill the dish; this had better be put in before adding the last layer of soaked crackers; bake three-quarters of an hour, and serve with pickles. Clam chowder is made in the same way.

552. Stuffed Oysters. TIME.—[TWENTY MINUTES.]

ARTICLES.—Twelve oysters with their shells, bread, yolks of two eggs, a little cayenne pepper and some butter.

DIRECTIONS.—Take the meat of the oysters, no juice, mince

them up fine, mix in the yolks of two eggs, then the bread crumbs to thicken, then the pepper and salt to taste, then fill the shells, rounding them, so as to hold it, brown in a quick oven. Eat hot or cold.

553. Minced Oysters. [Time.—To bake half an hour.]

ARTICLES.—Twenty-five oysters, bread crumbs or powdered crackers, a cupful of sherry wine, sweet oil, vinegar, cayenne pepper, and salt to taste and ten soda crackers

DIRECTIONS.—Take some fat oysters, mince them fine in their liquor, stir in some bread crumbs, sweet oil, vinegar, pepper, and salt to taste; put alternate layers of mince and crackers, first wet in the wine, in a pudding dish to bake, or a double boiler to boil, cook half an hour either way.

554. Oyster Fritters (French Style). [Time.—Five or six minutes.]

ARTICLES.—Two eggs, half a pint of milk, sufficient flour to make a batter and twenty-five oysters.

DIRECTIONS.—Beat two eggs and stir in half a pint of milk, and sufficient flour to make it a nice batter; dry some fine large oysters on a napkin, put a fork through the hard part, and dip each oyster twice into the batter, fry them in boiling lard or beef-dripping, and serve

555. Oysters in Marinade. [Time.—Six minutes.]

ARTICLES.—Oysters, pepper, salt, grated nutmeg, lemon juice and batter.

DIRECTIONS.—Pour the oysters (out of the shell) in cold water over the fire, and when it boils take them out, and throw them in cold water, and then lay them out upon a cloth to dry, spread them on a dish, sprinkle them with pepper, salt, and a little grated nutmeg, squeeze lemon juice over them, let them lie a little while, dip them in batter and fry them.

556. Indian Curried Oysters. [TIME.—TWENTY TO TWENTY-FIVE MINUTES.]

ARTICLES.—One hundred oysters, two small or one large onion, four dessertspoonfuls of curry powder, three ounces of butter, one cocoanut, juice of a lemon, a large sour apple, flour, salt, and a little warm water or broth.

DIRECTIONS.—Open the oysters and put them with their liquor into a basin, slice two small or one large onion as thin as possible, and put in a double boiler with a piece of butter to fry a nice brown; then stir in a piece of butter and the curry powder, adding, as you stir it, a little warm water or broth, very gradually; set it over the fire and mix in the grated cocoanut and the apple minced fine. Thicken it with a little flour made into a paste with water, and let it simmer until the cocoanut is tender. Then put in the oysters and their liquor strained, the juice of the lemon, and the milk from the cocoanut, and let it boil until the oysters are done, stirring it frequently. Serve it on a hot dish, with boiled rice on a separate dish.

557. Oyster Fritters. [TIME.—FIVE OR SIX MINUTES.]

ARTICLES.—One quart of oysters, half a pint of milk, two eggs, a little flour, and a little dripping or butter.

DIRECTIONS.—Open the oysters, strain the liquor into a basin, and add to it half a pint of milk and the eggs. Stir in by degrees flour enough to make a smooth but rather thin batter; when perfectly free from lumps put the oysters into it. Have some beef-dripping or butter made hot in a very clean frying pan and season with a little salt, and when it is boiling drop in the batter with a large spoon, putting one or more oysters in each spoonful. Hold the pan over a gentle fire until one side of the batter is a delicate brown, turn each fritter separately, and when both sides are done place them on a hot dish and serve.

558. Oyster Meat. [Time —Ten minutes to fry.]

ARTICLES.—Half a pint of oysters, five ounces of bread crumbs, one ounce of butter, the peel of half a lemon, a sprig of parsley, salt, nutmeg, a very little cayenne pepper, and one egg.

DIRECTIONS.—Wash the oysters well in their own liquor and mince them very fine, mix with the peel of half a lemon chopped small, a sprig of parsley, a seasoning of salt, nutmeg, and a very little cayenne pepper, and the butter in small pieces. Stir into these ingredients five ounces of bread crumbs, and when thoroughly mixed together, bind it with the yolk of an egg and part of the oyster liquor. Fry brown.

559. Devilled Oysters. [Time.—Ten minutes.]

ARTICLES.—Some fine shell oysters, one ounce and a half of butter, a little lemon juice, pepper, salt and cayenne.

DIRECTIONS.—Open a sufficient number of oysters for the dish, leaving them in their deep shells and their liquor, add a little lemon juice, pepper, salt, and cayenne, put a small piece of butter on each, and place the shells carefully on a gridiron over a clear, bright fire, to broil for a few minutes. Serve them with bread and butter.

560. Oyster Omelet. [Time.—Ten minutes to prepare.]

ARTICLES.—Eight oysters, six eggs, a wine-glassful of flour, a little milk, pepper, salt and butter.

DIRECTIONS.—The oysters chopped fine, eggs, flour, and milk, pepper, salt, and butter. Beat the eggs very light, add the oysters and the flour, which must be mixed to a paste with a little milk. Pepper and salt to the taste. Fry in hot butter but do not turn it. As soon as it is done slip it on a dish and serve it hot. The above is the usual mode of preparing oyster omelet; but the better way is to put your oysters in a double boiler, set them over the fire, and the moment they begin to boil take them out, drain them and dry them in a napkin.

They are not so watery when prepared in this manner, and consequently will not dilute the beaten eggs as much as the former mode. When they are cold, mince them and proceed as before.

561. Plain Oyster Patties. [TIME.—ALTOGETHER TWO HOURS.]

ARTICLES.—Round loaves, oysters, crumbs of bread, butter, black pepper, cayenne and cream.

DIRECTIONS.—Make little round loaves, make a hole in the top of each, and scrape out a portion of the crumb. Put some oysters into a double boiler with their own liquor, and add to them the crumbs of bread rubbed or grated fine, and a lump of butter. Season with black pepper, and a sprinkle of cayenne. Stew for five or six minutes, and then put in a spoonful of good cream. Fill the loaves, and cover with the bits of crust previously cut up. Set them in an oven for a few minutes to crisp.

Minced veal, lamb, poultry, game, etc., may be done in the same way as for paste patties.

562. Oyster Pie. [TIME.—AN HOUR TO BAKE.]

ARTICLES.—One hundred oysters; one gill of cream; one ounce and a half of butter; grated cracker, salt, cayenne pepper, two eggs and bread crumbs.

DIRECTIONS.—Take the oysters and dry them perfectly. Pour off half the liquor into a double boiler; salt it to your taste. Stir in the cream, then the butter rolled in grated cracker, and a little cayenne pepper. Boil two eggs hard, chop them up and mix them with as many bread crumbs as will cover the top of your pie. Season the bread and eggs with cayenne pepper and salt. Make a rich paste, line the sides of your pie dish, put in the oysters, pour the hot liquor over them, and strew the bread crumbs on the top; cover the whole with a lid of paste. Cut an opening in the center of the top crust, and ornament it with flowers or leaves made of the paste. As soon as the crust is done take the pie out of the oven.

563. Pickled Oysters. [TIME.—HALF AN HOUR.]

ARTICLES.—Two and a half quarts of oysters, vinegar, two tablespoonfuls of salt, one tablespoonful of mace; one tablespoonful of allspice; the same quantity of white pepper; and a teaspoonful of cloves.

DIRECTIONS.—Have ready the oysters with a pint of their liquor. Put the vinegar, salt, and liquor on to boil; when it comes to a boil skim it; then add the spices, give it another boil up, and then put in the oysters. Be careful they do not burn; to prevent this use the double boiler. They must be cooked over a quick fire and serve cold.

564. Scalloped Oysters. [TIME.—ABOUT FIFTEEN MINUTES.]

ARTICLES.—Shell oysters, bread crumbs, two ounces of butter, pepper and salt.

DIRECTIONS.—Open the oysters; leave each oyster in its own deep shell; sprinkle over it a little pepper and salt, and some crumbs of bread, and lay a little piece of butter on the top. Arrange the shells in a dish and put it in the oven. When the oysters are thoroughly hot they are done.

565. Scalloped Oysters (French style). [TIME.—A FEW MINUTES.]

ARTICLES.—Shell oysters; an ounce and a half of butter; a sprig of parsley; pepper, and a little lemon juice.

DIRECTIONS.—Throw the oysters into boiling water over the fire, and let them just bubble up, not boil. Roll them in butter, with minced parsley, pepper and lemon juice. Make some of the deep shells quite clean, arrange the oysters three or four in each, put them on the gridiron, and the moment the liquor bubbles at the side, take them up and serve them.

566. Oyster Catsup. [Time.—One hour.]

Articles.—One pint of oysters, one pint of sherry; one ounce of salt, and a little cayenne pepper.

Directions.—Rinse some fine fresh oysters in their own liquor, then pound them in a mortar, and to a pint of oysters put a pint of sherry. Boil them, add the salt and the cayenne pepper; boil the sauce up again, rub it through a sieve, and when cold put it in bottles and cork and seal them.

567. Oyster Cracker Salad. [Time.—Three minutes.]

Articles.—Oyster crackers (or any other kind), cabbage, celery, or lettuce, sweet oil, vinegar, pepper, mustard and salt to taste.

Directions.—Mix altogether, very fine. Good to eat with any of the above dishes.

568. Fish Chowder. [Time.—To prepare, half an hour; to cook, nearly an hour.]

Articles.—Four pounds of any fresh fish; pork, half a pound; milk, a pint; potatoes, twenty; onions, eight; hard crackers, one pound.

Directions.—Cut the pork into small pieces, fry it out, then pour it into the pot; then strew a layer of sliced onions, then a layer of sliced peeled potatoes, then a layer of fish, then a layer of crackers; repeat until all is in; season with pepper and salt; pour on hot water until it covers the contents; then let it boil until the potatoes are cooked; while the chowder is cooking, put a pint of milk in the double boiler to boil, and add enough flour to make it thick; let it boil until the chowder is done, then pour it over the top; do not stir the chowder, and take it up carefully. Clams and oysters can be used instead of fish.

LOBSTERS.

Lobsters are very fine shell-fish, and are caught in abundance along the shores of the New England States and Canada. The male lobster is distinguished by the narrowness of his tail; the female has a broader tail and small claws. All of the lobster is good to eat, except the stomach and a small intestine which runs through it. The flavor of the lobster is generally considered to be superior, in both purity and delicacy, to that of the other *crustacea*. They are a very agreeable and nutritive article of food, but are not suitable for dyspeptics or invalids. The usual way of cooking them has been to simply boil and eat them cold, with vinegar, or as a salad, but there are many other ways to cook these very economical fish, as will be seen by the following recipes.

569. To Choose Lobsters.

The heaviest are the best, and very often a good small-sized lobster will weigh heavier than a large one. The male is the best for boiling, the flesh is firmer, the shell of a brighter red. Hen lobsters are best for sauces or salads, on account of their coral. They are generally sent to market boiled; if you buy them alive, then proceed

570. To Boil a Lobster. [Time.—An hour.]

Put into a large kettle water enough to cover the lobster, with a quarter of a pound of salt to every gallon of water.

When it boils fast, put in the lobster, head first. If the head goes in first, it is killed instantly. Boil it briskly for an hour, then take it from the hot water, and lay it to drain. Wipe off all the scum from it. A lobster weighing a pound takes one hour to boil, others in like proportion, more or less. It will be a bright red, when done.

571. Plain Boiled Lobster.

After it is boiled and cold, break off the tail, cut it in two pieces with a sharp knife; remove the small intestine and remove the meat; break the claws up and remove their meat; then break off the small legs; open the body; take out everything but the stomach; cut the inner body open; arrange it all round a dish, and serve for breakfast, dinner, or supper. Use vinegar and pepper.

572. To Dress Lobsters.

When sent to the table, separate the body from the tail, remove the large claws, and crack them at each joint carefully, and split the tail down the middle with a sharp knife. Place the body upright in the center of a dish, and arrange the tail and claws on each side. Garnish it with parsley.

573. Lobster Salad. [TIME.—TWENTY MINUTES.]

ARTICLES.—A lobster; yolks of two eggs; a spoonful of made mustard; three tablespoonfuls of salad oil; vinegar; a little salt, and some fresh lettuce.

DIRECTIONS.—Pick all the meat out of the lobster; thoroughly beat the yolks of two eggs; beat in made mustard to taste, and, continuing to beat them, drop in the sweet oil; add whatever flavoring may be preferred, and some salt; mix in the vinegar to taste, and the soft part of the lobster; moisten the remainder of the lobster with this, and lay it at the bottom of the bowl; cut up the lettuce; take care that it is well rolled over in the dressing, and put it over the lobster. Mustard can be left out if it is not liked. The above quantity is given for the proportions and can be increased according to the lobster employed, or taste.

574. Scalloped Lobster. [TIME.—FIFTEEN MINUTES.]

ARTICLES.—One or two lobsters; a little pepper, salt, cayenne, and a tablespoonful of butter, or thin melted butter, and bread crumbs.

DIRECTIONS.—Pick out all the meat from one large or two middling-sized lobsters, and cut fine in a chopping tray, with a little pepper, salt, cayenne, and melted butter sufficient to moisten it. Split the empty shells of the tails and the bodies, and fill each of them neatly with the lobster. Cover them with grated bread, and put them into an oven.

575. English Way to Scallop Lobsters. [TIME.—TWENTY MINUTES.]

ARTICLES.—One large lobster; a teaspoonful of anchovy sauce; three tablespoonfuls of white sauce or cream; yolks of two eggs; some bread crumbs; a little nutmeg, and cayenne, and a lump of butter.

DIRECTIONS.—Cut a large fresh lobster into halves with a sharp knife; pound the spawn, pith, and coral in a mortar, with a lump of butter; then rub it through a sieve into a double boiler; add about three large spoonfuls of white sauce or cream, a teaspoonful of anchovy sauce, and a little cayenne and nutmeg; boil it for five minutes, stirring it constantly. Cut the meat of the lobster into small pieces and stir it into the sauce, with the yolks of two well-beaten eggs; make it thoroughly hot; fill the shells of the body and tail; strew over them some bread crumbs, and brown them.

576. Broiled Lobster. [TIME.—TWENTY MINUTES.]

After having boiled the lobster, split it from head to tail and lay it open; put pieces of butter over the meat; sprinkle it with pepper, and set the shells on a gridiron over the bright coals until nicely heated through. Serve in the shells.

577. Buttered Lobster. [TIME.—TWENTY MINUTES.]

ARTICLES.—One lobster; one wine-glassful of vinegar; a quarter of a pound of fresh butter; one saltspoonful of cayenne pepper; one saltspoonful of made mustard; three heads of lettuce; one hard-boiled egg.

DIRECTIONS.—Boil the lobster, take the meat from the shell and mince or chop it fine and put the coral and green inside; to the vinegar or hot water add the butter; add the pepper and mustard, and put it with the lobster into a double boiler. Stir it until it is thoroughly heated through.

Cut the heads of lettuce; wash them nicely and put them at the sides of a salad bowl; lay the hot lobster in the middle; garnish with the hard-boiled egg cut in circles, and serve hot.

578. To Stew Lobsters. [Time.—Twenty minutes.]

Articles.—One large or two small hen lobsters; one pint of water; one blade of mace; some whole pepper; some melted butter; a glass of white wine; juice of half a lemon.

Directions.—Pick the meat from one large or two small lobsters in large pieces; boil the shells in a pint of water, with a blade of mace, and some whole pepper. When all the strength is extracted from the shells and spice, strain the liquor; mix the coral and the rich part of the lobster with a few spoonfuls of melted butter, a wineglassful of white wine, and the juice of half a lemon strained; put in the picked lobster, boil it up, and serve.

579. Miroton of Lobster. [Time.—One hour and twenty minutes.]

Articles.—One large lobster; four eggs; one penny roll; three tablespoonfuls of cream; pepper, salt, and slices of fat ham.

Directions.—Pick out all the meat from a large hen lobster, and pound it in a mortar with the spawn and the crumb of a penny roll previously soaked in cream. Then stir in the yolks of three well-beaten eggs, and season it with pepper, salt, and a very little pounded mace. Beat an egg to a stiff froth, and add it to the pounded lobster. Line a pudding mould with some slices of fat ham, cut as thin as possible; fill the mould with the mixture, and boil it for an hour and twenty minutes. When done, turn it out carefully on a hot dish, and pour round it some good lobster sauce.

580. French Curry of Lobster. [Time.—One hour.]

Articles.—One lobster; one onion; a tablespoonful of

butter, a quarter of a lemon, a spoonful of flour, two spoonfuls of curry powder; one pint of water.

DIRECTIONS.—Pick out the meat from a large lobster; put the body into a double boiler with the water, cut the onion in slices, add the butter and a quarter of a lemon; then stir in the curry powder and the flour. When it is thoroughly done, strain the gravy from the body of the lobster; add a little pepper, salt, and the juice of a lemon, put in the picked lobster, first cut up in small pieces, let stand for an hour by the side of the fire, then boil up again, and serve hot.

581. Curry of Lobsters. [TIME.—ONE HOUR.]

ARTICLES.—Two small lobsters, half a blade of mace, four spoonfuls of meat gravy, four spoonfuls of cream, two teaspoonfuls of curry powder, one teaspoonful of flour, one ounce of butter, juice of half a lemon.

DIRECTIONS.—Pick the lobsters or spawns from their shells, put them into a stew pan with the mace, gravy, and the cream, rub smooth the curry powder, one ounce of flour, and an ounce of butter. Let it simmer for one hour, add a little salt, squeeze in the juice of half a lemon, and serve.

582. Lobster Fricasseed. [TIME.—EIGHT MINUTES TO PARBOIL, 10 EACH POUND THE SAME TIME]

ARTICLES.—Two lobsters, a pint of milk, juice of half a lemon, pepper, salt, and nutmeg.

DIRECTIONS.—Parboil two moderate sized lobsters, take out the meat from the claws and tail, and cut it into rather small pieces, put into a stew pan with the milk, cover the pan close, and stew it gently for the same time it has previously taken to parboil the lobsters. When on the point of boiling, stir in the juice of half a lemon quickly, just as it is removed from the fire. Serve it very hot.

583. To Roast a Lobster. [TIME.—HALF AN HOUR.]

DIRECTIONS.—Parboil a lobster, take it out of the water,

rub it over with butter, and put it in a dish before the fire; baste it well with butter until it has a fine froth, and serve.

584. Lobster Cutlets Fried in Batter. [TIME.—TWENTY MINUTES.]

Cook as below for cutlets, using batter instead of bread crumbs to fry them in.

585. Plain Lobster Cutlets. [TIME.—TO FRY, TWENTY MINUTES.]

ARTICLES.—A good-sized lobster; two eggs; crumbs of bread; cayenne; salt and nutmeg.

DIRECTIONS.—Cut the meat out of the tail and claws; slice them up about a third of an inch thick; dip them into beaten egg, then into very fine bread crumbs, which have first been seasoned with the pepper, salt and grated nutmeg; egg and crumb them twice; fry them quickly in butter until a light brown, and serve hot.

586. East India Lobster Cutlets. [TIME.—EIGHT MINUTES TO FRY.]

ARTICLES.—One large hen lobster and two small ones; two ounces of fresh butter; pepper and salt; one blade of mace, nutmeg and cayenne pepper; a dessertspoonful of anchovy sauce; four eggs, and bread crumbs. For the sauce, the coral of the lobster; a spoonful of anchovy sauce, and a small cupful of melted butter.

DIRECTIONS.—Pick the meat from a fine hen lobster and two small ones, and pound it in a mortar with part of the coral and a seasoning of pepper, salt, mace, nutmeg and cayenne pepper. Add the yolks of two well-beaten eggs, the white of one, and a spoonful of anchovy sauce; mix the above ingredients thoroughly together, and roll it out as you would paste, with a little flour, two inches thick. Cut it into cutlets; brush them over with the yolk of egg; dip them into bread crumbs, and fry a nice brown in butter, a spoonful of anchovy sauce,

CLOTHING.

319 Main Street. - 324 Washington Street.

RIEGEL & ROBINSON,

LARGEST EXCLUSIVELY CLOTHIERS IN WESTERN NEW YORK.

Separate Department for

BOYS' & CHILDREN'S CLOTHING

—{ Also for }—

MERCHANT TAILORING.

SPECIALTIES NEAT AND STYLISH RECEIVED DAILY IN BOTH DEPARTMENTS.

WE EMPLOY THREE FIRST-CLASS CUTTERS,

—{ AND }—

Over 100 Custom Tailors,

Which should be a Guarantee of Satisfaction in the Latter Branch.

319 MAIN STREET THROUGH TO 324 WASHINGTON STREET.

"HOUSEHOLD,"

SEWING MACHINE

— BUILT BY THE —

PROVIDENCE TOOL COMPANY.

This Machine fully sustains the high character of all goods manufactured by this celebrated manufactory, whose goods have been prominently in the market since 1836. They are the manufacturers of the celebrated "Peabody Martina" rifle, and have also had large experience in the manufacture of Sewing Machines prior to putting the

"HOUSEHOLD"
ON THE MARKET.

The "Household" is considered by experts the

ZENITH OF MECHANICAL PERFECTION IN SEWING MACHINES.

Light running, simple, durable, with "Automatic" or SELF REGULATING TENSION, self-setting needle, beautiful and substantial wood-work.

TRY IT BEFORE YOU BUY!

Needles, Attachments and Repairs for all Machines. Best Oil, warranted not to gum, 10 cents per bottle. Machines rented. Satisfaction guaranteed. All work warranted.

N. O. TIFFANY.   -   33 Niagara Street.

and the remainder of the coral. Pour it into the center of a hot dish, and arrange the lobster cutlets round it, as you would cutlets of meat, and place between each the horns of the lobster cut into short lengths.

587. Lobster Balls. [TIME.—EIGHT OR TEN MINUTES TO FRY.]

ARTICLES.—A fine hen lobster; two eggs; bread crumbs; two ounces of butter: pepper, salt, and a very little cayenne pepper.

DIRECTIONS.—Take the meat from a fine hen lobster, and pound it in a mortar with the coral and spawn. Mix with it not quite an equal quantity of bread crumbs, seasoned with pepper and salt and a little cayenne; bind the whole with two ounces of fresh butter warmed; roll the mixture into balls the size of large duck's eggs; brush them over with beaten egg; cover them with bread crumbs, and fry them lightly. Serve them hot, after draining the grease from them.

588. Lobster Pie. [TIME.—ONE HOUR.]

ARTICLES.—One lobster; a spoonful of vinegar; a table-spoonful of butter; some bread crumbs and puff paste.

DIRECTIONS.—Pick all of the meat out of the lobster, spawn and green; cut all up fine in a chopping tray, or beat it in a mortar; season it with pepper, salt, and vinegar; melt the butter; stir all together with a cupful of bread crumbs; put puff paste around the pie plate; put in the meat, covering it over with the paste; make a hole in the top, and bake it in a slow oven.

589. Minced Lobsters. [TIME.—TEN MINUTES.]

ARTICLES.—One lobster; a glass of white wine; pepper and salt; nutmeg; cayenne, and a wine-glassful of vinegar; two ounces of butter; one anchovy; yolks of eggs, and bread crumbs.

DIRECTIONS.—Pick the meat from a fresh lobster; mince it

very well, and put it into a stew pan with a seasoning of pepper and salt, a little cayenne, a wine-glassful of white wine, and one of vinegar. Set it over a clear fire to stew for about ten minutes; melt two ounces of butter, with an anchovy, and the yolks of two well-beaten eggs; stir it into the lobster, and thicken the whole with bread crumbs; place it in a dish, and garnish with the claws and double parsley.

590. Lobster Soup. [TIME.—ONE HOUR AND A QUARTER.]

ARTICLES.—One lobster; two or three plain soda biscuits; one quart of milk; one quart of water; one tablespoonful of salt; one teaspoonful of pepper, and a quarter of a pound of fresh butter.

DIRECTIONS.—Pick the meat from a lobster already boiled, and cut it into small pieces; roll the biscuits to a powder; put a quart of milk and a quart of water into a double boiler, with a tablespoonful of salt and a teaspoonful of pepper. When the milk and water are boiling hot, add the lobster and pounded biscuit mixed to the soup with a quarter of a pound of fresh butter; let it boil closely covered for half an hour; pour it into a tureen, and serve.

591. Lobster Croquettes. [TIME.—EIGHT MINUTES TO FRY.]

ARTICLES.—One large lobster; two tablespoonfuls of cream; some grated bread; a teaspoonful of anchovy sauce; one egg; juice of one lemon; pepper, salt, and nutmeg.

DIRECTIONS.—Pick the meat from a large lobster; mince it up, and mix with it the bread, anchovy sauce, cream, the juice of a lemon, pepper, salt, and a little grated nutmeg. Put it over the fire and make it very hot: turn it out, and stir in the yolk of a beaten egg. When cold, make it into balls; brush them over with egg; strew bread crumbs over them, and fry them in hot fat; pile them in a dish, and garnish with fried parsley.

FRIED PASTRY.
Cakes, Fritters, Crullers and Doughnuts.

We give below several of the best recipes known for frying pastry. When properly made and fried, there is nothing more palatable and universally desired than these dishes.

592. To Fry Pastry. [TIME.—SIX MINUTES.]

Use fresh sweet lard, have at least two or three inches in a deep frying pan to save burning, and to be handy use a frying sieve, which prevents the articles from touching the bottom of the pan, and is also handy to lift all in the pan out of the fat at once. In frying potatoes or small articles they can be tossed in it, instead of being turned with a fork; try your fat to see if it is hot with a small piece of dough; if it is hot enough it will rise quickly and soak no fat. Fry a delicate brown.

593. Raised Doughnuts. [TIME.—TO RISE SIX HOURS.]

ARTICLES.—One cup of warm milk; one cup of sugar; one yeast cake; fat, size of an egg; salt and flour. Cinnamon or other spice to taste.

DIRECTIONS.—Sift the flour, add a little salt, beat the milk and fat together, and add the yeast; make a stiff dough; when risen work in the spice, and cut out in any shape and fry.

594. Yeast Doughnuts. [TIME.—TO RISE ABOUT SIX HOURS.]

ARTICLES.—One quarter of a pound of butter; half a pound of sugar; two tumblerfuls of milk; two eggs; a teacupful of yeast; spice to taste and flour.

DIRECTIONS.—Prepare as above, beat the eggs well with the sugar, and add. Fry and when cold sprinkle powdered sugar over them.

595. Fine Doughnuts. [TIME.—TEN MINUTES TO PREPARE.]

ARTICLES.—Three eggs; two cups of sugar; one tablespoonful of butter; a large cup of sweet or sour milk; one nutmeg, and a scant teaspoonful of soda.

DIRECTIONS.—Beat the eggs well with the sugar and butter, spice to taste, add the milk and the soda mixed, and flour enough to roll. Fry at once.

596. Plain Cheap Doughnuts. [TIME.—TO PREPARE TEN MINUTES.]

ARTICLES.—A pint of milk; one egg; one cup of sugar; half a teaspoonful of soda; one teaspoonful of cream of tartar, and flour enough to roll.

DIRECTIONS.—Prepare and cook same as for fine doughnuts.

597. Fried Crullers. [TIME.—A FEW MINUTES.]

ARTICLES.—Four eggs; half a pound of sugar; three ounces of butter; one gill of milk; one teaspoonful of cinnamon, and flour and lard.

DIRECTIONS.—Prepare as for fine doughnuts; roll it out, cut the dough into strips, twist them and drop them in boiling lard.

598. Fried Crackers.

Prepare same as for recipe, No. 525, and fry in hot fat.

599. Wonders. [TIME.—TO MAKE, AN HOUR.]

ARTICLES.—A quarter of a pound of sugar; ten ounces of butter; one pound of flour; three eggs; a little nutmeg, and some yeast.

DIRECTIONS.—Work the sugar and butter together till quite soft, throw in the eggs that have been previously well beaten, then add the flour and a little nutmeg and yeast. Knead twenty minutes and let it rise, then roll between your hands into round balls, the size of a small potato, but do not add any more flour. Flour your pasteboard lightly, and roll each ball into a thin oval, the size of the hand; cut with a knife, three slits like bars in the center of the oval, cross the two center ones with your fingers, and draw up the two sides between; put your finger through and drop it into boiling lard. Turn as they rise, and when a nice brown take them up with a fork.

600. **Spanish Puffs.** [TIME.—TO FRY, TWENTY MINUTES.]

ARTICLES.—One pint of milk, one pint of flour, a little cinnamon, almond essence, four eggs, and sugar to your taste.

DIRECTIONS.—Put a pint of milk into a double boiler and let it boil, add the same quantity of flour by degrees, a teaspoonful at a time, stirring it together till it becomes a very stiff, smooth paste. Put it into a basin, add a little cinnamon, a little almond essence, and sugar to your taste. After you have put in all the ingredients, beat them well together for half an hour, adding, as you beat it, and by degrees, four eggs. Make some lard hot in a pan, drop into it pieces of this paste of about the size of a walnut, and fry them.

601. **Lemon Turnovers.** [TIME.—TO BAKE, TWENTY MINUTES.]

ARTICLES.—Three dessertspoonfuls of flour, one of powdered sugar; rind of one lemon; two ounces of butter; two eggs, and a little milk.

DIRECTIONS.—Mix the flour, sugar, and the grated rind of the lemon with a little milk to the consistency of batter, then add the eggs well beaten, and the butter melted, and fry.

602. **Snow Pancakes.** [TIME.—TO FRY, A FEW MINUTES.]

ARTICLES.—Four ounces of flour, a quarter of a pint of milk; a little grated nutmeg, a pinch of salt, sufficient flour to make a thick batter, and three large spoonfuls of snow to each pancake.

DIRECTIONS.—Make a stiff batter with the flour and milk, add a little grated nutmeg and the salt. Divide the batter into any number of pancakes, and add the snow to each. Fry them lightly, and serve quickly.

603. **Batter Pancakes.** [TIME.—TEN MINUTES TO MAKE.]

ARTICLES.—Three eggs; one pint of milk, sufficient flour, a pinch of salt; and a little nutmeg.

DIRECTIONS.—Beat the eggs and stir them into the milk, add the salt and sufficient flour to make it into a thick smooth batter. Fry them in boiling fat; roll them over on each side, drain and serve them very hot, with lemon and sugar.

604. Rye Flour Pancakes. [TIME.—TEN MINUTES TO MAKE.]

ARTICLES.—A pint of milk; two eggs; sugar; half a cup of flour to make a stiff batter; hot fat, a teaspoonful.

DIRECTIONS.—Same as for batter pancakes.

605. Irish Pancakes. [TIME.—TO MAKE TEN MINUTES.]

ARTICLES.—Yolks of four eggs; whites of four; one pint of milk; a little grated nutmeg; two ounces of sugar; peel of a lemon grated; three ounces of fresh butter; and six ounces of flour.

DIRECTIONS.—Warm the milk in a double boiler and strain into it the well-beaten eggs, with the sugar, a little nutmeg, and the peel of a lemon, grated; warm the butter and stir it into the milk. Then mix in the flour to form a smooth batter. Put a piece of butter at the bottom of the pan, pour in the batter, and fry the pancakes very thin. When done, place them on a hot dish, one over the other, and serve them quickly, and as hot as possible.

606. Fruit Fritters. [TIME.—TO FRY TEN MINUTES.]

ARTICLES.—One pound of flour; one ounce of yeast; a little milk; two ounces of loaf sugar; four eggs; three ounces of butter; the peel of half a lemon; marmalade, jam, or fruit.

DIRECTIONS.—Put the flour into a bowl, and put into the center the yeast; add sufficient milk to form a stiff dough, and set by the fire to rise. Melt the butter, add it to the sugar, beat it all well together, add it to the dough, and again beat it until it will separate from the bowl. Roll this mixture into a number of balls, any size you prefer, fill each with marmalade, fruit, or jam, and set them to rise, with a floured paper under them. Then put them into a large pan of boiling lard and fry them nicely.

607. Orange Fritters. [TIME.—A FEW MINUTES.]

ARTICLES.—Three oranges, butter, pounded sugar.

DIRECTIONS.—Peel the oranges, then cut them across into slices, pick out the seeds, and dip each slice of orange into a thick fritter batter. Fry them nicely, and serve them with sugar sifted over each. Any sliced fruit will answer as well.

608. Batter Fritters of all kinds. [TIME.—TO MAKE, TEN MINUTES.]

ARTICLES.—Eight ounces of flour; half a pint of water; two ounces of butter; whites of two eggs.

DIRECTIONS—Mix the flour with the water into a smooth batter, dissolve the butter over a slow fire, and then stir it by degrees into the flour; then add the whites of the eggs whisked to a stiff froth, and stir them lightly in. Any cooked vegetables can be covered with this batter, and fried.

609. Bread Fritters. [TIME.—A FEW MINUTES.]

ARTICLES.—Half a pound of currants; flour; half a pint of bread crumbs; a pint of milk; two ounces of butter; half a nutmeg; a quarter of a pound of sugar; a wineglassful of brandy; and six eggs.

DIRECTIONS.—Grate the bread crumbs into the boiling milk, in which the butter and currants have been stirred, cover the pan and let it stand for an hour. Then beat the mixture thoroughly and add half a nutmeg grated, with the white powdered sugar and the brandy. Beat the eggs till very light, and stir them by degrees into the mixture. It should be brought to the consistency of a thin batter; and if it turns out too thin, add a little flour, and fry brown.

610. Croquettes of Rice. [TIME.—AN HOUR.]

ARTICLES.—Half a pound of rice; one pint and a half of

milk; a quarter of a pound of butter; half a pound of sugar; one lemon; five eggs; and some bread crumbs.

DIRECTIONS.—Put the rice and milk into a double boiler, and let it simmer until quite tender. Rub the rind from the lemon with the sugar in a mortar, add it to the rice, and the yolks of the eggs well beaten, stirring it untilthe eggs thicken. When cold, form into small balls; whisk the eggs well in a basin, dip each ball into the egg, and then into the bread crumbs; smooth them with a knife, repeat the egg and crumbs, and put them into a frying sieve, and place it in a stew pan of boiling lard, and fry them lightly. When done, drain them from the fat and pile them on a dish; sift powdered sugar over them and serve hot.

611. Wafers. [TIME.—A FEW MINUTES TO MAKE.]

ARTICLES.—A quarter of a pound of butter; a pound of flour; three eggs; salt; a teaspoonful of cinnamon, and milk.

DIRECTIONS.—Make all into a batter, and bake same as for waffles.

612. Waffles. [TIME.—A MINUTE TO BAKE.]

ARTICLES.—Ten ounces of flour; five of sugar; two eggs; flavor with essences; half a cup of sherry wine, and milk.

DIRECTIONS.—Make a paste of the flour and milk, beat the sugar, eggs and wine together and flavor to taste. Warm your waffle-irons, then grease them, fill them nearly full, close them, and place them over a fire. Turn the irons so as to bake the waffles on both sides; when done, take out, butter, and sift sugar over them, and eat hot.

613. Yeast Waffles. [TIME.—TO BAKE, A MINUTE OR TWO.]

ARTICLES.—Flour, one pound; milk, one pint; butter, one ounce; yeast, and two eggs.

DIRECTIONS.—Beat the eggs, stir in the milk and butter, add the flour, beat quite smooth, add sufficient yeast to make it rise; then bake as directed above.

614. Egg Waffles. [TIME.—TO MAKE, A FEW MINUTES.]

ARTICLES.—Three eggs; a cup of butter; a quart of milk; flour; a teaspoonful of soda; two teaspoonfuls of cream of tartar.

DIRECTIONS.—Make a batter of the eggs, milk, and as much flour as will thicken it; add the cream of tartar and soda in the usual way. Bake in the waffle-irons at once.

615. Nonesuch. [TIME.—TO MAKE TEN MINUTES.

ARTICLES.—Yolks of five eggs; an even teaspoonful of salt; flour.

DIRECTIONS.—Beat the eggs light, add the salt, and flour enough to form a stiff dough. Roll as thin as paper, cut out with a round cake-cutter, cut stripes in the center and fry. While hot, sprinkle sugar over them.

616. Yankee Marvels. [TIME.—HALF AN HOUR.]

ARTICLES.—Four eggs; four tablespoonfuls of sugar; one tablespoonful of melted lard; flour enough to make a dough.

DIRECTIONS.—Prepare and fry as above.

617. Fried Patty Paste. TIME.—TWENTY MINUTES TO MAKE.]

ARTICLES.—One pound of flour; quarter of a pound of butter; half a pound of lard, and a little salt.

DIRECTIONS.—Rub a little of the flour into a bowl with a pinch of salt, then rub in a little lard, add water enough to make it into a stiff paste, then flour the pasteboard and with your hands take out the paste; flour the roller, roll it out into a thin flat surface, spread over it rows of lard and butter, fold it over, then roll it out again; sprinkle a little flour, and repeat six times; it is then ready for any kind of pies, short cakes, or patties.

618. Patties and Pies. [TIME.—THIRTY MINUTES.]

ARTICLES.—Some of the above paste; and any kind of meat,

poultry, or oysters. Fruit or vegetables may be used if desired.

DIRECTIONS.—Prepare the filling of meat, or any other article desired, to suit the taste; roll out the patty paste the thickness of pie crust, cut it with a cake cutter, put a tablespoonful of the filling in the center, twist the edges together, and fry them a nice brown in plenty of boiling lard.

619. Patties and Pies.

Use the patty paste. Line a dish with it and fill in with any meat or other articles, and bake; cut a hole in the top to let the steam out, and fill up with water.

620. Bread Patties. [TIME.—A QUARTER OF AN HOUR.]

ARTICLES.—Cooked mince meat; slice of bread; yolk of egg; bread crumbs; cupful of milk or cream.

DIRECTIONS.—Cut some stale bread into thick slices, hollow out the center, dip each into the milk, brush them over with the yolk of a beaten egg; strew bread crumbs over them and fry a light brown; fill the center of one with the mince meat and cover with the other, and serve.

Gingerbread, Cakes, Puffs, Puddings, etc.

Ginger is stimulating and aromatic, increases the secretion of gastric juices, and removes flatulency. Used in moderation it is a very healthy and valuable condiment, and removes faintness and sickness of the stomach.

Of all cakes none are more suitable for the nervous than gingerbread or ginger-cakes; they rarely disagree with any one.

621. Rich Gingerbread. [TIME.—THREE-QUARTERS TO ONE HOUR.]

ARTICLES.—Half a pound of butter; half a pound of sugar; half a pound of molasses; one pound of flour; half an ounce of ginger; one teaspoonful of carbonate of soda, and four eggs.

DIRECTIONS.—Put the butter, sugar, and molasses into a

double boiler together, and place it over the fire to melt. Then beat the eggs, and stir the melted butter, sugar, and molasses into the eggs, add the powdered ginger and carbonate of soda, then stir all together into the flour and bake.

622. Cheap Gingerbread. [TIME.—THREE-QUARTERS OF AN HOUR.]

ARTICLES.—One pound of flour; one pound of molasses; a quarter of a pound of butter; one egg; one ounce of ginger; a teaspoonful of soda, and a little milk.

DIRECTIONS.—Mix the ginger with the flour, warm the butter and molasses, and mix it well with the flour and ginger. Take a few spoonfuls of warm milk, dissolve a teaspoonful of soda in it, and mix the whole up lightly with the egg well-beaten, and bake in a long buttered tin for three-quarters of an hour. Just before it is removed from the oven brush it over with the yolk of an egg, well-beaten with a little milk, then put it back in the oven and finish baking. The time, of course, must be according to its size.

623. Gingercakes. [TIME.—HALF AN HOUR.]

ARTICLES.—One pound of moist sugar; half a pound of butter; a cup of milk; one pound and three-quarters of flour, and half an ounce of ginger.

DIRECTIONS.—Put the sugar, butter, and milk into a double boiler and let it boil until the butter is melted. While it is quite hot, mix it with the flour and ginger. Roll it out thin; prick it, and cut it into any shape you like. If the paste gets stiff before you have rolled it all out, set it before the fire a little. Bake these cakes in a slack oven.

624. Gingerbread Loaf. [TIME.—THREE-QUARTERS OF AN HOUR TO ONE HOUR.]

ARTICLES.—One pound of flour; one pound of molasses; six ounces of butter; four ounces of moist sugar; half an ounce of coriander seeds; half an ounce of caraway seeds; half a tablespoonful of soda; a quarter of a teacupful of cream, and four eggs.

DIRECTIONS.—Melt the molasses and the butter together, add the moist sugar, the coriander and caraway seeds ground together, and ginger to your taste. Mix with the flour; mix the soda with a very little cream; mix all well together. Beat the eggs and add them to the gingerbread the very last thing. Line a tin with paper, butter it, and put the mixture in it. Bake in a slow oven.

625. Honeycomb Gingerbread. [TIME.—TEN MINUTES.]

ARTICLES.—Half a pound of flour; half a pound of coarse sugar; a quarter of a pound of butter; one ounce of ginger; half an ounce of lemon peel; juice of one lemon; six ounces of molasses, and a quarter of an ounce of butter for the tin.

DIRECTIONS.—Add the flour and sugar, rub into it the butter and the ginger, and mix them; put half an ounce of lemon peel, well grated, over it, and pour in the juice of a whole lemon. Use enough molasses to make it into a very thin paste that will spread over a sheet of tin, first having rubbed the tin with butter. Bake it in a moderate oven, and watch it carefully. When it is baked enough cut it into strips upon the tin, and roll it around your finger like a wafer.

These rolls must be kept in a tin case; if they should chance to get moist they must be renewed in the oven when wanted.

626. Cocoanut or Almond Gingerbread. [TIME.—THREE-QUARTERS OF AN HOUR.]

ARTICLES.—One pound of syrup; one pound of flour; one ounce of ground ginger; half a pound of butter; half a pound of moist sugar; seven ounces of grated cocoanut or pounded almonds; peel of two small lemons, and one ounce and a half of candied orange peel.

DIRECTIONS.—Put the syrup into a double boiler with the butter, and when hot pour it into the flour, previously mixed with the sugar, grated ginger, lemon peel, and sliced citron. Beat the mixture well together, and set it to become cold; then stir or beat into it the cocoanut or sweet almonds pounded, beat it for a few minutes, and then drop the mixture from a tablespoon on a buttered tin, any size you prefer the cakes to be, and bake them in a slow oven.

627. Orange Gingerbread.

ARTICLES.—Two pounds of flour; two pounds of molasses; eight ounces of candied orange peel; a pound of moist sugar; two ounces of ground ginger; one ounce of allspice; a pound of butter; one teacupful of milk, and the yolk of one egg.

DIRECTIONS.—Mix with the flour the candied orange peel cut very small, the moist sugar, the ground ginger, and allspice, and molasses; melt the butter till it is oiled, mix it well with the flour, etc., and put it in a cool place for ten or twelve hours. Roll out about half an inch thick, cut it into any form you please, or cut it into pieces rather longer than square; brush them over with milk mixed with the yolk of the egg, and bake them in a cool oven. .

628. Gingerbread Nuts. [TIME.—TWENTY MINUTES.]

ARTICLES.—One pound of sugar; two pounds of molasses; three-quarters of a pound of butter; four pounds of flour; four ounces of ginger; one ounce of allspice; two spoonfuls of coriander seed; some candied orange peel; two spoonfuls of brandy, and the yolks of four eggs.

DIRECTIONS.—Mix the sugar, molasses, and butter, and melt all together; then stir in the flour, ground ginger, allspice, coriander seed, and the orange peel cut very small. Mix all into a paste with the eggs well beaten; add the brandy, and make them into nuts or cakes.

629. Sugar Ginger Crisps. [TIME.—TO BAKE ABOUT TEN MINUTES.]

ARTICLES.—One cupful of sugar, two of molasses, one of

butter; a teaspoonful of soda; ginger, and sufficient flour.

DIRECTIONS.—Mix all the ingredients together, and add ginger to your taste, and flour enough to make a stiff dough. Roll the dough very thin and cut with a wine-glass, and bake in a quick oven.

630. **Molasses Ginger Crisps.** [TIME.—ABOUT TEN MINUTES.]

ARTICLES.—Two cups of molasses, one of lard; one tablespoonful of ginger; one dessertspoonful of soda, and flour.

DIRECTIONS.—Mix all of the above articles together; dissolve the soda in a little hot water, and add enough flour to make a stiff dough, and roll thin.

631 **Fruit Ginger Cake.** [TIME.—NEARLY AN HOUR.]

ARTICLES.—One pound of flour; one cup of sugar; two of molasses; half a pound of butter; six eggs; one pound of currants; the same of raisins; half a pound of citron; one tablespoonful of ginger; one teaspoonful of cinnamon and allspice; one teaspoonful of soda and two of cream of tartar.

DIRECTIONS.—Mix all well together and bake.

632. **Soft Ginger Cake.** [TIME.—ABOUT HALF AN HOUR.]

ARTICLES.—One cup of sugar, three of molasses, one of butter, one of sweet milk; three eggs; seven cups of flour; one teaspoonful of soda beaten well into the molasses; ginger and spice to taste.

DIRECTIONS.—Mix all in the usual way and bake.

633. **Spice Ginger Cake.** [TIME.—ABOUT THREE QUARTERS OF AN HOUR.]

ARTICLES.—Five eggs; two teacupfuls of butter; four of flour; two of sugar; one teacup, not quite full, of molasses; teaspoonful of soda; a wineglassful of brandy; a tablespoonful of ginger; one of cinnamon, and one of allspice and cloves mixed.

DIRECTIONS.—Stir the soda into the molasses until it foams from the bottom ; add the whites of the eggs, frothed, last ; and next to the last add the molasses. Fruit may be added if desired.

634. Ginger Puffs. [TIME.—HALF AN HOUR.]

ARTICLES.—Half a pound of flour ; three eggs ; one teaspoonful of grated ginger ; a little nutmeg ; a tablespoonful of sugar ; half a glassful of white wine.

DIRECTIONS.—Add the grated ginger, sugar and nutmeg, to the flour, and mix all together with the eggs, well beaten, and the wine. Bake them in cups in a quick oven, and pour a little wine sauce over them before they are sent to the table.

635. Ginger Pudding. [TIME.—THREE HOURS.]

ARTICLES.—A quarter of a pound of suet ; half a pound of flour ; a quarter of a pound of moist sugar, and one full teaspoonful of ground ginger.

DIRECTIONS.—Chop a quarter of a pound of beef suet very fine ; mix it with the flour, sugar and ginger. Mix all dry, and put into a well-buttered double boiler ; boil three hours, and when done turn out and serve with white wine sauce.

636. Mrs. B.'s Best Cheap Pudding. [TIME.—TEN HOURS.]

ARTICLES.—Two quarts of bread, or crackers ; one pound of raisins or currants ; one cup of molasses ; cloves, allspice, and nutmeg to taste ; milk or water to soak the bread in, and salt.

DIRECTIONS.—Soak the bread in water (milk if you desire) until quite soft ; mix all the articles together ; put them in an earthen stone pot, then place the pot in a boiler or steamer, and steam from six to ten hours ; then put them in an oven and bake them slow four hours.

FANCY DISHES FOR DESSERT.

We give below a number of fine dishes for dessert, many of which are rare.

637. Custard with Jelly. [TIME.———

ARTICLES.—One pint of milk, three to five eggs, sugar and flavor to taste, and the peel of half a lemon.

DIRECTIONS.—Put into a double boiler the milk, sugar and the lemon peel cut thin ; when it boils pour it out, whisk the whites and yolks of the eggs, and stir them gradually into the milk ; pour it into a double boiler, and stir it over the fire one way until it thickens ; when cold pour it into custard glasses, and put a spoonful of clear jelly on some, and a dark colored jelly on the others ; place the cups on a dish and serve.

638. Tipsy Cake. [TIME.—ONE HOUR TO SOAK.]

ARTICLES.—One stale sponge cake, one glass of brandy, sufficient wine to soak it, juice of half a lemon, three ounces of sweet almonds, one pint of rich custard.

DIRECTIONS.—Place a large sponge cake in the glass dish in which it is to be served, make a small hole in the centre, and pour in over the cake a sufficient quantity of sherry wine (mixed with the brandy and the juice of the lemon) to soak it thoroughly; then blanch two or three ounces of sweet almonds, cut them into long spikes, stick them all over the cake, and pour around it a pint of very rich custard.

639. A Cake Trifle. [TIME.—AN HOUR.]

ARTICLES.—A Savoy cake, or a Naples cake, a pint of milk, yolks of four eggs, whites of two, two ounces of sugar, one teaspoonful of peach water, or any jam.

DIRECTIONS.—Take a Savoy or Naples cake, cut out the inside about an inch from the edge and bottom, leaving a shell ; fill the inside with a custard made of the yolks of the eggs beaten with the milk, sweetened with the sugar, and flavored with the peach water ; lay on it some strawberry, or any other jam you may prefer ; beat the whites of the eggs with a little sifted sugar, until they will stand in a heap, pile it up on the cake over the preserves, and serve.

HOUSE FURNISHING.

WALBRIDGE'S
HOUSE FURNISHING DEPOT,

317 and 319 Washington St., - BUFFALO, N. Y.

A Complete Assortment of

DINING ROOM AND KITCHEN UTENSILS,

Consisting in part of

Tin Ware,
Granite Iron Ware,
Larding Pins,
Meat Rests or Pan Grates,
Whip Cream Churns,
Jelly Moulds,
Ice Cream Freezers,
Dover Egg Beaters,
Fancy Vegetable Cutters,
Chinese Strainers,
Lustro and Electro Silicon,

Fine Carvers,
Fine Table Cutlery,
Cheese Scoops,
Fine Cork-screws,
Table Mats,
Knife and Fork Baskets,
Vienna Coffee Machines,
Coffee Biggins,
Chamois Skins,
Plate Brushes, Sponges,
Tea Trays,

Carved Bread Plates,
Bread Knives,
Crumb Brushes and Trays,
Children's Trays,
Carpet Sweepers,
Clothes Wringers,
Feather Dusters,
Gents' Blacking Cases,
Fluting Machines,
Polishing Irons,
Water Coolers.

——{ AN ELEGANT DISPLAY OF }——

SILVER PLATED WARE

Of New and Elegant Designs, from the Best Factories.

ATTENTION IS INVITED TO OUR

Fine Scissors and Pocket Knives.

If you have trouble with your Range or Cooking Stove try a

JEWEL RANGE,

Made by the Detroit Stove Works. The Heaviest, Most Substantial, and Most Thoroughly Made RANGE in the Market.

SOLD ONLY BY

C. E. WALBRIDGE,

WASHINGTON STREET, COR. S. DIVISION.

THE PLACE TO BUY

Crockery,
Glassware,
Fancy Goods,
PLATED WARE,
Lamps,
Chimneys,
Etc.

CHEAP AND GOOD,
—(IS AT)—
GEORGE E. NEWMAN'S
444 Main Street, -   - BUFFALO, N. Y.

640. Rice and Pears. [Time.—One hour and a half.]

Articles.—One breakfast cup and a half of rice, one pint of milk, a large tablespoonful of sugar, three eggs, a little cinnamon and nutmeg, and baked pears.

Directions.—Boil the rice till tender in the milk in a double boiler, then put in the cinnamon, sugar, and nutmeg; take it up, let it get nearly cold, beat the eggs well, mix them with the rice, tie it down tightly in a floured cloth, and let it boil for one hour; turn it out, lay around it baked pears; garnish it with slices of lemon stuck into the rice.

641. Orange Sponge. [Time.—To make, an hour.]

Articles.—One ounce of gelatine, one pint of water, juice of six or seven oranges, juice of one lemon, sugar to taste and the whites of three eggs.

Directions.—Dissolve the gelatine in the water, strain it and let it stand until nearly cold; then mix with it the juice of one lemon; add the whites of the eggs and sugar, and whisk the whole together until it looks white and like a sponge. Put it into a mould and turn it out the next day.

642. Apple Snow. [Time.—One hour and a half.]

Articles.—Eight apples, half a pound of sugar, juice of one lemon, and the whites of three eggs.

Directions.—Add to the pulp of the baked apples the sugar, the juice of the lemon and the whites of the eggs; whisk the whole together for one hour; put some cream or custard in a dish, and drop the whisked broth on it in large flakes; a pinch of alum makes the whisk firmer.

643. Apple de Par. [Time.———

Articles.—One pound of sugar, half a pint of water, the peel and juice of one lemon, a pound and a half of apples.

Directions.—To the sugar add the water and the peel of the lemon cut thin, let it boil about ten or fifteen minutes in the double boiler; take out the peel and put in the apples cut in slices, and the juice of the lemons; when they have boiled until soft enough to pulp, press them through a hair sieve, put them back into the double boiler, and let them boil until quite stiff, stirring all the time, then put it into small moulds, or into a soup plate, and cut it in slices of any form you please for dessert. If not boiled so stiff, it may be turned out of teacups, and custard poured over it as a second course dish.

644. Apple Hedgehog.

ARTICLES.—Fifteen or sixteen large apples, four or five pounds of boiling apples for marmalade, three ounces of sugar, the whites of three eggs, some apricots or strawberry jam, half a pound of sweet almonds, half a pint of water, half a pound of sugar for the syrup.

DIRECTIONS.—Pare and core the apples, make a syrup with the water and sugar, and simmer the apples until tolerably tender in a double boiler; drain them, and fill the part from which the core is taken with apricot or strawberry jam, then arrange them on a dish in the form of a hedgehog; stew the boiling apples down to a smooth, dry marmalade, and fill the spaces between the apples with it, covering it also entirely over them; whisk the whites of the eggs and sugar to a solid froth, spread it evenly over the hedgehog, and sift sugar over it; blanch and cut into long spikes the almonds, and stick them thickly over the surface; place the dish in a moderate oven to slightly color the almonds. and make the apples hot through.

645. Gooseberry Fool. [TIME.—TWO HOURS TO MAKE.]

ARTICLES.—Two quarts of gooseberries, one quart of water, sugar to taste, two quarts of new milk, yolks of four eggs, a little grated nutmeg.

DIRECTIONS.—Put two quarts of gooseberries into a double boiler with a quart of water; when they begin to turn yellow and swell, drain the water from them and press them with the back of a spoon through a colander, sweeten them to your taste, and set them to cool, put the milk over the fire, beaten up with the yolks of the eggs and a little grated nutmeg, stir it over the fire until it begins to simmer, then take it off and stir it gradually into the cold gooseberries, let it stand until cold and serve it. The eggs may be left out and milk only added. Half this quantity makes a good dishful.

646. Gateau de Pommes. [Time.—Three-quarters of an hour]

ARTICLES.—One pound of sugar, one pint of water, two pounds of apples, juice and peel of one large lemon, and some rich custard.

DIRECTIONS.—Boil the sugar in the water in a double boiler until the water has almost evaporated, then add the apples pared and cored, the juice of a large lemon and the peel grated; boil all together till quite stiff, then put it into a mould, and when cold, turn it out and serve it.

647. Stewed Fruit—A Compote. [Time.—Twenty minutes.]

ARTICLES —One pound and a half of fruit, three-quarters of a pound of sugar and one pint of milk.

DIRECTIONS.—The fruit should be freshly gathered. Make a syrup of the sugar in the water for each two pints and a half of fruit, let this syrup boil gently for ten or twelve minutes, and skim it thoroughly; then throw in the fruit, let it boil up quickly in a double boiler, and afterwards simmer until quite tender, which will usually be in about fifteen minutes. Be careful that the fruit does not crack.

648. Iced Fruits for Dessert. [Time.—To dry, about three hours.]

ARTICLES.—A quarter of a pint of water, pounded sugar, whites of two eggs and currants.

DIRECTIONS.—Procure some of the finest bunches of currants,

well beat the whites of the eggs and mix them with the water, dip each bunch of currants separately into the egg and water, drain them for two minutes and roll them in some finely powdered sugar, repeat the rolling in sugar, and lay them carefully on sheets of white paper to dry, when the sugar will become crystallized; arrange them on a dish with a mixture of any other fruit; plums, grapes, or any fruit may be iced in the same manner for dessert.

649. Stewed Plums. [TIME.—ONE HOUR TO STEW THE PLUMS SEPARATELY; ONE HOUR AND A HALF IN THE SYRUP.]

ARTICLES.—One pound and a half of plums, three-quarters of a pint of syrup, two tablespoonfuls of port wine, peel and juice of one lemon, and one pound of loaf sugar.

DIRECTIONS.—Stew the plums in a little water; when tender strain them, and add to the water the sugar; boil it for one-quarter of an hour in a double boiler, skimming it carefully; when clear, add the juice, put in the plums, and let the whole simmer very slowly for about an hour and a half; when done take out the plums in a glass dish and pour the syrup over them; set them in a cold place.

650. Stewed Pears. [TIME.—THREE OR FOUR HOURS.]

ARTICLES.—Nine or ten large pears, seven ounces of loaf sugar, seven cloves, six allspice, rather more than half a pint of water, a quarter of a pint of port wine, and a few drops of cochineal.

DIRECTIONS.—Pare and core nine or ten large pears, dividing them with part of the stalk on each, put them into a double boiler with the sugar and water, wine, cloves, allspice, and cochineal; let them stew gently over a clear fire until tender, and when done take them carefully out, and place the slices of pears in a glass dish; boil up the syrup for a few minutes, and when cool pour it over the pears and put them by to get cold; the peel of a lemon cut thin, is an improvement to their flavor.

PRESERVES.
Jams, Jellies, Marmalade.

For making preserves, a good sound fruit and good white (granulated is really the cheapest) sugar should be used.

651. The Fruit

should be sound, ripe, and good; any rind can be preserved, as well as many kinds of vegetables.

652. The Sugar.

We use for all purposes white granulated sugar; it is the most economical in the end, dry and handy.

653. The Preserving Kettles.

Most persons use a copper or brass kettle, but we prefer, for large lots, a porcelain one; for a quart or two use the double boiler. Never keep preserves in the kettle any longer than to cook them, as the metal will injure them.

654. The Proportion of Fruit and Sugar.

A pound of fruit to a pound of sugar is generally used; a tumblerful of water to a pound of sugar to make the syrup. Always skim off all the froth or scum.

655. To Keep Preserves Good.

Put them in stone jars or vessels of glass, earthen or stoneware; cover tightly and keep in a cool, dry place. Look at them every month; if they are turning, scald and return to the jars.

656. Damson Cheese. [TIME.—ONE HOUR AND A HALF TO BOIL.]

ARTICLES.—To every quart of plums allow a quarter of a pound of sugar, and to every pound of pulp add half a pound of sugar.

DIRECTIONS.—Gather the plums when full ripe, put them into a jar, and to every quart of plums add the sugar. Bake them in a moderate oven until they are soft; then rub them through a hair sieve. To every pound of pulp add half a pound of sugar beaten fine; boil it over a slow fire in a double boiler, and stir it all the time; pour it into shapes, tie brandy paper over them, and keep them in a dry place. They will not be fit to use for three or four months. All cheese may be made by this recipe except greengage, which does not require so much sugar.

657. Green Gooseberry Jam. [Time.—Forty-five minutes.]

ARTICLES.—Three pounds of gooseberries and two pounds and a half of sugar.

DIRECTIONS.—Pick off the stalks and buds from the gooseberries; bruise them lightly; put them into a preserving pan and boil them quickly for eight or ten minutes, stirring all the time; add the sugar to the fruit, and boil it quickly for three-quarters of an hour, carefully removing the scum as it rises. When done, put it into pots, cover it with brandy paper, and secure it closely down with paper moistened with the white of an egg.

658. Green Gooseberry Jelly—an Excellent Substitute for Guava Jelly. [Time.—One hour and twenty-five minutes to boil.]

ARTICLES.—Six pounds of gooseberries; four pints of water, and one pound of sugar to each pound of fruit.

DIRECTIONS.—Wash some green gooseberries very clean, after having taken off the tops and stalks; then to each pound of fruit pour three-quarters of a pint of water, and simmer them until they are well broken; turn the whole into a jelly-bag or cloth, and let the juice drain through; weigh the juice and boil it rapidly for fifteen minutes; draw it from the fire and stir into it, until entirely dissolved, an equal weight of sugar; then boil the jelly from fifteen to twenty minutes longer, or until it jellies strongly on the spoon. It must be perfectly cleared from scum. Then pour it into small jars, moulds or glasses. It should be pale and transparent.

659. Strawberry Jam. [TIME.—ONE HOUR.]

ARTICLES.—To six pounds of strawberries allow three pounds of sugar.

DIRECTIONS.—Procure some fine scarlet strawberries, strip off the stalks and put them into a preserving pan over a moderate fire; boil them for half an hour, keeping them constantly stirred. Mix the sugar with the berries after they have been removed from the fire; then place it again over the fire, and boil it for another half-hour very quickly. Put it into pots, and when cold cover it over with brandy paper, and a piece of paper moistened with the white of an egg over the top.

660. Strawberry Jelly. [TIME.—HALF AN HOUR.]

ARTICLES.—Equal weight of sugar and strawberry juice.

DIRECTIONS.—Press some ripe strawberries through a delicately clean cloth; then strain the juice very clean, and stir into it an equal weight of sugar. When the sugar is dissolved put into a double boiler over a clear fire, and let it boil for half an hour, skimming it carefully as the scum rises. Put into glass jars or pots, and when cold cover it over as above directed.

661. To Preserve Plums. [TIME.—THREE-QUARTERS OF AN HOUR.]

ARTICLES.—To three pounds of plums allow three pounds of sugar.

DIRECTIONS.—Prick the plums with a fine needle to prevent their breaking, put them into a preserving pan with only sufficient water to cover them and set them over a gentle fire until the water simmers; then take them out and set them on a sieve to drain; add to the water in which the plums were boiled the above-named quantity of sugar; boil it quickly, skimming it as the scum rises, until the syrup sticks to the spoon; then put in the greengages and let them boil until the sugar bubbles, then pour the whole into a basin and let it stand until the next day; drain the syrup from the fruit, boil it up quickly and pour it over the plums; then boil the fruit in it for five or six minutes, put them into jars, pour the syrup over them, and cover them over with brandy paper. The kernels must be blanched and boiled with the fruit.

662. Rhubarb Marmalade. [TIME.—THREE QUARTERS OF AN HOUR IF YOUNG RHUBARB, AND ONE HOUR AND A HALF IF OLD.]

ARTICLES.—To each pound of sugar, add one pound and a half of rhubarb stalks, and the peel of half a lemon.

DIRECTIONS.—Cut the rhubarb stalks into pieces about two inches long, and put them into a double boiler with the sugar, and the peel of the lemon cut thin. Boil the whole well together, put it into pots, and cover it as directed for other preserves.

663. Rhubarb and Orange Preserves. [TIME.—ONE HOUR.]

ARTICLES.—Six oranges, two pounds of rhubarb stalks, one pound and a half of sugar.

DIRECTIONS.—Peel the oranges carefully; take away the white rind and the pulps; slice the pulps into a double boiler with the peel cut very small; add the rhubarb cut very fine, and sugar. Boil the whole down in the usual way for preserves.

664. Peach Preserves without Boiling. [TIME.—ABOUT THREE-QUARTERS OF AN HOUR.]

ARTICLES.—One pound of sugar to three pounds of peaches; a quarter of a pint of water to each pound of sugar, and the white of an egg to every four pounds.

DIRECTIONS.—Pare and cut in halves some ripe peaches and dry them in a hot sun or warm oven for two days; then weigh them and make a syrup of the sugar, water and eggs. Stir it until it is dissolved, then set it over the fire; boil and skim it until the syrup is thick and clear ; put in the kernels blanched, and when cold put a piece of paper to fit the inside of the pots, or jars, dipped in thick sugar syrup, over the top of the preserves, and close it over securely with tissue paper moistened with the white of an egg.

665. Fruit Preserved without Cooking. [TIME.—ABOUT AN HOUR.]

ARTICLES.—Any fruit and double-refined sugar.

DIRECTIONS.—Take any fruit, and put it into a deep dish ; pour boiling water over to cover it, then cover the basin with a thickly folded towel, and let it remain until the water is nearly cold ; take out the fruit and rub the skins off with a coarse towel ; put a layer in a jar, cover thickly with the best double-refined sugar ; then put another layer of fruit ; and fruit and sugar alternately until the jar is full, the sugar being last ; close and seal them down immediately, and set the jar in a cool, dry, dark place.

666. Fruit Jam. [TIME.—ALTOGETHER, TWO HOURS AND A HALF.]

ARTICLES.—To every pound of fruit after being prepared three quarters of a pound of sugar, juice of one small lemon, and the peel of one large one grated.

DIRECTIONS.—Pare and core the fruit, cut it into very thin slices, and put into a double boiler ; let the fruit stew for about two hours ; then put it into a preserving pan with the sugar and the juice and grated peel of a lemon. Simmer the whole over a clear fire for about half an hour ; after it begins to simmer all over, carefully remove the scum as it rises, and when done put the preserves into pots. When cold cover them with paper dipped into white of an egg and stretched over the top, with a piece of oiled paper next the jam.

667. Fruit Ginger. [TIME.—FORTY-FIVE MINUTES.]

ARTICLES.—Two pounds of apples, pears, or other fruit ;

one pint and a half of water; two pounds of sugar; and a little ginger.

DIRECTIONS.—Put into a double boiler the sugar and the water; boil and skim it well, and then add the ginger; pare, core, and divide some fruit, and put them into a double boiler with the syrup; boil them quickly until very clear, then lay them carefully on a dish; put the syrup into a jar, and when cold put in the fruit, and tie it closely over to exclude the air.

PICKLING VEGETABLES AND FRUITS.

We do not consider pickles healthy for the well, and they are positively injurious to the weak and sick. Immense quantities are put up every year, sold and eaten, and they are considered a necessity of civilization. As many families desire to put them up, we give a number of good recipes.

668. The Vinegar.

Procure always the best apple, or white wine vinegar. The success of good pickling depends upon using good vinegar. Always boil the vinegar unless stated otherwise.

669. The Vegetables and Fruit

should be sound and good.

670. Cooking Utensils to use in Pickling.

Use saucepans or kettles lined with porcelain. If copper or tin is used to boil vinegar in, do not let it remain in them a moment longer than is necessary to boil them. Use wooden knives and forks.

671. The Bottles, Jars, or Vessels.

Use glass bottles for pickles. If jars are used they must be unglazed, as the glaze, acted upon by the vinegar, produces a strong poison. Wooden vessels for large quantities are best. Fill either of them three-quarters full of pickles, then fill with vinegar.

672. From July to October,

Cauliflowers, peppers, cucumbers, onions, garlic, melons, tomatoes, beans, cabbage, mushrooms, beets, artichokes, horseradish, peaches, plums, and barberries may be pickled.

673. Indian Pickle, to keep Ten Years. [TIME.—Two WEEKS TO PREPARE.]

ARTICLES.—One pound of ginger root, one pound of garlic, half a pound of ground mustard, quarter of a pound of mustard seed, two ounces of dry peppers, half an ounce of turmeric, same of cayenne pepper, a gallon of best vinegar.

DIRECTIONS.—Put the garlic in a strong brine for three days, soak the ginger over night, slice it, also slice the peppers and garlic, dry them, mash the mustard seed and turmeric; put all, with the vinegar, into a large stone jar stirring it well every day for ten days, and cover closely; do not boil the vinegar. You can add more vinegar as it is used up. Dry any vegetable and put in this pickle, and it will keep them.

674. East India Piccalilly. [TIME.—THREE DAYS TO PREPARE.]

ARTICLES.—A pound each of garlic and ginger, whole black pepper and mustard seed, an ounce of turmeric, half an ounce of cayenne pepper, and two quarts of vinegar.

DIRECTIONS.—Take a pound of ginger, let it lie in salt and water one night, then cut it in thin slices; take one pound of garlic, peel, divide, and salt it three days, then wash and dry it in the sun, on a sieve; take the pound of black pepper, the mustard seed and the turmeric bruised very fine, and a little cayenne pepper; put all these ingredients into a quart jar, with the vinegar boiled and poured over them, and when cold, fill the jar three parts full, and let it stand for a fortnight. Everything you wish to pickle must be salted and dried in the sun for three days. The jar must be full of liquor; and, after it is finished for use, stop it down for six weeks or two months before using it. The vinegar must be thrown over when the spices and garlic are hot.

675. To Pickle any Vegetables. [TIME.—TEN DAYS.]

ARTICLES.—Brine, vinegar, whole pepper, mustard seed, allspice, a small piece of alum and any vegetables.

DIRECTIONS.—Make a brine of salt and water which will bear an egg, let your vegetables remain in it for twenty-four hours, then take them from the brine and lay them on a pan; make a sufficient quantity of vinegar boiling hot, adding whole pepper, allspice and mustard seed; pour it over the pickles, and let them remain until the next day, then strain it off, boil it again, pour it over, and cover the pickles with a thickly-folded cloth; drain off the vinegar the next day, add to it a few bits of alum the size of a pea, make it boiling hot and again pour it over the pickles; let them remain for a day or two, then cut one across, and if it is not green through, scald the vinegar again, and pour it over them; in a few days, divide the pickles, and put those of an equal size into jars, cover them with the cold vinegar, and cover them down for use. Or they may be put into jars for immediate use, with a cloth folded over the top and a plate over the cloth.

676. To Pickle Plums like Olives. [TIME.—TWENTY-FOUR HOURS.]

ARTICLES.—Green plums, vinegar, mustard seed and salt.

DIRECTIONS.—Make a pickle of vinegar, mustard seed and salt; make it boiling hot, then pour it over green plums gathered before they begin to turn, or before the stone is formed; let them stand all night, then drain off the vinegar, make it hot again and pour it over the plums. When cold cover them closely over.

677. To Pickle Peaches. [TIME.—EIGHT OR TEN DAYS.]

ARTICLES.—Half a bushel of peaches, one gallon of vinegar,

four pounds of brown sugar, five or six cloves for each peach, and two ounces of cinnamon.

DIRECTIONS.—Take the sound peaches, remove the down with a brush, make the vinegar hot, add to it the sugar, boil and skim it well, stick five or six cloves into each peach, then pour the vinegar boiling hot over them, cover them over, and set them in a cold place for eight or ten days; then drain off the vinegar, make it hot, skim it, and again pour it over the peaches; let them become cold, then put them into glass jars, and secure them as for preserves. The cinnamon and cloves can be added to the peaches, and the hot vinegar poured over.

678. Sweet Green Tomato Piccalilly. [TIME.—TO BOIL, ABOUT ONE HOUR.]

ARTICLES.—A peck of green tomatoes, five tablespoonfuls of ground mustard, half a pint of mustard seed, two tablespoonfuls of ground cinnamon, one of cloves, one pound of brown sugar, three quarts of vinegar, and some celery tops.

DIRECTIONS.—Peel and slice the tomatoes, boil all together until all are done.

679. To Pickle Whole Tomatoes. [TIME.—TO PREPARE, THREE DAYS.]

ARTICLES.—One peck of tomatoes, a gallon of vinegar, one ounce of whole cloves, one of white pepper, one of cinnamon, and three ounces of mustard.

DIRECTIONS.—Prick each tomato with a fork to allow some of the juice to exude, put them into a deep pan, sprinkle some salt between each layer, and let them remain for three days covered, then wash off the salt and cover them with a pickle of cold water which has been boiled with the spices. It will be ready for use in ten or twelve days, and is an excellent sauce for roast meat of any kind.

680. To Pickle Beets. [TIME.—ONE HOUR.]

ARTICLES.—Three quarts of vinegar, half an ounce of mace,

half an ounce of ginger, some horseradish, and the beets.

DIRECTIONS.—Boil the beets the above time, cut them into any form you please, or gimp them in the shape of wheels and put them into a jar; boil three quarts of vinegar, with the mace, ginger, and a few slices of horseradish, and pour it while very hot over the beets; tie them over, and set them in a dry place.

681. To Pickle Cauliflowers.

ARTICLES.—Three ounces of coriander seed, one ounce of mustard seed, one ounce of ginger, half an ounce of mace, half an ounce of nutmegs and three quarts of water.

DIRECTIONS.—Gather on a fine day some of the whitest and closest cauliflower you can procure, break them into bunches, and scald them in salt and water, taking care they do not boil, as it would spoil their color; set them to cool, covering them over; then put them on a colander, sprinkle them with salt, and let them drain for a day and night; then place the bunches in jars, pour boiling salt and water over them, and let them remain all night; then drain them through a hair sieve, and put them into glass jars; boil the vinegar with the ginger, mustard, nutmeg, and coriander seeds, and when cold, pour it over the cauliflowers, and tie them closely over.

682. To Pickle Onions.

ARTICLES.—Onions, vinegar, ginger, and whole pepper.

DIRECTIONS.—Take some nice onions and throw them into a double boiler half full of boiling water, and let them remain ten minutes. Then take them out quickly and lay them between two cloths to dry; boil some vinegar with the ginger and whole pepper, and when cold, pour it over the onions in glass jars, and tie them closely over.

683. To Pickle Peppers.

ARTICLES.—Some peppers, vinegar, an ounce of nutmeg, salt and water, and one quart of vinegar to the spices.

PICKLES.

DIRECTIONS.—Pick some fine peppers with the stalks on just before they turn red, and remove the seeds by opening a small place at the side, set them in strong salt and water for three days, changing it three times, then take them out and place between a thick cloth to become dry, put them into a jar and cover them with vinegar, previously boiled with the mace and grated nutmeg, and let it get cold.

684. To Pickle Barberries.

Take a quantity of barberries not over ripe, pick off the leaves and dead stalks, put them into jars with a large quantity of strong salt and water, and tie them down with a bladder, when you see a scum rise on the barberries, put them into fresh salt and water, cover them close, and set them by for use.

685. To Pickle Cabbage.

ARTICLES.—To one quart of vinegar one ounce of whole pepper.

DIRECTIONS.—Remove the coarse leaves from some cabbage, and wipe them very clean; cut them in long thin slices or shreds and put them on a large sieve, well covering them with salt, and let them drain all night, then put them into stone jars, and pour over them some boiling vinegar and whole peppers; cover them over and set them by for use.

MANIOCA.

A delicious product from the East Indies. Try it with these recipes.

686. Manioca Pudding. [TIME.—HALF AN HOUR.]

ARTICLES.—Four tablespoonfuls of manioca, one quart of milk, a little salt, one tablespoonful of butter, four eggs, sugar, spice, or flavoring to the taste.

DIRECTIONS.—Mix the manioca in half the milk cold, and with the butter stir on the fire in a double boiler, until it thickens or boils; pour it quickly into a dish. Stir in the sugar and the remaining milk, and when quite cool add the eggs, spice and wine, or flavoring. This pudding may be varied by omitting the eggs and substituting currants, chopped raisins, or candied lemon, orange or citron sliced. Bake half an hour in a moderate oven.

687. Manioca Apple Pudding. [TIME.—BAKE HALF AN HOUR.]

ARTICLES.—Four tablespoonfuls of manioca, tablespoonful of butter, apples, lemon juice, one quart of water, a little salt, and seasoning.

DIRECTIONS.—Mix the manioca in the water, and boil in the double boiler; put a thick layer of apples with a little lemon juice, sweeten well, pour on the cooked manioca, and bake till nicely browned.

688. Manioca Blanc Mange. [TIME.—ABOUT HALF AN HOUR TO BOIL.]

ARTICLES.—Four tablespoonfuls of manioca, one quart of milk, a little salt, one tablespoonful of butter, sugar and flavoring.

DIRECTIONS.—Mix all together and boil till quite thick in a double boiler, pour into an earthen mould, turn out when cold and flavor to suit the taste. Eat with syrup, cream or jelly.

689. Caudle for Invalids. [TIME.—TWENTY MINUTES.]

ARTICLES.—Two spoonfuls of manioca, one quart of water, a bit of butter, two blades of mace, some grated lemon peel, honey or sugar, spice, and brandy or wine.

DIRECTIONS.—It is made with the manioca stirred in the water with the butter, the mace, and grated lemon peel. Boil it twenty minutes in a double boiler, stirring that it may be smooth, sweeten with refined honey or sugar if preferred, add spice to taste, and one glass of brandy or white wine. Should the mixture become too thick, stir in a little boiling water while the mixture is yet warm.

D. J. STICKNEY,

Dealer in

BEST GRADES

ANTHRACITE, BRIER HILL AND CANNEL

COAL!

Carefully Selected and Screened for

FAMILY USE.

OFFICE:

Cor. Niagara and Pearl Sts., - BUFFALO, N. Y

TOILET SOAPS.

ROBINSON BROS. & CO.,
MANUFACTURERS OF
SILVER, PUMICE, SHAVING, DENTAL, AND
FINE TOILET SOAP.

The INDEXICAL SOAPS are prepared from the choicest materials; all are boiled soaps, with lasting odors; they are durable, economical, and always mild and wholesome.

LARGE OVAL SOAPS.

Honey, Glycerine, White Glycerine, Brown Windsor, Turtle Oil, Oat Meal Glycerine, Almond Meal, Poncine, Zahater, Sunflower, Rice Flour, Baby, Palm Oil, Farina, Pure Almond, Bay Leaf, Musk, Windsor, Tar, Sand, Pumice, etc.

SILVER SOAP.

For cleaning Silver and Plated Ware, Gold and Plated Jewelry, Pearls and Precious Stones, Gold Chains, etc., etc.

GIANT SOAPS.

Honey, Glycerine, Pink Bath, Bee Bath, Oatmeal, Elder Flower. The Giants are half-pounds of the finest quality boiled and perfumed pure Soap, and the cheapest Toilet Soaps to be obtained anywhere.

SHAVING SOAPS.
Crown and Bay Rum.   Best in use.

FRENCH OVAL SOAPS.
Musk Rose, Lotus, Newport, etc.

690. Manioca Soup.

One or two dessertspoonfuls of manioca (first mixed in cold water) will greatly improve soup, and render it more nourishing for children or delicate persons.

JELLY ICE CREAMS.

The old way of making ice cream is with cream or milk, sugar, essence, and a large number of eggs. This plan made a fair, but expensive ice cream. If milk was used the result was a coarse ice cream, full of lumps of ice. What is required is a smooth rich cream, at a small expense; in order to do this we had to reduce the water to a jelly with the aid of new and cheap foods, so that the icy granules would not be formed. By our recipes this has been accomplished, and the cheapest, richest, smoothest, finest, most nutritious and healthy ice creams ever made, are now given to the public.

691. Jelly Ice Creams.

Are made by reducing gelatinous animal and vegetable preparations to a jelly, and adding sugar, eggs, and flavoring to taste. They are superior to any other.

692. Light Jelly Ice Creams.

Those wishing to have them light should eat them as soon as made.

693. To Improve Creams.

After they are made draw off the water from the wooden freezer, pack it full of broken ice and salt, take out the dasher if you have one in the tin part, scrape off the cream that adheres to the sides, cover it over with the cover, then pack any old blankets, or any other cloth covers, around the whole freezer, let it stand for two or three hours or longer, and it will be hard, rich, and smooth. Packed with salt and ice it will keep hard as long as desired.

We prefer condensed milk to make these creams, although

common milk will do. We give the recipes for common milk. If condensed is used, use one part milk and three parts water.

694. Gold Jelly Cream. [Time.—To prepare, half an hour.]

Articles.—Yolks of five eggs, one ounce of gelatine or isinglass, one quart of milk, one quart of ice water; sugar, quarter of a pound, or to suit the taste; essence, a tablespoonful, or to suit the taste.

Directions.—Dissolve the gelatine in the hot milk in the double boiler, add the ice water, then the yolks well beaten, sweeten and flavor to taste and freeze.

695. Silver Jelly Cream. [Time.—To prepare, half an hour.]

Articles.—The whites of five eggs, an ounce of gelatine or isinglass, a quart of milk, same of ice water, sugar and spice to taste.

Directions.—Dissolve the gelatine in boiling milk in the double boiler; after it is all dissolved, pour in the same quantity of ice water; add the whites well beaten, sugar and flavor to taste.

696. Gold and Silver Creams.

Made as above and served in moulds, or in glasses, are very pretty, and flavored with different flavors, are very delightful.

697. Tapioca Jelly Cream. [Time.—To boil, four hours.]

Articles.—Tapioca, four ounces; milk, one quart; water, a quart; one egg; sugar and flavor to taste.

Directions.—Soak the tapioca from two to ten hours, then boil it in the double boiler with the milk and water, until it is in a jelly, cool it with pieces of ice, beat up the eggs, the sugar and flavor, stir altogether and freeze.

698. Manioca Jelly Cream. [Time.—To soak, all night; to boil, three hours.]

Articles.—Manioca, two ounces; milk, a pint; water, a

pint; one egg; sugar and flavor to taste.

DIRECTIONS.—Soak the manioca all night; this softens it; then boil it in the double boiler with the water and milk until it is a jelly; when cold add the eggs, sugar and flavor, then freeze.

699. Cassava Jelly Cream. [TIME.—TO PREPARE, FOUR HOURS.]

ARTICLES.—Cassava, one ounce; milk, a pint; water, same; sugar and flavor to taste, and one egg.

DIRECTIONS.—Soak the cassava, boil it in the double boiler in water and milk until a jelly; then flavor to taste, and freeze.

700. Arrow-root Jelly Cream. [TIME.—TO PREPARE, QUARTER OF AN HOUR.]

ARTICLES.—Two tablespoonfuls of arrow-root, one pint of milk, one pint of water, sugar and flavor to taste.

DIRECTIONS.—Mix up the arrow-root in a little cold water, set the milk and water to boil in the double boiler, when hot add the arrow-root and sugar, let it boil ten minutes, let it get cold, and add the flavoring, and freeze.

701. Sago Jelly Ice Cream. [TIME.—HALF AN HOUR TO PREPARE.]

ARTICLES.—Quarter of a pound of sago, a quart of milk, same of water, three eggs, flavor, and sweeten with sugar.

DIRECTIONS.—Boil the sago in the double boiler until it is a jelly, add the water, eggs well beaten, sweeten and flavor to taste, and freeze.

702. Rice Jelly Ice Cream. [TIME.—TO PREPARE, HALF AN HOUR.]

ARTICLES.—Half a pound of rice flour, one quart of milk, one quart of water, three eggs, sugar and flavoring.

DIRECTIONS.—Boil the rice flour and milk to a jelly in the double boiler; when done pour in the cold water, the eggs well beaten, sugar and flavor, and freeze.

703. Farina Jelly Ice Cream.

ARTICLES.—Quarter of a pound of farina; milk, a quart; water, a quart; three eggs, sugar and flavoring.

DIRECTIONS.—Boil the farina to a jelly in water and milk, add the sugar; when cool, add the eggs and flavor

704. Maizena Jelly Ice Cream. [TIME.—TO PREPARE, HALF AN HOUR.]

ARTICLES.—Maizena, quarter of a pound; milk, two quarts; four eggs; sugar and flavoring to taste.

DIRECTIONS.—Mix the maizena in a little cold water, put the milk in the double boiler; when the milk is hot, stir in the maizena and sugar, and boil to a jelly, beating the eggs well; when the jelly is cold, add the eggs and flavoring, and freeze.

705. Corn Starch Jelly Cream

Can be made the same way, making more or less, but in the same proportions.

706. Calves' Feet Jelly Ice Cream. [TIME.—TO MAKE, TEN MINUTES.]

ARTICLES.—A pint of calves' feet jelly, a quart of milk, a quart of water, two eggs, sugar and flavor.

DIRECTIONS.—Prepare the jelly as directed in recipes 48 and 49. Boil the milk in the double boiler, add the jelly and sugar, beat the eggs well, when cold add them with the flavoring to the milk

707. Cocoanut Jelly Ice Cream. [TIME.—TO BOIL, FOUR HOURS.]

ARTICLES.—Half a pound prepared cocoanut, four ounces of tapioca, a quart of condensed milk, a quart of water, sugar, and four eggs.

DIRECTIONS.—Boil the cocoanut and tapioca in half the milk and water for four hours in the double boiler, then strain, add the rest of the milk, water and eggs well beaten, sugar to taste, and freeze.

708. **Grape Jelly Ice Cream.** [Time.—To prepare, ten minutes.]

Articles.—A quart of milk, a quart of water, four ounces of cassava or manioca, a quart of sound grapes, sugar, and half a pint of port wine.

Directions.—Boil the cassava or manioca in the double boiler with the milk and water until it is a clear jelly, then add the sugar, and when cold add the grapes and wine, then freeze.

709. **Banana Jelly Ice Cream.** [Time.—To prepare, half an hour.]

Articles.—Two ounces of tapioca, a pint of milk, same of water, three large bananas and sugar.

Directions.—Boil the tapioca, milk and water to a jelly; when icy cold, add the bananas mashed to a jelly, sweeten with sugar, and freeze.

710. **Wine Jelly Ice Cream (for Invalids).** [Time.—To prepare, half an hour.]

Articles.—Half a pint of sherry, or some other wine, half a pint of water, half a pint of milk, an ounce of isinglass or gelatine, juice of two oranges and sugar to taste.

Directions.—Put the isinglass in the hot water in the double boiler until it is dissolved, then stir in the juice of the oranges, the milk and wine, sweeten to taste, and freeze.

711. **Very Cheap Jelly Ice Cream.** [Time.—Twenty minutes to prepare.]

Articles.—A pint of water, a tablespoonful of syrup, a pint of milk, corn starch and flavoring.

Directions.—Boil the water and milk together in the double boiler, mix the corn starch in a little cold water, put in the boiler, let it boil five minutes, then sweeten with syrup, flavor to taste when cold, and freeze.

712. Irish Moss Jelly Ice Cream. [TIME.—AN HOUR TO BOIL.]

ARTICLES.—Two ounces of moss, a quart of milk, two eggs, sugar and flavoring.

DIRECTIONS.—Boil the moss in the water until it is a jelly, then add the milk and sugar; when cold, add the eggs well beaten, sweeten and flavor to taste.

RICH ICE CREAMS.

The old method of freezing involved hours of really hard work of whirling by hand the common freezer, With the modern inventions, it is but a few minutes' easy labor, which a child can perform.

To those who are compelled to remain in the city during the summer, its use is almost a necessity; even during the colder months it is a delicacy that is pleasant. These recipes are rich and delicious in flavor, and, of course, cost more than the common or jelly creams.

In freezing ice cream, the substance to be frozen should always be cold before putting it in the freezer, as it saves ice.

Use any common salt—not rock salt, as rock salt settles to the bottom of the tub.

Break the ice fine; a good way is to put it in a coarse sack, and break it with a mallet or round billet of wood.

713. Chocolate Cream.

ARTICLES.—Half a pint of strong made chocolate, one pint of milk, yolks of eight eggs, half a pint of thick cream, and half a pound of sugar.

DIRECTIONS.—Make the milk very hot, sweetened with the sugar, then stir carefully into it the yolks of the eggs and the chocolate; put it into a double boiler, and stir it one way until the eggs are set in the milk, but do not let it boil; then strain it through a fine silk, or hair sieve, and stir into it the cream, and freeze.

714. Coffee Cream.

ARTICLES.—One large cupful of made coffee, four ounces of sugar, three-quarters of a pint of milk, yolks of eight eggs, two ounces of gelatine.

DIRECTIONS.—Put the milk into a double boiler with the coffee, and add the well-beaten eggs and sugar; stir the whole briskly until it begins to thicken, and strain it through a sieve on the gelatine; mix it thoroughly together, and when the gelatine is dissolved in the double boiler, freeze.

715. Tea Cream.

ARTICLES.—A quarter of an ounce of hyson tea, half a pint of milk, half a pint of cream, two spoonfuls of rennet, and sugar to taste.

DIRECTIONS.—Boil the tea with the milk, cream, and rennet in a double boiler; when it is thick, it will be sufficiently done. Stir in sugar to taste, then freeze.

716. Velvet Cream. [TIME.—UNTIL THE GELATINE IS DISSOLVED.]

ARTICLES.—One ounce of gelatine, a breakfast cupful of white wine, juice of one large lemon, the peel rubbed with sugar, one pint of cream.

DIRECTIONS.—Put the gelatine into a double boiler, with the wine, the juice of a lemon, and sufficient sugar to sweeten it rubbed on the peel to extract the color and flavor; put it over the fire until the gelatine is dissolved, and then strain it to get cold; then mix with it the cream, and freeze.

717. Ratafia Cream.

ARTICLES.—Six bay leaves, one quart of new milk, a little essence of ratafia, yolks of four eggs, four spoonfuls of cream and sugar to taste.

DIRECTIONS.—Put the milk into a double boiler, with bay leaves and a little ratafia; when it has boiled up, take out the leaves, beat up the yolks of the eggs with the cream, and add sugar to your taste; stir it into the ratafia cream to thicken it, and heat again without allowing it to boil; keep stirring it all the time one way, or it may curdle, and then freeze.

718. Bohemian Cream.

ARTICLES.—One ounce and a half of gelatine, one pint of cream, half a pint of water, six ounces of sugar, one lemon and one pint of strawberries.

DIRECTIONS.—Rub through a sieve the strawberries, sugar, and the juice of the lemon; dissolve the gelatine in the water; mix these ingredients well together and freeze.

719. Chester Cream.

ARTICLES.—One pint of rich cream, peel of one lemon, a teaspoonful of the juice, one glass of sherry wine, sugar to taste and three ounces of macaroons.

DIRECTIONS.—Mix the lemon peel very fine with the cream, squeeze in the lemon juice, sugar to taste, add the wine, and freeze.

720. Spanish Cream. [TIME.—UNTIL VERY THICK.]

ARTICLES.—Three tablespoonfuls of sifted ground rice, yolks of three eggs, three spoonfuls of water, two of orange-flower water, one pint of cream and three spoonfuls of sugar.

DIRECTIONS.—Sift the rice, add to it the sugar, and mix it smooth with the water and orange flower water; then stir in gradually the cream and boil it in a double boiler till it is of a proper thickness, and then freeze.

721. Burnt Cream. [TIME.—TO BOIL TEN MINUTES.]

ARTICLES.—One pint of cream, peel of half a lemon, a stick of cinnamon, one ounce and a half of sugar and the yolks of four eggs.

DIRECTIONS.—Boil the cream with the peel of the lemon, and the stick of cinnamon in a double boiler; pour it very slowly on the well-beaten yolks of the eggs, stirring till half cold; add the sugar; take out the spice and lemon peel, pour it into a dish, and when cold, freeze.

722. Imperial Cream. [Time.—Ten minutes to boil the cream.]

Articles.—One quart of cream, peel of one lemon, juice of three and about eight ounces of sugar.

Directions.—Boil the cream with the thin peel of one lemon, in a double boiler, to extract the flavor, and then stir the cream until nearly cold, adding the sugar; strain the juice of the lemons into a glass dish, and pour the cream over it; mix it with the juice of the lemons, and freeze.

723. Pistachio Cream.

Articles.—Half a pound of pistachio nuts, one spoonful of brandy, yolks of two eggs, one pint and a half of cream, sugar to taste.

Directions.—Blanch the pistachio nuts, and pound them to a paste with the brandy; add the paste to the cream, sweeten it to your taste, and boil it in a double boiler until it becomes thick, and freeze.

724. Noyeau Cream. [Time.—Nearly half an hour.]

Articles.—Two ounces of gelatine, one quart of cream, peel of one lemon, juice of three lemons, a quarter of a pound of sugar, two glasses of noyeau.

Directions.—Dissolve the gelatine in a cupful of boiling water, with the peel of a lemon cut very thin; when the gelatine is dissolved, and the essence extracted from the peel, strain it into the cream, stirring it constantly to prevent its curdling; sweeten it with sugar, and add the noyeau; whisk the whole thoroughly together for a few minutes, and then freeze.

725. Spring Cream. [Time.—About twenty minutes.]

Articles.—One dozen sticks of rhubarb, peel of one lemon

two cloves, a piece of cinnamon, and as much moist sugar as will sweeten it, and two ounces of gelatine.

DIRECTIONS.—Clean the rhubarb, cut it into pieces and put it into a double boiler with the peel of a lemon grated, the cloves, a piece of cinnamon, and as much sugar as will sweeten it; set it over the fire and reduce it to a marmalade; pass it through a hair sieve and add to it the cream, and freeze.

726. German Cream.

ARTICLES.—One pint of cream, six ounces of sugar, the peel of half a lemon, and the juice of two, and one wineglassful of brandy.

DIRECTIONS.—Boil the cream with the sugar, and the peel of the lemon cut thin, in a double boiler. As soon as it boils take it off the fire and let it stand until nearly cold; then add the juice of two lemons and the brandy, and then freeze.

727. Almond Cream.

ARTICLES.—Five ounces of sweet almonds, six bitter almonds, one quart of cream, three ounces of sugar and the juice of two large lemons.

DIRECTIONS.—Blanch and pound both the sweet and the bitter almonds, and stir the paste into the cream sweetened with sugar, mixed with the strained juice of the lemons, or use the essence; whisk the whole and then freeze.

728. Sicilian Cream.

ARTICLES.—One pint of cream, one glass of noyeau, two ounces of gelatine, and five ounces of sugar.

DIRECTIONS.—Whip the cream, add to it the noyeau and sugar, with the gelatine; mix all and then freeze.

729. Snow Cream.

ARTICLES.—One quart of cream, whites of three eggs, two glasses of sherry wine, two ounces of sugar and the peel of half a lemon.

DIRECTIONS.—Beat well the whites of the eggs, and add to them the cream; stir them well together, and add the wine, sugar and lemon peel, and freeze.

730   Housewife's Cream.

ARTICLES.—Half a pint of cream, quarter of a pint of sherry, three ounces of sugar, peel and juice of one lemon.

DIRECTIONS.—Cut the peel of a lemon into small pieces, mix the cream, wine, white sugar, peel and juice of a lemon together, whisking it until quite thick, and freeze.

APPLES.

APPLES are our national fruit—generally the cheapest of all fruits. Some kinds can be kept until the new crop grows. Dried, they are the cheapest of dried fruits, if not the best. It is important that all should know how to use this wholesome, hearty, and excellent fruit. They can be used in many ways; and where the whole fruit cannot be had, use the dried.

HEALTHFULNESS OF APPLES.—There is scarcely an article of vegetable food more widely useful and more universally liked than the apple. Let every housekeeper lay in a good supply of apples, and it will be the most economical investment in the whole range of culinaries. A raw, mellow apple is digested in an hour and a half, while boiled cabbage requires five hours. The most healthful dessert that can be placed on the table is apples cooked in some form. If eaten frequently at breakfast, with coarse bread and butter, without meat or flesh of any kind, they have an admirable effect on the general system, often removing constipation, correcting acidities, and cooling off febrile conditions more effectually than the most approved medicines. If families could be induced to substitute apples—sound and ripe—for pies, cakes, and sweetmeats, with which their children are too frequently stuffed, there would be a diminution in doctors' bills, in a single year, sufficient to lay in a stock of this delicious fruit for the whole season's use.

731. To Choose Apples.

In choosing apples, be guided by the weight—the heaviest are the best; and those should always be selected which, on being pressed by the thumb, yield to it, with a slight crackling noise. Prefer large apples to small; for waste is saved in peeling and coring them.

732. How to Keep Apples.

Pick them carefully; place them one by one in a barrel, with holes in it, for air, or in a heap with straw; keep them in a cool, dry place; look them over once a month carefully; pack none but sound ones; if any are bruised or specked, pick them out and use them up.

733. To Save Specked Apples.

If you do not wish to use them by any of the recipes below, pare, core, and stew with cider and sugar; this makes a delicious sauce, will keep any length of time, and is equal to Shaker apple sauce, being the same way they make it. Any empty fruit cans can be filled with it.

734. Apple Dumplings Boiled. [TIME.—TO STEAM OR BOIL, ONE HOUR.]

ARTICLES.—Any apples and paste.

DIRECTIONS.—Pare, quarter, and core as many apples as required, and make a paste; roll it out a quarter of an inch thick; cover each apple with it; then steam or boil. Some wrap them in pieces of cotton cloth—they are better that way.

735. Apple Dumplings Baked. [TIME.—ONE HOUR.]

ARTICLES.—Apples, paste, sugar, cinnamon or spice.

DIRECTIONS.—Pare; take out the core; do not split the apples; fill the center of them with sugar and spices to taste; wrap them in paste; wet the edges to make them stick, and then bake.

736. Apple Custard Pies. [Time.—To bake, about half an hour.]

Articles.—Twelve apples ; to these add salt, sugar, nutmeg, two eggs well beaten, a pint of milk, a tablespoonful of melted butter, and one lemon.

Directions.—Stew or grate the apples to a pulp, the grated rind of the lemon, and its juice ; pour the mixture into plates lined with paste ; and then arrange strips over the top ; sift over them powdered sugar, and then bake until they become a light brown.

737. Dried Apple Pies. [Time.—To bake, about half an hour.]

Articles.—Dried apples, a pound ; butter, sugar, and spices to taste, and one lemon.

Directions.—Wash the apples clean in two waters, and put them to soak ; after soaking an hour put them into a preserving kettle, with the same water, and with the thin peel of a lemon chopped very fine ; boil them till tender ; when they rise, press them down, but do not stir them ; when they become tender, add sugar and boil twenty minutes longer.

738. Dried Apple Sauce.

Use the above recipe—of course, without the crust.

739. Sadie's Apple Fritters. [Time.—Six minutes to fry.]

Articles.—Three eggs ; one pint of new milk ; a little grated nutmeg ; a glass of brandy ; sufficient flour for the batter and six apples.

Directions.—Beat the eggs ; mix in the nutmeg, a pinch of salt, and a glass of brandy ; beat the mixture well, and then add flour to make a thick batter ; pare, core, and slice six large apples ; sprinkle powdered sugar over them ; dip each piece in the batter, and fry them in hot lard ; the lard should not be made too hot at first, but must become hotter as they are frying ; serve with sifted sugar over them.

740. Apple and Crumb Pudding. [Time.—To bake, half an hour.]

Articles.—Bread crumbs, apples, butter, sugar, and ground cinnamon.

Directions.—Put a layer of bread crumbs over a well-buttered and deep dish; on the crumbs small pieces of butter; then a layer of apples, pared, cored, and cut into slices; then sugar and the powdered cinnamon; repeat this, beginning with the bread crumbs, until your dish is full, and bake it in a moderate oven; when done, turn it out and serve it with sauce.

741. Italian Apple Marmalade. [Time.—Forty minutes.]

Articles.—One peck of apples, one gallon of water to every quart of pulp, one pound of sugar.

Directions.—Take the apples, quarter them, and take out the cores; but do not pare them; put them into a preserving pan with the water, and let them boil moderately until you think the pulp will run or suffer itself to be squeezed through a cloth, only leaving the peels behind; then to each quart of pulp add sugar, and boil it altogether, keeping it stirred; then put it into pots.

742. Clear Apple Jelly. [Time.—One hour and a half to boil the apples; a quarter of an hour, the jelly.]

Articles.—Two dozen and a half of apples; one quart of water to every pint of juice, three-quarters of a pound of sugar; ten ounces of isinglass, and the peel of one small lemon.

Directions.—Pare, core, and boil the apples in water, with the lemon; when they are tender, pour the juice from the apples, and strain it through a jelly bag; then put the strained juice, the sugar and the isinglass boiled till dissolved, in half a pint of water; boil the whole for about fifteen minutes, and then pour it into moulds.

743. Chinese Apple Ginger. [Time.—One hour.]

Articles.—Two pounds of apples, one pint and a half of

water, two pounds of sugar, and a little Chinese ginger.

DIRECTIONS.—Put into a preserving pan the sugar and water; boil and skim it well, and then add the ginger, pare, core, and divide some apples, and put them into the preserving pan with the syrup, boil them quickly until they are very clear; then lay them carefully on a dish, put the syrup into a jar, and, when cold, put in the slices of apples, and tie it closely over to exclude the air.

744. Ida's Apple Jelly. [TIME.—RATHER MORE THAN ONE HOUR.]

ARTICLES.—Apples, ten ounces of sugar to every pound of pulp, and the peel of half a lemon.

DIRECTIONS.—Pare and core some apples; cut them into slices, and boil them with a little water to a pulp, boil the sugar with a little water to a thick syrup; add it to the apple pulp, with the lemon grated, put the whole over a clear fire, and boil it for about twenty minutes, or until the apples are a thick marmalade, stirring it all the time; then put it into a mould, which has been previously soaked in cold water; when cold and set, turn the jelly out.

745. Apple Mould and Cream. [TIME.—TO BOIL ABOUT HALF AN HOUR.]

ARTICLES.—Four apples, two pounds of sugar; one pint of cream or new milk; yolks of two eggs; peel and juice of one lemon; a little cinnamon, and a spoonful of extract.

DIRECTIONS.—Boil the sugar in water, and as the scum rises, carefully take it off; when clear, put in the apples, pared and cored, cut into quarters, with the juice of a lemon, and the peel cut very thin; set the stew pan over a clear fire, and stew it until it is boiled to a thick jam; put it into a mould, and when cold turn it out; add the yolks of the eggs and the thin peel of a lemon; boil it for a few minutes, stirring it constantly, and when cold pour it round the apple extract.

746. French Apple Meringue. [TIME.—FOUR OR FIVE HOURS TO STEW; ONE HOUR TO BAKE.]

ARTICLES.—Twelve large apples, some preserved wine-sours, sugar to your taste, some sugar icing.

DIRECTIONS.—Pare and core the apples, stew them gently for four or five hours, sweeten them to your taste; place a layer on a souffle dish, then add a layer of preserved wine-sours (stoned), then the remainder of the apples; bake, and a short time before it is wanted put on an icing of fine white sugar; put it again in the oven to brown, and send it up quite hot, as a remove at second course.

747. Apple Mince Meat. [TIME.—ABOUT AN HOUR.]

ARTICLES.—One pound of currants, one pound of peeled and chopped apples, one pound of suet chopped fine, one pound of moist sugar, quarter of a pound of raisins stoned and cut in two, the juice of four oranges, and two lemons, with the chopped peel of one; add of ground mace and allspice each a spoonful, and a wine-glassful of brandy.

DIRECTIONS.—Mix all well together, and keep closely covered.

748. Apple and Almond Pudding. [TIME.—HALF AN HOUR, OR UNTIL NICELY BROWNED.

ARTICLES.—Five ounces of sweet almonds, five ounces of sugar, four eggs, one large lemon, some stewed apples.

DIRECTIONS.—Pare, core, and stew to a pulp, some baking apples, and place them at the bottom of a baking tin or mould, blanch and pound five ounces of almonds with the sugar, and stir into them the yolks of the eggs, the peel of a large lemon grated, and the juice strained, thicken it with two dessertspoonfuls of flour; mix all thoroughly together, and then add the whites whisked to a very stiff froth, pour this over the stewed apples, and bake it in a moderate oven.

749. Apple Sauce. [TIME.—TWENTY MINUTES.]

ARTICLES.—Eight apples, a small piece of butter and sugar.

HATS, CAPS AND FURS.

(ESTABLISHED 1845.)

C. & F. GEORGER,

Importers and Manufacturers of

SEAL SACQUES AND DOLMANS,

AND ALL STYLES OF

FUR-LINED GARMENTS.

THE LATEST STYLES IN

MUFFS, COLLARS AND CAPES.

The Largest Assortment of

FUR TRIMMING

OF ANY HOUSE WEST OF NEW YORK, ON HAND AND MADE TO ORDER.

CHILDREN'S FURS,

Seal Caps, Seal Gloves and Mittens.

FANCY SLEIGH ROBES.

The Newest Shapes and Nobbiest Styles in

MEN'S, BOY'S AND CHILDREN'S HATS AND CAPS

ALWAYS ON HAND.

508 MAIN STREET, - BUFFALO, N. Y.

GINGER ALE.

—THE—
ORIGINAL IMPORTED

ALSO

ROSS'S ROYAL BELFAST
Soda Water, Lemonade and Lime-Juice.

FOR SALE BY

DINGENS BROTHERS,
333 MAIN STREET, - BUFFALO, N. Y.

DIRECTIONS.—Pare, core and cut into slices, eight apples, put them into a sauce pan, with sufficient water to moisten and prevent them from burning, boil them until sufficiently tender to pulp; then beat them up smoothly with a piece of butter, and add sugar to your taste.

750. French Apple Souffle. [TIME.—TEN MINUTES TO BAKE.]

ARTICLES.—Six or eight apples, some white sugar, yolks and whites of three eggs, a quarter of a pint of new milk, one tablespoonful of brandy, and sugar to taste.

DIRECTIONS.—Peel and cut the apples, boil them with a little white sugar, and mash them smooth, make a custard with the yolks of the eggs and the milk, and the brandy, white sugar to taste; have the apples and custard ready, make a ring around the dish with the apples, and put the custard in the middle, whisk the whites of the eggs to a stiff froth, and put them over the custard and apples, sift sugar over it, and bake in a moderate oven.

751. Apple Tart and Custard. [TIME.—TO BAKE THREE-QUARTERS OF AN HOUR.]

ARTICLES.—Two pounds of apples, a quarter of a pound of sugar, peel of half a lemon, one tablespoonful of lemon juice, one pint of custard, and puff paste.

DIRECTIONS.—Make about a pound of good puff paste, put a border of it round the edge of a pie-dish, and fill it with the apples pared, cored, and cut into slices; add the sugar, the grated lemon peel, and the juice, with a small quantity of water, cover it with a crust, cut the crust close round the edge of the dish, and bake it. When done, cut out the middle of the crust, leaving only a border at the edge of the dish, pour in a good boiled custard, grate a little nutmeg over the top, and serve it up cold.

752. Apples for Dessert. [TIME.—ABOUT AN HOUR.

ARTICLES.—Apples. A thin syrup of sugar and water, strawberry, or any other pink-colored jelly which may be desired.

DIRECTIONS.—Peel and core as many apples as will fill a dish, and put them into the double boiler, with a thin syrup of sugar and water; boil until tender, and set to cool. Lay them on a dish, pour the syrup round them, and fill the centre of the apples with any jelly.

753. Grace's Apple Trifle. [TIME.—ONE HOUR.]

ARTICLES.—Twelve apples, peel of one lemon, sugar to taste, three-quarters of a pint of milk, quarter of a pint of cream, yolks of two eggs, and whipped cream.

DIRECTIONS.—Pare, core, and scald the apples, with the peel of a lemon grated, and sugar to taste. When tender, beat them to a pulp, and put them at the bottom of a dish; add the milk and cream to the eggs, with a few lumps of sugar, stir it in a double boiler until it thickens, and when cold lay it over the apples and pile a whipped cream over the whole.

754. Apple Suet Pudding. [TIME.—BOIL AN HOUR AND A QUARTER.]

ARTICLES.—One pint of bread crumbs, half a dozen of apples, half a pound of suet, one egg, juice and rind of one lemon, and a little salt, mixed to the consistency of drop-cake with milk and water. Cook as below.

755. French Apple Pudding. [TIME.—BOIL AN HOUR AND A QUARTER.]

ARTICLES.—Apples, sifted flour, one quarter of a pound of finely chopped beef suet, a little salt, cold water, and sugar.

DIRECTIONS.—Line a pudding bowl, fill with tart apples, cut in quarters, sprinkle the sugar on the top, cover with paste, and then boil, turn out, and serve with a sweet liquid pudding sauce, spiced with lemon and ginger.

756. Green Apple Pie.

Grate six good apples, add a cup of sugar, three tablespoonfuls of melted butter, and spice to taste.

THE SICK ROOM.

Hints for Attendants in the Sick Room.

Do not get out of temper, but strive to make the sick chamber the pleasantest and yet the quietest portion of the house.

Do not converse in whispers; invalids generally are suspicious, and will imagine all sorts of things if they hear, but do not understand, a conversation in the room.

Do not urge the invalid to eat and drink when he does not feel like it.

Allow no unpleasant smells to pervade the room; prevent this by a thorough ventilation; let in fresh air and sunshine freely and frequently; never raise a dust, but wipe the floor or carpet with a damp cloth, and pick up bits as needed; do not let lamp or sunlight shine directly in the eyes, and when the patient desires to sleep a little, darken the room somewhat; do not wear rustling dresses.

Keep everything that is used by the patient perfectly clean.

Do not allow the nauseating medicine bottles to stand in the sight of the patient.

Study all the peculiarities of your patient, and instead of opposing them by argument or otherwise, humor them, whenever by so doing you do not interfere with the physician's instructions.

Do not allow flowers or plants to be kept in the room too long, and especially over night.

Proper nursing is an art, and should be studied as assiduously as any other.

A cheerful, merry heart is indispensable in the sick room, and there is nothing better than a keen sense of the humorous to arouse a smile, and if the patient is not too weak, a laugh, which is worth more than many drugs. No long faces should be seen in the sick room, and no impatience or petulance. If, after having taken the utmost pains to have the food perfect, and served on the instant, do not be vexed if the poor worn and nervous patient should refuse the food, but put the matter in such facetious light that the patient will perhaps forget his lack of appetite, and may taste the food and eat it with a relish. Prepare only a small amount of anything, and never discuss it beforehand; a surprise will often rouse a flagging appetite.

Never leave any article of diet in the sick room; it is a good means of destroying the appetite, which should be encouraged and not weakened.

Whatever is served, let great attention be paid to giving the dish, after it is properly cooked, a dainty appearance. Place it on the choicest ware in the house, with the cleanest of napkins and the brightest of silver, even if that consists only of a teaspoon.

If tea and toast be served, put the tea freshly drawn into the daintiest of teacups (every family might well afford to buy one little, thin china cup and saucer, to use in case of illness,) and serve with cut loaf sugar. A few drops of cream are easily saved for the patient's tea from a small quantity of milk; and cream in small quantities is considered more digestible than milk.

757. Tea.

Tea is best made in the sick room. With a small table at the side of the invalid's bed, it is a decidedly pleasant little diversion to make tea in this manner, being sure at the same time that it is perfectly fresh. But, however it is made, do not present a cupful of tea to the sufferer, with a part of it spilled in the saucer.

758. Toast.

All cooks think they can make toast. There is about one person in ten who really knows how; there is quite a difference between a thin and well yellowed crisp piece of toast with crust cut off, just from the fire, and a thick unshapely slice, unevenly crisped on the outside and of doughy softness inside: one is appetizing and digestible; the other not.

To make it properly, the bread should not be too fresh. It should be cut thin, evenly and in good shape, half an inch in thickness or even less—never more; the crust edges should be cut off, these pieces can be dried and saved for various purposes.

Present each side of the bread to the fire for a few moments to warm, without attempting to toast it; then turn the first side to the fire but at some distance from it, so that it may slowly and evenly receive a golden color over all the surface; repeat the same with the other side. To insure success the coals should be clear and hot. Serve the moment it is done, on a warm plate.

759. To Make Gruel.

Pour a quart of hot water into a clean earthen or tin vessel over a brisk fire; when it boils, add two large tablespoonfuls of corn or oatmeal; mix it smooth in just enough water to thicken it; put a small lump of butter into the water, and when melted, add the meal and stir for about half an hour; then add a teacupful of sweet milk, and when it boils again, throw in the upper crust of hard baked bread cut into small pieces; let it boil some time, and add a little black pepper, a little salt, a pinch of grated nutmeg, a little more butter and a teaspoonful of French brandy. The butter, spices, and brandy, should be omitted when the case is a serious one.

760. Beef Tea.

Take a pound of lean beef, cut it fine, put it in a bottle corked tightly, and put the bottle into a kettle of warm water; the water should be allowed to boil for a considerable time; the bottle should then be removed and the contents poured out. The tea may be salted a little, and a teaspoonful given each time.

Another way of preparing it is as follows: Take a thick steak, broil slightly on a gridiron until the juices have started, and then squeeze thoroughly with a lemon squeezer. The juice thus extracted will be highly nutritious.

761. Toast Water.

Toast slightly a piece of bread, and add to it boiling water; if preferred, sweeten. It may be flavored with lemon or orange peel.

762. Flax Seed Tea.

Take an ounce of flax seed and a little pounded liquorice root, and pour on a pint of boiling water; place the vessel near a fire for four hours; strain through a linen or cotton cloth.

763. Barley Coffee.

Roast barley until well brown, and boil a tablespoonful of it in a pint of water for five minutes; strain, and add a little sugar, if desired. A nourishing drink toward the close of fever and during convalescence.

764. Oat Meal Coffee.

Mix common oatmeal and water to form a cake; bake and brown it, powder it, and boil in water five minutes. Good for checking obstinate vomiting, especially in cholera morbus.

765. Egg Brandy.

Take the yolks of two eggs, beat well, and add half an ounce of white sugar, and a little cinnamon water, or two drops of oil of cinnamon. Mix well, and add a wineglassful of French brandy.

766. Milk Punch.

A teaspoonful of sugar and enough water to dissolve it; pour in two gills or teacupfuls of milk, and then in a small stream stirring constantly, a tablespoonful or two of brandy or rum.

767. Egg Nog.

A teaspoonful of sugar well beaten with an egg, a gill or a teacupful of milk, and one or two tablespoonfuls of good French brandy. Flavor with grated nutmeg.

768. Sage Tea.

Dry leaves of sage, half an ounce; boiling water, one quart; infuse for half an hour, strain and add sugar and lemon juice as required by the patient. Balm and other teas are made in the same manner.

769. Rice Water.

Rice, two ounces; water, two quarts; boil an hour or so, and add sugar and nutmeg.

770. Refreshing Drinks in Fevers.

Put a little sage, two sprigs of balm, and a little sorrel into a stone jug; peel a small lemon, slice it, and put in, together with a small piece of the rind; then pour in three pints of boiling water, sweeten, and cover it close.

ANOTHER.—Take half an ounce of prunes, or dried plums, an ounce of cranberries, half an ounce of stoned raisins, and a quart of water; boil down to one pint, strain, and flavor with lemon peel, or essence of lemon. Keep it closely covered.

ANOTHER.—Take one ounce each of currants, raisins, and tamarinds or prunes, and boil in one quart of water down to one pint. Flavor with lemon peel, or essence of lemon.

771. Fruit Drinks for Invalids.

Currants, cranberries, and prunes make refreshing drinks, when added to water, and sweetened to suit the patient's taste.

772. Water Gruel.

Corn, or oatmeal two tablespoonfuls; water, one quart; boil for ten or fifteen minutes, and add sugar or salt, if desired by the patient.

773. Rice Gruel.

Ground rice, one heaping tablespoonful; ground cinnamon, half a teaspoonful; water, one quart; boil slowly for fifteen or twenty minutes, add the cinnamon near the conclusion of the boiling, strain and sweeten.

774. Cooling Drink for Fevers.

Take vinegar, one teacupful; water, six teacupfuls; and honey, two teacupfuls. Mix together. If honey does not agree with the person, use molasses or syrup.

775. Quince Wine.

Take six quinces, slice them and pour on half a gallon of boiling water; let them stand over night, and in the morning boil fifteen minutes and add one pound of sugar. Let the liquid ferment, and add one pint of whisky or brandy; strain and keep in closely corked bottles or jugs.

776. Gum Arabic Mixture.

Dissolve four ounces of gum Arabic, in three teacupfuls of boiling water; sweeten and flavor as desired. Useful in cases of inflammation of the stomach and bowels.

777. Panada.

White bread, one ounce; water, one pint; ground cinnamon, one teaspoonful; boil until well mixed, and add a little sugar and nutmeg. Wine may be added if desirable.

778. Sago Gruel.

Sago, two tablespoonfuls; water, one pint; boil until it thickens, frequently stirring. Wine, sugar, and nutmeg may be used, if desirable.

779. Mucilage of Elm Bark.

Place a small quantity of elm bark in cold water. May be drunk after an hour or two. If desired it may be flavored with lemon juice, or essence of lemon, or other essence. It may be drunk freely in cases of inflammation of the bladder, stomach, etc.

780. Tapioca Jelly.

Tapioca, two tablespoonfuls; water, one pint; boil slowly for an hour, until it becomes of a jelly-like appearance; add sugar, wine, and nutmeg, to suit the taste of the patient. Lemon juice may also be added.

781. Irish Moss Jelly.

Irish moss, half an ounce; fresh milk, one and a half pints; boil down to a pint, strain, and add a sufficient amount of sugar and lemon juice, or peach water, to give it an agreeable flavor.

782. Arrow Root Gruel.

Add a tablespoonful of arrow root, to half a pint of boiling water; mix well, add half a pint of milk, and boil together for two or three minutes; sweeten to the taste. Wine may be added if suited to the case.

783. Milk Porridge.

Add two tablespoonfuls of cornmeal, to a pint each of milk and water; mix the meal with a small quantity of cold water, so as to form a thin paste; pour the milk and water together and as soon as they commence boiling, add the paste, and stir. It may be flavored with cinnamon, nutmeg, sugar, or wine.

784. Isinglass Jelly.

Isinglass, one roll, boiled in one pint of water until dissolved, then strain, and add one pint of sweet milk. Put it again over the fire, and let it just boil up. Sweeten with sugar, and grate nutmeg upon it. If properly made, it resembles custard.

785. Apple Water.

Cut two large apples into slices and pour on them a quart of boiling water; after standing two or three hours, sweeten slightly.

786. Boiled Flour.

Tie one pound of flour in a linen bag; dip this a number of times into cold water, and then sprinkle flour upon the outside to form a crust, which will prevent the water from entering inside while boiling; place the bag thus prepared, in some water, and boil until it becomes a hard, dry mass. A little of this may be grated, and prepared in the same manner as arrow root gruel.

787. Vegetable Soup.

Take one turnip, one potato, one onion, and slice and boil them in one quart of water for an hour, add salt as agreeable, and pour the whole upon a piece of dry toast.

788. Mutton Tea.

Take one pound of mutton, remove the fat, and cut the meat into small pieces; pour half a pint of boiling water over it, let it stand near a fire for half an hour, and then boil for one hour, strain through a sieve or cloth, and add salt to suit the taste. A very nourishing diet.

789. Mutton Broth.

Take one pound of good mutton, remove the fat, and put in a vessel with three pints of boiling water; simmer for two hours; then cut up into slices three carrots, three turnips, and three onions; boil them in a quart of water for half an hour, strain, and add the vegetables to the mutton liquor, season with salt, and simmer slowly for four hours.

790. Chicken Broth.

Take half a chicken, remove all the fat, cut the meat up into small pieces, and bread the bones; put into a vessel with three pints of boiling water; boil for one hour, season with salt, and strain. Very nourishing.

791. Rennet Whey.

New milk, one quart; rennet, a large spoonful; heat the milk and then add the rennet; boil until the curd separates, which is to be taken off.

792. Vinegar Whey.

Milk, one pint; vinegar, one tablespoonful; boil for a few minutes and separate the curd.

793. Alum Whey.

To a pint of milk, add a teaspoonful of powdered alum, boil and strain; useful in diarrhœa, dysentery, and inflammation of the stomach. The curd forms an excellent poultice for inflammation of the eye.

794. Mustard Whey.

Mustard seed, one tablespoonful; milk, one pint; boil together for a few minutes and separate the curd. A useful drink in dropsy.

795. Calves' Feet Jelly.

Take two calves' feet, and add to them one gallon of water; boil down to one quart; strain, and when cold, skim off the fat; add to this the whites of six or eight eggs well beaten, a pint of wine, a half pound of sugar and the juice of four lemons. Mix well. Boil them a few minutes, stirring constantly, and strain through flannel.

796. Orange Whey.

Milk, one pint; the juice of one orange with a portion of the peel; boil the milk, then add the orange to it, and let it stand until coagulation takes place, and strain.

797. Sweet Whey.

Skimmed milk, two quarts, and a piece of calves' rennet. Mix, and put in a warm place until it coagulates, and then strain.

798. Wine Whey.

Milk, two-thirds of a pint; water, one-third of a pint; Madeira or other wine, one gill; sugar, one dessertspoonful; put the milk and water together in a deep pan on the fire, and at the moment when it begins to boil, pour in the wine and the sugar, stirring constantly; boil ten or fifteen minutes; when boiled, strain through a sieve. This may be drunk either cold or warm, a wineglassful at a time. An excellent thing in all forms of fever.

799. Sippets.

On an extremely hot plate put two or three slices of bread, and pour over them some of the juice of boiled beef, mutton or veal, and sprinkle over them a little salt.

800. Chicken Panada.

Take the white meat of a chicken, having removed the skin and fat, and boil in a small quantity of water until the flesh is soft; pound the flesh in a mortar until pulpy, and then add an equal weight of stale, wheat bread, gradually adding some of the water in which the chicken was boiled, until the whole forms a thin fluid paste; boil this paste for ten minutes, frequently stirring, and season to suit the taste.

801. French Milk Porridge.

Stir together some oatmeal and water, and let the mixture stand until clear, and pour off the water; then put some more water to the meal, stir it well, and let it stand until the next day; strain through a fine sieve, and boil the water, adding the milk while doing so. The proportion of water must be small.

Additional Recipes for dishes appropriate for the sick, will be found in various parts of the book, and are so marked.

HOUSEHOLD REMEDIES.

802. Mosquito Ointment.—(*Prof. Linden.*)

One-half dram carbolic acid, one ounce sweet oil; mix well, and rub on hands and face.

803. Diarrhœa Mixture.—(*Mrs. Cady.*)

One teaspoonful of ordinary salt, one teaspoonful of flour, one tablespoonful of vinegar; mix well and take in one dose.

804. Tooth Powder.—(*Dr. Cook.*)

Two ounces prepared chalk, one ounce powdered orris root, and mix well.

805. Remedy for Burns.

If the skin is not broken, wash with fluid turpentine, then cover with cotton batting or soft linen to exclude the air; repeat the wash when the skin becomes dry; this remedy will remove pain almost instantly. Another good remedy, when the skin is not broken, consists of applying cloths wet with essence of peppermint mixed with whisky or spirits; one part peppermint to three of whisky. Peppermint and sweet oil is equally good, put on with cotton. The simplest and best remedy, however, in case the skin is broken, is to cover the burns with common wheat flour.

806. Lait de Poule.—(For Colds.) [TIME.—TEN MINUTES.]

ARTICLES.—Half a pint of milk, one egg, and one tablespoonful of sugar.

DIRECTIONS.—Beat the yolk of the egg and the sugar together, and the white separately; mix the beaten yolk and sugar with the milk boiling hot; stir very fast to prevent curdling; then add the white next, stirring very rapidly; drink as hot as possible, just before going to bed.

REMARKS —This is an excellent and old French remedy for a cold, and produces a gentle perspiration when other means fail.

807. Eau Sedatif. (*Raspail.*)

Dissolve two small handfuls of ordinary salt in one quart of water; add one small wineglassful of spirits of camphor, and two small wineglassfuls of spirits of ammonia, mix well together, then filter through filtering paper or common brown wrapping paper and keep well corked.

REMARKS.—This is an old recipe from the eminent French physician, Raspail, and is used as an emollient for bruises, (when the skin is not broken) Rheumatism, Headache, etc. When used for Headache, reduce it one-half with water, wet a cloth and lay it on the head. When used for bruises, lameness, etc., rub the parts affected briskly with the mixture pure, and then rub with camphor lard.

808. Camphor Lard. (*Raspail.*)

One part clear lard, } By weight.
Two parts pulverized camphor. }

Let it simmer slowly, till the camphor is dissolved, stir occasionally, especially just before pouring it into vessels to keep.

809. To Stop Bleeding of the Nose.

Find the artery on both sides of the face where it crosses the jaw, some two or three inches above the point of the chin, press it closely against the bone with the thumb and forefinger ; observe which nostril bleeds most freely, and press harder on that side. This gives speedy relief, and is far more agreeable than rolls of paper pressed above the front teeth, or cold keys and cold water applied to the back of the neck.

810. Advice in Cases of Poisoning.

Stir into a glass of water a heaping teaspoonful each of salt and mustard, and drink immediately. One or more doses will cause vomiting, and cleanse the stomach. To overcome the effects, swallow the whites of two or three eggs, and drink a cup or two of strong coffee.

Sweet oil, taken freely, is excellent in cases of poisoning.

NURSERY RECIPES.

811. For Dysentery or Cholera Infantum.

To the white of one egg beaten stiff add three drops of brandy and one lump of sugar ; mix well together and give a quarter of a teaspoonful every two hours. *For Babies over six months old*, mix a quarter of a teaspoonful of brandy with the egg and give a teaspoonful for a dose.

812. For Taking Scurf. (*From the head of an Infant.*)

Burn butter and apply like glycerine at night.

813. Earache.

Take a bit of cotton batting, put upon it a pinch of black

pepper, gather it up and tie it, dip it into sweet oil and insert it in the ear ; put a flannel bandage over the head to keep it warm ; this will give immediate relief.

814. Stings of Hornets, Wasps and Bees.

Cover the sting with wet earth. the relief is instantaneous.

VARIOUS HOUSEHOLD RECIPES.

815. To Remove Grease Spots from Carpets.

Rub dry buckwheat flour on the stain. renew the flour and rubbing till the stain is removed.

816. Kid Glove Cleaning Fluid.

ARTICLES.—One gallon deodorized benzine ; one-half ounce sulph. ether; one-half ounce chloroform. and one ounce alcohol.

DIRECTIONS.—Any kind of perfume if desired ; pour a small quantity in a plate, lay the glove in it and rub gently with a flannel cloth ; lay a napkin or towel on a table, stretch the glove on it and rub gently with a towel till dry ; if the glove is very much soiled, wash it twice, but dry it only once ; this same fluid is excellent for removing grease spots from any fabric.

817. Washing Fluid.

ARTICLES.—One pound of potash dissolved in three gallons boiling water, strain it off clear, add one ounce salts of ammonia and one ounce salts of tartar ; bottle and cork tight.

DIRECTIONS.—Put half a cupful of the fluid in three pails of water ; soak the clothes over night, soaping, however, the parts that are mostly soiled. The clothes require much less rubbing by the use of this fluid.

818. Bedbug Exterminator.

The whites of two eggs and ten cents' worth of quicksilver ; beat well together and apply to cracks and crevices with a feather. Warranted to be a perfect exterminator of bugs and their eggs, etc.

819. RATES OF POSTAGE.

Letters.—Letters go to any part of the United States for three cents per half ounce, or fraction thereof, if prepaid.

Unpaid letters are sent to the Dead Letter Office, at Washington.

Newspapers.—Publishers are now required to prepay all postage on newspapers; only one copy to each actual subscriber residing within the county in which the same is published goes free through the mails.

Miscellaneous Matter of the Third Class.—Books, pamphlets, and all printed matter of the third class, except unsealed circulars, one cent for each two ounces, or fraction thereof. Unsealed circulars, types, cuttings, roots, seeds, merchandise, metals, ores and minerals, and all mailable matter of the third class, except that mentioned above, one cent for each ounce, or fraction thereof.

Money Orders.—Money orders can be obtained only at designated Money Order Offices. Money can be sent to any part of the country with absolute safety, by obtaining a money order, for which the fees are: Not exceeding $15, 10 cents; over $15, and not exceeding $30, 15 cents; over $30, and not exceeding $40, 20 cents; over $40, and not exceeding $50, 25 cents. No order issued for more than $50.

Registration.—It costs ten cents extra, besides the regular postage, to register a letter. Letters may be registered at any post office.

820. Value of Foreign Money.

ON A GOLD BASIS.

Pound Sterling, of England		$4.84
Guinea,	"	5.05
Crown,	"	1.21

Shilling, "		.22
Napoleon, of France		3.84
Five Francs "		.93
Franc, "		.18½
Thaler, of Saxony		.68
Guilder, of Netherlands		.40
Ducat, of Austria		2.28
Florin "		.48½
Doubloon, of Spain (1800,)		15.54
Real, "		.05
Five Rubles, of Russia		3.95
Ruble, "		.75
Franc, of Belgium		.18½
Ducat, of Bavaria		2.27
Franc, of Switzerland		.18½
Crown, of Tuscany		1.05½

821. Business Laws.

It is not legally necessary to say on a note "for value received."

A note drawn on Sunday is void.

A note obtained by fraud, or from a person in a state of intoxication, cannot be collected.

If a note be lost or stolen, it does not release the maker; he must pay it.

A note given by a minor is void.

Notes bear interest only when so stated.

Principals are responsible for the acts of their agents.

Each individual in a partnership is responsible for the whole amount of the debts of the firm.

Ignorance of the law excuses no one.

It is a fraud to conceal a fraud.

The law compels no one to do impossibilities.

An agreement without consideration is void.

Signatures made with a lead pencil are good in law.
A receipt for money paid is not legally conclusive.
The acts of one partner bind all the others.
Contracts made on Sunday cannot be enforced.
A contract made with a minor is void.
A contract made with a lunatic is void.

WEIGHTS AND MEASURES

822. Legal Weight of Bushel as prescribed by the Statutes of New York State.

Bush.	Lbs.	Bush.	Lbs.
African Peanuts	32	Malt	38
Barley	48	Millet Seed	50
Blue Grass Seed	14	Oats	32
Bran	20	Onions	55
Buckwheat	48	Peas	60
Castor Beans	46	Plastering Hair	8
Clover Seed	60	Rye	56
Corn Meal	48	Salt	56
Corn in the ear	70	Shelled Corn	58
Dried Apples	22	Stone Coal	80
Dried Peaches	32	Sweet Potatoes	60
Flax Seed	55	Timothy Seed	44
Ground Peas	20	Turnips	55
Hemp Seed	40	Unslacked Lime	30
Hungary Grass Seed	48	Wheat	60
Irish Potatoes	60	White Beans	60

TABLES OF WEIGHTS, MEASURES, Etc.

823. Linear or Long Measure

Is used in measuring lines or distances. A line has only one dimension—length.

ONE INCH.

TWO INCHES.

THREE INCHES.

TABLE.

12 inches equal to 1 foot.
3 feet " 1 yard.

WEIGHTS AND MEASURES.

5½ yards or 16½ feet	"	1 rod.
40 rods	"	1 furlong.
8 furlongs or 320 rods	"	1 mile.
5,280 feet	"	mile.

The inch is generally divided into halves, quarters, eighths, sixteenths, and sometimes in tenths and twelfths. Civil and mechanical engineers, and others, use decimal divisions of the foot and inch.

The following denominations are also in use:

3 barley corns make 1 inch, used by shoemakers.

4 inches make 1 hand, used in measuring the height of horses at the shoulder.

9 inches make 1 span; among sailors, 8 spans make 1 fathom.

6 feet make 1 fathom, used in measuring depths at sea.

120 fathoms make 1 cable's length.

3 feet make 1 pace.

1,152⅔ common miles make 1 geographical mile, used to measure distances at sea.

3 geographic miles make 1 league.

60 geographic or 69.16 statute miles make 1 degree of latitude on a meridian or of longitude on the equator.

360 degrees make the circumference of the earth.

A knot is a geographical or nautical mile, used to measure the speed of vessels.

824. Surveyors' Long Measure.

A gunter's chain, used by land surveyors, is 4 rods or 66 feet long, and consists of 100 links.

TABLE.

7-92 inches equal to		1 link.
25 links	"	1 rod.
4 rods	"	1 chain.
80 chains	"	1 mile.

825. Square Measure.

Square measure is used in computing areas or surfaces, as of land, boards, painting, plastering, paving, etc.

144 square inches equal to 1 square foot.
9 square feet   "   1 square yard.
30¼ square yards   "   1 square rod or perch.
160 square rods   "   1 acre.
36 square miles (6 miles square) equal to 1 township.

826. Wood Measure

Is used to measure wood and rough stone. Cubic or solid measure is used in estimating the contents of solids.

27 cubic feet make 1 cubic yard.
16 cubic feet equal to 1 cord foot.
8 cord feet or } " 1 cord.
128 cubic feet }
24¾ cubic feet   "   1 perch of stone or masonry.

A cubic yard of earth is called a load.

A pile of wood 8 feet long, 4 feet wide and 4 feet high contains one cord.

A perch of stone or of masonry is 16½ feet long, 1½ feet wide and 1 foot high.

827. Liquid Measure

Is used in measuring liquids.

4 gills equal to 1 pint.
2 pints   "   1 quart,
4 quarts   "   1 gallon.
31½ galls.   "   1 barrel.
63 gallons   "   1 hogshead.

828. Apothecaries' Fluid Measure.

60 minims or drops equal to 1 fluid drachm. (ƒ ʒ)
8 fluid drachms   "   1 fluid ounce.   (ƒ ℥)
16 fluid ounces   "   1 pint.   (O)
8 pints   "   1 gallon.   (Cong.)

The minim is equivalent to a drop of water. A pint of water weighs a pound.

829. Dry Measure

Is used in measuring dry articles such as grain, fruit, salt, etc.

    2 pints equal to 1 quart.
    8 quarts " 1 peck.
    4 pecks " 1 bushel.

MEASURES OF WEIGHT.
830. Troy Weight

Is used in weighing gold, silver and jewels.

TABLE.

  24 grains equal to 1 pennyweight. (*pwt.*)
  20 pennyweights " 1 ounce.   (*oz.*)
  12 ounces " 1 pound.   (*lb.*)

A carat is a weight of about 3 and 2-10 Troy grains and is used to weigh diamonds and precious stones. The term carat is also used to express the fineness of gold, and means a twenty-fourth part. Thus gold is said to be 18 carats fine when it contains 18 parts of pure gold and 6 parts of alloy or baser metal.

831. Apothecaries' Weight

Is used by physicians and apothecaries in prescribing and mixing dry medicines.

TABLE.

  20 grains (*gr.*) equal to 1 scruple. (℈)
  3 scruples " 1 dram. (ℨ)
  8 drams   " 1 ounce. (℥)
  12 ounces " 1 pound. (℔)

Medicines are bought and sold by avoirdupois weight; the pound, ounce and grain are the same as those of Troy weight, the ounce being differently divided. Physicians write prescriptions according to the Roman notation, using small letters, preceded by the symbols, writing j for i, when it terminates a number. Thus 6 ounces is written ℥ *vj*; 8 drams, ℨ *vij*; 14 scruples, ℈ *xiv*; etc. ℞ is an abbreviation for recipe, or take; $\bar{a}$, *aa*, for equal quantities; *ij*, for 2; *ss*, for semi, or half;

gr. for grain ; *P.* for particular, or little part ; *P. aeq.* for equal parts ; *p. q.* as much as you please.

832. Avoirdupois Weight

Is used for weighing all coarse and heavy articles.

TABLE.

16 ounces *(oz.)* equal to 1 pound.	*(lb.)*
100 lbs. " 1 hundred weight.	*(cwt.)*
20 cwt. " 1 ton.	*(T.)*

The following denominations are also in use :

100	pounds of grain or flour make	1 cental.
100	"	dry fish	"	1 quintal.
100	"	nails	"	1 keg.
196	"	flour	"	1 barrel.
200	"	pork or beef	"	1 barrel.
240	"	lime	"	1 cask.
280	"	salt at N. Y. S. Works make 1 barrel.

The weight of the bushel of certain grains and roots has been fixed by statute in many of the states ; and these statute weights must govern in buying and selling, unless specific agreements to the contrary are made.

SIZE OF NAILS.

2 penny,	1 inch	557	nails to the pound
4 "	1¼ "	353	"	"
5 "	1¾ "	232	"	"
6 "	2 "	167	"	"
7 "	2¼ "	141	"	"
8 "	2½ "	101	"	"
10 "	2¾ "	68	"	"
12 "	3 "	54	"	"
20 "	3½ "	34	"	"
Spikes,	4 "	16	"	"
"	4½ "	12	"	"
"	5 "	10	"	"

833. Counting.

The following table is used in counting certain classes of articles :

VARIOUS TABLES.

```
12 units or things equal to  1 dozen.        (doz.)
12 dozen              "      1 gross.        (gro.)
12 gross              "      1 great' gross. (g gro.)
20 units or things    "      1 score.        (sc.)
```

834. Table for the Paper Trade.

```
24 sheets equal to  1 quire.
20 quires     "     1 ream.
 2 reams      "     1 bundle.
 5 bundles    "     1 bale.
```

835. Table for the Book Trade.

The terms, folio, quarto, octavo, etc., indicate the number of leaves into which a sheet of paper is folded.

When a Sheet is Folded Into	The Book is Called	And one Sheet of Paper Makes
2 leaves	a folio	4 pp. (pages.)
4 "	a quarto or 4to	8 "
8 "	an octavo or 8vo	16 "
12 "	a duodecimo or 12mo	24 "
16 "	a 16mo	32 "
18 "	an 18mo	36 "

Clerks and copyists are usually paid by the *folio* for making copies of legal papers, records, and documents.

    72 words make 1 folio or sheet of common law.
    90 "   " 1 "   "   " Chancery.

836. DISTANCES FROM BUFFALO, N. Y.
— TO THE —
PRINCIPAL POINTS OF THE GLOBE.

Compiled from official records, via shortest routes, by Land
and Water, giving the most desirable route
to commence the trip.

From Buffalo, N. Y. to
MILES.

Aberdeen, Scotland, via New York City	4222
Acapulco, Mexico, via New York City	5348
Adrian, Michigan, via Lake Shore Railway	327
Alexandria, Egypt, via New York City and Liverpool	6816
Albany, New York, via New York Central Railroad	298
Algiers, Africa, via New York City	4633
Altoona, Pa., via Erie Railway	343
Alton, Illinois, via Lake Shore Railway	712
Ann Arbor, Michigan, via Great Western Railway	291
Archangel, Russia, via New York City	4753
Aspinwall, Panama, via New York City	2771
Athens, Greece, via New York City	5233
Atlanta, Georgia, Erie Railway via Washington, D. C.	1218
Atlanta, Georgia, via Lake Shore Railway	1023
Auburn, New York, via New York Central Railroad	147
Auckland, New Zealand, via San Francisco & S. Isl'ds.	8825
Augusta, Maine, via New York Central Railroad	672
Augusta, Ga., Erie Railway, via Washington, D. C.	1047
Austin, Minn., via Great Western Railway	832
Bainbridge, Florida, Erie R'y, via Washington, D. C.	1438
Baltimore, Maryland, via Erie Railway	405
Bangor, Maine, via New York Central Railroad	744
Batavia, New York, via New York Central Railroad	37
Belfast, Ireland, via New York City	3652

Bellefontaine, Ohio, via Lake Shore Railway.......... 323
Binghamton, New York, via Erie Railway............ 208
Bitter Creek, W. T., Lake Shore or Gt. Western R'ys.. 1815
Bombay, India, via New York City and Liverpool...... 10896
Boston, Mass., via Erie Railway..................... 667
Boston, Mass., via New York Central Railroad........ 498
Bowling Green, Kentucky, via Lake Shore Railway.... 662
Bradford, Pa., via Erie Railway..................... 79
Bremen, Prussia, via New York City................. 4003
Bridgeport, Conn., via Erie Railway................. 480
Bryan, Texas, via L. S., and New Orleans........... 1902
Bryan, W. T., via L. S. or G. W. Railways.......... 1889
Brunswick, Maine, via New York Central Railroad..... 636
Buenos Ayres, S. A., via New York City............ 6552
Bull Run, Va., Erie Railway, via Washington, D. C.... 476
Buffalo, New York, (Voyage around the world,) via Union Pacific Railroad and California to Sandwich Islands, 5020—to Hong Kong, 4800—to Singapore, 1380—to Calcutta, 1680—to Madras, 780—to Bombay, 1340—to Alexandria, via Red Sea, 2740—to Malta 840—to Gibraltar, 960—to Liverpool, 1500—to Buffalo, via New York City, 3519. Whole distance........... 24559
Burlington, Iowa, via Great Western Railway......... 744
Burlington, Vermont, via New York Central Railroad.. 433
Cairo, Illinois, via Lake Shore Railway............... 831
Cairo, Egypt, via New York City................... 5433
Calcutta, India, Un. Pac. Railroad via California...... 12502
Callao, Lima, via New York City and Panama........ 3933
Canary Islands, via New York City................. 3373
Canton, China, via New York City and Isthmus...... 10600
Canton, China, via New York City and Cape Horn.... 21500
Canton, China, via Lake Shore and U. P. Railroads.... 9400
Canandaigua, New York, via New York Central R'd.... 98
Cape Horn, via New York City..................... 8653

Cape of Good Hope, via New York City	6371
Carlin, Nevada, via Lake Shore or G. W. Railways	2358
Cedar Rapids, Iowa, via Great Western Railway	805
Cedar Falls, Iowa, via Great Western Railway	824
Charlotte, N. C., Erie R'y via Washington, D. C.	855
Charleston, S. C., Erie R'y via Washington, D. C.	1030
Charles City, Iowa, via Great Western Railway	865
Chattanooga, Tenn., via Lake Shore Railway	884
Chelsea, Mass., via New York Central Railroad	502
Cherbourg, France, via New York City	3558
Cheyenne, W. T., via L. S. or G. W. Railways	1545
Chillicothe, Mo., via Lake Shore Railway	901
Chicago, Illinois, via Lake Shore Railway	538
Chicago, Illinois, via Great Western Railway	537
Chicago, Ills., via Canada Southern Railway	538
Cincinnati, Ohio, via Lake Shore Railway	441
Cleveland, Ohio, via Lake Shore Railway,	183
Columbus, Ohio, via Lake Shore Railway	321
Columbia, S. C., Erie R'y via Washington, D. C.	962
Concord, N. H., via New York Central Railroad	537
Constantinople, Turkey, via New York City	5573
Corinth, Miss., via Lake Shore Railway	916
Corning, New York, via Erie Railway	132
Cork, Ireland, via New York City	3799
Corry, Pa., via Lake Shore Railway	91
Council Bluffs, Iowa, via L. S. or G. W. R'ys	1025
Crestline, Ohio, via Lake Shore Railway	258
Culpepper, Va., Erie Railway, via Washington, D. C.	532
Cynthiana, Kentucky, via Lake Shore Railway	507
Danville, Va., Erie Railway via Washington, D. C.	714
Davenport, Iowa, via Great Western Railway	720
Darwin, Minn., via Great Western	1005
Dayton, Ohio, via Lake Shore Railway	401
Decatur, Illinois, via Lake Shore Railway	619

TO PRINCIPAL POINTS. 249

Des Moines, Iowa, via Great Western Railway	894
Detroit, Michigan, via Great Western Railway	253
Detroit, Michigan, via Grand Trunk Railway	258
Detroit, Mich., via Canada Southern Railway	253
Dixon, Illinois, via Great Western Railway	638
Dover, N. H., via New York Central Railroad	569
Dublin, Ireland, via New York City	3299
Dubuque, Iowa, via Great Western Railway	726
Duluth, Minnesota, via Lake Shore Railway	1089
Duluth, via Union Line of Steamers	1216
Dunkirk, New York, via Lake Shore Railway	40
Dunleith, Illinois, via Great Western Railway	725
Easton, Pa., via Erie Railway	459
Edinburgh, Scotland, via New York City	4122
Elmira, New York, via Erie Railway	149
Erie, Pa., via Lake Shore Railway	88
Evansville, Ind., via Lake Shore Railway	684
Exeter, N. H., via New York Central Railroad	548
Florence, S. C., Erie Railway via Washington, D. C.	928
Fond du Lac, Wis., via Great Western Railway	714
Fortress Monroe, Va., Erie R'y via Washington, D. C.	689
Fort Harker, Kan., via Lake Shore Railway	1256
Fort Riley, Kan., via Lake Shore Railway	1176
Fort Dodge, Iowa, via Great Western Railway	917
Fort Wayne, Ind., via Lake Shore Railway	389
Fort Howard, Wis., via Great Western Railway	779
Frankfort, Kentucky, via Lake Shore Railway	558
Franklin, Mo., via Lake Shore Railway	765
Freeport, Illinois, via Great Western Railway	658
Fredericksburgh, Va., Erie R'y via Washington, D. C.	513
Galesburg, Illinois, via Great Western Railway	700
Galway, Ireland, via New York City	3164
Galveston, Texas, L. S., via New Orleans	1752

Gardiner, Maine, via New York Central Railroad	665
Geneva, New York, via New York Central Railroad	121
Gettysburg, Pa., Erie R'y via Washington, D. C.	389
Gibralter, via New York City and Liverpool	5016
Glasgow, Scotland, via New York City	3522
Goldsboro, N. C., Erie Railway via Washington, D. C.	799
Goderich, Ont., via Grand Trunk Railway	160
Grand Haven, Mich., via Great Western Railway	442
Grand Island, Neb., via L. S. or G. W. Railways	1183
Great Falls, N. H., via New York Central Railroad	572
Great Bend, Pa., via Erie Railway	222
Greensboro, N. C., Erie Railway via Washington, D. C.	762
Greenland, via New York City	2233
Groton Junc., Mass., via New York Central Railroad	482
Guayaquil, Ecuador, via New York City and Panama	3233
Halifax, New York Central Railroad, via Boston	885
Hamilton, Ont., via Great Western Railway	67
Harrisburg, Pa., via Erie Railway	320
Harper's Ferry, Va., via Erie Railway	414
Hornellsville, N. Y., via Erie Railway	91
Hartford, Conn., via New York Central Railroad	426
Havre, France, via New York City	3581
Havana, Cuba, via New York City	1933
Havana, Cuba, via Lake Shore and New Orleans	1733
Haverhill, Mass., via New York Central Railroad	531
Hong Kong, China, via N. Y. City, Liverp'l & E. Ind.	14736
Hot Springs, Ark., via Lake Shore Railway	1075
Houston, Texas, Lake Shore via New Orleans	1802
Hudson, New York, via N. Y. C. Railroad	328
Humboldt, N. T., via L. S. or G. W. Railways	2519
Humboldt, Tenn., via Lake Shore Railway	843
Iceland, via New York City	2933
Indianapolis, Indiana, via Lake Shore Railway	465
Iowa City, Iowa, via Great Western Railway	774

TO PRINCIPAL POINTS. 251

Isle of Man, via New York City 3598
Ithaca, New York, via Erie Railway 206

Jackson, Mich., via Great Western Railway 329
Jackson, Miss, via Lake Shore Railway 1125
Jacksonville, Fla., Erie R'y via Washington, D. C. .. 1463
Jacksonville, Ill., via Lake Shore Railway 691
Japan, via Union Pacific and California 7680
Jefferson City, Mo., via Lake Shore Railway 853
Junction City, Kan., via Lake Shore Railway 1179

Kalamazoo, Mich., via Great Western Railway 397
Kansas City, Mo., via Lake Shore Railway 1010
Kenosha, Wis., via Great Western Railway 588
Kingston, Jamaica, via New York City 1635
Kingston, Ont., via Grand Trunk Railway 267
Knoxville, Tenn., via Lake Shore Railway 991

LaGrange, Kentucky, via Lake Shore Railway 521
Lancaster, Pa., via Erie Railway 357
Lansing, Mich., via Great Western Railway 366
Lafayette, Ind., via Lake Shore Railway 498
Laramie, W. T., via L. S. or G. W. Railways 1602
Lawrence, Mass., via New York Central Railroad .. 524
Leavenworth, Kan., via Lake Shore Railway 1037
Lexington, Kentucky, via Lake Shore Railway 540
Liberia, via New York City 4933
Lima, S. A., via New York City 3700
Little Rock, Ark., via Lake Shore Railway 1035
Littleton, N. H., New York Central Railroad 650
Liverpool, England, G. T. Railway, via Quebec ... 3179
Liverpool, England, via New York City 3519
Lockport, New York, via New York Central Railroad ... 28
Logansport, Ind., via Lake Shore Railway 461
London, England, via New York City 3658
London, Ont., via Great Western Railway 142

Londonderry, Ireland, via New York City............ 3602
Louisville, Kentucky, via Lake Shore Railway......... 548
Lowell, Mass., via New York Central Railroad........ 524
Lynchburg, Va., Erie R'y via Washington, D. C....... 621

Macon, Ga., via Lake Shore Railway................. 1125
Macon, Mo., via Lake Shore Railway................. 841
Madison, Wis., via Great Western Railway........... 675
Malta, via New York City and Liverpool.............. 5976
Mammoth Cave, Kentucky, via Lake Shore Railway.... 638
Manassas Junction, Va., Erie R'y via Washington, D. C. 477
Manilla, Phillippian Is'ds, via N. Y. City and Isthmus.. 11183
Mankato, Minn., via Great Western Railway.......... 1019
Manchester, N. H., via New York Central Railroad.... 515
Mattoon, Illinois, via Lake Shore Railway............ 594
Mazatlan, Mexico, via New York City and Panama..... 5158
Melbourne, Australia, via N. Y. City and Panama...... 11165
Memphis, Tenn., via Lake Shore Railway............. 925
Mendota, Ill., via Great Western Railway............ 621
Meridian, Miss., via Lake Shore Railway............. 1110
Michigan City, Ill., via Great Western Railway........ 482
Milwaukee, Wis., Gt. Western via Grand Haven....... 527
Minneapolis, Minn., via Gt. Western Railway......... 944
Mobile, Ala., Erie R'y via Washington, D. C.......... 1696
Mobile, Ala., via Lake Shore Railway................ 1383
Montrose, Scotland, via New York City.............. 4093
Monrovia, Liberia, via New York City............... 4283
Montreal, Quebec, via G. W. or G. T. Railways....... 439
Montpelier, Vt., via New York Central Railroad....... 473
Montgomery, Ala., via Lake Shore Railway........... 1197
Mouth of Rio Grande river, via L. S. and N. Orleans... 1948
Murfreesboro, Tenn., via Lake Shore Railway......... 765

Nangasaki, Japan, via New York City................ 9800
Nashville, Tenn., via Lake Shore Railway............ 733

Nashua, N. H., via New Central Railroad	500
Natural Bridge, Va., Erie R'y via Washington, D. C.	636
New Bedford, Mass., via New York Central Railroad	557
Newberne, N. C., Erie R'y via Washington, D. C.	858
Newburyport, Mass., New York Central Railroad	534
New Haven, Conn., via Erie Railway	499
New Orleans, La., via Lake Shore Railway	1308
New Orleans, La., Erie R'y via Washington, D. C.	1683
New Orleans, La., via Str. from New York City	2133
Newport, R. I., via New York Central Railroad	547
New York City, via Erie Railway	423
New York City, via New York Central Railroad	440
Niagara Falls, N. Y., via New York Central Railroad	22
North Platte, Neb., via L. S. or G. W. Railways	1320
Norfolk, Va., Erie R'y via Washington, D. C.	676
Ogdensburg, N. Y., via N. Y. Central Railroad	330
Ogden, U. T., via L. S. or G. W. Railways	2061
Oil City, Pa., via Lake Shore Railway	136
Omaha, Neb., via Great Western Railway	1929
Oswego, N. Y., via New York Central Railway	185
Owego, N. Y., via Erie Railway	186
Palatka, Fla.	1538
Palmer, Mass., via New York Central Railroad	415
Panama, Isthmus, via L. S. and New Orleans	2902
Pana, Illinois, via Lake Shore Railway	633
Paris, France, via New York City	3732
Paris, Ont., via Grand Trunk Railway	84
Peekskill, N. Y., via New York Central Railroad	400
Pensacola, Fla., via Lake Shore Railway	1355
Peoria, Ill., via Lake Shore Railway	633
Pernambuco, Brazil, via New York City	6353
Petersburgh, Va., Erie R'y via Washington, D. C.	595
Philadelphia, Pa., via Erie Railway	426

Pittsburgh, Pa., via Lake Shore Railway	236
Pittsfield, Mass., via New York Central Railroad	347
Plymouth, N. H., via New York Central Railroad	588
Portsmouth, N. H., via New York Central Railroad	554
Portland, Maine, via New York Central Railroad	609
Poughkeepsie, N. Y., via N. Y. Central Railroad	368
Prairie du Chien, Iowa, via Great Western Railway	720
Promontory, U. T., via L. S. or G. W. Railways	2113
Providence, R. I., via New York Central Railroad	497
Quebec, Prov. Quebec, via Grand Trunk Railway	597
Quincy, Ill., via Lake Shore Railway	771
Raleigh, N. C., Erie R'y via Washington, D. C.	751
Rawlings, W. T., via L. S. or G. W. Railways	1740
Reading, Mass., via New York Central Railroad	510
Reading, Pa., via Erie Railway	374
Richmond, Va., Erie R'y via Washington, D. C.	573
Rochester, N. Y., via New York Central Railroad	67
Rock Island, Illinois, via Great Western Railway	719
Rome, N. Y., via New York Central Railroad	188
Rome, Italy, via New York City	4633
Rutland, Vt., via New York Central Railroad	366
Sacramento, Cal., via L. S. or G. W. Railways	2803
Sacramento, Cal., via N. Y. City and Cape Horn	19280
Saginaw, Mich., via Great Western Railway	351
Salt Lake City, U. T., via L. S. or G. W. R'ys	2108
Salem, Mass., via New York Central Railroad	514
San Francisco, Cal., via L. S. or G. W. R'ys	2925
Sandwich Islands, via New York City	7590
Sandwich Islands, via Un. Pac. and Cal.	5020
Sanford, Fla.	1656
Saratoga, N. Y., via N. Y. Central Railroad	303
Sarnia, Ont., via Grand Trunk Railway	195
Sauk Rapids, Minn., via Great Western Railway	1011

Savannah, Ga., Erie R'y via Washington, D. C. 1202
Schenectady, N. Y., via New York Central Railroad ... 281
Scranton, Pa., via Erie Railway............................ 372
Sheridan, Kan., via Lake Shore Railway................. 1442
Sidney, Neb., via L. S. or G. W. Railways 1443
Singapore, India, via New York City.................... 13356
Sioux City, Iowa, via Lake Shore Railway 1080
Skowhegan, Maine, via N. Y. Central Railroad......... 709
Society Islands, via San Francisco and S. Islands...... 7410
Southampton, England, via New York City............. 3316
Springfield, Mass., via New York Central Railroad..... 400
Springfield, Ill., via Lake Shore Railway 657
St. Augustine, Fla. 1522
St. Catharines, Ont., via Great Western Railway....... 41
St. Joseph, Mo., via Lake Shore Railway............... 977
St. Louis, Mo., via Lake Shore Railway 728
St. Paul, Minn., via Great Western Railway 933
St. Petersburg, Russia, via New York City............. 4850
Stamford, Conn., via Erie Railway 458
Stratford, Ont., via Grand Trunk Railway............. 115
Syracuse, N. Y., via New York Central Railroad....... 150

Tampico, Mexico, via New York City 2933
Terre Haute, Ind., via Lake Shore Railway 538
Titusville, Pa., via Lake Shore Railway................ 118
Touno, Nev., via L. S. or G. W. Railways............. 2244
Tolono, Ind., via Lake Shore Railway.................. 581
Toledo, Ohio, via Lake Shore Railway 295
Toronto, Ont., via Great Western Railway............. 105
Trenton, N. J., via Erie Railway........................ 456
Troy, N. Y., via New York Central Railroad........... 301
Truckee, Cal., via L. S. or G. W. Railways............ 2683

Utica, N. Y., via New York Central Railroad 203
Vera Cruz, Mexico, via New York City................. 2633

Vicksburg, Miss., via Lake Shore Railway	1170
Vincennes, Ind., via Lake Shore Railway	603
Wabash, Ind., via Lake Shore Railway	431
Wahsatch, Utah, via L. S. or G. W. Railways	1997
Wardsworth, Nev., via L. S. or G. W. Railways	2614
Washington, D. C., via Erie Railway	443
Watertown, N. Y., via N. Y. Central Railroad	260
Waterbury, Conn., via N. Y. Central Railroad	489
Waterville, Me., via New York Central Railroad	692
Waverly, N. Y., via Erie Railway	167
Wells River, Vt., via New York Central Railroad	630
Welden, N. C., Erie Railway via Washington, D. C.	659
Westfield, Mass., via New York Central Railroad	390
White River Junction, N. H., via N. Y. C. Railroad	537
White Mountains, N. H., via N. Y. C. Railroad	580
Wilmington, N. C., Erie R'y via Washington, D. C.	821
Wilmington, Del., via Erie Railway	454
Williamsport, Pa., via Erie Railway	227
Winnemacea, Nev., via L. S. or G. W. Railways	2476
Worcester, Mass., via New York Central Railroad	454
Xenia, Ohio, via Lake Shore Railway	340
Yokohama, China, via New York City	12500
Yonkers, N. Y., via New York Central Railroad	426
Zanesville, Ohio, via Lake Shore Railway	330

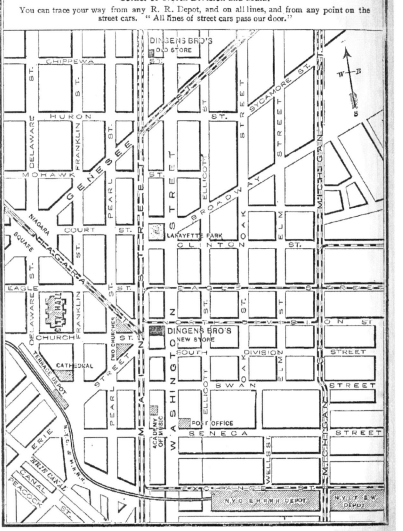

EPICUREAN DEPOT!!

READ CAREFULLY THIS

DESCRIPTIVE LIST AND CATALOGUE

OF STAPLE AND

FANCY GROCERIES,

IMPORTED AND DOMESTIC.

TABLE DELICACIES,

Wines, Liquors, Cigars, Mineral Waters, Etc., Etc.,

ON SALE BY

DINGENS BROTHERS,

IMPORTERS AND GROCERS,

No. 333 MAIN STREET, S. E. COR. OF NORTH DIVISION,

OPPOSITE THE TWO CHURCHES, HEAD OF NIAGARA STREET,

BUFFALO, N. Y.

SEE INDEX, PAGE 6.

It will pay you to visit our Store and see the Neatest, the Cheapest and Best Arranged Store west of New York City, carrying the Greatest Variety of

PURE AND FIRST CLASS GOODS

IN OUR LINE TO BE FOUND IN BUFFALO.

Read our Instructions "How to Buy,"—Page 4.

To our Patrons and the Public.

In presenting this "Descriptive list," of our Goods, **we beg leave to call your attention to the following facts :**

FIRST : This list necessarily cannot describe our whole stock, as we are daily adding novelties in the shape of Imported and Domestic Table Delicacies and staple goods as fast as they appear in the market. It only describes such goods as we had in stock at the time of publication.

SECOND : We could not quote prices on all goods, they fluctuate so frequently that it would occasion confusion ; but the Public can rest assured that we will continue to maintain our reputation of selling (quantity and quality considered), as low as the lowest. We receive no worthless or adulterated goods, because they are cheap, and to offer at seemingly good bargains to catch the unwary and careless buyer, but handle only sound, pure goods, *in qualities however, to suit both large and small purses.*

THIRD : We carry a larger variety of goods in our line than any house in Buffalo ; this fact is becoming generally known to the people of *Buffalo and vicinity*, and the liberal patronage received up to the present time, shows that there was a want of an establishment like ours in this city, and that it is appreciated.

It has always been our earnest endeavor to merit in every respect the confidence bestowed on us, by supplying the best, and *the best only*, of everything pertaining to our line of business, and that we have by so doing gained a liberal and constantly increasing patronage and popularity, is to us a matter of considerable pride.

With many thanks for past patronage, and soliciting a continuance of same, with the assurance that we will strive to maintain our present position of the

Leading Grocery House of Buffalo,

We are yours, most respectfully.

DINGENS BROTHERS.

How to Buy and Where.

There are two ways in which to supply your wants: One, to find a reliable merchant and make use of him whenever you have need; the other, to go in search of so called "bargains" offered by adventurers. In one case you will get your money's worth of honest goods—no more; in the other you will be served with spurious goods and only learn your loss, when your health tells you, you have been deceived.

WHAT ADVANTAGES CAN WE OFFER?

We buy for cash and sell for cash, therefore no losses or bad debts are added to the cost of goods—to be paid by the purchaser—a saving of ten per cent. at least. Our large sales enable us to buy large quantities, a saving of from 2 to 5 per cent., the benefit of which accrues to our patrons. Owing to rapid sales you are sure of getting Fresh Goods.

We give our patrons the option of the following modes of ordering:

To those who cannot visit us personally, to get our prices and leave their orders, we will state, that they can send us their orders by mail for about the quality of goods they want, and can rest assured that the order will be filled at the lowest market price, on day of receipt of order, or we will cheerfully quote prices on such goods as may be enquired for or wanted, and hold prices open for a reasonable length of time, and should the prices decline before shipment, our patrons will receive the benefit.

Our method of payment is as follows:

1. To responsible parties, furnishing satisfactory reference, goods will be shipped, subject to remittance after they have been received and examined.

2. C. O. D. by freight, to our firm name, and draft accompanied by Bill of Lading, made on the party ordering, through a Bank or Express Co.

3. C. O. D. by Express, (light packages, as teas, spices, etc., etc).

4. Cash, or Draft or Post Office Money Order to accompany the order for goods.

N. B. Make Checks, Post Office Orders or Drafts payable to the order of DINGENS BROTHERS.

When Clubs order from us, we parcel each one's goods separately, (if desired) and mark the names and contents plainly on each package, and pack in a barrel or box. **No charge for package, nor for cartage to depots.**

Address simply, DINGENS BROTHERS, Buffalo, N.Y.

SEE INDEX, PAGE 6.

NOTE THESE FACTS.

WE ARE HEAD-QUARTERS FOR "TEAS AND COFFEES."

Our combination "Java and Mocha Coffee" is acknowledged to be **The Coffee, Par Excellence,** and is acquiring a reputation that we are PROUD OF, and will endeavor to maintain at any cost.

The SECRET of its popularity is due, first, to the careful blending of the finest grades of Mocha and Java, in such proportions as to give a certain tone to the too mild properties of the Java (when used alone), by a sufficient quantity of the strong and subtle Mocha. *Independent* of this secret of the proper proportions, when we find the coffees that produce the desired result, we purchase the entire line, thereby insuring a continued similarity in our combination. Again, these large purchases which enable us to procure the goods at prices way below the price paid by Grocers who purchase only from second or third hands, enable us to give a better quality for the price we ask, than the generality of dealers.

Not one Grocer in ten, buys the green coffee and has it roasted, but sells you a coffee purchased from Spice Dealers, called Java and Mocha, and he nor you can tell what you are getting.

Last but not least, our large sales enable us to send out coffees freshly roasted. **We Roast Daily.**

We earnestly solicit a trial order of this **celebrated combination coffee,** feeling confident that its merits will be quickly recognized by the most fastidious.

Our Sugars and Syrups are strictly pure, and not adulterated with Glucose or Grape Sugar.

Our strictly Pure Ground Spices can be relied upon as represented.

Dingens Brothers' Catalogue.

INDEX.

By using the Index, customers will be greatly aided in making their selections.

A
67 Alum.
71 Ales.
13 Alkethrepta.
23 Anchovies.
28 Anchovy Paste.
17 Apple Butter.
22 Arrow Root.

B
27 Baking Powders.
22 Barley.
49 Baskets.
67 Bath Brick.
68 Bay Rum.
22 Beans.
67 Beeswax.
71 Beer.
25 Beef Salad.
67 Bird Food.
67 Bird Gravel.
55 Biscuits, (Fancy).
40 Blackings.
67 Blueings.
62 Bottles.
67 Borax.
73 Brandies.
48 Bread.
27 Bread Preparations.
13 Broma.
65 Brooms.
66 Brushes.
48 Butter.
22 Buckwheat Flour.

C
29 Capers.
26 Calves' Foot Jelly.
39 Canary Seed.
39 Caraway Seed.
36 Canton Ginger.
28 Catsups.
63 Candles.
67 Can Openers.
61 Castile Soaps.
23 Caviar.
39 Celery Seed.
67 Chloride of Lime.
14 Cheese.
23 Chowders.
10 Chocolates.
11 Chocolate Pastes.
5 Chicory.
67 Chamois Skins.
A 72 Cider.
16 Citron.
87 Cigars.
50 Clothes Lines.
2 Coffees.
3 Condensed Coffee.
12 Cocoa.
4 Coffee Extract.
22 Corn Meal.
69 Corks.
85 Cordials.
74 Cognacs.
51 Crocks.
55 Crackers.
67 Cream Tartar.
67 Cuttle Bone.
29 Curry Powder.
18 Currants.

D
52 Demijohns.

E
67 Electro Silicon.
48 Eggs.
24 Extract of Beef.

F
22 Farinaceous Goods.
22 Farina.
49 Faucets.
23 Fish, Canned.
23 do Dried.
23 do Salted.
23 do Smoked.
23 do In Oil.
22 Flours.
31 Flavoring Extracts.
19 Fruits, Green.
15 do Canned.
20 do In Glass.
20 do Preserved.
16 do Candied.
26 do Jellies.
17 do Butter & Jams.
18 do Dried.
20 do In Brandy.
16 do Dessicated.
26 do Marmalades.
21 Fruit Syrups & Juices.

G
70 Gelatine.
36 Ginger, all styles.
72 Ginger Ales.
22 Granum, Imperial.

H
59 Honey.
58 Hops.
22 Hominy.
58 Herbs, dried.
39 Hemp Seed.

I
35 Imported Table Delicacies.

J
26 Jellies.
51 Jugs.

INDEX.

L
48 Lard.
67 Laurel Leaves.
16 Lemon Peel.
22 Lentils.
21 Lime Juice.
67 Lye.

M
22 Manioca.
44 Matches.
22 Macaroni.
26 Marmalades.
71 Malthoptonique.
24 Meats, canned.
25   do smoked.
25   do dried, pickled,&c
86 Mineral Waters.
48 Milk, Condensed.
11 Milk Chocolate.
9 Mixed Spices.
8 Molasses.
57 Mustard, prepared.
35 Mushrooms.

N
56 Nuts.

O
22 Oat Meal.
41 Oils, table.
53 Olives.
23 Oysters.

P
68 Perfumery, etc.

47 Pickles.
67 Potash.
71 Porter.
67 Polishes.
58 Poultry Dressing.
24 Potted Meats.
18 Prunes.
48 Provisions.
77 Punches, prepared.
46 Puddings.

R
18 Raisins.
29 Relishes.
67 Rennet Liquid.
22 Rice.
67 Rock Candy.
85 Rock Candy & Rye.

S
67 Sal Soda.
23 Sardines.
67 Saleratus.
54 Salt.
28 Sauces.
25 Sausage.
42 Salad Dressing.
22 Sago.
67 Saltpeter.
39 Seeds.
30 Soaps, laundry.
60 Soaps, toilet.
64 Soups, canned.
9 Spices, whole.
9 Spices, ground.
6 Sugars.
38 Starch.

67 Sundries.
23 Shrimps.
7 Syrups.

T
22 Tapioca.
67 Tacks.
45 Tapers.
1 Teas.
67 Tooth Picks.
68 Toilet Sundries.
35 Truffles.
67 Twine.

V
33 Vegetables, green.
32   do canned.
34   do evaporated.
22   do dried.
32   do in glass.
22 Vermicelli.
43 Vinegars.

W
79 Wines.
26 Wine Jellies.
78 Whiskies.
49 Wooden Ware.
67 Whiting.
65 Whisk Brooms.

Y
37 Yeasts.

ADDITIONAL GOODS.

A
88 Ales and Beer.

C
89 Champagnes.
90 Cider.
91 Cordials.

92 Chocolates.
93 Coffee, Cocoa and Chocolate prepared.
94 Delicacies—Various.
95   " Imported.
96 Fruits in Glass.

97 Fruits in Glass, Imp'd.
98 Mustard and Mixed Spices.
99 Soap, Laundry.
100 " Castile.
101 Sundries.

REMEMBER

We handle *only Pure,* sound and first quality goods. Competitors may claim to sell as low or lower. Do not rely upon such arguments. A comparison of the goods both as to quality, quantity, and brand is the only reliable test.

1—TEAS.

Ah Yes!! Teas, next to our combination Java and Mocha Coffees—Teas are our hobby, and we invite the especial attention of consumers "to these facts." Our stock is large and we can suit any taste; our facilities for procuring the choicest and newest Teas to be had are unrivalled. We pack our Teas in tin canisters of one pound, and in fancy caddies of two to twenty pounds. No charge for package. Original packages hold from fifty to seventy-five pounds. T'is true we give no cheap chromos, crockery, or glass ware, but guarantee to give you *Quality and Full Weight,* which will leave you sufficient margin to buy better things than are given by concerns who hold out such inducements to catch the unwary and ignorant, besides evading the chances of being poisoned by inferior, spoiled or adulterated goods. We offer

Original packages contain about 65 lbs.

Young Hyson—Fair.
  do Good.
  do Choice.
  do Choice Moyune.
  do Choicest Moyune.
Old Hyson—Fine.

Original packages contain about 55 lbs.

Japan—Fair.
  do Good.
  do Choice.
  do Choicest.
Japan Siftings.—Good.
  do Choicest.

Chests about 65 lbs.

Basket Fired Japan.—Extra Choice.
Gunpowder—Choice.
  do Choicest.

Chests about 40 lbs.

Oolong—Amoy Fair.
  do do Choice.
  do do Extra Choice.

Formosa—Extra.
  do Extra Choice.
English Breakfast—Choice.
  do Extra Choice.

2—COFFEES.—Green.

Bags hold about 135 lbs.

Rio—Fair.
 do Choice.
 do Extra Fancy.

La Guayra—Extra.

Maracaibo—Choice.
  do Extra Choice.

Mats about 68 lbs.

Java Old Gov.—Fair.
  do do Extra.
  do do Fancy Mandehling.

¼ and ½ pockets, 25 to 50 lbs.

Mocha—The Best.

Roasted Coffees.

In sacks of about 100 lbs.

Rio—Fair.
 do Choice.
 do Extra Fancy.

Maracaibo—Choice.
  do Extra.
Old Gov. Java—Fine.
  do do Fancy Mandehling.
Mocha—Finest.
Our Combination Java and Mocha.

See argument, page 5.

Ground Coffee.

In 1 lb. sealed glass jars.

Cafe des Gourmets.

Our Liquid Java and Mocha Combination Coffee

Is prepared in an instant, with either hot water or hot milk; no waste of time, nor loss of material.

In pint bottles, $3.00 per doz.

3—CONDENSED COFFEE.

Borden's—¼ lb. Tins.
" 1 lb. Tins.

4—COFFEE EXTRACT.

German, in Foil.

5—CHICORY.

Chicory.—Loose.
   do   German, in Yellow Paper.

6—SUGARS.

Cut Loaf.
Crushed.
Granulated.
Powdered.
Coffee A.
Coffee B.
Coffee C.
Yellow.

Barrels contain from 280 to 300 lbs.

Maple Sugar.

In bricks of about 5 lbs.

7—SYRUPS.

Rock Candy Drips.
Loaf Sugar Syrup.
Silver Drips.
Golden Drips.

Maple Syrup.—1 Gallon Cans.
               ½ Gallon Cans.
               ¼ Gallon Cans.
               ¼ Bottles.

8—MOLASSES.

Porto Rico.
New Orleans.

9—SPICES, WHOLE.

Allspice.
Cinnamon.
Cloves.
Mace.
Nutmegs.

Pepper, Common.
   do   Shot.
   do   White.
Ginger, Jamaica.
   do   African.
Mixed Spices—Durkee's.

Spices Ground, Loose.
Allspice.
Cinnamon or Cassia.
Cloves.
Mace.
Mustard.
Pepper, Shot.
   do   White.
   do   Cayenne.
Ginger—Ground, Jamaica.
   do   do   African.

Spices in Packages.

ALLSPICE—¼ lb. Tins.
            ¼ lb. Bottles.
            ½ lb. do
            1 lb. do

CINNAMON—¼ lb. Tins.
             ¼ lb. Bottles.
             ½ lb. do
             1 lb. do

CLOVES—¼ lb. Tins.
          ¼ lb. Bottles.
          ½ lb. do
          1 lb. do

MACE—¼ lb. Bottles.

PEPPER—Common, ¼ lb. Tins.
   do   Singapore (Shot), black.
   do   do   do   ¼ lb. Bottles.
   do   do   do   ½ lb. do
   do   do   do   1 lb. do
   do   White,   ¼ lb. do
   do   do   ½ lb. do
   do   do   1 lb. do
   do   Cayenne, 1 oz. do
   do   do   2 oz. Cruets.

The Spices in Glass are the famous Pinckney Pure Spices.

10—CHOCOLATE.

Baker's Premium, not sweet.
Brooks' do   do
Maillard's do   do
   do   Sweet.
   do   do triple Vanilla.

Menier's Chocolates, Etc
See No. 02.

11—CHOCOLATE PASTES.

Wallace's, Vanilla Cream, 1 ℔ pots.
Mack's Milk Chocolate, 1 ℔ tins.
N. B.—These Chocolate Pastes are ready for immediate use, requiring simply the addition of hot water. A spoonful of the paste makes a cup of chocolate.

12—COCOA.

Baker's, ½ ℔ foil.
Brooks', ½ ℔ tins.
Epps' Breakfast Cocoa, ½ lb tins.
Maillard's ½ ℔ tins.
Brooks' Breakfast Cocoa, ½ lb tins.
Baker's Cocoa Shells, 1 ℔ packages.

13—BROMA.

Baker's ½ ℔ foil.
Brooks' ½ ℔ tins.
Alkethrepta, 1 ℔ tins.

14—CHEESE.

American Dairy.
Edam, Holland, Imported.
Cheddar, English, Imported.
Cheddar, American.
Creme de Brie, Imported.
Fromage de Menauta, Imported in tins,
Fromage de Brie, Imported.
French Cream Cheese, Imported,
Neufchatel, Imported.
Parmasan, C. & B. grated, in bottles for Macaroni and Sandwiches, Imported.
Swiss, Gruyere, Imported.
Sap Sago, Imported.
Pine Apple.
Young America.
Roquefort, Imported.
Old Brandy Cheese, in foil, 20 cts. each.
Hamburgh Dairy.

15—FRUITS, CANNED.

Apricots, California, 3 ℔.
Apples, 3 ℔.
Blackberries, E. H., 2 ℔.
Cherries, California White Wax, 3 ℔.
  do   Black Tartarian, E. H., 2 ℔.
  do   White Wax.
  do   Pitted Sour, E. H., 2 ℔.
  do   do   E. H., 2 ℔.
Grapes, California, 3 lbs.
Nectarines, California, 3 lbs.

Peaches, Cottage, 3 lbs.
  do   White Heath, 3 lbs.
  do   Extra Yellow, 3 lbs.
  do   California, 3 lbs.
Pine Apple, 2 lbs.
  do   whole.
Plums, California Egg, 3 lbs.
  do   do   Golden Drop, 3 lbs.
  do   do   Green Gages, 3 lbs.
  do   do   Damson, 3 lbs.
Pears,   do   Bartlett, 3 lbs.
  do   do   2 lbs.
Quinces, California, 3 lbs.
  do   2 lbs.
Raspberries, Red, E. H., 2 lbs.
Raspberries, Black, E. H., 2 lbs.
Strawberries, E. H., 2 lbs.

16—FRUITS.

Candied and Dessicated.

Assorted, Imported, ½ and 1 lb. cartoons
Candied Ginger, loose.
  do   do   1 lb. tins.
  do   lemon peel.
  do   orange peel.
  do   citron.

Cocoanuts.

Dessicated, ½ lb. and 1 lb. cartoons.
  do   1 lb. tins fancy caddies.

17—FRUIT BUTTERS & JAMS.

Apple Butter.
Plum   do
Lake Superior Rasp'y. Jam, 1 Gal. Jugs.
Scotch Raspberry Jam, Dundee, in pots.
  do   do & Currant Jam, Dundee, in small pots.
  do   Strawberry Jam, Dundee.
West India Tamarinds in small stone Jars.

18—FRUITS, DRIED.

Apples, evaporated.
Apricots, do
Blackberries.
Cherries.
Peaches.
Raspberries, red and black.
Citron.
Currants.
Dates.
Figs, loose.
  do in boxes or baskets, assorted sizes.
Lemon Peel.

Orange Peel.
Prunelles, loose.
   do   small boxes.

PRUNES.

Turkish, loose.
French, fair.
  do   choice.
  do   choicest.
  do   2 lb. glass jars.
  do   in brandy.

RAISINS.

Valencia, cooking, loose.
Loose Muscatel,   do
London Layer,   do
  do   do   ¼ boxes.
Dehesa, loose.
  do layer, ¼ boxes.
Sultana, seedless.

19—FRUITS—Green.

Bananas, red and yellow.
Cranberries.
Lemons.
Oranges, Florida.
  do   Valencia.
  do   Messina.
Grapes, Malaga.

20—FRUITS IN GLASS.

Apricots, (au Jus), imported, pts.
  do (au Jus) do   qts.
Blackberries, G. & D.
Cherries,   do
Citron,   do
Damsons,   do
Figs,   do
Ginger,   do
Green Gages, do
Limes,   do
Peaches,   do
Raspberries, do
Strawberries, do
Tamarinds,   do
Green Figs, (au Jus) imported pints.
Prunes,   do   do   do
Pears,   do   do   do
Mirabelles, do   do   do
Pine Apple, K. & D., quarts.
Pears, Perry's Bartlett, quarts.
  do   do   ½ gall.
  do   do   1 gallon.
Pitted Red Cherries, pints and quarts.
Red Raspberries,   do   do
Quinces, Perry's,   do

Peaches in brandy.
Prunes in brandy.

21—FRUIT SYRUPS & JUICES.

Blackberry Juice.
    do   Syrup.
Cherry Juice.
Lime Juice.
Raspberry Juice.
    do   Syrup.
Lemon do

22—FARINACEOUS GOODS.

Arrow Root, (Bermuda) ¼ lb. papers.
Beans, Navy.
  do   Marrowfat.
  do   Black Turtle, imported, for soups
Barley.
Buckwheat flour, Binghampton, loose and 12½ and 25 lb. sacks.
Corn Meal, white.
  do   yellow.
Corn, (Shakers' dried).
  do Pop.
Crushed Indian.
Farina, Hecker's, 1 lb. papers.
  do Akron,   do
Fancy Pastes for soups, stars and crescents.
Flour, Epicurean, New Process.
  do T. & C. Best.
  do Banner.
  do Globe Mills.
At Mill Prices, in bbls., ½ bbls., ¼ bbls. and ⅛ bbls.
Granum, Imperial, ½ lb. and 1 lb.
Graham Flour, loose.
        do in 10 lb. sacks.
Hominy, coarse and fine, 2 and 5 lb. packages.
Lentils, loose.
Manioca, 1 lb. papers.
Macaroni, 1 lb. packages, Italian.
    do   6 lb. cartoons, French.
Oat Meal, Akron Mills loose.
  do   2 and 5 lb. packages.
  do   Irish.
  do   Scotch.
Peas, split, loose.
Pumpkin Flour, 1 lb. tins.
Rice, Carolina.
  do   fancy.
Rice flour, 1 lb. papers.

Steam Cooked Oats.
   do   do   Wheat.
Sago, German White, loose.
Tapioca, flake.
   do   Pearl.
Vermicelli, 1 lb. packages.
   do   6 lb. Cartoons.
Wheat, Cracked Pearl, 2 lb. packages.
Wheat Meal, 10 lb. sacks.

23—FISH.

Anchovies, in salt, glass.
   do   in oil,   do
   do   in kegs, spiced.
   eo   Pot Luck in tins.
Bloaters, Yarmouth.
Caviar, Russian, ½, 1 and 2 lb. cans.
Clams, 1 and 2 lb. cans.
Clam, (chowder) 3 lb. cans.
Codfish, whole.
   do   boneless, loose.
   do   do   in 5 lb. cartoons.
Codfish balls, 2 lb. cans.
Chowder, fish, 3 lb. do
Eels, in jelly, Hamburg, 1 and 2 lb. cans.
Finnan Haddies.
Halibut, smoked.
Herring, salt, Holland, in kegs.
   do   smoked boneless.
   do   broiled, soused, in tins.
   do   do   tomato sauce, in tins.
Lobster, 1 and 2 lb. cans.
Mackerel, Extra Mess, salt, loose.
   do   Breakfast, 5 and 10 lb. tins.
   do   No,1 Shore,15 and 20 lb. kits.
   do   No. 2 do 15   do.
   do   No.1 Extra Mess, 15 & 18 lb. kits.
   do   Fresh broiled tomato sauce, tins.
   do   do   mustard do   do.
   do   do   soused do   do.
   do   do   1 and 2 lb. cans.
Oysters, Cove, 1 and 2 lb. tins.
   do   pickled, glass reservoir jars.
   do   do   in glass bottles.
Salmon, 1 and 2 lb. cans.
   do   spiced, 2 lb. cans.
Sardelles, in glass jars and kegs.

SARDINES.

LeMarchand, boneless, half boxes.
A. G.,   do   do.
Penanross,   do   do.
Alex. Eyquem, do   do.
Sardines Marinees, spiced do.
Sardines, with bones, assorted brands.
Sardines, with bones, assorted brands, quarter boxes.
Shrimps, (for salads) 1 lb. cans.
Trout, Sea, broiled, tins.
   do   Brook, do   do
English Breakfast Herring, broiled.

24—MEATS—Canned.

Cooked Corned Beef, 1 lb., 2 lb., 4 lb., 6 lb., 10 lb. and 14 lb. tins.
R. & R., Lunch Ham.
   do   do   Tongue.
   do   do   Turkey.
   do   Roast Turkey.
   do   Potted Ham.
   do   do   Tongue.
   do   do   Turkey.
   do   do   Chicken.
C. & B. Imported Potted Beef.
   do   do   do   Tongue.
   do   do   do Strasbourg Meats.
Underwood's Deviled Ham.
   do   do   Tongue.
   do   do   Turkey.
Huckin's Sandwich Ham.
   do   do   Tongue.
   do   do   Turkey.
   do   do   Chicken.
English Brawn, 2 lb. tins.
Lamb's Tongue, fresh, 1 lb. tins.
Cocks' Combs, Imported, in glass jars.

Extracts of Beef.

Liebig's, 2 oz. jars.
   do   4 do.

25—MEATS.

Smoked, Dried and Pickled.

Miles Jones' Sons Hams.
   do   Bacon.
Royal Hams.
Westphalia, Imported Hams.
Boneless Ham in sacks.
Cervelat Sausage.
Saveloy   do
Imported Liver Sausage, Truffled, in tins.
Dried Beef, sliced and whole.
Ox feet and snout salad, in glass jars.
Pickled Tripe   do
   do   Pigs' feet   do
   do   Tongues, in glass jars.
Beef Salad.

26—JELLIES & MARMALADES.

Apple Jelly, a la Vanille, Imported.
Red Currant various sizes tumblers.
   do   G & D   do
Black Currant do   do
Raspberry   do   do
Grape   do   do
Strawberry   do   do
Blackberry   do   do
Apple   do   do
Crab Apple   do   do
Orange   do   do
Lemon   do   do
Quince   do   do
Cherry   do   do
Cranberry, tin pails.
Guava Jelly, ½ and whole Boxes.
Calves' Foot Jelly, C. & B. quart Bottles.
  do do & Wine do   do   do
Apricot Marmalade.
Orange   do Scotch, Dundee.
  do   do   Thurber's.

The Celebrated Wine Jellies of F. S. Siegrist & Co., California.

Port Wine—Quarts Flagons.
Dry Muscat   do   do
Golden Tokay do   do
Angelica   do   do
Madeira   do   do

27—BAKING POWDER
and Bread Preparations.

Our Baking Powders can be relied upon as being strictly pure. We handle no cheap and worthless brands.

ROYAL BAKING POWDER.

¼, ½, and 1 lb. Tins.
Holman's, ¼, ½, and 1 lb. Cartoons.
De Land's 1 lb. Tins.
Moon's, Loose.
Baking Soda, 1 lb. papers.
Saleratus, 1 lb. papers.
Cream Tartar, ¼ lb., ½ lb. 1lb. & papers.

28—SAUCES AND CATSUPS.

Anchovy Sauce, C. & B.
  do   Paste,   do fancy jars.
  do   Butter, French.
Bengal Chutney Sauce.
Halford Sauce.
John Bull Sauce.
Sultana Sauce.
Tomato Sauce.
Mushroom Sauce.
Tobasco Sauce.
Walnut Sauce.
Worcestershire L. & P. Sauce.
Monticello's Tomato Catsup, ½ pts.
    do   do   pts.
Cayuga   do   ½ pts.
    do   do   pts.
C. B. Imperial do   qts.
G. & D.   do   qts.
C. & B. Mushroom Catsup, ½ pts.
    do Walnut do   ½ pts.

29—RELISHES.

Curry Powder, C. & B., glass bottles.
Celery Salt, in cruets.
Capers, Capotte, large bottles.
  do   Nonpareil, do
  do   do   half do
Horse Radish, grated, in glass.

30—SOAPS—LAUNDRY.

R. W. Bell & Co.'s Soaps.

Extra family, long bar, 40 bars per box.
Favorite, 1 lb. do 70 do   do
New Era, ¾ lb. do 100 do   do

Lautz Bros. & Co.'s Soaps.

Extra dry family, long bar, 40 bars per box
Extra   do   do   40 do do
Master,   ¾ lb. bar, 100 do do
Acme,   1 lb. do   70 do do

B. T. Babbitt's Soaps.

Best Soap, ¾ lb. bars, 100 bars per box.

American Laundry.

1 lb. bars, 75 bars per box.

Miller's Yankee Laundry.

The Finest Laundry Soap made, for the price asked.
1 lb. bars, 70 bars per box.

Colgate's Laundry Pure.

¾ lb. bars, 12 bars per box.

Dobbins' Electric.
¼ lb. bars, 60 bars per box.

"Kitchen" Crystal.
1 lb. bars, 60 bars per box.

Enoch Morgans' Sons Sapolio.

31—FLAVORING EXTRACTS.
Burnett's Extracts.
Vanilla, 2 oz. bottle.
do   5 oz.   do
do   8 oz.   do
Lemon, 2 oz. do
do   5 oz.   do
do   8 oz.   do
Almond, 2 oz. do
Cloves, 2 oz. do
Celery, 2 oz. do
Cinnamon, 2 oz. do
Ginger, 2 oz. do
Orange, 2 oz. do
Peach, 2 oz. do
Rose, 2 oz.

Colton's Extracts.
Vanilla, 2 oz. bottle.
do   4 oz.   do
do   8 oz.   do
Lemon, 2 oz. do
do   4 oz.   do
do   8 oz.   do

Lupin's.
Vanilla, 2 oz. bottle.
Lemon, 2 oz. do

Pickering's Extracts.
Vanilla, 2 oz. bottle.
Lemon, 2 oz. do

32—CANNED VEGETABLES.
Asparagus, G. & D.
    do   Oyster Bay.
Beans, string, E. H. 2 lbs.
    do   do   Baltimore, 2 lbs.
    do   stringless, Imported, 2 lbs.
    do   Lima, Baltimore, 2 lbs.
    do   Boston Baked, 3 lbs.
    do   Perry's, in glass jars.
Corn, E. H. 2 lbs.
    do   Perry's, in glass jars.
Okra, 3 lbs.

Pumpkin, 3 lbs.
Peas, Marrowfat, E. H. 2 lbs.
    do   Champion, 2 lbs.
    do   Early, 2 lbs.
    do   E. H., French, 1 lb.
    do   Imported Moyene.
    do   do   Extra.
    do   do   Extra Choix.
Succotash, E. H., 2 lbs.
Tomatoes, E. H., 3 lbs.
    do   E. H., Solid Meats, 3 lbs.
    do   E. H., Standard, 3 lbs.
    do   do   1 Gallon.

33—VEGETABLES, Green.
Onions.
Potatoes,

34—VEGETABLES, Evaporated.
Mixed, (for Soups,) 1 lb boxes.

35—IMPORTED TABLE DELICACIES.
Cocks Combs in glass.
Mushrooms, in tins, choice.
    do   extra   do
    do   extra choice button.
    do   in glass—choice.
Pates de Fois Gras—tins.
Truffles—in glass.
    do   in tins.
Truffled Liver Sausage—tins.

36—GINGER ROOT.
African, whole—loose.
Jamaica, do   do
African, ground, do
Jamaica, do   do
    do   ¼, ½, and 1 lb. bottles.
Canton, preserved—¼ pots.
    do   do   ½ pots.
    do   do   whole pots.
Candied—loose.
    do   1 lb. tins and 7 lb tins.

37—YEASTS.
Fleischmann's, compressed.
Twin Brothers, dry.
National, dry.

38—STARCH.
Kingsford's Oswego Gloss Starch—40 lb. boxes, loose.
Kingsford's Oswego Silver Gloss—6 lb. boxes.

Kingsford's Oswego Silver Starch—3 lb. boxes.
Kingsford's Oswego Silver Starch—1 lb. papers.
Kingsford's Oswego Corn Starch—1 lb. papers.
Gilbert's Patent Gloss Starch—40 lb. boxes
Gilbert's Patent Gloss Starch—6 lb. boxes.
Gilbert's Patent Gloss Starch—1 lb. papers.
Gilbert's Patent Corn Starch—1 lb. papers.
Niagara Gloss Starch—1 lb. papers.
   do   do   do.   6 lb. boxes.
   do   Corn do.   1 lb. boxes.
Buffalo Grape Sugar Starch—loose.
Buffalo Grape Sugar Gloss Starch—6 lb. boxes.
Buffalo Grape Sugar Gloss Starch—1 lb. boxes.
Buffalo Grape Sugar Corn Starch—1 lb. boxes.
Dobbin's Starch Polish.

39—SEEDS.
Canary.
Caraway.
Celery.
Hemp.
Mustard (white).
Mustard (black).
Mixed bird seed (1 lb. boxes).
Rape seed.

40—BLACKING.
Day & Martin's Liquid English.
Small bottles.
Medium do.
Large do.
Jacquot's French.
Nos. 2, 3, 4, 5, tins.
Japanese Liquid Polish, bottles, designed for ladies' fine shoes.
Wyat's American Blacking, Nos. 2 and 4—tins.

41—OLIVE OILS.
Boutellau fils—full pints.
   do   do quarts.
Barton and Guestier—pints.
   do   do   quarts.
Bertrand freres—pints.

E. Loubon, Nice—pints and half-pints.
Italian, Wicker'd bottles.

42—SALAD DRESSING.
Monticello—pints and half-pints.
Durkee's—large pints.
Gordon & Dilworth's—pints.

43—VINEGARS.
Bottled, Wine Vinegar, quarts.
C & B Malt Vinegar, quarts, imported.
Louit Freres, a l'estragon, quarts.
   do   au Naturel quarts.
Imported wine vinegar on draught,
Native   do   do.   do.
Pure Cider   do   do.
Grape, white,   do   do.

44—MATCHES.
S & C Sulphur No. 4.
   do   do   No. 4½
   do   do   No. 7.
   do Parlor 80 s.
   do   do   200 s.
   do   do   500 s.
   do   do in tins of 1 doz., 500 s, $1.
   do   do   do., 1 gross, 80 s., $3.25

45—TAPER.
S & C, Wax ¼ lb. boxes.

46—PLUM PUDDING.
R & R, 1 lb. cans.
   do   2 do   do
   do   3 do   do

47—PICKLES.
Domestic.
Obelisk, small glass jars.
Windsor M. Picolos, small glass jars.
   do   onions, do do do
Brooks mixed, quart glass jars.
   do Gherkins, do do do
Monticello.
Chow-chow, quarts and pints.
Mixed Pickles, do   do
Gherkins do   do
Autumn Clusters, "   do
Stuffed Mangoes, "   do
Tiny tins, pints and ½ pints.
Cauliflower, pints.
Picklette, pints.

Dingens Brothers' Catalogue.

IMPORTED.

C. & B. Chow Chow, pts and qts.
do Piccalilli, do do
do Cauliflower, do do
do Mixed Pickles, do do
do Girkins, do do
do Walnuts, do do
do Onions, do do

48—PROVISIONS, &c.

Butter.

We make a specialty of the choicest family Butter, both in crocks and one pound prints. We receive every second day the fresh churnings of the Allen Creamery Co., of Grand Island, made from the milk of the finest breed of Alderney cows, and consumers of this butter are assured of having fresh, clean and handsomely ornamented prints, pleasing to the eye and delightful to the palate.

Eggs.

Warranted fresh and at market prices.

Bread, French.
do Vienna.
Lard, 3 lbs, tin pails.
do 5 do
do 10 do
Milk, condensed.
Borden's Eagle Brand.
Swiss, Imported.
Mince Meat.
Potatoes, Sweet.
do Irish.
do Saratoga Chips.

49—WOODEN WARE.

Baskets.

Market Baskets.
Grocers' do
Bushel do
Willow Clothes Baskets.
Covered Baskets.

Pails.

Wooden, 2 hoops.
do 3 do
Red Cedar, 3 Brass Hoops.
White do 3 do do
Horse pails.

Tubs.

Large.
Medium.
Small.
Keelers.

Washboards.

Zinc.
Combination.
Wooden.
Mop Sticks.
Clothes Pins.
Rolling Pins.
Faucets, small.
do medium.
do large.
do metal keys.
do for ice boxes.
Potato Mashers.
Chopping Boards.

50—CLOTHES LINES.

Hemp.
Jute.
Manilla.
White Cotton, 40, 60, 80 and 100 feet.

51—CROCKS and JUGS, (stone.)

1 gallon Butter Crocks.
2 do do do
3 do do do
4 do do do
5 do do do
6 do do do
1 quart stone Jugs.
½ gallon do do
1 do do do
2 do do do
3 do do do

52—DEMIJOHNS.

¼ gallon.
½ do
1 do
2 do
3 do
5 do

53—OLIVES.

Selected Queen, Monticello, 20 oz.
do do do 30 do
do do G. & D. 27 do
do do W. & R. 27 do
do do S. & V. quarts.
do do do pints.

French Crescent "Lucques" pints.
French Verdales, G. & D.   do
Stuffed Olives.
Louit Freres, Olives Farcies, pints.
  do   do   half pints.

54—SALT.
Celery Salt in Cruets.
Imported Table Salt, C. & B. Stone Jars.
  do   Liverpool, 5 lb sacks.
  do   do   10 do do
  do   Ashland, 1 bushel sacks.
Dairy Salt, 5 lbs sacks.
  do   10 do do
  do   1 bushel sacks.
  do   in barrels.

55 CRACKERS and BISCUITS.
Imported.
Albert Biscuits, in Tins.
Carlsbad's Wafers, do
Sugar Wafers, P. F. & Co., do Lemon.
  do   do   do   do Vanilla.

Domestic, (not sweet.)
Bent's Cold water Crackers.
Boston Butter Crackers, Kennedy's.
Butter Crackers, Ovens'.
Cream   do   Kennedy's.
Champion cream Crackers.
Climax Soda   do
Graham Wafers, Kennedy's.
Milk Biscuit, Ovens'.
Moravian Pretzels.
Oat meal Wafers, Kennedy's.
Oyster Crackers. Fox's.
  do   do   Ovens'.
Soda   do   "
Thin Water Biscuits, 3 lb. tins.
Zephyr, or Pastry Wafers.

Sweet Biscuits.
Animals.
Balmorals.
Cream Cracknels.
Cornhills.
Cocoanut Taffy.
Egg Biscuits.
Egg Jumbles.
Fruit Biscuits.
Ginger Snaps.
Honey Jumbles.
Jumbles, assorted.
Kindergarten.

Lemon Snaps.
Maccaroons.
Menagerie.
Oswego, 1 lb. tins.
Perkins, or Nut Cookies.
Vanilla Bar.

We are continually adding new varieties and can suit almost any taste.

56—NUTS.
Almonds, Princess Paper shells.
  do   Lisbon.
  do   Tarragona.
  do   shelled, Sicily sweet.
  do   do   bitter.
Brazil Nuts.
Cocoanuts.
Filberts.
Hickory Nuts.
Pecan Nuts.
Walnuts, Grenoble.

57—MUSTARDS, Prepared.
Imported.
Dijon, large and small fancy pots.
Bordeaux,   do   do   do
Bordelaise, large and small glass jars.
Anchovy Mustard, glass jars.

58—HERBS.
Hops, ½ and 1 lb. papers.
Marjorum, ¼ lb. tins.
Summer Savory, ¼ lb. Tins.
Sage, ¼ lb. tins.
Thyme, ¼ lb. tins.
Bell's Poultry Seasoning, small cans.
  do   do   do   large do

59—HONEY.
In the comb, small boxes.

Strained, in tumblers.
  do   pints, glass jars.
  do   quarts, do do
  do   ½ gallon glass jars.

60—SOAPS, TOILET.
We have a full assortment varying in price from 4 cents per cake, upwards.

Almond Meal Soap.
Baby   do
Brown Windsor do
Bay Leaf   do
Bay Rum   do

Elder Flower, giant Soap.
   do   do diamond do
   do   do in Bars.
Glycerine, white Soap.
   do   pure   do
   do   No. 19, do
   do   Giant   do
   do   Imperial Soap.
Honey No. 1, Soap.
   do   pure   do
   do   No. 18, do
Hand Sapolio   do
London Toilet   do
Mineral   do
Musk Windsor   do
Musk Rose   do
Naiad Queen   do
Newport Glycerine Soap.
   do   Honey   do
   do   Windsor do
Oatmeal Glycerine do
   do   in Bars,   do
Palm Oil   do
   do do in Bars, do
Palace   do
Rice Flower   do
Silver   do
Shaving   do
Sand   do
Transparent Glycerine Soap.
Tar and Glycerine   do
Turtle Oil   do
Zahater   do

61—CASTILE SOAPS.

White, Conti Brand
  do   A. G.
Mottled.

62—BOTTLES.

Half pint Flasks, amber.
Pint   do   do
Half do do green.
Pint   do   do
N. Y. Wines, amber, sixes
  do   do   do fives.
Champagnes, quarts.
     do   pints.
Clarets, fives.
Hocks, do

63—CANDLES.

Common Stearine, 6 to the pound.

Adamantine, Hotel, 12 do do
     do   6 do do
Parrafine Wax, 12 do do
  do   do   6 do do
  do   do   4 do do
  do   do assorted colors, 6 to the lb.
  do   do   do   4 do do
Patent Sperm, 6 to the pound.
  do   do   4 do do

64—SOUPS, (canned.)

Huckins' Beef,   3 lb. cans.
  do   Chicken, do do
Consomme,   do do
Green Turtle,   do do
Haricot Mutton, do do
Irish Stew,   do do
Julienne,   do do
Mock Turtle,   do do
Mutton Broth,   do do
Mulligatawney, do do
Ox Tail,   do do
Okra,   do do
Tomato,   do do
Green Turtle stock, do do

Brunswick Soups.
Each Tin contains stock for 5 pints of excellent soup.
Beef.
Vegetable
Ox Tail.
Mock Turtle.
Kidney with Mushrooms.

65—BROOMS.

Whisk Brooms, No. 00   wood handles.
  do   do   do 2 B. H. do   do
  do   do   do 2 O. K. do   do
  do   do   do 3 O. K. do   do
  do   do   small, medium, large Broom, whisk handles.
Carpet do Extra.
  do   do No. 7.
  do   do do 6.
  do   do do 5.
Stable do
Street do
Ceiling do
Children's Brooms.

66—BRUSHES.

Shoe Brushes, in sets, 3 pieces.
  do   Fancy.
  do   No. 1 and No. 2.
  do   Daubers.

Clothes Brushes, No. 1.
Horse   do   Leather Back.
Scrub   do   Nos. 1 and 2.
  do   do   Fancy.
  do   do   Root, Nos. 1 and 2.
Stove   do

67—SUNDRIES.

Alum.
Bath Brick.
Beeswax.
Bird Food, small boxes.
Bird Gravel   do
Blueing, dry, small boxes.
   "   liquid 4 oz. pts and qts. glass.
Borax, Powd'd Persian, ½ and 2 lb pkgs
Can openers.
Chloride of Lime. ¼, ½ and 1 lb boxes.
Chamois Skins.
Cream Tartar. Loose, ¼, ½ and 1 lb
   packages.
Cuttle Bone.
Electro Silicon.
Nutmeg Graters.
Pickle Forks.
Laurel Leaves.
Liquid Rennet, ½ pts Glass.
Lye, in 1 lb Tins.
Potash, in Balls.
   do   1 lb Tins.
Rock Candy, White.
   do   Yellow.
   do   Red.
Scouring Polish, Dobbins'.
Sal Soda, Granulated, loose.
Saleratus, 1 lb papers.
Saltpeter, loose.
Stove Polish, Dixon's.
   do   Prescott's.
Tacks.
Tooth Picks, wood.
Twine.
Whiting.

68—TOILET SUNDRIES.

Bay Rum, sprinkle tops, ½ pts.
   do   do   pints.
Burnett's Triple Cologne.
4 oz. Wicker bottles.
8 oz. do   do
16 oz. do   do
4 oz. Glass do
8 oz. do   do
16 oz. do   do
Magnolia Florida Water.

69—CORKS.

Taper, all sizes, from No. 4, 5-8 in. in diameter, to No. 22, 1¾ in. in diameter.

Fine wine corks, x and xx, No. 9, 1½ in,, 1¾ and 2 in long.

70—Gelatine.

Cox's Imported, small packages.
Chalmer's, do.
Nelson's Sheet Gelatine, loose.

SEE LAST PAGE FOR ADDITIONAL GOODS.

71—ALES, &c.
Imported.

Packed in barrels of 8 doz pints.
   do   do   4 do quarts.
   do   cases of 4 do pints.
Bass' Pale Ale, pints.
   do do do quarts.
Younger's Scotch Ale, pints.
Guinness' Extra Dublin Stout and Porter pints.
Burton's Malthoptonique, pints.

Imported Lager Beer.
Kaiser pints.
Pilsner pints.
Erlanger pints.

Domestic Lager Beer.
Milwaukee pints, Patent Stoppers.
Niagara Falls, pints,   do
Buffalo,   do   do

72—GINGER ALE.

We are the wholesale agents for Buffalo and vicinity for Ross' Celebrated Belfast Ginger Ale, packed in casks of 10 doz. bottles—$1.40 per dozen. Discount according to quantity.
Cantrell & Cochrane's Belfast Ginger Ale.
Vincent Hathaway's Boston Ginger Ale.
At lowest market prices.

A 72 Bottled Cider—Refined and sparkling.
Russet and Pippin, qts. per doz. $3 50
   do   do   pts. do do   2 00
Crab Apple,   do do do   2 50

We quote prices for pure goods only. The older the vintage the higher the price.

73—BRANDIES.
Domestics.
Per Gallon.
Cooking............... $2 00 to $3 00
California............. 4 00 to 5 00
Catawba............... 4 00 to 5 00
Cherry Brandy........ 1 50 to 2 50
Peach Brandy......... 3 00 to 5 00
Blackberry Brandy.... 2 00 to 3 00
Raspberry do ...... 2 50 to 3 50
Grape   do ...... 3 00 to 5 00
White Brandy, for pickling fruit............. 3 00 to 5 00

The older the vintage the higher the price.

74—COGNAC BRANDIES.
Imported.
Per Gallon.
A. Seignette........... $4 50 to $6 50
Otard, Dupuy & Co.... 5 50 to 7 50
E. Remi Martin....... 6 00 to 8 00
J. Hennessey & Co. ... 6 00 to 8 00
J. & F. Martell........ 6 00 to 9 00
Jules Robin & Co......   12 00
Special quotations to the trade.

The older the vintage the higher the price.

75—VARIOUS IMPORTED SPIRITS.
Per Gallon.
Gin, De Kuyper....... $4 00 to $6 00
  do Cabinet.......... 3 00 to 5 00
  do E. B. & C.........   4 00
London Dock Jamaica Rum................ 5 00 to 8 00
St. Croix Rum......... 5 00 to 8 00
Zwetschenwasser...... 3 00 to 8 00
Batavia Arrack........   8 00
Kirschenwasser....... 4 00 to 8 00
Old Tom London Cordial Gin 6 00
Scotch Whiskey ...... 4 00 to 8 00
Irish   do .... 4 00 to 8 00

76—VARIOUS DOMESTIC SPIRITS.
Per Gallon.
Cherry Bounce .... $1 50 to $2 00
New England Rum..... 2 50 to 4 00
Medford Rum .... 2 00 to 3 00
Domestic Jamaica Rum. 2 50 to 4 00
  do   St. Cruz do 2 50 to 4 00
Cordial Gin........... 2 00 to 3 50
French Gin...........   3 00
Domestic Gin......... 1 50 to 2 50
Berlin Doppel Kuemel.. 1 50 to 2 00
Napoleon Bitters,....   2 00
Pickwick Bitters.......   1 50
Napoleon Cocktail Bitters,   4 00
Stoughton Bitters ..... 2 00 to 3 00
Ginger Wine .... 1 50 to 2 00
  do   Cordial .... 1 50 to 2 00
Peppermint Cordial ... 1 50 to 2 00
  do   Essence.... 3 00 to 4 00
Raspberry Syrup....... 2 00 to 3 00
Lemon Syrup.......... 2 00 to 3 00
Plain Gum Syrup, white,   1 50

77—PREPARED PUNCHES
For Hot Drinks.
READY FOR IMMEDIATE USE.

Per Gallon.
Jamaica Rum Punch	$3 00 to $4 00
Arrack Punch	3 00 to 4 00
Nectar Punch	3 00 to 4 00
Scotch Whiskey Punch	3 00 to 4 00
Cognac Punch	3 00 to 4 00

78—WHISKIES.
UNDER OUR OWN BRANDS AND TRADE MARKS.

1860—Mortan & Co., Extra Ky. Bourbon	$6 00
1865—Mortan & Co., Fine Ky. Bourbon	5 00
Old Kentucky Bourbon	2 00 to 4 00
Persymons Bourbon	2 50 to 3 50
Persymons Rye	2 50 to 4 00

The Persymons Whiskies are distilled by a peculiar process, whereby all deleterious oils and acids are extracted. See argument.

Old Monongahela Rye	$2 50 to $3 50
Mortan & Co., Ky. Rye	2 00 to 3 00
Extra Old Rye	1 75 to 2 50
Magnolia Rye	1 50 to 2 00
Ohio Cabinet Rye	1 25 to 1 75
Old Q Whiskey	1 00 to 1 20
Tennessee White Wheat Whiskey	2 00 to 3 50

Two Stamp Whiskies.
Cedar Chief Rye	1 75 to 2 50
E. N. Cook & Co., Copper Rye	2 00 to 3 00
E. N. Cook & Co., Copper Bourbon	2 00 to 3 00
Rohrer Bourbon	2 50 to 3 50
Lancaster Bourbon	2 50 to 3 50
Hermitage Rye	3 00 to 8 00
do Bourbon	3 00 to 6 00
Old Crow do	4 00 to 6 00
Kentucky Club	4 00 to 6 00
Guckenheimer Rye	3 00 to 6 00
Cheektowaga Malt (Jan. 1873) unsurpassed for Toddy	6 00
Canada Malt Whiskey	3 00 to 4 00

79—WINES.
THE OLDER THE VINTAGE THE HIGHER THE PRICE.

Native Wines.
California Hock (Dry White Wine) per gal.	$1 25 to $2 00
California Riesling (Dry White Wine) per gal	1 50 to 2 25
California Zeinfadel (Dry Claret Wine) per gal	1 50 to 2 00
California Port Wine (Sweet and Dry) p g'l	2 00 to 4 00
California Muscat (Sw't) per gal.	2 50 to 3 50
California Angelica, (Sweet), per gal	2 00 to 3 00
Kelly Island Sweet	1 25 to 1 75
Hammondsport Sweet Catawba	1 50 to 3 00
Sandusky Bay Islands, (Dry) per gal	1 25 to 2 00

The older the Vintage the higher the price.

80—FOREIGN WINES.
Port Wines.
Tarragona Port	$2 00 to $4 00
A. B. Burgundy, per gal	2 00 to 3 00
C. B. Pure Juice, do	2 50 to 3 50
"S" Superior Port do	3 00 to 4 00
Oporto "Real," do	3 00 to 5 00
G & A Oporto, light and delicate, per gal	4 00 to 5 00
G & A Oporto, extra vintage, per gal	6 00

Sherry Wines.
Double Crown (cooking) per gal	$1 75 to $2 50
Juarez, Pale Dry Table Wine, per gal	2 50 to 3 50
"R" Superior Rudolf Sherry	3 00 to 4 00
"O P" Rudolf Sherry	3 50 to 5 00
"S.O.P." Rudolf Sherry extra old and fine	6 00

Madeira Wines.
"R" Old Stock Madeira	$3 75 to $4 50
"S.O.B." Sicily do	5 00 to 7 00

Italian Wines.

"G" Sweet Malaga .... $2 75 to $3 50
Sweet Muscat .... 3 00 to 4 00
Dry Marsala ..... 3 00 to 4 00

Hungarian Wines.

Matrai, old, choice, p gal., $4 00 to 6 00

French Wines. (clarets.)

Medoc, per gal ..... $1 25 to $1 75
St. Julien, do ..... 1 50 to 2 00
Margaux, do ..... 2 00 to 2 50

French White Wines,

Sauternes, per gal ..... $1 75 to 2 50
Cette, do ..... 1 50 to 2 00

81—BOTTLED & CASED GOODS.
Wines, (our own bottling).

	per bottle	per doz.
Angelica, 5 s	$ 80	$8 00
California Claret, 5 s		3 50 to 6 00
do Hock, 5 s		3 50 to 5 00
do Riesling, 5 s		4 00 to 7 00
do Muscat, 5 s	80	8 00
do Port, 5 s	80 to 1 00	8 00 to 12 00
Dry Catawba, 5 s		3 50 to 5 00
Sandusky Bay Islands, 5 s		3 50 to 5 00
Sweet Catawba, 5 s	50	4 00 to 6 00
Ginger Wine, 5 s	50	5 00
Italia Muscat, 5 s	1 00	9 00
Sweet Malaga, 5 s	1 00	9 00
Madeira Wines, 5 s	1 25 to 2 00	10 00 to 18 00
Sherry Wines, 5 s	1 00 to 2 00	7 00 to 18 00
Port Wines, 5 s	1 00 to 2 00	7 00 to 18 00
Hungarian Port Wines, 5 s	1 50	15 00

French White and Claret Wines.
OUR OWN BOTTLING.

St. Emilion, per doz .... $4 00 to $5 00
St. Julien, do .... 5 00 to 6 00
Chateau Margaux, p'r doz 6 00 to 8 00
Cette, per doz ..... 4 00 to 5 00
Sauternes, do ..... 6 00 to 8 00

We allow 50 cents per doz. for the empty bottles returned.

French Red and White Wines.

Imported in Glass. From the celebrated House of Cruse & Fils, Freres Bordeaux.

All bottled wines sent out by Cruse & Fils, Freres, have a patent wire cover around each bottle, which guarantees the genuineness of their Wines.

Red Wines.

	Per case 12 qts.	Per case 24 pts.
Medoc	$ 7 00	$ 8 00
Chateau Bouliac	8 00	9 00
St. Julien	9 00	10 00
St. Remi	10 00	11 00
St. Estephe	10 00	11 00
Margaux	10 00	11 00
Chateau Laujac	12 00	13 00
Pontet Canet	12 00	13 00
La Rose	13 00	14 00
Leoville	14 00	15 00
Lafitte	14 00	15 00

White Wines.

	Per case 12 qts.	Per case 24 pts.
Sauterne	$ 8 50	$ 9 50
Chateau Latour Blanche, (1867)	18 00	19 00
Chateau Yquem, (1869)	25 00	26 00

Rhine Wines.

Deidesheimer, per doz $ 7 00 to $ 9 00
Forster Riesling, do 8 00 to 10 00
Liebfrauenmilch, do 8 00 to 12 00
Rudesheimer, do 10 00 to 12 00
Ungsteiner, do 12 00
Ruppertsberger, do 14 00

Hungarian Wines.

Imported in glass. From the celebrated house of Anton Szeifriz.

FUENFKIRCHEN.

White Wines.

Dom Eigenbau, St. Mikloser, Auslese, per doz $12 00
Seminar Eigenbau, Szilvaser, Auslese, per doz 14 00
Funfkirchner Riesling Cabinet, per doz 16 00

Red Wines.

Villanyer Cabinet, "Grand vin"	$15 00
Villanyer Ausstich, "Vin d'amour" (a sweet wine)	18 00

We are the sole agents in the United States for this House.

Other Hungarian Wines.

Szegszardi, (red) per doz	$9 00
Egri, (red) do	10 00
Villanyi, (red) do	10 00
Pesti, (white) do	8 00
Somlyai, do do	10 00
Tokajy Maslas, (white) per doz	18 00
Matrai, (Hungarian Port) do	15 00

Burgundy Wines.

Macon, qts. per doz	$9 00
Beaujolais, do do	10 50
Chablis, do do	15 00
Chambertin, do do	20 00
Chablis, pts. 24 bottles, per case	16 00

82—CHAMPAGNES.

Our sparkling wines are always fresh and sold at lowest market prices.

Piper Heidsieck, baskets, 12 qts.
   do   do   do   24 pts.

G. H. MUMM & CO.

Dry Verzenay, cases, 12 qts.
  do do do 24 pts.
Extra Dry, do 12 qts.
  do do do 24 pts.

GREAT WESTERN, cases, 12 qts.
  do do do 24 pts.
Pleasant Valley, extra dry, cases, 12 qts.
  do do do do 24 pts.
America, do do 12 qts.
  do do do 24 pts.

The older the vintage the higher the price.

83—COGNAC BRANDIES, (bottled).

	Case of 12 qts.	Case of 24 pts.	per Bottle qts.	per Bott. pts.
J. Hennessy & Co.,	$16 00	$18 00	$1 50	$ 85
J. & F. Martell	18 00	20 00	1 75	1 0
Otard, Dupuy & Co	15 00	17 00	1 50	8
Jules Robin, (1858)	26 00	28 00	2 50	1 25
E. Remy, Martin & Co	18 00		1 75	
Southern Vineyard	15 00		1 50	
Veuve, Martin & Fils, glass bbls	20 00		2 00	
Pinet, Castilion		18 00		1 00
Arnoux & Co	9 00	11 00	1 00	60
Eug. Dulon & Co	9 00	11 00	1 00	60

84—GINS, (bottled.)

	Cases of 15 large bottles	Cases of 12 qts.	per bottle
J. De Kuyper & Son	$18 00	1 75	1 25 50
Van der Wuyk & Zoon	17 50		
French Gin, fancy white Glass		10 00	1 00
Old Tom Gin		9 00 to 12 00	1 00 to 1 50
London Cordial Gin		10 00 to 15 00	1 00 to 1 75

85—ASSORTED GOODS IN CASES.

Of 1 dozen Bottles each; handsomely labeled and capped or sealed. Amber bottles, 5 to the gallon.

	per Case.	per Bottle
Persymons Rye Whiskey	$9 50	$1 00
Persymons Bourbon Whiskey	9 50	1 00
Old Rye Whiskey	6 00 to 8 00	65 to 1 00
Old Monongahela	7 00 to 10 00	75 to 1 00
Old Bourbon	7 00 to 10 00	65 to 1 50
Hermitage Rye	9 00 to 15 00	1 00 to 1 50
Old Malt Whiskey	8 00 to 12 00	1 00 to 1 50
Old Scotch Whiskey	9 00 to 15 00	1 00 to 1 50
Old Irish Whiskey	9 00 to 15 00	1 00 to 1 50
Old Jamaica Rum	9 00 to 15 00	1 00 to 1 50
Old St. Croix Rum	9 00 to 15 00	1 00 to 1 50
Old White Wheat Whiskey	7 00 to 9 00	80 to 1 00
Ginger Cordial	6 00	50
Blackberry Brandy	7 50 to 9 00	80 to 1 00
Cherry Brandy	5 00 to 7 00	65 to 80
Rock Candy and Rye	10 00	1 00
Chectowaga Malt 1873	15 00	1 50
Kentucky Club	10 00 to 15 00	1 00 to 1 50
Old Crow	10 00 to 15 00	1 00 to 1 50
Hermitage Bourbon	10 00 to 15 00	1 00 to 1 50
Rye, Bourbon, Gin and Brandy, in pint flasks, white glass, glass stoppers, either all one kind of Liquor or assorted, 24 bottles per case		$10 00
Same in half pints, 24 bottles		$6 00
Berliner Doppel Kuemmel, qts		8 00
Bay Rum, green glass, sixes		6 00
Essence of Peppermint green glasses, 6s		8 00
Essence of Wintergr'n, green glasses, sixes		8 00
Stoughton Bitters, green glass, 6 s		8 00
Raspberry Syrup, green glass, 6 s		6 00

Dingens Brothers' Catalogue.

Lemon Syrup, green glass, sixes	6 00
Sirop de Gomme, green glass, 6 s	5 00
Napoleon Bitters	7 00 to 8 00 80 to 1 00
Napoleon Cocktail Bitters	10 00 1 00

The most unique Bottle and finest Bitter for a Cocktail in the market.

Cordials and Liquers.

	per doz.	per Bottle.
Creme de Rose (in fancy	$10 00	$1 00
Creme de Anise { white	10 00	1 00
Essence de Peppermint (glass bot)	10 00	1 00
Kirchenwasser	18 00	1 50
Zwetschenwasser	16 00	1 50
Chartreuse, per case, 24 pts	26 00	1 30
Benedictine, do	15 00	1 50
Vermouth, do	9 00	1 00
Curaco, white, qts., stone jugs, 12 qts	18 00	1 75
Prunelle, pts., stone jugs, 24 pts	24 00	1 25

Dingens' Prepared Punches.

In cases of one dozen fancy white glass bottles, unique in shape and design.

		per Bottle.
Scotch Whiskey Punch,	$10 00	$1 00
Arrack	10 00	1 00
Cognac	10 00	1 00
Nectar	10 00	1 00
Jamaica Rum	10 00	1 00
Assorted, as per desire	10 00	

(One bottle will make 20 hot punches),

Family Liquor Cases.

Containing one dozen bottles assorted Wines and Liquors, of fine quality and guaranteed pure.

Each case contains:

- 1 Bottle Cognac Brandy
- 1 do London Dock Jamaica Rum
- 1 Bottle French Gin
- 1 do Napoleon Bitters
- 1 do Old Port Wine
- 1 do Old Madeira
- 2 do Fine Old Sherry
- 2 do Persymons Rye Whiskey
- 2 do Persymons Bourbon

Per Case, $12 00.

86—MINERAL WATERS

We are headquarters for various celebrated Springs and sell you at Importer's prices.

Apollinaris.

	Per Hamper or Case.	Per Dozen.
In hampers of 50 stone qt. jugs.		
do do 50 do pt. do		
In Cases of 50 glass qts.		
do do 100 do pts.		

Friederichschall Bitter Water.

per Case. per Doz.
In Cases of 24 pts., glass

Hathorn Spring.

per Case. per Doz.
In Cases of 4 doz., qts., glass
do of 4 do pts., do

Hunyadi Janos.

per Case. per Doz.
In Cases of 50 glass bottles

Champion Spring.

Saratoga quarts, glass

German Selters.

Hampers of 50 stone qts

Vichy, Grande Grille.

In Cases of 50 glass qts.

Eau de Cesar.

In Cases of 60 glass qts.

Congress.

In Cases of 2 doz. glass qts.
"   " 4 "   " pts.

Empire Springs.

In Cases of 2 doz. glass qts.
"   " 4 "   " pts.

Lake Auburn.

(Effervescent.)

In Cases of 4 doz. pts., glass	$6 00	1 75
" " 8 " pts. "	12 00	1 75
On draught, per gallon,		30
In Bbls. of 32 gallons, per Bbl.,		6 00

87—CIGARS.

We call the especial attention of Smokers to our Cigar Department.

Our Imported and Key West Cigars are received weekly, hence can always be relied upon as being fresh. We do not handle low priced or inferior brands of these goods, they are N. G. A better low priced clear Havana Spanish made cigar can be procured here than can be imported; smokers are becoming aware of this fact and are giving the home-made goods the preference. In Domestic Cigars of all grades we guarantee satisfaction; in short, taking the whole department through, we guarantee the finest Cigar in the City for the price asked. Try us.

N. B.—We are continually adding new brands of true merit only, and handle NO TENEMENT HOUSE MADE GOODS.

SPECIAL DISCOUNT TO THE TRADE.

Imported.

No. Cigars per box.		Per Box.
50	Lopez, "Conchas finas,"	$ 5 50
50	do do especial,"	6 00
100	do "Reina Victoria"	17 00
50	Romeo and Juliet, "Concha Regalia"	6 00
100	La Competentia, "Princessa"	8 50

Key West.

No. Cigars per box.		Per Box.
50	La Belle Senora, "Conchitas"	$ 3 50
100	do do "Opera Reinas"	7 00
50	do do "Non plus Ultra"	4 25
50	Hermanos, "Concha de Regalo"	4 25

Spanish Make, Clear Havanas.

No. Cigars per box.		Per Box.
100	Lozana, Pendas & Co., H. CLAY, "Reina Fina"	$ 8 00
50	do do do "Concha Regalia"	4 75
25	do do do "Rothschilds"	3 00
50	do do ESCEPCION, "Regalia Favorita"	4 50
100	do do do "Reina Victoria," extra	15 00
100	do do MANUEL LOPEZ, "Reg. Brittannica"	12 00
50	Sanchez Y Hyas, "Reinas"	4 00
25	do do "Para la Nobleza"	3 50
50	C. S., H. CLAY, "Conchas Especiales"	3 75
50	do do "Non plus Ultra"	4 25

Fine Seed and Havana Hand Made Cigars.

La Buena Fe.

No. Cigars per box.		Per Box.
50	Sublimes, banded	$ 3 50
25	do do	1 75
25	Comme il faut, banded	2 00
100	Reina Victoria	10 00
50	Selecto, Concha del Rey	3 25
50	Audubon Club, Concha Grandes	3 25
50	Stella, Concha	2 75
50	Fortuna, "Sublimes," banded	2 50
50	Black and Tan	2 00
50	Dark Horse, Infantes	2 00

Choice, Connecticut Seed.

No. Cigars per box.		Per Box.
50	Gen. Garfield, "Brilliantes"	$ 1 50
50	A. De Villar, "Regalia Chica"	1 50
50	Mansanilla, "Conchas Especiales"	1 50
50	Southern Cross, "Conchas"	1 25

Additional Brands.

No. Cigars per box.		Per Box.
25	En're la Rosas,	$4 75
50	Bolero,	2 50
100	Preciosa,	5 00
50	Par Value, Panetelas,	2 00

ADDITIONAL GOODS.

88—ALES AND BEER.

Smith's India Pale Ale, superior to the Imported, and less in price—in casks of 10 dozen pint bottles.
Imported Lager Beer—Budweiser, pints, glass.
      Liebotschaner, " "

89—CHAMPAGNES.

Piper Sec. Cases of 12 quarts. Cases of 24 pints.
A. Roederer, Superior Extra Dry, white flint glass bottles, cases of 12 quarts, and cases of 24 pints.

90—CIDER.

Farnsworth & Gillette, pure, sparkling and sweet. Cases of 12 quarts, and Cases of 24 pints.

91—CORDIALS.

		Per Case.	Per Bottle.
Absinthe,	Cases of 12 quarts,	$15 00	$1 50
Anisette,	" " 12 "	12 00	1 25
Carmelite,	" " 12 "	18 00	1 75
Creme de Cacao,	" " 12 "	12 00	1 25
Curaçoa, Triple Sec,	" " 12 "	12 00	1 25
Curaçoa, Dubb. Orange,	" " 12 Stone Jugs,	15 00	1 25
Eau de Vie de Dantzick,	" " 12 quarts,	15 00	1 50
Maraschino, fino,	" " 12 "	12 00	1 25
Maraschino, fino, Antonio Rosett,	" " 12 Stone Jugs,	20 00	2 00

92—CHOCOLATE.

Menier's Sante, fine quality, yellow wrapper, ½ lb. papers.
 " Vanilla, demi fine, red " " "
 " " fine green   " " "
 " " superfine, bronze, " " "
 " Chocolate Confections, Nos. 1, 2, 3.
 " " Croquettes for breakfast, in tins, Nos. 1 and 2.
 " Breakfast Cocoa, ½ lb. tins.
 " Essence of " 1 " "

93—PREPARED COFFEE, CHOCOLATE, Etc.

Prepared Coffee and Milk in tins, T. & H. Smith & Co., London and Edinburgh.
 " Cocoa and Milk in tins, " " " "
 " Chocolatine, " " " " "

94—VARIOUS TABLE DELICACIES.

Boneless Chicken, (Oneida Community,) in tins.
"   Duck,   "   "   "
"   Turkey, "   "   "
Roast Chicken, (Cumberland,)   "
"   Duck,   "   "   "
"   Turkey, "   "   "
Whole Roast Chicken,   "
R. & R. Boneless Cooked Ham, in tins, various weights.
Whole Tongue, cooked, L. McN. & L., in 2 lb. tins.
Beef   "   "   compressed, Wilson's, in 2 lb. tins.
Lambs   "   pickled, in glass jars.
Clams, spiced, in glass jars.
Mussels, "   "   "
Shrimps, pickled "   "
Lobster, "   "   "
Mackerel, fresh broiled, in 1 and 2 lb. square tins.
Findon Haddocks, Imported in tins.
Kippered Herring,   "   "
Mushrooms,   " in ½ tins.
Liebig's Extract of Beef, 8 oz. jars.
Mackie's Edinburgh Abernethy Biscuit, Imported in tins.
Alden's Evaporated Codfish, ¼ and ½ lb. cartoons.
Brazilian Cassava, in 1 lb. papers.
Rio Tapioca,   " 1 " "
Rose's Lime Juice Sauce, the finest Table Sauce in the world.
   Half pints, glass stoppered bottles.
   Pints,   "   "   "
Piccadilly Sauce, in pints and ½ pints.

95—IMPORTED TABLE DELICACIES—In fancy packages.

Preserved Ginger, in Wedgwood Ware Vases.
   "   "   Fuchia   "   "
Royal Table Sauce, in Wedgwood   "   "
Sultana "   "   "   "   "
John Gray & Son's, Edinburgh, Scotch Jams, Marmalades, Etc.
   In glass pitchers.   In Majolica pitchers.   In Majolica Vases.
J. Moir & Sons, Scotch Jams.
   Greengage.   Damsons.   Plum.   Black Currant.
Preserved East India Fruit.
   Mandarins, in pots.   Stuffed Prunes, small boxes.

96—FRUITS IN GLASS.

Mrs. S. W. Youngs, LaSalle, N. Y,, Fruits, Jellies, Jams, Etc.
   Apple Jelly, in tumblers.   Blackberries, quarts and pints, in glass.
Blackberry Jam, in ½ lb., 1 lb., and 2 lb., glass jars.
Blackberry Jelly, in tumblers.   Cherries, quarts and pints, in glass.
Currants and Raspberries, pints and quarts, in glass.
   Currant Jelly, in tumblers.   Crab Apple Jelly in tumblers.
      Cranberry Jelly, in tumblers.   Grape Jelly in tumblers.

Peaches, pints and quarts, in glass jars.   Pears, pints and quarts, in glass jars.
Plums,   "   "   "   Quinces, "   "   ".
Quince Jelly, in tumblers.   Raspberries, Black, in pints and quarts, glass.
Raspberry, Black, Jam, ½ lb., 1 lb. and 2 lb. glass jars.
   "   "   Jelly, in tumblers.
   "   Red, pints and quarts, in glass.
   "   "   Jam, ½ lb., 1 lb. and 2 lb., in glass jars.
   "   Jelly, in tumblers.
Strawberries, quarts and pints, in glass.
Strawberry Jam, ½ lb., 1 lb. and 2 lb., in glass jars.
   "   Jelly, in tumblers.
R. & R. Assorted Dessert Fruit Preserves in tins.

97—GERMAN PRESERVED FRUIT—In Glass, Imported.

Cherries,	per bottle,	.	.	.	.	.	$1 00
Prunes,	" "	.	.	.	.	.	1 00
Quinces,	" "	.	.	.	.	.	1 00
Strawberries,	" "	.	.	.	.	.	1 00
Mixed,	" "	.	.	.	.	.	1 00

98—MUSTARD.

H. F. A. Pinckney's, 1 lb., ½ lb. and ¼ lb., in glass bottles.
   "   "   Loose.
Colman's, Double Superfine, Imported, in 1 lb., ½ lb. and ¼ lb. tins, and loose.
Durkee's Mixed Ground Spices, in ¼ lb tins.

99—SOAP.

Miller's Yankee Laundry, in Boxes of 30 bars.

100—CASTILE SOAP.

Green Imported.   Blue Mottled, Imported.

101—SUNDRIES.

Silver Sheen Liquid, 4 oz. bottles.   Household Ammonia, pint bottles.
  Insect Powder, in sifting tins.   Essence Jamaica Ginger, Brown's.
    Burnett's Florimel.   Rye Meal, 10 lb. sacks.
    Burnett's Rose Water.   Champagne Faucets or Syphons.
Fruit Jars, lightning fasteners, qts. & pts.   Cork Screws.
  Patent Bottle Locks.   Table Wine Baskets.
    Christmas Candles, in 1 lb. Boxes, containing each, 36, 48, 72, & 96 Candles.
    Dobbins' Starch Polish.

WINES, LIQUORS, CIGARS, Etc.

— OUR —

WINES, LIQUORS, ALES,
BEER, CORDIALS AND CIGAR

Department is complete in every detail. Upwards of

Thirty Years' Experience

In this line of business has demonstrated the advantages and necessity of handling only articles of good quality and known purity. The knowledge we have obtained by experience, and the facilities we have acquired for procuring the best goods,

FROM THE PRODUCERS DIRECT,

Enable **us** to not only guarantee **Quality and Purity,** but to offer them at prices that no ordinary house can compete with. Competitors may claim to offer similar goods at our prices.

Comparison is One Test.

Confidence in the house is the true test, and for the latter we can refer to thousands who have honored us with their patronage for the past quarter of a century.

On goods where the prices are liable to fluctuate, no price is quoted, but patrons can be assured of the lowest market price.

Special Quotations Given to the Trade.

Receiving all our Imported Goods and Fine Whiskies in Bond, we can guarantee absolute purity.

GOODS SOLD IN BOND,

or duty and tax paid, at option of purchaser.

PERSYMONS'
RYE & BOURBON WHISKIES.

The grains from which American Whiskies are distilled, contain finer oils as regards aroma and taste, than any material used in the distillation of imported spirits; but, UNFORTUNATELY, also oils, ethers and acids that are injurious to the health. The theory that age causes these injurious properties to evaporate is exploded.

IT WON'T!

Distillers have in vain sought to rid Whiskies of these oils. It was left for a French Distiller, (**M. Persymons,**) to perfect a still that accomplishes this.

DINGENS BROTHERS, OF BUFFALO, N. Y.,

In 1871, obtained this secret, and then first made Whiskies by this process. They tested them for more than two years, in every conceivable manner, and satisfied that the product was a Whiskey

PURE AND UNPREJUDICIAL TO THE NERVES,

only then offered it to the public under the title of

"OLD PERSYMONS WHISKEY," RYE OR BOURBON.

The Genuine bears our Signature and Seal.

NAPOLEON BITTERS

Are prepared from a formula obtained by Mr. J. A. DINGENS, from an eminent French Physician, and have been acknowledged by the entire medical Faculty of Europe, where they have been known and extensively used for the past 50 years, as the best compound for a gentle

STIMULANT, ALTERATIVE and APPETIZER

ever produced in the world. They are infallible as a remedy for

Dyspepsia,
    Fever and Ague,
        Indigestion,
            Loss of Appetite,
                Costiveness,
                    Sick and Nervous Headache,
                      Sea Sickness,
                        Lassitude,
                          Nervous Debility,

and all maladies arising from a disordered state of the stomach or liver; and as a preventive of the ill effects arising from a change of water or diet, or exposure to night air in malarious districts, they are invaluable.

In Europe these Bitters are found in all Hotels and Cafes, and at the sideboard of all well regulated families. They are exceedingly pleasant to the taste, and as a beverage, either straight or to flavor any liquor, they have no equal. For sale everywhere in the United States.

Introduced in America by

DINGENS BROS.,
BUFFALO, N. Y.

Our NAPOLEON COCKTAIL BITTERS have a World-wide reputation.

PREPARED PUNCHES

—⟨ FOR ⟩—

HOT OR COLD DRINKS.

After deep research and manifold experiments, we have succeeded in producing an article or compound, the want of which has long been felt, namely: a method of preparing a FRAGRANT PUNCH, equal to the best prepared in the usual old style, and conceded by many far superior, at a saving of labor, material and cost amounting to from 50 to 100 per cent. *No Lemons! No Sugar!* nothing but water needed. How often a merchant, a mechanic or a laborer, returning home, cold and weary, after his day's labor, feels the need of a stimulant. How invigorating and soothing would a punch feel, but "no lemons in the house," "crushed sugar just out," no punch to be had. But hold! Here is a bottle of **Dingens' Nectar, Cognac, Scotch Whiskey** or other **Prepared Punch!** "How handy!" exclaims the good housewife, and in a moment a fragrant punch, possessing all the requisite flavor, is prepared, and health and happiness is the result. Many imitations of our Prepared Punches, under different names, have been thrown into the market; but when compared with the genuine Dingens' Prepared Punches, the difference was so palpable that it has only strengthened public opinion in our favor. For sale by the trade generally.

A DOLLAR BOTTLE WILL PRODUCE OVER 20 PUNCHES.

BEWARE OF IMITATIONS.

PART II.

PART II.

————:o:————

There are natural cooks as well as natural musicians, and there is a charm in both that can never be reached by art. The delicate taste that decides whether there shall be a grain more of this or that in the seasoning of a soup; the eye that discerns, as by intuition, whether the gravy is of the proper thickness, the rolls just light enough for the oven, and the jelly of perfect shade and stiffness; are like an exquisite ear, beautiful taste, and graceful touch in music. They are rare gifts, however, and the majority of those who would excel in either art must accept the necessity of scales and measures. For exactness of proportions it is safer to weigh solids and measure fluids; to weigh even by ounces and half ounces, and to measure even by gills and half gills.

Teacups and tablespoons, dessert and teaspoons vary in size, and it is, moreover, difficult to know how closely the butter, flour, or brown sugar may lie in them. If a recipe says "heaping" it is very indefinite, as a teaspoon may be heaped from one-third to double its even quantity; and the "scant cup of butter" may have an easy range, varying in weight from half an ounce to an ounce and a half. It seems impossible, however, to avoid using a tablespoon and teaspoon as measures, a tablespoonful of flour being less than half an ounce, and a teaspoonful of the same still more difficult to weigh. Many cooking spoons hold very much more than tablespoons, and cannot be used for this purpose. The true tablespoon measure is one-eighth of a gill, and the teaspoon used in these recipes holds one-third of a tablespoonful. No rule is given in which the measure is heaped. In many cases the word *even* precedes the measure, but it is simply for the safety of those who may not have read this explanation. But with all this exactness in measuring and weighing, it must be remembered that *good ingredients* are indispensable to success; the best cooking cannot make a good dish of a joint of meat too recently killed or too long hung, nor a palatable omelette from eggs that are not perfectly fresh; nor with the utmost skill can good bread be made from poor flour, nor good cake with any other than sweet butter.

TABLE OF WEIGHTS AND MEASURES.

4 tablespoonfuls	equal to	½ gill.
8 "	"	1 gill.
2 gills	"	½ pint.
4 "	"	1 pint.
2 pints	"	1 quart.
4 quarts	"	1 gallon.
½ gallon	"	¼ peck.
1 "	"	½ peck.
2 "	"	1 peck.
4 "	"	½ bushel.
8 "	"	1 bushel.

A common-sized tumbler holds half a pint.

A common-sized wineglass holds half a gill.

One quart of sifted flour equals one pound.

One quart of cornmeal equals one pound and two ounces.

One quart of closely-packed butter equals two pounds.

One quart of powdered sugar equals one pound and seven ounces.

One quart of granulated sugar equals one pound and nine ounces.

A bit of butter the size of an egg weighs about two ounces.

SOUPS.

837. Stock.

A diversity of opinion exists as to the quality of soups and dishes prepared from stock. While some cook-books are silent upon the subject, most of them advocate the preparation of stock, and claim that no kitchen should be without it; true, it is useful in the preparation of some sauces and is economical, but to us there is a sameness of flavor in all dishes prepared from stock, that reminds one of hotel soups and dishes, which all taste alike. However, as our aim is to suit all tastes, we give the best methods of preparing stock, also full recipes for the production of soups without the use of stock. In the preparation of stock THE FIRST ESSENTIAL is a tightly-covered kettle, either tinned iron or porcelain lined, holding not less than two gallons; three being a preferable size. Whether cooked or uncooked meat is used it should be cut into small bits, and all bones broken or sawn into short pieces, that the marrow may be easily extracted.

To every pound of meat and bone allow one quart of cold water, one even teaspoonful of salt, and half a saltspoonful of pepper. Let the meat stand till the water is slightly colored with its juice; then set it upon the fire, and let it come slowly to a boil, skimming off every particle of scum as it rises. The least neglect of this point will give a broth in which bits of dark slime float about, unpleasant to sight and taste. A cup of cold water, thrown in as the kettle boils, will make the scum rise more freely. Let it boil steadily, but very slowly, allowing an hour to each pound of meat. The water will boil away, leaving, at the end of the time specified, not more than half or one-third the original amount. In winter this will become a firm jelly, which can be used by simply melting it, thus obtaining a strong, clear broth; or can be diluted with an equal quantity of water, and vegetables added for a vegetable soup.

The meat used in stock, if boiled the full length of time given, has parted with all its juices, and is therefore useless as food. Strain, when done, into a stone pot or crock kept for the purpose, and, when cold, remove the cake of fat which will rise to the top. This fat, melted and strained, serves for many purposes better than lard. If the stock is to be kept several days, leave the fat on till ready to use it. Fresh and cooked meat may be used together, and all remains of poultry or game, and trimmings of chops and steaks, may be added, mutton being the only meat which cannot well be used in combination; though even this, by trimming off all the fat, may also be added. If it is intended to keep the stock some days, no vegetables should be added, as vegetable juices ferment very easily.

In order to prepare soup, it is only necessary just before dinner each day, to cut off some of the jelly and heat it. It is very good with nothing additional; but one can have a change of soup each day by adding different flavorings, such as onion, macaroni, vermicelli, tomato, tapioca, sago, spring vegetables (which will make a *Julienne*), poached eggs, fried bread, asparagus, celery, green peas, etc. Stock is also valuable for gravies, sauces, and stews.

The secret of a savory soup lies in many flavors, none of which are allowed to predominate, and careful and frequent tasting is very essential to insure success.

RECIPES FOR SOUPS FROM STOCK.

838. Beef Soup with Vegetables. [Time.—An hour and a quarter.]

ARTICLES.—Two quarts of stock, one small carrot, a turnip, a small parsnip, two onions, all chopped fine; a cupful of chopped cabbage; two tablespoonfuls of barley or rice; six fresh tomatoes sliced, or half a can of canned tomatoes, and a saltspoonful each of pepper and curry powder.

DIRECTIONS.—Place the stock on the fire to boil; as soon as it boils add the vegetables, let boil half an hour, then add rice or barley, previously washed in cold water, next your seasoning, and let all boil together about half an hour.

839. Julienne Soup. [Time.—One hour.]

ARTICLES.—Two quarts of stock, two medium sized carrots, a medium sized turnip, a piece of celery, the core of a head of lettuce, and an onion; cut them into thin pieces about an inch long, add a pinch of salt and a teaspoonful of sugar.

DIRECTIONS.—Fry the onions in butter over a moderate fire; do not let them burn; add the carrots, turnip and celery—raw if tender, if not, boil them separately for a few minutes. After frying all slowly for a few minutes, season with the salt and sugar, then moisten with about a gill of your stock, and boil until reduced to a glaze; now add your stock, and let boil slowly; a quarter of an hour later add the lettuce.

840. Mullagatawny Soup. [TIME.—ONE HOUR AND A HALF.]

ARTICLES.—Two quarts of stock, one fowl or rabbit cut in small joints, four thin slices of lean ham, one ounce of pounded almonds, one clove of garlic, six small onions, two tablespoonfuls of curry powder, a pinch of salt and one of pepper.

DIRECTIONS.—Slice and fry the onions to a delicate brown, and slightly brown the joints of the fowl or rabbit, line the stew pan with the ham and put in the onion, garlic, fowl and stock, let it all simmer till tender, skim, and when the meat is done add the curry powder, rubbed smooth with a little of the stock, also the almonds pounded with a few drops of stock added occasionally and season to taste.

841. Sago and Tomato Soup. [TIME.—FORTY MINUTES.]

ARTICLES.—Two quarts of stock, two quarts of peeled sliced tomatoes, a sliced onion, one and one-half pints boiling water, four tablespoonfuls of sago, two teaspoonfuls of salt, three teaspoonfuls of sugar, half a teaspoonful of pepper, and four cloves.

DIRECTIONS.—Boil the tomatoes and sliced onion till half cooked, pour the water on the sago and let boil ten minutes; add it to the tomatoes, next add the stock well warmed, then the seasoning, and boil the whole ten minutes.

842. Asparagus Soup. [TIME.—FORTY-FIVE MINUTES.]

ARTICLES.—Two quarts of beef stock, one onion, four small

bunches of asparagus, a little mint, one ounce of flour, two ounces of butter, salt and cayenne pepper to taste, and one gill of cream.

DIRECTIONS.—Boil the asparagus and mint fifteen minutes until tender, cut off the heads about one inch in length and set them aside, boil the stems till very tender, pass through a sieve and mix with the stock well heated, add the flour, rubbed smooth with the butter, next the seasoning, then the cream; let it simmer until the flour is cooked, then add the heads of the asparagus and serve. If the soup is not green enough, color with juice pressed from fresh spinach.

843. Sorrel Soup (French). [TIME.—TWENTY-FIVE MINUTES.]

ARTICLES.—Four quarts of stock, a piece of butter the size of an egg, three sprigs of parsley, a little mint, three leaves of lettuce, one onion, one pint of sorrel, a little nutmeg, pepper and salt, the yolks of four eggs, two tablespoonfuls of flour, and a cup of cream.

DIRECTIONS.—Chop the parsley, lettuce, sorrel, mint and onion fine, place in a saucepan with the butter and seasoning, cover and let them cook or sweat ten minutes, then add the flour, mix well, and add gradually your stock, let it boil ten minutes; beat the yolks of the eggs, mix with a small cup of cream, and stir into the soup when ready to serve.

844. Leek Soup (Scotch). [TIME.—THREE HOURS.]

ARTICLES.—One dozen leeks, four quarts of stock, half a teaspoonful of pepper, two teaspoonfuls of salt and one small fowl.

DIRECTIONS.—Carefully wash the leeks, cut them into pieces about an inch long, drain them through a colander, put them into the beef stock, season, and let it boil gently, adding the fowl in time for it to be well boiled.

845. Puree of Carrots (French). [Time.—Two hours and a half.]

Articles.—Seven or eight carrots, one onion, one turnip, two or three slices of lean ham or bacon, a bunch of parsley, two bay leaves, two dessertspoonfuls of flour, one-quarter pound butter, one pint of water, five pints of stock, one teaspoonful of sugar, and seasoning.

Directions.—Scrape and cut into very thin slices all the red part of seven or eight carrots, slice a small onion and a turnip, which you put into a stewpan with a bunch of parsley and a couple of bay leaves, and fry in one-quarter of a pound of butter, then add the scraped carrots with a pint of water, and let all stew till tender; pour in the stock with a little salt and two dessertspoonfuls of flour, stir it over the fire, and let it boil for twenty minutes; strain through a sieve, give it a boil again for ten minutes, and serve with fried bread cut into dice in the tureen.

846. Macaroni Soup. [Time.—Thirty minutes.]

Articles.—Three quarts of stock and one-quarter pound macaroni.

Directions.—Break the macaroni in pieces two to three inches long, boil twenty minutes in two quarts of water to which has been added a teaspoonful of salt, then drain in a colander; place your stock in the kettle; when well warmed, add the macaroni, let it simmer five minutes and serve.

847. Vermicelli Soup. [Time.—Fifteen minutes.]

Articles.—Three quarts stock and two ounces of vermicelli.

Directions.—Place your vermicelli in a colander, pour a quart of water over it, let it drain, add to the stock when warm, let it simmer a few minutes and serve.

848. White Soup with Almonds. [Time.—Thirty minutes.]

Articles.—One quart of beef stock, one pint of cream, two

ounces of sweet almonds, blanched and pounded to a paste, (using a little water to prevent their becoming oily), two ounces of butter, three tablespoonfuls of flour, quarter of a teaspoonful of pepper, half a teaspoonful of salt, and the rind of one lemon.

DIRECTIONS.—Put the cream over in a double boiler, when warm add the lemon rind, heat your stock in a saucepan, when hot pour it gradually into the cream; add all the other ingredients and let it simmer fifteen minutes. Take out the lemon when the soup is sufficiently flavored.

SOUPS NOT MADE FROM STOCK.

849. Venison Soup. [TIME.—THREE HOURS.]

ARTICLES.—Three pounds of venison, (what are considered the inferior parts will do), one pound corned ham or pork, one onion, one head of celery, one tablespoonful of butter, one tablespoonful of browned flour, a tablespoonful of walnut or mushroom catsup, a teaspoonful of Worcestershire sauce, a good sized wineglassful of sherry or Madeira wine, two or three blades of mace, and six whole peppers.

DIRECTIONS.—Cut up the meat, chop the vegetables and place in the pot with sufficient water to cover them, keep on the lid of the pot all the while and stew slowly for one hour; then add two quarts of boiling water, with the mace and pepper, boil two hours longer, salt and strain; return the liquid to the pot, stir your flour and butter together with a little warm water into a thin paste, then stir into the soup, then add the catsup, sauce and wine, let it simmer five minutes and serve immediately.

850. Plain Chicken Soup. [TIME.—THREE HOURS.]

ARTICLES.—One old chicken, four quarts of cold water, a teacupful of rice, and a sprig of parsley.

DIRECTIONS.—Cut up the chicken and break all the bones; put it in the water and let simmer three hours, skimming it well; the last hour add the rice and parsley, giving it an hour to cook; when done, let the kettle remain quiet for a few moments on the kitchen table; then skim off every particle of fat; then pour all on a sieve placed over some deep dish, pick out all the bones, meat and parsley and press the rice through the sieve; then mix the rice with the soup until it resembles a smooth *puree*, and season with pepper and salt to taste. Straining off the soup may be omitted, and it may be served with the addition of *croutons*, that is, thin slices of bread cut into dice and browned in the oven; the *croutons* or dice are added just before serving.

851. Ox Tail Soup. [Time.—Four hours.]

ARTICLES.—Two ox tails, a good sized carrot, two onions, one stalk of celery, a little parsley, and a small cut of pork, pepper and salt to taste, three cloves, and four quarts of water.

DIRECTIONS.—Cut the ox tails at the joints, slice the vegetables (except one onion) and mince the pork; put the pork into a stewpan, when hot add first the sliced onion, when it begins to color add the ox tails, let them fry a very short time, now cut them to the bone that the juice may run out in boiling, put both the ox tails and the fried onions in a soup kettle with the water, let simmer about four hours, then add the other vegetables, with the cloves stuck in the other onion, salt and pepper to taste; as soon as the vegetables are well cooked the soup is done; strain it and select some of the joints (about one for each plate) trim, and serve them with the soup. Joints may be left out if preferred.

852. Mock Turtle Soup. [Time.—Six hours.]

ARTICLES.—One calf's head well cleaned, with the skin on it, two onions, one bunch of sweet herbs, five tablespoonfuls of butter, and five of browned flour, one teaspoonful of pepper, two of salt, two raw eggs, a little flour, two glasses of sherry wine, one tablespoonful of mushroom or walnut catsup, five quarts of cold water, and one lemon.

DIRECTIONS.—Soak the calf's head one hour in cold water, then put over to boil in five quarts of water, until the bones can be removed from the flesh, leave the broth and bones in the pot, lay aside the tongue, the cheeks and fleshy parts of the scalp to cool, chop the rest, including the ears, very fine, reserve four spoonfuls of this for forcemeat balls, season the rest with the pepper, salt, onion and herbs, and put back into the pot; cover closely and cook two hours; should the liquor sink to less than four quarts, replenish with boiling water. Just before straining the soup take out half a cupful; put into a frying pan; heat, and stir in the browned flour, (first made into smooth thin paste with cold water,) also the butter, simmer ten minutes stirring constantly. Strain the soup, scald the pot, and return the broth to the fire; have ready the tongue and fleshy parts of the head, cut (after cool) into small squares; also about fifteen balls made of the chopped meat highly seasoned and worked into the proper consistency with a little flour and bound with the raw eggs beaten into the paste; they should be as soft as can be handled; grease a pie pan, flour the balls and set in a quick oven until a crust forms upon them, then cool; next thicken the strained broth with the mixture in the frying pan, stirred in well; then drop in the dice of tongue and fat meat, cook slowly for five minutes; put the forcemeat balls and thin slices of a peeled lemon, in the tureen, pour the soup upon them, add the catsup and wine, cover five minutes and then serve.

853. Oyster Soup. [TIME.—FIFTEEN MINUTES.]

ARTICLES.—Two quarts of oysters, one quart of milk, a tablespoonful of salt, half a teaspoonful of pepper, a piece of butter the size of an egg, and one-quarter pound oyster crackers.

DIRECTIONS.—Strain the liquid from the oysters and add an equal amount of water, then the milk, the butter and the seasoning; let it come to a boil, skimming well; let boil about two minutes; add the oysters and let boil up once; place the crackers in the tureen, pour the soup over them and serve.

854. French Oyster Soup. [TIME.—TWENTY-FIVE MINUTES.]

ARTICLES.—One quart of oysters, one pint of water, a piece of butter the size of an egg, five cloves of garlic, half a teaspoonful of salt, and one-quarter teaspoonful of pepper.

DIRECTIONS.—Fry the garlic in a saucepan with the butter till they have acquired a light brown color, strain the liquid from the oysters, put in the kettle with the water, garlic and butter, let boil up once, put in the oysters and let boil one minute, serve with crackers as in the above recipe, or the soup may be served without crackers.

855. Clam Soup. [TIME.—FORTY-FIVE MINUTES.]

ARTICLES.—Fifty clams, one quart of milk, one pint of water, two tablespoonfuls of butter, and seasoning.

DIRECTIONS.—Drain the liquor from the clams and put it over the fire with a dozen whole peppers, a half a dozen blades of mace, and salt to taste; let it boil for ten minutes, then put in the clams and boil for half an hour quite fast, keeping the pot closely covered; if you dislike to see the whole spices in the tureen, strain them out before the clams are added; at the end of the half hour add the milk, which has been heated to scalding, not boiling, in another vessel; boil up again, taking care the soup does not burn, and put in the butter; then serve without delay. If you desire a little thicker soup stir a heaping tablespoonful of rice flour into a little cold milk and put in with the quart of hot.

856. Clam Soup, No. 2. [TIME.—THREE HOURS.]

ARTICLES.—A knuckle of veal, fifty clams, one onion, butter the size of an egg, a tablespoonful of flour, the yolks of two eggs, a little parsley, and one-half a pint of milk.

DIRECTIONS.—Boil for three hours a knuckle of veal with a goodly portion of water; when the scum rises, skim it, and add the onion; strain and add the liquor of the fifty clams; thicken with a tablespoonful of flour, well rubbed with a piece of butter the size of a small egg; have your clams cut in three pieces; beat the yolks of two eggs very light and put them into the tureen with a little parsley and one-half pint milk; just before serving drop the clams into the boiling soup, letting them boil up once, and then pour into the tureen, stirring well its contents while doing so.

857. Nantucket Soup. [TIME.—THIRTY MINUTES.]

ARTICLES.—Half a pint of codfish, picked fine, two quarts of water, one quart of milk, three ounces of butter, one ounce of flour, half a teaspoonful of pepper, and three eggs.

DIRECTIONS.—Boil the codfish slowly in the water for fifteen or twenty minutes, soften the butter with a little of the boiling water, and mix it until smooth with the flour and pepper; put it in the soup and after boiling a minute or two add the milk; when it boils again stir in the beaten eggs and serve with bread dice strewn over the top.

858. Noodles (plain). [TIME.—ONE HOUR AND A HALF.]

ARTICLES.—Three eggs, a little salt, and flour to make a stiff dough.

DIRECTIONS.—Add to the three eggs (slightly beaten) two tablespoonfuls of water, a little salt and enough flour to make a rather stiff dough; work it well for fifteen or twenty minutes, adding flour when necessary; when pliable cut off a portion at a time, roll it thin as a wafer, sprinkle with flour and roll it into a tight roll; with a sharp knife cut it from the end into very thin slices about one-sixteenth of an inch in thickness, and let them dry an hour or so. They will keep quite a while, if well dried, and may be used to add to plain beef or veal soup.

859. Noodles, to Serve Boiled. [TIME.—FIFTEEN MINUTES.]

ARTICLES.—Three cups of fresh noodles, three quarts of

salted boiling water (a good tablespoonful of salt will salt three quarts sufficiently,) butter the size of an egg, and half a cupful of bread crumbs.

DIRECTIONS.—When the salt water is boiling, strew them in the water a few at a time, stirring them continually to prevent them from matting together; ten minutes should cook them; skim them out when done and keep on a warm dish in a warm place; place the butter in a pan and fry half a cupful of bread crumbs to a light brown color, pour the butter and bread crumbs over the top of the noodles and serve; or some of the noodles may be fried brown and strewn on top, it may also be served with a sauce, (see noodle sauce.)

860 Noodle Soup.

Add to the water in which the noodles were boiled, a piece of butter the size of an egg, a tablespoonful of chopped parsley, half a cupful of sweet cream, if you have it—and half a cup of noodles; season with more salt if necessary; let boil up once and serve.

861. Beef or Veal Noodle Soup.

Add to plain beef or veal soup a small handful of the dried or fresh noodles, about twenty minutes before serving, which will be long enough time to cook them.

862. Eel Soup. [TIME.—ONE HOUR.]

ARTICLES.—Three to three and one-half pounds of eels, one-half pound salt pork, one pint milk, two eggs, one head of celery, or a small bag of celery seed, a little parsley, one small carrot, one small onion, and a piece of butter the size of a walnut.

DIRECTIONS.—Skin and clean the fish and cut them up, chop the pork into small pieces, put them together in the pot with two quarts of water; add the herbs, etc.; season with salt and pepper to taste; let boil one hour, then strain, return to the pot and add the milk already heated; next the eggs beaten to a froth; next a lump of butter the size of a walnut; boil up once, and serve with dice of toasted bread in the tureen. Pass sliced lemon or pickled walnuts with the soup.

863. Lobster Soup. [TIME.—THREE HOURS, INCLUDING THE TIME REQUIRED TO PREPARE THE BROTH.]

ARTICLES.—Two quarts of veal or chicken broth, two eggs, boiled hard, and one large lobster.

DIRECTIONS.—Boil the lobster, and extract the meat; if you purchase a boiled lobster, of course this is not necessary; extract the meat, setting aside the coral, cut or chop up the meat found in the claws, rub the yolks of the boiled eggs to a paste with a teaspoonful of butter; pound and rub the claw meat in the same manner and mix with the yolks; beat up a raw egg and stir into the paste, season with pepper and salt, and if you like with a little mace; make into forcemeat balls and set away with the coral to cool and harden; by this time the stock should be well heated, when put in the rest of the lobster meat cut into square bits; boil fifteen minutes, during which time reduce the coral to a fine smooth paste in a bowl, with a few spoonfuls of the broth, of about the consistency of boiled starch, stirring carefully into the hot soup; then drop in the forcemeat balls, after which do not stir, lest they should break; simmer a few minutes, but do not allow it to boil, or the beautiful rosy hue of the soup will change to a dingy brown.

864. Crab Soup

Is made the same way, excepting the coloring process; crabs do not contain coral.

865. Green Turtle Soup. [TIME.—FIVE HOURS.]

ARTICLES.—A turtle, (or canned turtle,) a wineglassful of Madeira or sherry wine, two onions, a bunch of sweet herbs, juice of one lemon, and five quarts of water.

DIRECTIONS.—Chop up the coarser part of the turtle meat and bones, add to them four quarts of water, and stew four hours with the herbs, onions, pepper and salt; stew very slowly

BARNUM'S
GREAT VARIETY STORE.

TEA POTS,
  Special kinds, *only* from Japan.
SILVER PLATED TABLE WARE,
  Standard Goods only.
JAPANESE,
  Crumb Trays, Bread and Cracker Boats.
SALAD FORKS AND SPOONS,
  Bread Boards and Knives.
FEATHER DUSTERS,
  Ostrich, Turkey and Chicken.
CARPET SWEEPERS,
  That are warranted to give satisfaction.
BASKETS,
  For the Nursery, Kitchen, Parlor, Traveling, etc.
BRUSHES,
  Cloth, Hair, Tooth, Nail, Shoe, Counter and Floor.
BLACKING,
  Shoe and Stove Blackings and Polishes.
LEAD PENCILS,
  Dixon's Pencils—best in the world.
WRITING PAPER,
  Pens—Stylographic and Steel.
HOYLE'S BOOK,
  Games, Playing Cards, etc.
SCISSORS,
  Shears, Sewing and Pocket Knives.
MACHINE SILKS,
  Threads, Needles, Bobbins, etc.
EMBROIDERY SILKS,
  Threads, Crewels, Yarns, etc.

Useful Articles and Novelties arriving daily in every department which we offer at lowest competing prices. Mail orders solicited.

265 and 267 Main Street,   -   BUFFALO, N. Y.

FLOUR.

IF YOUR BREAD DOES NOT SUIT,

—TRY—

SCHOELLKOPF & MATHEWS'

PATENT ROLLER

SPRING WHEAT FLOUR,

—MADE FROM—

MINNESOTA HARD WHEAT.

—EVERY BARREL—

Guaranteed to make Perfect Bread.

MILL BRANDS,

"NIAGARA FALLS" and "SURPRISE,"

—AND SOLD BY—

DINGENS BROTHERS,

UNDER THEIR SPECIAL BRAND

"EPICUREAN."

but do not let it cease to boil during this time; at the end of four hours strain the soup, and add the finer parts of the turtle and the green fat, which has simmered for one hour in two quarts of water; thicken with browned flour, return to the soup pot, and simmer gently an hour longer; if there are eggs in the turtle, boil them in a separate vessel for four hours, and throw into the soup before taking it up; if not, put in forcemeat balls, then the juice of the lemon, and the wine; some cooks add the finer meat before straining, boiling all together five hours; then strain, thicken, and put in the green fat cut into lumps an inch long; this makes a handsomer soup than if the meat is left in; for the mock eggs take the yolks of three hard boiled eggs, and one raw egg well beaten; rub the boiled eggs into a paste with a teaspoonful of butter, bind with the raw egg, roll into pellets the size and shape of turtle eggs, and lay in boiling water for two minutes before dropping into the soup. To make forcemeat balls for the above take six tablespoonfuls of turtle meat chopped very fine; rub to a paste with the yolks of two hard boiled eggs, a tablespoonful of butter and, if convenient, a little oyster liquor; season with cayenne, mace, and half a teaspoonful of white sugar, bind with a well beaten egg, shape into balls, dip in egg, then powdered cracker, fry in butter, and drop into the soup when it is served.

866. Beef Kidney Soup. [Time.—Six hours.]

ARTICLES.—One bullock's kidney, three sticks of celery, three or four turnips, three or four carrots, a bunch of sweet herbs, pepper and salt, a spoonful of mushroom catsup, and the liquor in which a leg of mutton has been boiled.

DIRECTIONS.—Add to the liquor from a boiled leg of mutton a bullock's kidney, put it over the fire, and when half done take out the kidney, and cut into pieces the size of dice; add three sticks of celery, three or four turnips, and the same of carrots, all cut small, and a bunch of sweet herbs tied together;

season to your taste with pepper and salt; let it boil slowly for five or six hours, adding the catsup; when done take out the herbs and serve the vegetables in the soup.

867. Veal Soup with Macaroni. [TIME.—THREE HOURS.]

ARTICLES.—Three pounds of veal knuckle, or scrag, with the bones broken and meat cut up, three quarts of water, and one-quarter pound macaroni.

DIRECTIONS.—Boil the meat alone in the water for nearly three hours until it is reduced to shreds; boil the macaroni also alone in a separate vessel until tender; the pieces should not be more than one inch in length; add a little butter to the macaroni when nearly done; strain the meat out of the soup, season to your taste, put in the macaroni, also the water in which it was boiled, let it boil up and serve.

868. Cream Soup. *(J. D.)* [TIME.—TEN MINUTES.]

ARTICLES.—One quart water, one-half dozen slices bread, a piece of butter the size of an egg, one teaspoonful of salt, and a cup of cream.

DIRECTIONS.—Cut the bread into small pieces, place in the kettle with the water, the salt and the butter, let it boil five minutes, add the cream and serve immediately.

869. Bouillon for Luncheons, (for a Party of Ten). [TIME.—FIVE HOURS.]

ARTICLES.—Six pounds of beef and bone, (soup bones,) two quarts of cold water, salt and pepper.

DIRECTIONS.—Cut up the meat and break the bones, put it in the pot with two quarts of cold water, simmer slowly about five hours, strain it through a fine sieve, removing every particle of fat; should there be more than ten cupfuls of bouillon, reduce it to that quantity by boiling; season only with salt and pepper. It is served in bouillon cups at luncheons, or evening parties, Germans, etc.

870. Green Pea Soup. [Time.—Three hours.]

Articles.—Four pounds of beef cut into small pieces, one-half peck of green peas, one gallon of water, one-half cupful of rice flour, salt, pepper and chopped parsley.

Directions.—Boil the empty pods of the peas in the water one hour before putting in the beef, strain them out, put in the beef and boil slowly for one and one-half hours longer; one-half an hour before serving, add the shelled peas, and twenty minutes later the rice flour, with salt, pepper and parsley; after adding the rice flour, stir frequently to prevent scorching, and strain into a hot tureen.

871. Dried Split Pea Soup. [Time.—Two hours.]

Articles.—One gallon of water, one quart of split peas, which have been soaked over night, one pound of salt pork cut into pieces, one inch square, one pound of beef, also cut into pieces one inch square, celery, sweet herbs, and fried bread.

Directions.—Put over the fire and boil slowly for two hours; pour into a colander and press the peas through with a wooden spoon, return the soup to the pot, add a small head of celery chopped up, a little parsley, or, if preferred, a little summer savory or sweet marjoram; scatter your fried bread, in small, thin slices upon the surface of the soup after it is poured into the tureen and just before serving.

872. Potato Soup. [Time.—Two hours and a quarter.]

Articles.—Twelve large, mealy potatoes, two onions, one pound of salt pork, three quarts of water, one tablespoonful of butter, one cup of milk or cream, one egg, and one chopped onion.

Directions.—Boil the pork in the clear water one hour and a half, then take it out; have ready the potatoes, which have been peeled, sliced and soaked in cold water for half an hour; throw them into the pot with the chopped onion, cover and boil three-quarters of an hour, stirring often; beat the butter, egg and milk or cream together, add it gradually, stirring while adding, let it boil up once and serve.

873. Summer Tomato Soup. [TIME.———]

ARTICLES.—Two and one-half pounds veal or lamb, one gallon water, two quarts of tomatoes peeled and cut fine, one tablespoonful of butter, one teaspoonful of powdered sugar, pepper, salt and chopped parsley.

DIRECTIONS.—Boil the meat to shreds and the water down to two quarts, strain the liquor, put in the tomatoes, stirring them very hard that they may dissolve thoroughly, and boil half an hour; season with parsley or any other green herb you may prefer, pepper and salt; strain again and stir in the butter and sugar before pouring into the tureen; the soup is more palatable if made with chicken broth.

874. Winter Tomato Soup. [TIME.—TWO AND THREE-FOURTHS HOURS.]

ARTICLES.—Three pounds of beef, one quart of canned tomatoes, one gallon of water, a small onion, pepper and salt to taste.

DIRECTIONS.—Boil the meat and water two hours, till reduced to a little more than two quarts, next stir in the tomatoes and stew all slowly for three-fourths of an hour longer, season to taste, strain and serve.

875. Turtle Bean Soup, No. 1. [TIME.———]

ARTICLES.—One pint of turtle beans, three quarts of water, one-quarter pound of salt pork, one-half pound of lean beef, one carrot, two onions cut fine, one tablespoonful of salt, and a pinch of cayenne pepper.

DIRECTIONS.—Wash, and then soak the beans in cold water over night; put them in a pot with three quarts of cold water, add the pork, beef, carrot, onions, salt and cayenne pepper; cover closely and boil four or five hours; add sufficient water from time to time, as it boils away, to preserve the original quantity, viz.: three quarts; then rub it through a colander; place in the tureen three hard boiled eggs cut into slices, one lemon sliced thin, half a glass of sherry wine, pour in the soup and serve; or it can be served with small sausages which have been boiled in the soup ten minutes, then skinned, and used either whole or cut up into bits and put in the tureen with the eggs, etc.

876. Turtle Bean Soup, No. 2. *(Miss B.)*

ARTICLES.—One gallon of water, one quart of turtle beans, three pounds of salt pork, two stalks of celery, and a sliced lemon.

DIRECTIONS.—Soak the beans over night, put them on the fire with the water and pork, and boil three hours; then take out the pork, strain the soup, add two stalks of celery and a sliced lemon.

877. To Brown Flour for Soups and Gravies.

Put a pint of flour in an iron saucepan on the stove, and when it begins to heat, stir constantly until it is dark brown, but be very careful not to let it burn; when cold put it in a covered jar or large mouthed bottle, and keep it from the air. More of this is required for thickening a gravy than of flour that has not been browned.

878. Forcemeat Balls for Soup.

ARTICLES.—Twelve ounces of veal, three ounces of salt pork, two ounces of grated bread, three tablespoonfuls of sweet cream, one tablespoonful of salt, half a teaspoonful of pepper, half a teaspoonful of summer savory, and one egg beaten with the cream.

DIRECTIONS.—The veal and pork must be chopped as fine as possible, well mixed with the other ingredients, and made into smooth, round balls a little larger than an ordinary marble roll them in egg, then in fine grated bread, place them in the frying basket and fry in deep lard. When the soup is ready to serve lay a dozen or more in the tureen and pour the soup on them.

879. Another Recipe for Forcemeat Balls.

ARTICLES.—Any kind of meat, chicken, or broth, (the kind of meat used in making the soup for which the forcemeat balls are required may also be used,) salt, pepper, parsley, thyme, or a little parsley and fried onion, or thyme alone, or parsley alone, a little lemon juice and grated peel, one egg, and a little flour.

DIRECTIONS.—Chop the meat very fine, season it with the pepper and salt, add your chopped herbs or onion, lemon juice and rind, break in the raw egg and stir in a little flour, enough to make a soft paste, roll in little balls, the size of pigeons eggs, fry them in a little butter, or they may be cooked in boiling water, or they may be egged, and bread crumbed, and fried in boiling lard. Just before serving the soup, place them in the tureen and pour the soup on them.

880. Croutons or Bread Dice for Soups.

Cut moderately thick slices of stale bread, take off the crust and cut the rest into small dice, put them in the frying basket, sink it into hot lard or drippings and remove it as soon as the bread is browned and let it drain. They may be served with the soup, in a dish alone, or scattered over the top in the tureen.

881. Egg Balls for Soups.

ARTICLES.—The yolks of two hard boiled eggs, the raw yolk of one egg, one tablespoonful of melted butter, a little salt and pepper, and enough sifted flour to make it consistent enough to handle.

DIRECTIONS.—Mix together, sprinkle a little flour on the board, roll out your mixture, about half an inch thick, cut it into dice and roll each one into little balls in the palm of the hand; put these into the soup to cook, about five minutes before serving.

FISH.

882. To Select Fish.

The most essential point in choosing fish is their freshness, and this is determined as follows : if the gills are red, the eyes prominent and full, and the whole fish stiff, they are good ; but if the eyes are sunken, the gills pale, and the fish flabby, they are stale and unwholesome, and, though often eaten in this condition, lack all the fine flavor of a freshly-caught fish.

The fish being chosen, the greatest care is necessary in cleaning. If this is properly done, one washing will be sufficient ; the custom of allowing fresh fish to lie in water after cleaning, destroys much of their flavor.

Another very essential point is this : fish to be palatable and healthy must be THOROUGHLY COOKED.

Fresh-water fish, especially the cat-fish, have often a muddy taste and smell. To get rid of this, soak in water strongly salted ; say, a cupful of salt to a gallon of water ; letting it heat gradually in this, and boiling it for one minute ; then drying it thoroughly before cooking.

All fish for boiling should be put into cold water, with the exception of salmon, which loses its color unless put into boiling water. A tablespoonful each of salt and vinegar to every two quarts of water, improves the flavor of all boiled fish, and also makes the flesh firmer. Allow ten minutes to the pound after the fish begins to boil, and test with a knitting needle or sharp skewer. If it runs in easily, the fish can be taken off. If a fish-kettle with strainer is used, the fish can be lifted out without danger of breaking. If not, it should be thoroughly dredged with flour, and served in a cloth kept for the purpose. In all cases drain it perfectly, and send to table on a folded napkin laid upon the platter.

In frying, fish should, like all fried articles, be immersed in the hot lard or drippings. Small fish may be fried whole ; larger ones boned, and cut in small pieces. If they are egged and crumbed, the egg will form a covering, hardening at once, and absolutely impervious to fat.

Pan-fish, as they are called—flounders and small fish generally—can also be fried by rolling in Indian meal or flour, and browning in the fat of salt pork.

Baking and broiling preserve the flavor most thoroughly.

Cold boiled fish can always be used, either by spicing as in the rule to be given, or by warming again in a little butter and water. Cold fried or broiled fish can be put in a pan, and set in the oven till hot, this requiring not over ten minutes; a longer time giving a strong, oily taste, which spoils it. Plain boiled or mashed potatoes are always served with fish where used as a dinner course. If fish is boiled whole, do not cut off either tail or head. The tail can be skewered in the mouth if desired; or a large fish may be boiled in the shape of the letter S by threading a trussing needle, fastening a string around the head, then passing the needle through the middle of the body, drawing the string tight and fastening it around the tail.

883. Baked Fish.

ARTICLE.—Bass, fresh shad, blue-fish, pickerel, etc., may be cooked in this way.

DIRECTIONS.—See that the fish has been properly cleaned. Wash in salt water, and wipe dry. For stuffing for a fish weighing from four to six pounds, take four large crackers, or four ounces of bread crumbs; quarter of a pound of salt pork; one teaspoonful of salt, and half a teaspoonful of pepper; one teaspoonful of chopped parsley, or a teaspoonful of thyme. Chop half the pork fine, and mix with the crumbs and seasoning, using half a cup of hot water to mix them, or, if preferred, a beaten egg. Put this dressing into the body of the fish, which is then to be fastened together with a skewer. Cut the remainder of the pork in narrow strips, and lay it in gashes cut across the back of the fish about two inches apart. Dredge thickly with flour, using about two tablespoonfuls. Put a tin baking-sheet in the bottom of a pan, as without it the fish can not be easily taken up. Lay the fish on this, pour a cup of boiling water into the pan, and bake in a hot oven for one hour, basting it very often that the skin may not crack ; and, at the end of half an hour, dredging again with flour, repeating this every ten minutes till the fish is done. If the water dries away, add enough to preserve the original quantity. When the fish is done, slide it carefully from the tin sheet on to a hot platter. Set the baking pan on top of the stove. Mix a teaspoonful of flour with quarter of a cup of cold water, and stir into the boiling gravy. A tablespoonful of walnut or mushroom catsup, or of Worcestershire or lime juice sauce, may be added if liked. Serve very hot.

Before sending a baked fish to table, take out the skewer. When done, it should have a handsome brown crust. If pork is disliked, it may be omitted altogether, and a tablespoonful of butter substituted in the stuffing. Basting should be done as often as once in ten minutes, else the skin will blister and crack. Where the fish is large, it will be better to sew the body together after stuffing, rather than to use a skewer. The string can be cut and removed before serving.

If any is left it can be warmed in the remains of the gravy, or, if this has been used, make a gravy of one cup of hot water, thicken with one teaspoonful of flour or corn starch stirred smooth first in a little cold water. Add a tablespoonful of butter and any catsup or sauce desired. Take all bones from the fish ; break it up in small pieces, and stew not over five minutes in the gravy. Or it can be mixed with an equal amount of mashed potato or bread crumbs, a cup of milk and an egg, with a teaspoonful of salt and a saltspoonful of pepper and baked until brown, about fifteen minutes, in a hot oven.

884. To Bake Fish with Wine.

Stuff a fish with the following dressing : soak some bread in water, squeeze it dry, and add an egg well beaten. Season it with pepper, salt, and a little parsley or thyme; grease the baking pan (one just the right size for holding the fish) with butter; season the fish on top and put it into the pan with about two cups of boiling water; baste it well, adding more boiling water when necessary. About twenty minutes before serving, pour over it a cup of claret or Sauterne wine (or if sherry or port wine is used, only half a cupful) add a small piece of butter, two or three tablespoonfuls of lime juice sauce or Worcestershire sauce to the wine and stir it well together before pouring over the fish, put half a lemon sliced into the gravy; baste the fish again well; when it is thoroughly baked remove it from the pan; garnish the top with the slices of lemon; finish the sauce in the baking dish by adding a little butter rubbed to a paste in some flour; strain, skim and serve in a sauce boat.

885. To Boil Fish.

General directions have already been given. All fish must boil very gently, or the outside will break before the inside is done. In all cases salt and a little vinegar, a teaspoonful each, are allowed to each quart of water. Where the fish has very little flavor, the following recipe for boiling will be found exceedingly nice:

Mince a carrot, an onion, and one stalk of celery, and fry them in a little butter. Add two or three sprigs of parsley, two tablespoonfuls of salt, six pepper-corns, and three cloves. Pour on two quarts of boiling water and one pint of vinegar, and boil for fifteen minutes. Skim as it boils, and use, when cold, for boiling the fish. Wine may be used instead of vinegar; and, by straining carefully and keeping in a cold place, the same mixture can be used several times.

886. To Broil Fish.

If the fish is large, it should be split, in order to ensure its being cooked through; though notches may be cut at equal distances, so that the heat can penetrate. Small fish may be broiled whole. The gridiron should be well greased with dripping or olive oil. If a double wire gridiron is used, there will be no trouble in turning either large or small fish. If a single-wire or old-fashioned iron one, the best way is to first loosen with a knife any part that sticks; then, holding a platter over the fish with one hand, turn the gridiron with the other, and the fish can then be returned to it without breaking.

Small fish require a hot, clear fire; large ones, a more moderate one, that the outside may not be burned before the inside is done. Cook always with the *skin-side down* at first, and broil to a golden brown,—this requiring, for small fish, ten minutes; for large ones, from ten to twenty, according to size. When done, pepper and salt lightly; and to a two-pound fish allow a tablespoonful of butter spread over it. Set the fish in the oven a moment, that the butter may soak in, and then serve. A teaspoonful of chopped parsley, and half a lemon squeezed over shad or any fresh fish, is a very nice addition. Where butter, lemon, and parsley are blended beforehand, it makes the sauce known as *maitre d' hotel* sauce, which is especially good for broiled shad.

In broiling steaks or cutlets of large fish,—say, salmon, halibut, fresh cod, etc., the same general directions apply. Where very delicate broiling is desired, the pieces of fish can be wrapped in buttered paper before laying on the gridiron; this applying particularly to salmon.

887. To Fry Fish.

Small fish—such as trout, perch, smelts, etc., may simply be rolled in Indian meal or flour, and fried either in the fat of salt pork, or in boiling lard or drippings. A nicer method, however, with fish, whether small or in slices, is to dip them first in flour or fine crumbs, then in beaten egg,—one egg, with two tablespoonfuls of cold water and half a teaspoonful of salt, being enough for two dozen smelts; then rolling again in crumbs or meal, and dropping into hot lard. The egg hardens instantly, and not a drop of fat can penetrate the inside. Fry to a golden brown. Take out with a skimmer; lay in the oven on a double brown paper for a moment, and then serve.

Filets of fish are merely flounders, or any flat fish with few bones, boned, skinned, and cut in small pieces; then egged and fried.

To bone a fish of this sort use a very sharp knife. The fish should have been scaled, but not cleaned or cut open. Make a cut down the back from head to tail. Now, holding the knife pressed close to the bone, cut carefully till the fish is free on one side; then turn, and cut away the other. To skin, take half the fish at a time firmly in one hand; hold the blade of the knife flat as in boning, and run it slowly between skin and flesh. Cut the fish into small diamond-shaped pieces; egg, crumb, and put into shape with the knife; and then fry. The operation is less troublesome than it sounds, and the result most satisfactory.

The bones and trimmings remaining can either be stewed in a pint of water till done, adding half a teaspoonful of salt, a saltspoonful of pepper, and a tablespoonful of catsup; straining the gravy off, and thickening with one heaping teaspoonful of flour dissolved in a little cold water; or they can be broiled. For broiled bones, mix one saltspoonful of mustard, as much cayenne as could be taken up on the point of a penknife, a saltspoonful of salt, and a tablespoonful of vinegar. A tablespoonful of olive-oil may be added, if liked. Lay the bone in this, turning it till all is absorbed; broil over a quick fire, and serve very hot.

Fish may also be fried in batter, or these pieces, or *filets*, may be laid on a buttered dish; a simple drawn butter or cream sauce poured over them; the whole covered with rolled bread or cracker crumbs, dotted with bits of butter, and baked half an hour. A cup of canned mushrooms is often added.

888. To Stew Fish, or Fish en Matelote.

Any fresh-water fish is good, cooked in this way; cat-fish which have been soaked in salted water, to take away the muddy taste, being especially nice. Cut the fish in small pieces. Boil two sliced onions in a cup of water. Pour off this water; add another cupful, and two tablespoonfuls of wine, a saltspoonful of pepper, and salt to taste (about half a teaspoonful). Put in the fish, and cook for twenty minutes. Thicken the gravy with a heaping teaspoonful of flour, rubbed to a cream with a teaspoonful of butter. If wine is not used, add a sprig of chopped parsley and the juice of half a lemon.

These methods will be found sufficient for all fresh fish, no other special rules being necessary. Experience and individual taste will guide their application. If the fish is oily, as in the case of mackerel or herring, broiling will always be better than frying. If fried, let it be with very little fat, as their own oil will furnish part.

889. To Boil Salt Codfish.

The large, white cod, which cuts into firm, solid slices, should be used. If properly prepared, there is no need of the strong smell, which makes it so offensive to many, and which comes only in boiling. The fish is now to be had boned, and put up in small boxes, and this is by far the most desirable form. In either case, lay in tepid water *skin side up*, and soak all night. If the skin is down, the salt, instead of soaking out, settles against it, and is retained. Change the water in the morning, and soak two or three hours longer; then, after scraping and cleaning thoroughly, put in a kettle with tepid water enough to well cover it, and set it where it will heat to the scalding point, but not boil. Keep it at this point, but never let it boil a moment. Let it cook in this way an hour; two will do no harm. Remove every particle of bone and dark skin before serving, sending it to table in delicate pieces, none of which need be rejected. With egg sauce, mashed or mealy boiled potatoes, and sugar beets, this makes the New England "fish dinner" a thing of terror when poorly prepared, but both savory and delicate where the above rule is closely followed.

Fish balls, and all the various modes of using salted cod, require this preparation beforehand.

890. Salt Cod with Cream.

Flake two pounds of cold boiled salt cod very fine. Boil one pint of milk. Mix butter the size of a small egg with two tablespoonfuls of flour, and stir into it. Add a few sprigs of parsley or half an onion minced very fine, a pinch of cayenne pepper, and half a teaspoonful of salt. Butter a quart pudding dish, and put in alternate layers of dressing and fish till nearly full. Cover the top with sifted bread or cracker crumbs, dot with bits of butter, and brown in a quick oven about twenty minutes. The fish may be mixed with an equal part of mashed potato, and baked; and not only codfish, but any boiled fresh fish can be used, in which case double the measure of salt given will be required.

891. Spiced Fish.

Any remains of cold fresh fish may be used. Take out all bones or bits of skin. Lay in a deep dish, and barely cover with hot vinegar in which a few cloves and allspice have been boiled. It is ready for use as soon as cold.

892. Potted Fish.

Fresh herring or mackerel or shad may be used. Skin the fish, and cut in small pieces, packing them in a small stone jar. Just cover with vinegar. For six pounds of fish allow one tablespoonful of salt, and a dozen each of whole allspice, cloves, and pepper corns. Tie a thick paper over the top of the cover, and bake five hours. The vinegar dissolves the bones perfectly, and the fish is an excellent relish at supper.

893. Fish Chowder.

ARTICLES.—Three pounds of any sort of fresh fish may be taken; but fresh cod is always best; six large potatoes and two onions, with half a pound of salt pork.

DIRECTIONS.—Cut the pork into dice, and fry to a light brown. Add the onions, and brown them also. Pour the remaining fat into a large saucepan, or butter it, as preferred. Put in a layer of potatoes, a little onion and pork, and a layer of the fish cut in small pieces, salting and peppering each layer. A tablespoonful of salt and one teaspoonful of pepper will be a mild seasoning. A pinch of cayenne may be added, if desired. Barely cover with boiling water, and boil for half an hour. In the meantime boil a pint of milk, and, when at boiling point, break into it three ship biscuit or half a dozen large crackers; add a heaping tablespoonful of butter. Put the chowder in a platter, and pile the softened crackers on top, pouring the milk over all. Or the milk may be poured directly into the chowder; the crackers laid in, and softened in the steam; and the whole served in a tureen. Three or four tomatoes are sometimes added. In clam chowder the same rule would be followed, substituting one hundred clams for the fish, and using a small can of tomatoes if fresh ones were not in season.

894. Fish au Gratin.

This is one of the favorite methods employed by the French in cooking fish, it being served in the same dish in which it is cooked. The *gratin* dish is an oval silver plated platter, but is also made of block tin. Put into a saucepan a piece of butter the size of an egg, then a handful of shallots, or one large onion minced fine, let it cook ten minutes, then mix in half a cupful of flour; then mince three-fourths of a cupful of fresh mushrooms, or a can of canned mushrooms, add a teacupful of water (or stock if you have it) to the saucepan, then a glass of claret or Sauterne wine, salt and pepper to taste; after mixing well in the saucepan add the minced mushrooms and a little minced parsley; skin the fish, cut off the head and tail, split in two, laying bare the middle bone; slip the knife under the bone removing it smoothly; now cut the fish in pieces about an inch long, moisten the *gratin* dish with butter, arrange the cuts of fish tastefully on it, pour over the sauce, then sprinkle the whole with bread crumbs which have been dried and grated; put little pieces of butter over all and bake. The dish may be garnished with little diamonds of fried or toasted, and buttered bread around the edge.

895. Fish à la Crème.

Boil a fish weighing four pounds in salted water, when done remove the skin and flake it, leaving out the bones; boil one quart of rich milk, mix a piece of butter the size of a small egg with three tablespoonfuls of flour, stir it smoothly in the milk, adding also two or three sprigs of parsley, half an onion chopped fine, a little cayenne pepper, and salt, stir it over the fire until it has thickened; butter a *gratin* dish, put in first a layer of fish, then of dressing, and continue in alternation until all the fish is used, with dressing on top; sprinkle sifted bread crumbs over the top and bake half an hour; garnish with parsley and slices of hard boiled eggs.

896. Broiled Fresh Mackerel.

Clean the mackerel, wash, and wipe dry; split it open, so that when laid flat, the backbone will be in the middle; sprinkle lightly with salt, and lay on a buttered gridiron over a clear fire, with the inside downward, until it begins to brown; then turn the other; when quite done, lay on a hot dish and butter it well; turn another hot dish over the lower one, and let it stand two or three minutes before sending to the table.

897. Broiled Salt Mackerel.

Soak over night in lukewarm water, skin side up, change

HERMITAGE AND OLD CROW WHISKIES.

THE HERMITAGE AND OLD CROW

WHISKIES,

Are strictly Pure, Old-Fashioned, Hand-Made, Fire Copper,

SOUR MASH WHISKIES

And are acknowledged by Connoisseurs, to be the

FINEST WHISKIES IN THE MARKET.

W. A. GAINES & CO.,

DISTILLERS,

FRANKFORT, - - **KENTUCKY.**

FOR SALE BY THE TRADE GENERALLY.

DINGENS BROS.,

333 Main Street, - **BUFFALO, N. Y.,**

Have on hand a variety of old Vintages.

T. V. DICKINSON,
Watchmaker and Jeweler,

Removed from the German Ins. Building, to

458 MAIN STREET, - Opp. Tifft House.

Fine Watches, Rich Jewelry,

DIAMONDS, SOLID SILVER AND PLATED WARE,

FRENCH AND AMERICAN CLOCKS.

THE WORKING DEPARTMENT

IS STOCKED WITH ALL TOOLS NECESSARY FOR THE REPAIRS OF

Fine and Complicated Watches,

FRENCH AND AMERICAN CLOCKS,

The old style "GRANDFATHER" Solid Silver,

Plated Ware, Bronzes, Fine Fans, Opera Glasses, Etc.

DIAMOND MOUNTING A SPECIALTY.

WEDDING RINGS MADE TO ORDER.

458 MAIN STREET, - - Opp. Tifft House,

T. V. DICKINSON.

this early in the morning for very cold water, and let the fish lay in it until time to cook, then proceed as with the fresh mackerel.

898. Halibut Steak.

Wash and wipe the steaks dry, beat up two or three eggs, and roll out some soda crackers until they are quite fine; salt each steak, then dip it into the beaten eggs, then into the cracker crumbs; fry in hot lard, or you can broil the steak upon a buttered gridiron, over a clear fire, first seasoning with salt and pepper; when done, lay in a hot dish, butter well and cover closely.

899. Stewed Sturgeon.

Boil five pounds of sturgeon, well covered with water, to extract the oil; (this is necessary whether the fish is to be baked, fried, or stewed); to one-quarter of a pound of butter add red and black peppers, mustard, salt, and vinegar to the taste; when the ingredients are well incorporated, stir in the sturgeon, which having been boiled until perfectly tender is picked very fine; heat the whole together and serve very hot. The above dressing may be used for baked sturgeon.

900. Sturgeon Steak.

Skin the steak carefully and lay it in the salted water (cold) for an hour to remove the oily taste so offensive to most palates; then wipe each steak dry, salt, and broil over hot coals on a buttered gridiron, serve in a hot dish and when you have buttered and peppered them, serve garnished with parsley and accompanied by a small glass dish containing sliced lemon; or you can pour over them a sauce prepared this way: put a tablespoonful of butter into a frying pan and stir it until it is brown (not burned), add half a teacupful of boiling water in which has been stirred a tablespoonful of browned flour previously wet with cold water; add salt, a teaspoonful of Worcestershire or anchovy sauce, the juice of a lemon, let it boil up well, and pour over the steaks when you have arranged them in the dish.

v

901. Baked Sturgeon.

A piece of sturgeon weighing five or six pounds is enough for a handsome dish; skin it and let it stand in salt water for half an hour; parboil it to remove the oil; make a dressing of bread crumbs, minute pieces of fat salt pork, sweet herbs and butter; gash the upper parts of the fish quite deeply and rub this forcemeat well in, put into a baking pan with a little water to keep it from burning and bake for an hour; serve with a sauce of drawn butter in which has been stirred a spoonful of caper sauce and another of catsup.

902. Baked Haddock. *(Mrs. E. Meyer.)* [TIME.—THIRTY TO SIXTY MINUTES, DEPENDING ON SIZE OF FISH.

ARTICLES.—Haddock, and veal stuffing.

DIRECTIONS.—Thoroughly clean and dry the haddock, fill the inside with veal stuffing, sew it up, and curl the tail into its mouth; brush it over with egg, and strew bread crumbs over it; set it in a warm oven to bake for about half an hour; serve it on a dish without a napkin, and with any sauce you please, anchovy, melted butter, etc.

903. Turbot. *(Mrs. Geo. Dorr.)* [TIME.—HALF AN HOUR.]

ARTICLES.—One white fish, one pint of milk, one-half a cupful of butter, one teaspoonful finely chopped onion, one of parsley and thyme, two tablespoonfuls of flour, one egg, a teaspoonful of water, and bread crumbs.

DIRECTIONS.—Boil a white fish weighing about three pounds; when cold, take out all the skin and bones, cut the fish in pieces not very fine, boil one pint of milk and stir in one teaspoonful of finely chopped onion, and one of parsley and thyme together; after the milk boils, add two tablespoonfuls of flour, rubbed into half a teacupful of butter, and let it boil a few minutes; beat one egg, add one teaspoonful of water to it, stir into the milk and remove it from the fire; fill a baking dish with alternate layers of fish and dressing, cover the top with bread crumbs and pieces of butter, and serve promptly.

904. Bread Stuffing for Fish.

Soak half a pound of bread crumbs in water, when the bread is soft, press out all the water; fry two tablespoonfuls of minced onion in some butter, add the bread, some chopped parsley, a tablespoonful of chopped suet, and pepper and salt; let it cook a moment, take it off the fire and add an egg.

905. Meat Stuffing for Fish.

This stuffing is best made with veal, and almost an equal quantity of bacon chopped fine; put in a quarter of its volume of white, softened bread crumbs, add a little chopped onion, parsley, or mushrooms and season highly.

SHELL FISH.

906. Oyster or Clam Fritters.

Chop twenty-five clams or oysters fine and mix them with a batter made as follows: One pint of flour in which has been sifted one heaping teaspoonful of baking powder and half a teaspoonful of salt, one large cup of milk, and two eggs well beaten; stir eggs and milk together; add the flour slowly and last the clams or oysters; drop by spoonfuls into boiling lard; fry to a golden brown and serve at once, or they may be fried like pancakes in a little hot fat. Whole clams or oysters may be used instead of chopped ones and fried singly.

907. Oysters for Pies or Patties.

Put one quart of oysters on to boil in their own liquor, turn them while boiling into a colander to drain; melt a piece of butter the size of an egg in the saucepan, add a tablespoonful of sifted flour, stir one minute, and pour in the oyster liquor slowly, which must not be less than a large cupful; beat the yolks of two eggs thoroughly with a saltspoonful of salt, a pinch of cayenne pepper and one of mace, add to the boiling liquor, but do not let it boil, put in the oysters and either use them to fill a pie or patties the forms for which are already baked, or, serve them on thin slices of buttered toast.

908. Oyster Omelet.

ARTICLES.—Twelve large or twenty-four small oysters, six eggs, one cup of milk, one tablespoonful of butter, chopped parsley, salt and pepper.

DIRECTIONS.—Chop the oysters very fine and beat the yolks and whites of the eggs separately; stir the yolks with the milk and seasoning, next put in the chopped oysters, and mix well, then add the tablespoonful of butter first melted; finally whip in the whites lightly, and with as few strokes as possible; while you are preparing the batter have your frying-pan ready with three tablespoonfuls of butter, melted and hot; then place your mixture in the pan; do not stir it, but when it begins to set, slip a broad-bladed, round-pointed knife around the sides and under the omelet that the butter may reach every part; as soon as the centre is fairly set turn into a hot dish bottom upward.

909. Oysters and Macaroni.

Lay some stewed macaroni in a deep dish, put upon it a thick layer of oysters, seasoned with cayenne pepper and grated lemon rind; add a small teacupful of cream; strew bread crumbs over the top, brown it in a pretty quick oven, and serve hot with a piquante sauce.

910. Oysters Vol-au-Vent.

Quarter some sweetbreads after they have soaked and blanched, put them into a stew pan with a very little veal gravy, and the liquor strained off two dozen oysters, adding a very little salt; then put two ounces of butter into a stew pan, stir it and thicken it with flour, and when the sweetbreads are sufficiently stewed add them with the gravy; after a few minutes put in the oysters, let them stew until heated through, and just before serving add a wineglassful of cream.

911. Oysters and Tripe.

A delicious stew may be made of oysters and tripe, substituting tripe for sweetbreads, and omitting the veal gravy, and proceeding in the same manner as above.

912. Oysters and Chestnuts.

Dip some oysters into a savory batter, bread crumb them and fry brown; in the same manner treat a number of blanched Spanish chestnuts; make a sauce with the oyster liquor, a piece of butter rubbed in flour, and two glasses of white wine; stew the chestnuts in this, add some yolk of egg to thicken and pour it upon the oysters.

In Part I. will be found over thirty different recipes for oysters.

CLAMS.

913. Clams Cooked with Cream.

Chop fifty small clams (not too fine) and season them with pepper and salt; put into a stew pan a piece of butter the size of an egg, and when it bubbles sprinkle in a teaspoonful of flour, which cook a few minutes; stir gradually into it the clam liquor, then the clams, which stew about two or three minutes, then add a cupful of boiling cream and serve immediately.

914. Clam Chowder, No. 1. [Time.————]

ARTICLES.—One-quarter pound fat pickled pork, one small onion, one quart of thinly sliced potatoes, washed in at least two waters, one large teaspoonful of salt, one small teaspoonful of black pepper, one pint of water from the clams, one quart of cold water, one quart of solid clams, one pint of milk, two and one-half ounces of flour, and crackers or pilot bread if desired.

DIRECTIONS.—Blanch the fat pork in hot water, drain, cut into small dice, and fry brown in a porcelain-lined kettle; shred the onion and brown it; remove from the fire and add the potatoes, salt, pepper, a pint of juice from the clams and a quart of cold water; replace upon the fire and boil until the potatoes are cooked; test by breaking with a fork, then add the clams, now mix smoothly one pint of milk with two and one-half ounces of flour, and add it to the chowder; let the whole boil up, remove from the fire and serve; crackers or pilot bread may be added if desired just after the clams are put in; clams may be chopped fine or not, as preferred.

915. Clam Chowder, No. 2.

ARTICLES.—Two hundred clams, one large onion, twenty large crackers, one can of tomatoes, some parsley chopped fine, half a pound of butter, one large teaspoonful each of sweet marjoram, thyme, sage, and savory, half a teaspoonful of ground cloves, half a teaspoonful of curry powder, half a pint of milk, and half a pint of sherry wine.

DIRECTIONS.—Put the clams with their liquor in the kettle, add all the ingredients but the milk and wine, boil well and then add the milk and wine just before serving.

CRABS, LOBSTERS AND FROGS.

916. Soft Shell Crabs.

Dry them, sprinkle with pepper and salt, roll them first in flour, then in egg (half a cupful of milk mixed with one egg) then in cracker dust and fry them in boiling lard.

917. Crabs a la Russe.

Boil them half an hour with a little salt; when done wipe dry, take off the shell, take out the blue veins, and what is called the lady fingers, as they are unwholesome; send to the table cold, garnish with parsley or sliced lemon or both.

918. Devilled Crabs.

Remove the meat from the shell, mix it with bread crumbs —about one-quarter will be sufficient, add white pepper, salt, a little cayenne, a little grated nutmeg, to taste; replace the mixture in the shells adding a small piece of butter to each, squeeze lemon juice over each, lay a thick coat of bread crumbs over all and bake.

919. Lobster Patties.

ARTICLES.—A minced lobster, four tablespoonfuls of bechamel sauce, six drops of anchovy sauce, lemon juice, and cayenne to taste; the patties.

DIRECTIONS.—Line the patty pans with puff paste and put into each a small piece of bread, cover with paste, brush over with egg, and bake of a light color; take as much lobster as is required, mince the meat very fine, add the sauces, lemon juice and cayenne to taste; stir it over the fire about five minutes, remove the lids of the patty cases, take out the bread, fill with the mixture, replace the covers and serve.

See Part I. for twenty-five more recipes for lobsters.

920. A White Fricasse of Frogs.

Cut off the hinder legs, strip them of the skin, and cut off the feet; boil them tender in a little veal broth with whole pepper, a little salt, with a bunch of sweet herbs, and some lemon peel; stew them with a shallot till the flesh is a little tender, strain off the liquor and thicken it with cream and butter; serve them hot with mushrooms pickled and tossed up with the sauce.

921. Frogs Fried.

Put them in salted boiling water, with a little lemon juice, boil them three minutes, wipe them, dip them first into cracker dust, then in eggs, (half a cupful of milk mixed in two eggs and seasoned with pepper and salt) then again in cracker crumbs; when they are all breaded, clean off the bone at the end with a dry cloth; put them in a wire basket and dip them in boiling lard to fry; place them on a hot platter in the form of a circle, one overlapping the other, with French peas in the center, and serve immediately while they are still crisp and hot.

TERRAPINS, TURTLES AND TORTOISES.

922. Terrapins.

They must be boiled and picked; they are "diamond backs," and sold in the markets by *counts*, which are so called from the width of the bottom shell, each count measuring three inches; any terrapin that will go a count is a female, and is preferred for being more tender, and on account of the eggs. Throw the terrapin into scalding water, with a little salt; when boiled, after cooling, the under shell becomes detached; the only things to be taken out of the terrapin are the gall and the sand bag, which are near together and about the center of it; the contents of the shell are broken up, and a small quantity of Madeira wine, pepper and salt added to the taste, and serve hot.

Another method adopted by fishermen and hunters.—After being boiled the bottom shell is detached, gall and sand bag removed, the meat detached from the shell, broken up or minced, dressed with wine or brandy, or simply seasoned with salt and pepper, place a small piece of butter and some cracker or bread crumbs on top and bake in the shell. This is considered by connoisseurs as the only way in which the full flavor of the terrapin can be obtained.

923. Turtle or Tortoise, How to Roast.

Take a piece of about five or six pounds, lay it in salt and water for two hours, then stick a few cloves in it and fasten it to the spit; or lay it in the pan and place in your oven, baste it with wine and lemon juice, then dredge some flour over it with the raspings of bread sifted, and then baste it well either with oil or butter, strewing on from time to time, more flour and raspings, then take the liquor in the pan, and pouring off the fat, boil it with some lemon peel and a little sugar and salt, pour it over the turtle and serve hot.

CARVING.

One who is born with no mechanical genius should never torment himself or distract his family by attempting to carve at the table; the office should be assumed by some one of the family more favored of the gods, who may, by daily practice and close attention, soon become a proficient in the art. Or it may be done in the kitchen before the repast and brought on the table at the proper time, and served by the host, or it may be served a la Russe—that is, by a servant passing the dish with the carved meat thereon to each guest. The arrangement of the meat on the plate, like that of flowers or dress, is a matter where taste is appreciated and usefully brought in. To save strength, time, and patience, a very sharp knife is an absolute necessity; it is impossible to cut thin, beautiful slices without it; as a general rule cut *across* the grain.

POULTRY.

If care is taken in picking and dressing fowls or birds, there is no need of washing them; in France it is never done, unless there is absolutely something to wash off, then it is done as delicately as possible.

Directions for selecting poultry will be found in Part 1, page 19.

924. Roast Turkey.

The secret to have a good roast turkey is to baste it often and to cook it long enough. A small turkey of seven or eight pounds (the best selection if fat) should be roasted or baked about three hours; a very large turkey will take four hours; if properly basted they will not become dry; after the turkey is dressed, season it well, sprinkling pepper and salt on the inside; stuff it, and tie it well in shape; either lard the top or lay slices of bacon over it; wet the skin and sprinkle it well with pepper, salt, and flour; pour a little water into the bottom of the dripping-pan. The excellence of the turkey depends much upon the frequency of basting it; occasionally baste it with a little butter, oftener with its own drippings; just before taking it out of the oven, put on more melted butter, this will make the skin more crisp and brown. While the turkey is cooking, boil the giblets well, chop them fine, and wash the liver, and when the turkey is done, put it on a hot platter; put the dripping pan on the fire, dredge in a little flour, and when cooked stir in a little boiling water, add the giblets, and season with salt and pepper. If chestnut stuffing is used, add some boiled chestnuts to the gravy; besides the gravy always serve cranberry, currant or plum jelly with turkey; roast turkey is frequently garnished with little sausage balls.

925. Stuffing for Roast Turkeys, Chickens, Ducks and Geese.

That ordinarily used is made as follows: Two onions, five ounces of soaked and squeezed bread, eight sage leaves, one ounce of butter, pepper, salt, one egg, a little piece of pork minced. Mince the onions, and fry them before adding them to the other ingredients. Some chopped celery is always a good addition.

926. Chestnut Stuffing

Is made by adding chestnuts to the ordinary stuffing; shell, and boil them in very salted water, remove the skin and add either whole, or minced, as you like; some may also be added to the sauce.

927. Oyster Stuffing

Is made by adding about a quart of raw oysters to the ordinary stuffing; the filling should be well seasoned, or the oysters will taste insipid.

928. Boiled Turkey.

If a boiled turkey is not well managed it will be quite tasteless; choose a hen turkey; if not well trussed and tied, the legs and wings of a boiled fowl will stick out in all directions;

cut the legs at the first joint and draw them into the body, fasten the small ends of the wings under the back, and tie them securely with strong twine; sprinkle over plenty of salt, pepper, and lemon juice, and put it into *boiling* water; boil it slowly for two hours, or until quite tender; it is generally served in a bed of rice, with oyster, caper, cauliflower, parsley or *Hollandaise* sauce; pour part of the sauce over the turkey, reserve the giblets for giblet soup. It can be stuffed or not, the same as for roasting.

929. Turkey Galantine, or Boned Turkey.

Choose a fat hen turkey; when dressing it leave the crop skin (the skin over the breast) whole, cut off the legs, wings and neck; now slit the skin at the back, and carefully remove it all around; cut out the breasts carefully and cut them into pieces about an inch square, season with pepper, salt, a little nutmeg, mace, pounded cloves, sweet basil, and a little chopped parsley, all mixed; now make a forcemeat with a pound and a quarter of lean veal or fresh pork, well freed from skin and gristle; mix this with the meat of the turkey, (all but the breasts) and chop it well; then chop an equal volume of fresh bacon, which mix with the other chopped meat, season this with the condiments last mentioned and pound it in a mortar to a paste; cut up one pound of truffles, half a pound of cooked pickled tongue, and half a pound of cooked fat bacon into small dice, seasoning them also; spread the turkey skin on a board, make alternate layers on it, first of half of the forcemeat, then half of the turkey breasts, then half of the dice of tongue, truffles and bacon, then turkey fillets and dice again; and save some of the forcemeat to put on the last layer; now begin at one side and roll it over, giving it a round and long shape; sew up the skin, wrap it, pressing it closely in a napkin; tie it at the extremities and also tie it across in two places, to keep it in an oval shape with round ends; boil the galantine gently for four hours in boiling water (or better, in stock), with the bones of the turkey thrown in ; at the end of that time take the stew pan off the fire and let the galantine cool in the liquor one hour, then drain it and put it on a dish with a weight on it; when cold take the galantine out of the napkin, put it at the end of an open oven for a few minutes to melt the fat, which wipe off with a cloth, glaze it or sprinkle it with a little egg and fine bread crumbs and bake it a few minutes. It is, of course, to be sliced when eaten, and is generally served, placed on a wooden standard.

930. A Simple way of Preparing Boned Turkey or Chicken.

Boil a turkey or chicken in as little water as possible, until the bones can easily be separated from the meat ; remove all of the skin, slice and mix together the light and dark parts; season with pepper and salt; boil down the liquid in which the turkey or chicken was boiled, and then pour it on the meat; shape it like a loaf of bread, wrap it tightly in a cloth, and press it with a heavy weight for a few hours. When served it is cut into thin slices.

CHICKENS.

931. Spring Chickens, How to Improve.

The excellence of spring chickens depends as much on feeding as on cooking them. If there are conveniences for building a coop, say five feet square, on the ground, where some spring chickens can be kept for a few weeks, feeding them with the scraps from the kitchen, and grain, they will be found plump, the meat white, and the flavor quite different from the thin, poorly fed chickens just from the market.

932. Spring Chickens Baked.

Cut them open at the back, spread them out in a baking pan, sprinkle on plenty of pepper, salt and a little flour ; baste them well with hot water which should be in the bottom of the pan, also at different times with a little butter; when done, rub butter over them, as you would beefsteak, and set them in the oven for a moment before serving.

933. Broiled Chicken.

Cut it through the back, clean, wash and wipe it dry; spread it on the gridiron, and cook slowly with the inside towards the fire, and keep it so until nearly done; the chicken cooks more thoroughly in this way, and the surface being seared, the juice is retained; it must be nicely browned on both sides, then served on a hot platter with a little butter, pepper and salt.

934. Roasted and Boiled Chickens.

Chickens are roasted and boiled the same as turkeys. A large tough chicken is very good boiled; just before serving, pour over a good pickle or caper sauce; of course the chicken should be put into *boiling water* and should not stop boiling until well done; the water in which it has boiled should always be saved for soup; the boiled chicken may be served on a platter and surrounded by a bed of boiled rice.

935. Fricasseed Chicken.

ARTICLES.—Two chickens weighing about two and one-half pounds each, one and one-half ounces of flour, two ounces of butter, one pint of cold water, two gills of cream, one teaspoonful of mace, two teaspoonfuls of salt, one-third of a teaspoonful of cayenne pepper, one-third of a nutmeg grated, one onion, and the yolks of four eggs.

DIRECTIONS.—Cut the chickens and sprinkle the pieces with the salt, pepper and spices; put the water in the kettle, and lay in the chicken, the skin side down; slice the onion over them, cover closely, and let them simmer until done; take out the chicken, arrange it on the platter, and keep it hot, while the gravy is being thickened; there should be nearly a pint of it; rub the butter and flour smoothly together, adding a little of the gravy to soften and help mix them; stir it in the gravy, and let it boil two or three minutes; pour in the cream, and as soon as it boils pour the whole on the well beaten yolks, return it to the saucepan, let it get thoroughly hot, without boiling, and pour it at once over the chickens.

936. Chicken Croquettes.

ARTICLES.—Two chickens, two sets of brains, both boiled; one teacupful of suet, chopped fine; two sprigs of parsley, chopped; one nutmeg, grated; an even tablespoonful of onion, after it has been chopped as fine as possible; the juice and grated rind of one lemon, salt, and black and red pepper to taste.

DIRECTIONS.—Chop the meat very fine, mix all well together, add cream until it is quite moist or just right for moulding; this quantity will make two dozen croquettes; then mould them into shape, dip them into beaten egg, then roll them in pounded cracker and fry in boiling hot lard.

DUCKS, GEESE AND GAME BIRDS.

937. Roast Ducks.

Truss and stuff them with onions as you would a goose; if they are ducklings, roast them from twenty-five to thirty minutes; epicures say they like them quite underdone, yet at the same time, very hot. Full-grown ducks should be roasted one hour, and frequently basted; serve with them the brown giblet gravy or apple sauce, or both; green peas should accompany the dish; many parboil ducks before roasting or baking them; if there is suspicion of advanced age, parboil them.

938. Wild Ducks.

They should be cooked rare, with or without stuffing; baste them a few minutes at first with hot water, to which has been added one onion, and salt; then baste with butter, and a little flour to brown them; the oven should be quite hot; twenty to twenty-five minutes should cook them; a brown gravy made with the giblets should be served with them. Currant jelly may also be served with them, and garnish the dish with slices of lemon.

939. Stewed Duck.

Cut the duck into joints; put the giblets into a stew pan, adding water enough to cover them for the purpose of making a gravy; add two onions, chopped fine; two sprigs of parsley, three cloves, a sage leaf, pepper and salt; let the gravy simmer until it is strong enough, then add the pieces of duck, cover, and let them stew slowly for two hours, adding a little boiling water when necessary; just before they are done, add a small glassful of port wine, and a few drops of lemon juice; put the duck on a warm platter, pour the gravy around, and serve with diamonds of fried bread placed around the dish.

940. Roast Goose.

The goose should be absolutely young; green geese are best, *i. e.*, when they are about four months old; in trussing, cut the neck close to the back, leaving the skin long enough to turn over the back; beat the breast-bone flat with a rolling-pin, and tie the legs and wings securely; stuff the goose with the following mixture: Four chopped onions, ten sage leaves, one-quarter of a pound of bread crumbs, one and one-half ounces of butter, salt and pepper to taste, one egg, and one slice of pork, chopped; now sprinkle the top of the goose well with salt, pepper and flour; if it be a green one, roast it one and one-half hours, if an older one it would be preferable to bake it in an oven, with plenty of hot water in the baking pan; it should be basted very often with this water, and when it is nearly done baste it with butter and a little flour; bake it three or four hours, decorate the goose with water cresses, and serve it with the brown giblet gravy in the sauce boat. Always serve an apple sauce with this dish.

941. Goose Stuffing. *(Soyer.)*

Take four apples peeled and cored, four onions, four leaves

of sage, and four of thyme; boil them with sufficient water to cover them; when done, pulp them through a sieve, removing the sage and thyme, then add enough pulp of mealy potatoes to cause the stuffing to be sufficiently dry, without sticking to the hand; add pepper and salt and then stuff the bird.

942. Pigeons Stewed in Broth.

Unless pigeons are quite young, they are better braised or stewed in broth than cooked in any other manner; tie them in shape, place slices of bacon at the bottom of a stew pan, lay in the pigeons, side by side, their breasts uppermost; add one sliced carrot, one onion with a clove stuck in, one teaspoonful of sugar, and some parsley, pour in enough stock to cover them; if you have no stock use boiling water; now place some thin slices of bacon over the tops of the pigeons, cover them as closely as possible, adding boiling water or stock when necessary; let them simmer until very tender; serve each pigeon on a thin slice of buttered toast, with a border of spinach, or make little nests of spinach on each piece of toast, and put a pigeon into each nest.

943. Roast Pigeon.

Never roast pigeons unless they are young and tender; after they are well tied in shape, drawing the skin over the back, tie thin slices of bacon over the breasts, and put a small piece of butter inside each pigeon; place them in a pan, put into the oven, roast until thoroughly done, and baste well with butter.

944. Broiled Pigeon.

Split the pigeons at the back, and flatten them, season, roll them in melted butter, and bread crumbs, and broil them, basting them with butter; or, cut out the breasts, and broil them alone; serve them on thin slices of toast; make a gravy of the remaining portions of the pigeons and pour it over them.

945. Prairie Chicken or Grouse, or Partridge.

These are generally split open at the back and broiled, rubbing

MEATS.

[ESTABLISHED 1845.]

AUGUSTUS F. WEPPNER'S
MEAT MARKET,

582 MAIN STREET.

TELEPHONIC COMMUNICATION.

ORDERS FILLED PROMPTLY AND WITH DISPATCH.

DOING OUR OWN

KILLING AND CURING,

We are enabled to provide our patrons with the

CHOICEST OF MEATS.

Lard and Sausage of our own Production

ALWAYS ON HAND.

We make a specialty of choice

HAMS, BREAKFAST BACON, TONGUES AND VEAL LOAF.

STARCH.

KINGSFORD'S OSWEGO CORN STARCH

Is the most delicious of all preparations for

PUDDINGS, BLANC-MANGE, CAKE, Etc.

KINGSFORD'S
OSWEGO

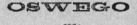

PURE AND

STARCH!

Is the Best and Most Economical in the World.
Is perfectly Pure—free from Acids, etc., that injure Linen.
Is Stronger than any other—requiring much less in using.
Is Uniform—stiffens and finishes work always the same.

To avoid gross imposition, see that

T. KINGSFORD & SON

IS ON EACH BOX AND ON EACH PACKAGE.

them with butter, but as all but the breast is generally tough, it is better to fillet the chicken, or cut out the breast, and the remainder of the chicken is cut into joints and parboiled; these pieces are then broiled with the breasts, after rubbing butter over them all; as soon as they are all broiled, sprinkle them with pepper and salt, and put a small piece of butter on top of each piece, which then place for a few moments in the oven to soak the butter, and serve with currant jelly. For fine entertainments the breasts alone are served; each breast is cut into two pieces, so that one chicken is sufficient for four persons; if the dish is intended for breakfast, serve each piece on a small square of fried mush; if for dinner, serve each piece on squares of buttered toast, with currant jelly on top of each piece of chicken, and garnish the plate with any kind of leaves, or with water cresses.

946. Quails Parboiled and Baked.

Tie a thin slice of bacon over the breast of each bird; put the quails into a baking dish, with a little boiling water; cover it closely, and set it on top of the range, letting the birds steam ten or fifteen minutes; this plumps them; then take off the cover and the pork, put the birds into the oven, basting them often with butter, brown them, and serve with currant jelly.

947. Quails Roasted.

Cover the breasts with very thin slices of bacon, or rub them well with butter, before placing them in the oven, basting them often with butter; cook twenty minutes, and serve on a hot dish the moment they are taken from the oven, and sprinkle them with salt and pepper.

948. Bread Sauce for Game. *(Mrs. Crane.)*

First roll one pint of dry bread crumbs, and pass half of them through a sieve; put one small onion into one pint of milk, and when it boils remove the onion, and thicken the milk with the one-half pint of sifted crumbs; take it from the

W

fire, and stir in one heaping teaspoonful of butter, a grating of nutmeg, pepper, and salt; put a little butter into a frying pan, and when hot, throw in the one-half pint of coarser crumbs which remained; stir them over the fire until they assume a light brown color, taking care that they do not burn, and stir into them a small pinch of cayenne pepper; they should be rather dry; for serving, put a plump roast quail on a plate, pour over it a tablespoonful of the white sauce, on this place a tablespoonful of the crumbs; the sauce boat, and the plate of crumbs may be passed separately, or the host may arrange them at the table before the birds are passed.

949. Scollops of Quails with Truffles.

Remove the fillets or breasts of six quails, cut each fillet in two, and trim the parts to a round shape; cook one-half of a pound of truffles in Madeira wine, and cut them into slices; put the scollops of quail into a frying pan with some butter; fry them until done, and mix with the truffles; put a nice border on the dish, pile the center with the scollops and truffles, pour in some Espagnole or brown sauce, flavored with a little Madeira, and serve. Truffles can be procured canned.

950. Snipe and Woodcock Fried.

Dress and wipe them clean, tie the legs close to the body, skin the heads and necks, and tie the beaks under the wings; tie also a very thin slice of bacon around the breast of each bird, and fry in boiling lard for five minutes; season and serve on toast.

951. Plovers

Are cooked the same way as quails or partridges.

VENISON.

952. Roast Saddle of Venison.

Make rather deep incisions, following the grain of the meat from the top, and insert pieces of pork about one-third of an inch square and one to one and one-half inches long, sprinkle over salt and a little flour, place in a hot oven for about two hours for an eight pound roast, baste often and serve with currant jelly.

953. Broiled Venison Steak.

Have the gridiron hot, broil and put on a hot dish, rub over them butter, pepper, salt and a little melted currant jelly; some cooks add a tablespoonful of Madeira, sherry, or port wine to the melted currant jelly; if one does not wish to serve the jelly, garnish simply with lemon slices.

954. Stewed Venison.

Cut it into steaks, spread over them a thin layer of stuffing made with bread crumbs, minced onion, parsley, pepper, salt, and a little pork chopped fine; now roll them separately, and tie them each with a cord; stew them in boiling water or stock, thicken the gravy with flour and butter mixed, and add one or two spoonfuls of sherry or port wine.

RABBITS.

955. Baked Rabbits.

After they are skinned, dressed, and hung over night, put them into a baking pan, sprinkle over pepper, and salt, and put also a thin slice of bacon on the top of each rabbit; now pour some boiling water into the bottom of the pan, and cover it with another pan of equal size, letting the rabbits steam fifteen or twenty minutes; then take off the cover, baste them with a little butter and let them brown. Rabbits are much improved by larding.

956. Stewed Rabbits or Hasenpfeffer. *(a la Mrs. D.)*

Skin, dress, and wash a rabbit nicely, cut into pieces, put into a pan with a large tablespoonful of lard, fry it a light brown on both sides, add salt and pepper to taste, one onion, four cloves of garlic, half a dozen sprigs of parsley, a little celery if handy, cover with water and stew gently for two hours ; do not let the water boil down to less than one-half. About fifteen minutes before serving, add half a cupful of vinegar, (pure wine vinegar is preferable) the gravy may be thickened with a little flour if desired. This method of stewing a rabbit is much superior to the German style of preparing a *Hasenpfeffer*, namely : soaking the rabbit in spiced vinegar a few days, a process that renders the meat tasteless.

MEATS.

957. Roast Beef.

To twelve pounds, or a "tenderloin roast," add one pint of water, one tablespoonful of salt, and one teaspoonful of pepper ; mix the salt and pepper, rub them well into the beef, lay it in the dripping pan with the water and roast two hours, basting it often ; when the beef is taken up, pour the fat from the dripping pan, and see that the gravy is well seasoned, put a few spoonfuls over the beef, and serve the rest in a gravy boat, thickened, if preferred, with browned flour.

958. Beef a la Mode.

Bone a round of beef, lard it with fat bacon, make several incisions, and fill them with a savory dressing of bread, in which there is a little chopped pork, and stuff it with the same, skewering it well together; tie it in good form with twine, put some pieces of pork in a pot, and when fried to a crisp take them out, lay in the beef and turn it until nicely browned all over ; then add hardly enough water to cover it, with a large onion, chopped, one sliced carrot, (several carrots may be used, with the addition of a little more water,) one dozen cloves, a small bunch of sweet herbs, pepper and salt ; cover closely and let it stew gently, but steadily for several hours, until very tender ; the water must boil down to make the gravy rich, but be careful that it does not burn ; it may be strained, and thickened with browned flour, or not, as preferred.

959. To Broil a Beefsteak.

It should be thick and tender, lay it on a gridiron, before or over a clear coal fire, and as soon as seared, turn it and sear the other side, to prevent the escape of the juice; if there is then danger of burning, the fire may be somewhat reduced by sprinkling ashes over it; turn the steak often, and serve the moment it is cooked; have the platter hot, and put small bits of butter, with a little pepper and salt over the steak, this may be garnished with fried sliced potatoes, or with the steak placed in the center of the dish, have browned potato balls, the size of a marble, in a pyramidal pile at each end.

960. Another Method of Broiling Beefsteak.

Put it on the gridiron before a clear fire; have two ounces of butter (more, if the steak is large), with an even teaspoonful of salt, and one-half as much pepper, on the end of a hot platter, when the steak is browned on one side, lay it on the platter and press the juice from it; return it to the gridiron, mix the gravy, and when the beef is sufficiently cooked take it up, turn it two or three times in the gravy, wipe the edge of the platter and serve, stewed mushrooms or tomatoes may be served with it if liked, or it may be garnished with shaved horse-radish; when the steak is broiled, many prefer leaving it covered in the oven a few moments before serving, and many serve it without butter.

961. Beefsteak Smothered in Onions.

Cut six onions quite fine, and stew them in a saucepan with one pint of water, two ounces of butter, one teaspoonful of salt, and one-half as much of pepper, dredge in a little flour, stew until the onions are quite soft, then add a well-broiled beefsteak, let it simmer about ten minutes, and serve very hot.

962. Beefsteaks for Extra Company.

Use only the fillets, that is, the tender parts of the porter.

house or tenderloin steak; cut in even shapes round or oval, and from one inch to one and one-half inches thick; broil, and serve in individual dishes, surrounded with Saratoga or fried potatoes in any form, or with water cresses, or mushrooms, or stuffed tomatoes, or green peas.

963. Beef Roll. *(Cannelon de Bœuf.)*

Chop two pounds of lean beef very fine, chop and pound into a mortar one-half of a pound of fat bacon, and mix it with the beef; season it with pepper and salt, (it will not require much salt,) one small nutmeg, the grated rind of one lemon, the juice of one-quarter of it, one heaping tablespoonful of parsley, minced fine; or, it can be seasoned with an additional tablespoonful of onion; or, if no onion, or parsley, be at hand, with summer savory and thyme; bind all these together with two eggs, form them into a roll, surround the roll with buttered paper, which tie securely around it, then cover it with paste made of flour and water, and bake two hours; remove the paper and crust, and serve it hot with tomato sauce or brown gravy.

964. Beef Croquettes.

There is no more satisfactory manner of using cold cooked beef than for croquettes, which may be served with tomato or any of the brown sauces, or may be served without sauce at all, as is generally the case; they are made in the same manner as is described for chicken croquettes, merely substituting the same amount of beef for the chicken, and of rice for the brains.

VEAL.

The best pieces of veal are the loin and the fillet, but a variety of dishes can be made with the cutlets and their different accompaniments; it is always better cooked with pork or ham, and should always be thoroughly cooked.

965. Roast of Veal. The Fillet.

Take out the bone of the joint, make a deep incision

between the fillet and the flap; then fill it with stuffing made as follows two cupfuls of bread crumbs, one-half a cupful of chopped pork, one-half a lemon peel grated, a little juice of the lemon, thyme, and summer savory, or any herbs to taste; bind the veal into a round form, fasten it with skewers and twine, sprinkle over pepper and salt, and cover it with buttered paper; baste well and often, just before it is done, remove the paper, sprinkle over a little flour, and rub it over with a little butter, this will give a frothy appearance to the surface of the meat; when done, add to the gravy in the pan a little flour, and boiling water, and, when cooked, some lemon juice; strain it, remove the grease, and pour it around the roast, or serve in a gravy boat, fry some pieces of ham cut in diamond shape, place these in a circle around the roast, each piece alternated with a slice of lemon.

966. Fricatelle. *(Mrs. B.)* [Time.—One hour.]

Articles.—Two pounds of lean veal, one large onion, six cloves of garlic, some parsley, two pounds of lean pork, five eggs, three-fourths cupful of flour, and salt and pepper to taste.

Directions.—Chop both veal and pork very fine, mince the onion, garlic and parsley fine, add your seasoning to the meat and mix well, mix the eggs with the mixture, and last the flour, kneading it well together, place in shallow pans about one and one-half inches thick and bake about one hour, serve cold, sliced and decorated with sprigs of parsley or chervil.

967. Veal Cutlets Broiled.

The rib cutlets should always be neatly trimmed, the bone scraped at the end, so that it will look smooth and white, broil them on a moderate fire, basting them occasionally with butter, and turning them often, dish them in a circle with tomato sauce.

968. Sweetbreads, How to Prepare.

Veal sweetbreads are the best, but spoil very soon, therefore the moment they come from the market they should be put into cold water to soak for about an hour, then lard them, or rather draw a lardoon of pork through the center and put them into salted boiling water and let them boil about twenty minutes, or until they are thoroughly done; throw them then into cold water for a moment only, and they will be firm and white; remove carefully the skin and little pipes and put the sweetbreads away in a cool place until ready to cook again; the simplest and best way to cook them is as follows:

969. Fried Sweetbreads.

Take them prepared as above, cut them into even sized pieces, sprinkle with pepper and salt, egg and bread crumb them and fry in hot lard; they are often immersed in boiling lard, and yet oftener fried in a frying pan, if so, when done put them on a hot dish, turn out part of the lard from the frying pan, leaving about one-half a teaspoonful; pour in a cupful of milk, thickened with a little flour; let it cook, stirring it constantly, season with salt and pepper, strain and pour over the sweetbreads.

970. Sweetbreads with Tomatoes.

Fry the prepared sweetbreads as above; stew either fresh tomatoes in the usual manner, strain through a sieve and pour hot over the sweetbreads, of course omitting the white sauce mentioned in the recipe for fried sweetbreads.

971. Vol-au-Vent of Sweetbreads and Oysters.

Prepare three or four sweetbreads as indicated in recipe No. 968; when cold cut into dice, salt, pepper and dredge them with flour; have in a basin two or three dozen stewed, drained oysters, a small teacupful of stewed button mushrooms, one dozen or more olives, pared in one piece close to the kernel; put one-quarter pound of butter in a stew pan, melt it, and add two tablespoonfuls of flour, stirring well and pouring in stock gradually until the sauce is of a creamy consistency, season with salt, pepper or cayenne, and add a *very little* grated nutmeg; put in the sweetbreads, stirring to prevent browning; when thoroughly heated add one after the other, the oysters, mushrooms and olives, and a tablespoonful of wine vinegar; stir and heat up again but do not let it boil; serve in a *vol-au-vent* crust, after gently warming it. See recipe for *vol-au-vent*

972. Fourchette.

ARTICLES.—Bits of nice salt pork about one-third of an inch thick and two or three inches square, and bits of calf liver the same size.

DIRECTIONS.—Put these alternately on a long skewer, beginning and ending with pork, lay it in the oven across a dripping pan, and roast as you would a bird, basting occasionally; when done, slide the pieces from the skewer, and serve on a platter.

973. Pork and Liver Brochette. *(Madame Grimard.)*

ARTICLES.—Bits of nice salt pork about one-quarter inch thick and about one inch square, and bits of calf liver the same size.

DIRECTIONS.—Put these alternately on a long skewer, beginning and ending with pork, broil over a clear, hot fire till nicely done, and serve hot on the skewers.

See Part I. for recipes for calves' head, feet and liver.

MUTTON.

The best roasts are the leg, the saddle and the shoulder, and are all roasted according to the regular rules of roasting; they are also good braised. Currant jelly is usually served with the roast, and the dish may be garnished with stuffed potatoes.

974. Boiled Leg of Mutton.

This should be quite fresh; put it into well-salted boiling water, which do not let stop boiling until the meat is thoroughly done; the rule is to boil it one-quarter hour for each pound of meat; caper sauce should be served with this dish, either in a sauce boat or poured over the mutton, and garnished with parsley.

975. Stuffed Leg of Mutton.

Take out the bone and fill the cavity with a stuffing made of bread crumbs, seasoned with pepper, salt, a little summer savory, two ounces of salt pork chopped fine, and a bit of butter half the size of an egg; skewer the ends, sprinkle the mutton with a teaspoonful of salt and half a teaspoonful of pepper; lay it in the dripping pan with a little water, and put it in a brisk oven; when it begins to roast, put a little butter over it, and dredge it lightly with flour; watch it very closely, keep an even heat and baste it thoroughly every fifteen minutes; a piece weighing six pounds will roast in one and one-half hours.

976. Mutton Cutlets.

Trim them well, scraping the bones; roll them in a little melted butter, or olive oil, season and broil them; or they are nice, egged, bread crumbed and fried; serve around a bed of mashed potatoes, which they help to season; tomato sauce is also a favorite companion to the cutlets; they can also be served with almost any kind of vegetables, peas or string beans placed in the center of the dish and the cutlets arranged in a circle around.

977. Mutton Stew. [TIME.—TWO HOURS AND A HALF.]

ARTICLES.—One and one-half pounds of mutton, two ounces of butter, one and one-half ounces of flour, one quart of boiling water, two teaspoonfuls of salt, one-half teaspoonful of pepper, a pinch of summer savory, two onions with two cloves stuck in each, and turnips.

DIRECTIONS.—Cut the mutton into bits and fry in the butter about fifteen minutes, dredge over it the flour and let it brown; add the boiling water, the salt, pepper, the onions cut in halves, cover closely and let simmer three-quarters of an hour;

form sixteen cork-shaped pieces of turnip with an apple corer, they should be of uniform length from two to three inches; fry them brown in one ounce of butter, drop them in the stew, cover, and continue boiling one hour longer; then drop in eight or ten potatoes, cut down to the size of a black walnut when the potatoes are cooked, the stew is finished; take out the onion, see that the gravy is well seasoned, pour the whole into a hot platter and serve. The bits of turnip and potato left from the cutting will do for soup, or with a little addition, may be cooked as vegetables.

978. English Mutton Stew.

Slice in thin small pieces, the cold roasted or boiled mutton left over from dinner, barely cover it with cold water, add pepper, salt and a small bit of butter, and let it simmer a few minutes; thicken the gravy with a little flour and brown it with a browned flour; add half a tumblerful of currant jelly and the same of port wine; simmer a little longer and serve. This makes a very dark colored dish.

979. Irish Stew. [TIME.—ONE HOUR AND A HALF.]

ARTICLES.—Two pounds of sliced potatoes, two pounds of *scrag* mutton, two sliced onions, and seasoning to taste.

DIRECTIONS.—Cut the mutton into six or eight pieces, put into the stew pan and cover with one pint of cold water, add the potatoes and onions, let it come slowly to the boiling point, then skim well; let it simmer one hour and a half, season to taste, and serve.

980. Mutton Haricot.

Trim mutton chops, but leave the bone; brown them on both sides in a hot pan with a very little butter; then drop them into boiling water deep enough to cover them, add two sliced carrots and let them stew until the carrots are tender; while stewing, brown half a sliced onion in the pan where the chops were fried, add to the carrots, and season with pepper and salt.

LAMB.

The best roasts are the fore and hind quarters, and the rules applying to veal will apply to lamb.

981. Lamb Chops a la Royal.

Trim them neatly, scrape the ends of the bones nicely, roll them in a little melted butter, and broil them carefully; when done rub more butter over them, season them with pepper and salt, and slip little paper ruffles over the ends of the bones. They may be served with a center of almost any kind of vegetables, a smooth mound of mashed potatoes, spinach, peas, beans, cauliflower, or stuffed baked tomatoes, or with a tomato sauce, and make a favorite company dinner dish.

982. Lamb Croquettes

Are made the same as chicken croquettes, only substituting cold cooked lamb for the chicken. Many prefer the lamb to the chicken croquettes, even for dinner or lunch parties.

SAUCES FOR MEATS.

The foundation of a large proportion of sauces is in what the French cook knows as a *roux*, and we as "drawn butter." As our drawn butter is often lumpy, or with the taste of the raw flour, we give the French method of preparing it.

983. Roux or Drawn Butter Sauce.

Melt in a saucepan a piece of butter the size of an egg, and add two even tablespoonfuls of sifted flour, one ounce of butter to two of flour being a safe rule; stir till smooth and pour in slowly one pint of milk, or milk and water, or water alone; with milk it is called *cream roux*, and is used for boiled fish and poultry; where the butter and flour are allowed to brown it is called a *brown roux*, and is thinned with the soup or stew which it is designed to thicken, and when made with the flour, butter and water only, it is called a *white roux*.

984. Caper Sauce.

Capers added to a *white roux*, which is the butter and flour with water added, as above, gives us a caper sauce. Pickled nasturtiums are a good substitute for capers.

985. Pickle Sauce.

Add two or three tablespoonfuls of pickles chopped or minced fine to a *white roux*, (see *roux* or "drawn butter" sauce.)

986. Boiled Egg Sauce.

Add to half a pint of *white roux*, three hard boiled eggs, chopped, but not very fine.

987. Anchovy Sauce.

Add to half a pint of *white roux* two teaspoonfuls of anchovy extract or anchovy paste.

988. Shrimp Sauce.

To half a pint of *white roux* add half a can of shrimps, whole or chopped a little, let it simmer, not boil, a few minutes, and just before removing from the fire add a few drops of lemon juice and a very little cayenne pepper. Some add a teaspoonful of anchovy paste, it is a matter of taste.

989. Sauce Hollandaise or Dutch Sauce.

This is one of the best sauces ever made for boiled fish, asparagus or cauliflower. Pour four tablespoonfuls of wine vinegar into a small stew pan, add some pepper corns and salt; let the liquid boil until it is reduced one half, let it cool, then add to it the well beaten yolks of four or five eggs, also four ounces (the size of an egg) of good butter, more salt, if necessary, and a very little nutmeg; set the stew pan on a very slow fire, and stir the liquid until it is about as thick as cream, and immediately remove it; now put this cup or stew pan into another pan containing a little warm water kept at the side of the fire; work the sauce briskly with a spoon or a little whisk, o as to get it frothy, but adding little bits of butter, in all about three ounces, (say about the size of half an egg); when the sauce has become light and smooth it is ready for use.

990. Mushroom Sauce.

Put a piece of butter the size of a walnut, into a small stew pan or tin basin, and when it bubbles add a teaspoonful of flour (not heaping); when well cooked stir in a cupful of stock, (reduced and strong,) and half a teacupful of the mushroom juice from the can; let it simmer for a minute or two, then after straining it, add half or three-quarters of a can of mushrooms, pepper, salt, and a few drops of lemon juice, and when thoroughly hot it is ready to pour over the meat.

991. Sauce aux Fines Herbes.

ARTICLES.—Half a pint of good stock, three tablespoonfuls of mushrooms, one tablespoonful of onion, two of parsley, and one shallot all chopped fine.

DIRECTIONS.—Fry the shallot and onion in a little butter until they assume a light yellow color, then add a teaspoonful of flour and cook it a minute, stir in the stock, mushrooms and parsley, simmer for five minutes, then add a little Worcestershire or lime juice sauce, and salt to taste.

992. Bechamel Sauce.

Put butter the size of a walnut into a stew pan, and when it bubbles stir in an even tablespoonful of flour, which cook thoroughly without letting it take color; mix into this a cupful of strong veal broth (*i. e.* veal put into cold water and boiled four or five hours) add next a cupful of boiling cream and one grating of nutmeg, let it simmer, stirring it well for a few minutes, then strain and it is ready for use. The sauce would be improved if the usual soup bunch of vegetables were added to the stock while it is being made.

993. A Simple Brown Sauce, (Sauce Espagnol.)

Put into a saucepan a tablespoonful of minced onion, and a little butter; when it has taken color, sprinkle in a heaping tablespoonful of flour, stir it well, and when brown add a pint of stock, cook it a few minutes and strain.

994. Sauce Poivrade.

To the above sauce add a cupful of claret wine, two cloves, a sprig of parsley, one of thyme, a bay leaf, pepper and salt; boil all two or three minutes and strain.

995. Sauce Piquante.

Make same as the poivrade sauce, omitting the claret wine, and adding instead a tablespoonful each of minced pickles, vinegar and capers.

996. Noodle Sauce. *(M. F. Friederich.)* [TIME.—ABOUT FIFTEEN MINUTES.]

ARTICLES.—A piece of butter the size of an egg, one-half an onion, two laurel leaves, salt and pepper, a little flour, two tablespoonfuls of vinegar, the yolk of one egg, and a cup of water.

DIRECTIONS.—Put the butter and onion in a saucepan and fry till brown, stir in about a teaspoonful of flour, then add the water, stirring all the time, next the laurel leaves, salt and pepper to taste, and next the vinegar, let it simmer about fifteen minutes, dan just before removing from the fire beat up the yolk of an egg and stir it in; serve hot in a gravy boat.

997. Chili Sauce. *(Mrs. Geo. Dorr.)* [TIME.—THREE HOURS—SLOW FIRE.]

ARTICLES.—Thirty ripe tomatoes, eight tablespoonfuls of brown sugar, eight onions, eight tablespoonfuls of vinegar, salt to taste, and eight green peppers.

DIRECTIONS.—Cut up the tomatoes, peppers and onions in a kettle, add vinegar, sugar and salt, simmer three hours, bottle and seal.

998. Tomato Catsup. [Time.—Three hours.]

ARTICLES.—To one-half bushel tomatoes add one quart of vinegar, one pound of salt, one-quarter pound of ground black pepper, one-quarter pound of ground allspice, two pounds of brown sugar, one ounce of cayenne pepper, one ounce of ground cloves, and six large onions.

DIRECTIONS.—Put all together and boil for three hours, stirring it to keep from burning; when cool strain through a fine sieve or coarse cloth, and bottle it for use.

VEGETABLES.

Part I. contains many recipes for preparing vegetables of all kinds. We add, however, a few not found there.

999. Lyonnaise Potatoes.

ARTICLES.—Half a pound of cold boiled potatoes, two ounces of onion, a heaping teaspoonful of minced parsley, and butter the size of an egg.

DIRECTIONS.—Slice the potatoes, put the butter into a saucepan, and when hot throw in the onion, minced, which fry to a light color, add the sliced potatoes, which turn until they are thoroughly hot, and of light color also, then mix in the minced parsley, and serve immediately while they are quite hot.

1000. Potatoes a la Neige.

Take mashed potatoes prepared in the usual manner, press through a colander into the dish they are to be served in, they will then resemble rice or vermicelli; they will be very light and nice and make a pretty dish, but must be served very hot. This makes a favorite accompaniment to venison and is often served around a rolled rib roast of beef.

1001. Saratoga Potatoes.

ARTICLES.—Raw potatoes and hot lard.

DIRECTIONS.—Pare and slice some raw potatoes *very thin*, lay them in cold water for half an hour, wipe dry in two cloths,

Gaff, Fleischmann & Co.'s
COMPRESSED YEAST,

FACTORY DEPOT: 30 EAST GENESEE ST.,

BUFFALO, N. Y.

ALL CORRESPONDENCE PROMPTLY ANSWERED.

SOLD BY ALL GROCERS.

To ensure the best results, always use

GAFF, FLEISCHMANN & CO.'S
COMPRESSED YEAST

IN ALL RECIPES WHERE YEAST IS REQUIRED.

LIME JUICE SAUCE.

L. ROSE & CO'S.,

TRADE MARK

LIME JUICE SAUCE,

Used with Hot or Cold Meats,

SOUPS, GRAVIES, FISH, OYSTERS, etc.

An Excellent Stomachic, Assisting Digestion.

Containing all the Valuable Properties of

ROSE'S CELEBRATED LIME JUICE CORDIAL.

Cooling and Purifying the Blood, as opposed to the Fiery Heating Sauces hitherto in use.

ROSE & CO.'S Preparations from the Lime Fruit, are highly recommended by the London Lancet, as also by principal Scientific and Trade Journals and by eminent Analysts.

———o———

SOLD BY

Messrs. DINGENS BRO'S,

And by Dealers in Fine Groceries generally.

———o———

W. FLEMING & CO.,

(Sole Agents for L. Rose & Co., of London, England,)

NEW YORK.

spreading them upon one and pressing the other upon them; have ready in a frying pan some boiling lard, fry a light brown, sprinkle with salt, and serve in a napkin laid in a deep dish, and folded over the potatoes; to dry them of the fat take from the frying pan as soon as they are brown with a perforated skimmer, put into a colander and shake for an instant. They should be crisp and free from grease.

1002. Baked Tomatoes. *(Mrs. M. Westerhold.)* [TIME.— HALF AN HOUR.]

ARTICLES.—Large, smooth tomatoes, bread crumbs, and salt pork

DIRECTIONS.—Take large, smooth tomatoes, wipe them and cut a thin slice from the blossom end, take out the seeds and fill each tomato with a forcemeat made of bread crumbs, some salt pork, chopped very fine, seasoning well with salt and pepper, put a bit of butter in each, fit on the top, place them in a deep dish and bake about half an hour.

1003. Asparagus on Toast. [TIME.—HALF AN HOUR.]

ARTICLES.—Asparagus, salt, butter, and toasted bread.

DIRECTIONS.—Tie the stalks in small bunches, boil them in a very little salted water about half an hour, toast as many slices of bread as there are bunches of asparagus, lay a bunch on each slice, add butter to the water sufficient to make a rich gravy, thicken with a little flour, season with pepper, pour over the asparagus and serve.

1004. Oyster Plants Stewed.

As you scrape them, throw them into a bowl of cold water in which is mixed a tablespoonful of vinegar; when all are scraped, cut them either into half inch lengths, or lengthwise into four pieces, which again cut into three inch lengths, throw them into boiling water, in which you have placed one-half teaspoonful of salt and one-third teaspoonful of sugar to one quart of water; when done, drain, and mix them with white sauce, either drawn butter or a simple bechamel sauce at pleasure.

1005. Cauliflower with White Sauce.

Trim off the outside leaves, and put the cauliflower into well salted boiling water; be careful to take it out as soon as tender, to prevent it dropping into pieces; make in a saucepan a white sauce as follows: put butter the size of an egg into a saucepan and when it bubbles stir in a scant half teacupful of flour, stir with an egg whisk until cooked, then add two teacupfuls of thin cream, some pepper and salt, stir it over the fire until perfectly smooth, pour the sauce over the cauliflower, and serve. Many let the cauliflower simmer in the sauce a few moments before serving. The *sauce Hollandaise* is very fine for cauliflower.

1006. Spinach.

Having washed it thoroughly put it into just enough salted boiling water to cover it; when it is tender, squeeze out all the water, and press it through a colander; then fry it for a few minutes, with a little butter, pepper and salt; serve with sliced hard boiled eggs on top; or, if used for a garnish for lamb, add a little lemon juice and a spoonful of stock; or, it is nice served as a course by itself, arranged as follows: put a circle of thin slices of buttered toast (one slice for each person at the table) around the dish, and on each slice put a cupful of spinach, neatly smoothed into shape; press the half of a hard boiled egg into the top of each pile of spinach, leaving the cut part of the egg uppermost.

1007. Beets.

If they are winter beets, soak them over night, in any case be careful not to prick or cut the skin before boiling, as they will lose their color, put them into boiling water and boil until tender; if they are served hot, pour a little melted butter, pepper and salt over them; they may be served cold, cut into slices with some vinegar over them, or cut into little dice and mixed with other cold vegetables for a winter salad, if desired.

1008. Artichokes.

Cut off the outside tough leaves and trim the bottom, throw them into boiling salted water, with a few drops of vinegar; when quite done, drain and serve with drawn butter, or still better with *sauce Hollandaise*.

1009. To Cook Cranberries.

Add one teacupful of water to a quart of cranberries, and put them over the fire; after cooking ten minutes add two heaping cupfuls of sugar, and cook about ten minutes longer, stirring them often; pour them into a bowl or mould, and when cold they can be removed as a jelly; the berries will seem very dry before the sugar is added, but if more water is used they will not form a jelly.

OMELETS.

Part I. contains many recipes for plain and fancy omelets; we add a few more.

1010. Omelets with Mushrooms.

Boil the mushrooms in a little water or stock, to which add pepper, salt, a few drops of lemon juice and a little flour to thicken it slightly; make the plain omelet and just before turning one half over the other, place part of the mushrooms in the center; when the omelet is turned, of course the mushrooms will be quite enveloped; when you serve it pour the remainder of the mushrooms around it with the juice.

1011. Omelets with Shrimps.

Inclose some canned shrimps in the center of the omelet, same as you have the mushrooms, and garnish the omelets with shrimps around it in the dish.

1012. Omelets with Oysters.

Scald the oysters in their own liquor; when just about to

boil, plump them by throwing them into cold water, and beat them into the eggs before cooking your omelet, leaving a few oysters out to garnish the plate.

1013. Sweet Omelet for Dessert.

Add a little sugar to the eggs, instead of pepper and salt, make it then as a plain omelet, enclosing in the center any kind of preserves, marmalade or jam; when it is turned upon the dish sprinkle sugar on the top.

1014. Omelet with Rum.

Add a little sugar to the eggs, say a sherry glassful to six eggs and make as a plain omelet; when turned upon the dish sprinkle a little handful of sugar over the top and pour five or six tablespoonfuls of Jamaica or Santa Cruz rum over it, set it on fire and serve it at the table burning.

1015. Omelet Soufflé.

ARTICLES.—Six whites and three yolks of eggs, three ounces of pulverized sugar or three tablespoonfuls, and vanilla or lemon flavoring.

DIRECTIONS.—Beat the yolks and sugar to a light cream and add the flavoring—only a few drops; then beat the whites into the stiffest possible frost, have the yolks in a deep bowl, turn the whites over them, and with a spoon, giving it a rotary motion, cut the two, mixing them carefully together; turn this upon a baking dish, either of earthen or tin, with sides two or three inches high and slightly buttered; smooth over the top, sprinkle over sugar and put it into a moderate oven. If it has to be turned or moved in the oven, do it as gently as possible. When it has risen well and is of a fine yellow color, it is ready to be served, and should be served at once, or it might fall.

SALADS.

A Frenchman thinks he cannot eat his dinner without his salad. It would be well if every one had the same appreciation of this most wholesome, refreshing, and at the same time, most economical dish. It is an accomplishment to know how to dress a salad well, which is especially prized by the fashionable world. The materials used for salads are generally those shown in the following list:

Lettuce,	Onions,	Cold boiled potatoes,
Celery,	Garlic,	Cabbage,
Endive,	Radishes,	Cives,
Garden-cress,	Beet-root,	Tarragon,
Sorrel,	Pepper-grass,	Nasturtium blossoms;

or salads of mixed vegetables *(salades en macedoine)*, selected from this list of vegetables:

Cold boiled potatoes,	Olives,	Cucumbers,
String beans,	Tomatoes,	Carrots,
Navy-beans,	Pease,	Truffles,
Lima beans,	Cauliflower,	Turnips.
Beet-root,	Asparagus-tops,	

Salads are also made of cold boiled fowls or fish, as follows:

Chickens,	Salmon,	Shrimps,
Lobster,	Prawns,	Sardines.

There are two kinds of dressing which are the best and oftenest used: the *Mayonnaise* and the French dressing. Epicures prefer the simple French dressing for salads served without fish or fowl. For chicken and fish salads, and some vegetables, as tomatoes and cauliflowers, they use the *Mayonnaise* sauce. This arrangement of dressings is almost universal in London and Paris. In America we use the *Mayonnaise* for all salads. The simple salad with the French dressing is, after all, the most refreshing and satisfactory, if one has a heavy dinner served before it. The recipes are as follows:

1016. Mayonnaise Sauce.

Put the uncooked yolk of an egg into a cold bowl; beat it well with a silver fork; then add two saltspoonfuls of salt, and one saltspoonful of mustard powder; work them well a minute before adding the oil; then mix in a little good oil, which must be poured in very slowly (a few drops at a time) at first, alternated occasionally with a few drops of vinegar. In proportion as the oil is used, the sauce should gain consistency. When it begins to have the appearance of jelly, alternate a few drops of lemon juice with the oil. When the egg has absorbed a gill of oil, finish the sauce by adding a very little pinch of cayenne pepper, and one and a half teaspoonfuls of good vinegar; taste it to see that there are salt, mustard, cayenne, and vinegar enough. If not, add more very carefully. These proportions will suit most tastes; yet some like more mustard and more oil. Be cautious not to use too much cayenne.

By beating the egg a minute before adding the oil, there is little danger of the sauce curdling; yet if, by adding too much oil at first, it should possibly curdle, immediately interrupt the operation. Put the yolks of one or two eggs on another plate; beat them well, and add the curdled *Mayonnaise* by degrees, and finish by adding more oil, lemon juice, vinegar, salt, and cayenne according to taste. If lemons are not at hand, many use vinegar instead.

1017. Red Mayonnaise Sauce.

Pound some lobster coral, pass it through a sieve, and mix it with the *Mayonnaise* sauce.

1018. French Dressing.

ARTICLES.—One tablespoonful of vinegar, three tablespoonfuls of olive oil, one saltspoonful of pepper, one saltspoonful of salt, and one even teaspoonful of onion scraped fine.

DIRECTIONS.—Pour the oil, mixed with the pepper and salt, over the salad; mix them together, then add the vinegar and mix again. Many different combinations can be made to suit the fancy, from the list of salad materials. We give certain combinations oftenest seen. It must be remembered that salad is never good unless perfectly fresh. It should not be mixed, or brought into the dining-room, until the moment when it is to be eaten. When preparing lettuce salad, choose the crisp, tender, center leaves of head lettuce.

COMBINATIONS.

1019. Lettuce (French Cook).

Rub garlic in the dish in which lettuce, with French dressing (without onion), is to be served. Leave no pieces of the garlic —merely rubbing the dish will give flavor enough. The French often use garlic in salads. We would advise, however, the use of the simple French dressing with onion to be mixed with the lettuce leaves, and dispense with the garlic. Use plain vinegar. Nasturtium blossoms have a most pleasant, piquant flavor, and make a beautiful garnish for a salad.

2. Lettuce, with water-cresses or pepper-grass mixed, and small radishes placed around for a garnish. French or *Mayonnaise* dressing.

3. Lettuce, with cives mixed, and olives placed around for garnish. French dressing.

4. Lettuce, with celery mixed (most excellent). Cut the celery into pieces, an inch and a half long; then slice these lengthwise into four or five pieces. Mix with lettuce. French dressing.

5. Lettuce and sorrel mixed. French dressing.

6. Lettuce, with anchovies (cut into thin strips as celery) and chopped cives. To vary this dish, prawns and shrimps are used for a garnish, or the anchovies may be left out. French dressing.

7. Endive alone. French dressing.

8. Endive, mixed with water-cress. French dressing.

9. Endive, with celery, beets, and hard-boiled eggs in slices. French dressing. Endive in center, row of eggs

around, then row of beets, then an edge of fringed celery.

10. Water-cress is good mixed with cold boiled beets. Cut the beets into little dice; garnish with olives. French dressing.

11. Lettuce and dice of cold boiled potatoes, and cold boiled beets. Potatoes piled in the center, beets next, and lettuce around the edge of the dish. French dressing.

1020. Potato Salad.

New small onions sliced, mixed with cold boiled potatoes cut into dice. French dressing. This potato salad is very nice.

Another way is to rub the dish with garlic in which the salad is made. Mix chopped parsley with the potatoes cut into dice. French dressing.

1. Sliced cucumbers, and sliced new onions. French dressing.

2. Cabbage alone, with French or *Mayonnaise* dressing.

1021. Cold Slaw.

Cut the cabbage not too fine; sprinkle pepper and salt over it, and set it on ice, or in a cool place, to keep it crisp.

DRESSING.—Beat the yolks of three eggs, or the whole of two eggs, with five tablespoonfuls of good strong vinegar, two heaping teaspoonfuls of sugar (three, if the vinegar is very strong), half a teaspoonful of made mustard, and butter size of an almond. Put these ingredients into a tin cup, and stir them over the fire until they are about to boil, or until they become a smooth paste. Put the mixture one side to become cold, and to remain until just before it is wanted at table; then mix it well with the cold cabbage, and garnish the top with slices of hard-boiled egg.

Cold slaw is especially nice served with fried oysters. Place it in the center of the warm platter on a folded napkin (a too warm platter would injure it), then make a circle of fried oysters around it. This makes a nice course for dinner.

The salads of vegetables are generally better with the French dressing. They present a better appearance by cutting them with a small vegetable-cutter.

1022. Salad of Vegetables (Salade de Legumes).

Mix cold boiled pease, string-beans, pieces of cauliflower, asparagus tops, or almost any one of the small vegetables; do not cut the larger ones too fine. French dressing.

2. Cold boiled potatoes, lima beans, beets, and carrots. French dressing.

3. Cold baked navy beans, with *Mayonnaise* sauce.

1023. Mayonnaise of Cauliflower.

Place some cauliflowers into just enough boiling water to cover them; add a little salt and butter to the water. When cooked, let them become cold; then season them with a marinade of a little salt and pepper, three spoonfuls of vinegar, and one spoonful of oil. Let them then remain for an hour. When ready to serve, pile them on the dish to a point; then mask them with a *Mayonnaise* sauce.

1024. Tomatoes a la Mayonnaise.

This is a truly delicious dish; it would, in fact, be good every day during the tomato season.

Select large, fine tomatoes and place them in the ice-chest; the colder they are, the better, if not frozen; skin them without the use of hot water, and slice them, still retaining the form of the whole tomato. Arrange them in uniform order on a dish, with a spoonful of *Mayonnaise* sauce thick as a jelly on the top of each tomato. Garnish the dish with leaves of any kind. Parsley is very pretty.

Some marinate the tomato slices, *i. e.*, dip them into a mixture of three spoonfuls of vinegar to one spoonful of oil, pepper, and salt; and then, after draining well, mix them in the *Mayonnaise* sauce.

1025. String Beans in Salad (French Cook).

String the beans and boil them whole; when boiled tender, and they have become cold, slice them lengthwise, cutting each bean into four long slices; place them neatly, the slices all lying in one direction, crosswise on a platter. Season them an hour or two before serving, with a marinade of a little pepper, salt, and three spoonfuls of vinegar to one spoonful of oil. Just before serving, drain from them any drops that may have collected, and carefully mix them with a French dressing. This makes a delicious salad.

1026. Chicken Salad.

Boil a young, tender chicken, and when cold separate the meat from the bones; cut it into little square blocks or dice; do not mince it. Cut white tender stalks of celery into about three-quarter inch lengths, saving the outside green stalks for soups; mix the chicken and celery together; and then stir well into them a mixture in the proportion of three tablespoonfuls of vinegar to one tablespoonful of oil, with pepper, salt, and a little mustard to taste. Put this aside for an hour or two, or until just before serving; this is called marinating the chicken; it will absorb the vinegar, etc. When about to serve, mix the celery and chicken with a *Mayonnaise* sauce, leaving a portion of the sauce to mask the top. Reserve several fresh ends or leaves of celery with which to garnish the dish. Stick a little bouquet of these tops in the center of the salad, then a row of them around it. From the center to each of the four sides sprinkle rows of capers. Sometimes slices or little cut diamonds of hard-boiled eggs are used for garnishing.

Chicken salad is often made with lettuce instead of celery. Marinate the chicken alone; add it to the small tender leaves (uncut) of the lettuce the last moment before serving; then pour *Mayonnaise* dressing over the top. Garnish with little center-heads of lettuce, capers, cold chopped red beets if you choose, or sliced hard boiled eggs. Sometimes little strips of anchovy are added for a garnish. When on the table it should all be mixed together. Many may profit by this recipe for chicken salad, for it is astonishing how few understand making so common a dish. It is generally minced, and mixed with hard-boiled eggs, etc., for a dressing.

1027. Chicken Salad. *(Careme's Recipe.)*

Take some tender pullets; fry them in the *saute* pan, or roast them; when cold, cut them up, skinning and trimming them neatly. Put the pieces into a tureen, with some salt, pepper, oil, vinegar, some sprigs of parsley, and an onion cut into slices; mix all well together, cover, and let stand for some hours, then, just before serving, drain the salad, taking care to remove all bits of onion, etc., and place it tastefully on lettuce leaves, with the hearts of the lettuce on top, and cover with a *Mayonnaise* dressing.

1028. Mayonnaise of Salmon.

Remove the skin and bones from a piece of salmon, boiled and cooled, and cut it into pieces two inches long. Marinate them, *i. e.*, place them in a dish, and season them with salt, pepper, a little oil, and, in this case, plenty of vinegar, some parsley, and a little onion cut up; then cover, and let them stand two or three hours. In the mean time, cut up some hard boiled eggs into four or eight pieces for a border. Cover the bottom of the salad dish with lettuce leaves, seasoned with a French dressing; place your salmon slices in a ring on the lettuce, pouring in the center a *Mayonnaise* sauce. Sprinkle capers over the whole.

Other kinds of fish, such as pike, blue-fish, and flounders, make very good salads, arranged in the same way. Careme, Gouffe, and Francatelli fry their fish and fowl in a *saute* pan, instead of boiling them. If you do not make use of remnants of salmon left from the table, you can form better-shaped slices by cutting the fish into little shapes before it is boiled. If you wish to boil them, immerse them in warm water (with vinegar and salt added) in a wire basket, or drainer.

1029. Salad a la Filley.

ARTICLES.—Cottage cheese, hard-boiled egg, and cives.

DIRECTIONS.—Arrange cives on a salad dish in such a manner as to form a nest; put into the nest whole hard boiled eggs (shelled), one for each person at table, alternated with little round cakes of cottage cheese. In serving, place upon each plate an egg, a cake of cottage cheese, and some of the cives. Each person cuts all together, and puts on the French dressing of oil, vinegar, pepper and salt.

1030. Shrimp Salad.—(*Maimy.*)

ARTICLES.—One can of shrimps, two or three sticks of celery, three tablespoonfuls of oil, three of vinegar, a teaspoonful of mustard, one-half teaspoonful of salt, one-quarter teaspoonful of pepper, two tablespoonfuls of capers, one lemon peeled, two hard boiled eggs.

DIRECTIONS.—Make a sauce of the vinegar, mustard, oil, salt and pepper; put the shrimps, celery, lemon, eggs and capers in a chopping bowl, chop up, then mix the sauce well with it; put it in a salad bowl or dish, spread over the salad a thin layer of salad dressing; (Durkee's or Gordon and Dilworth) decorate the top with slices of lemon, a few whole shrimps, capers, and pieces of hard boiled egg.

1031. Potato Salad. (*Mrs. W.*) [TIME.—HALF AN HOUR.]

ARTICLES.—Twelve common sized potatoes, one-quarter onion, little celery, two cups of thick, sour cream, one-half cup of vinegar.

DIRECTIONS.—Twelve common sized potatoes boiled unpeeled, let them cool and peel, cut in thin slices, chop the onion very fine with salt on; also chop the celery fine, and mix well with the pepper, cream and vinegar; garnish the dish nicely with hard boiled eggs and parsley, and serve with cold meats.

1032. Salad Dressing. *(Mrs. Ditto.)*

ARTICLES.—One tablespoonful of oil or melted butter, two of milk, six of vinegar, one teaspoonful of sugar, one of mustard, one of salt and two eggs.

DIRECTIONS.—Blend the ingredients well, put them on the fire, stirring constantly until the mixture has become thick then remove from the fire, and continue stirring until smooth.

1033. Lobster Salad with Cream Dressing.

ARTICLES.—One fine lobster, boiled, and when cold picked to pieces, or two small lobsters, one cup best salad oil, one-half cup sweet cream, whipped light to a cupful of froth, one lemon—the juice strained, one teaspoonful of mustard wet up with vinegar, one tablespoonful powdered sugar, one teaspoonful of salt, a pinch of cayenne pepper, four tablespoonfuls of vinegar, and the beaten yolks of two eggs.

IRECTIONS.—Beat the eggs, sugar, salt, mustard, and pepper until light, then add very gradually the oil; when the mixture is quite thick, whip in the lemon, and beat five minutes before putting in the vinegar; just before the salad goes to the table add half the whipped cream to this dressing and stir well into the lobster; line the salad bowl with lettuce leaves, put in the seasoned meat and cover with the rest of the whipped cream. Lobster salad should be eaten as soon as possible after the dressing is added. If you use canned lobster, open, and turn out the contents into a crockery dish several hours before you mix the dressing, that the close airless smell may pass away.

PUDDINGS, CUSTARDS, Etc.

Part I. contains numerous recipes; we add a few more.

1034. Plum Pudding with Rum or Brandy. [TIME.—FOUR HOURS.]

ARTICLES.—Three-quarters of a pound of chopped suet,

three-quarters of a pound of stoned raisins, three-quarters of a pound of currants, one-quarter pound citron, three-quarters of a pound of sugar, three-quarters of a pound of bread crumbs, two apples cut into small dice, the grated peel of a lemon, three pounded cloves, a pinch of salt, six eggs, and one-half a gill of rum or brandy.

DIRECTIONS.—Mix the above ingredients together, butter a pudding mould, fill it with the mixture and tie a cloth over the top, place a plate at the bottom of a kettle which is three-fourths full of boiling water, put the pudding in, and boil for four hours, keeping the pot replenished with boiling water, turn out the pudding on a hot dish and sprinkle sugar over it, pour over half a pint of warm rum or brandy, and light it when putting the pudding on the table.

1035. German Sauce for Plum Pudding. [TIME.——]

ARTICLES.—The yolks of eight eggs, one-quarter pound of sugar, three gills of Madeira or sherry wine, and the grated peel of half a lemon.

DIRECTIONS.—Mix the above ingredients together and stir over a fire till the spoon is coated, and serve in a sauce boat.

1036. Roly-Poly Pudding Boiled.

Make a biscuit dough and roll it out into a square about a fourth of an inch thick, spread over it (leaving an inch uncovered at the edges) almost any kind of fruit, or berries, such as strawberries, raspberries, etc. sweetened, or preserves, and roll it tight, sew it in a cloth giving it room to swell, and boil or steam it one hour, and serve with almost any kind of pudding sauce.

1037. Suet Pudding. (*Mrs. D.*)

ARTICLES.—Three-quarters of a pound of flour, one-half pound of suet, four eggs, one-quarter of a pint of milk, one-quarter pound raisins, and one-quarter pound currants.

DIRECTIONS.—Mix the suet with the flour, then add the milk

and eggs and beat well together; next add the raisins and currants; boil in a floured bag one hour, and serve with the following sauce: One tablespoonful of butter, one tablespoonful of flour, a piece of butter the size of an egg; let the butter melt in a pan on the stove, mix the flour with it, then add sufficient water to make a thick sauce; next add one wine glassful of brandy, a little ground nutmeg, one-half a cupful of sugar, and mix well.

1038. Eve's Pudding.

ARTICLES.—Six ounces of bread crumbs, six ounces of sugar, six ounces of raisins or currants, six ounces of butter cut into small pieces, or beef suet chopped fine, six large apples chopped, one tablespoonful of flour, six eggs, one tablespoonful of cinnamon, one teaspoonful of ground cloves.

DIRECTIONS.—Flour the fruit; mix the eggs and sugar together, and the suet and apples, then mix all, adding the beaten white of the eggs the last thing; boil it in a form or bag three hours, or bake it two hours, and serve with brandy sauce.

1039. Cottage Pudding.

ARTICLES.—One cup of sugar, one tablespoonful of butter, two eggs, one cup of sweet milk, three cups of flour, or enough to make a tolerably stiff batter, one-half teaspoonful of soda, one teaspoonful of cream of tartar sifted with the flour, and one teaspoonful of salt.

DIRECTIONS.—Rub the butter and sugar together, beat in the yolks, then the milk and soda, the salt and the beaten whites, alternately with the flour; bake in a buttered mould; turn out upon a dish, cut into slices, and eat with any liquid sweet sauce.

1040. "Jinks' Pudding." *(Mrs. Palmer.)* [TIME.—FORTY MINUTES.]

ARTICLES.—One pint of rice, one quart of milk, one teacupful of sugar, and four oranges, with sufficient cream.

DIRECTIONS.—Boil the rice till tender, place it in a deep dish, peel, slice and seed the oranges, spread the oranges and sugar over the rice, and serve hot or cold; an addition of cream will make it much richer.

1041. Albany Pudding. *(Mrs. Geo. Dorr.)* [TIME.—FOUR HOURS.]

ARTICLES.—One cup of butter, one cup of molasses, three cups of flour, one cup of milk, one teaspoonful of soda, one-half pound of currants, one-half pound of raisins, one teaspoonful nutmeg, one teaspoonful of cloves, one teaspoonful of cinnamon, and a little salt.

DIRECTIONS.—Mix the butter with the molasses, dissolve the soda in the milk, and add alternately with the flour; then add the fruit which must be chopped, lastly the spice; boil four hours and serve with wine sauce.

1042. Tapioca Cream Pudding. [TIME.—ONE HOUR.]

ARTICLES.—Three tablespoonfuls of tapioca, one cup of sugar, one quart of milk, a little salt, and four eggs.

DIRECTIONS.—Soak three tablespoonfuls of tapioca in water or milk over night, then add a quart of milk, and steam it gently in a double boiler until it comes to a boil, or is soft, then add a little salt, the beaten yolks of four eggs, scalded in, and also a cupful of sugar; set it away to cool in the dish in which it is to be sent to the table; flavor with vanilla; when ready to use cover with the whites of the eggs beaten to a froth.

1043. Snow Pudding. *(Mrs. W.)*

ARTICLES.—One-half box of gelatine, one pint boiling water, two cups sugar, whites of three eggs, two teaspoonfuls extract of lemon.

DIRECTIONS.—Take one-half box gelatine, pour on water enough to cover it; add one pint of boiling water, let it dissolve, add two teaspoonfuls of extract, two cups of sugar, and

BUFFALO EVENING NEWS

BUFFALO, NEW YORK, U. S. A.

LEADING NEWSPAPER OF WESTERN NEW YORK.

LIVE, FEARLESS, NEWSY, INDEPENDENT

The EVENING NEWS has the largest circulation of any paper in the State, west of New York, and

MORE THAN THREE TIMES

That of any other paper in Buffalo, except the SUNDAY NEWS. Printed on a Lightning Hoe Press from Stereotype Plates.

IT CONTAINS ALL THE NEWS,

Local and telegraphic by Associated Press, and special correspondents in the State and National Capitals, and in the principal cities of the country.

The NEWS Building is the only newspaper establishment in Buffalo lighted from composition to business office with the

ELECTRIC LIGHT.

The NEWS has telephone connection with all the principal business houses, banks, municipal and county buildings, Board of Trade, marine and shipping offices, and is centrally located on the principal business street of Buffalo.

NO "DEAD ADS."

The NEWS publishes no dead ads, and gives no puffs. All business is for cash over the counter.

ADVERTISING RATES MADE KNOWN AT THE OFFICE.

4 Editions Daily. $3.00 Per Year.   Price One Cent.

THE BUFFALO SUNDAY NEWS.   THE EVENING NEWS.
BRADFORD (Pa.) SUNDAY NEWS.

E. H. BUTLER, Prop'r,

218 Main St.,   -   BUFFALO, N. Y.

To make a good Soup requires great skill and experience. Owing to their unvarying excellence

HUCKINS' SOUPS

have obtained a great popularity.

The different varieties are

Tomato,	Chicken,
Mock Turtle,	Mutton Broth,
Ox Tail,	Beef,
Julienne,	Okra and Gumbo,
Pea,	Soup and Bouilli,
Macaroni,	Mullagatawney,
Vermicelli,	Green Turtle,
Consomme,	Terrapin.

In hermetically sealed quart cans and ready for the table at a moment's notice, only requiring to be heated before serving. They are rich and delicious.

let it stand till cold ; beat the whites of three eggs to a froth, and add the gelatine, beat all one hour in as cool a place as you can ; of the yolks make a boiled custard sauce ; for the custard, take the yolks of two more eggs, three tablespoonfuls of sugar, one teaspoonful extract of lemon, and one quart of milk ; place the snow on a dish and the custard poured around. This is a delicious dessert.

1044. Minute Pudding,

ARTICLES.—One quart of milk, salt, two eggs, and about one pint of flour.

DIRECTIONS.—Beat the eggs well, add the flour and enough milk to make it smooth, butter the sauce pan, and put in the remainder of the milk well salted ; when it boils, stir in the flour, eggs, etc., lightly ; let it cook well ; it should be of the consistency of thick corn mush. Serve immediately with the following simple sauce, viz. ; milk sweetened to taste and flavored with grated nutmeg or vanilla.

1045. Plum Pudding.

ARTICLES.—One cupful of butter, one cupful of sugar, one-half a cupful of cream, one half a cupful of rum, one cupful of ale, one cupful of suet, (chopped,) one cupful of raisins and currants, half a cupful of candied orange peel cut fine, six eggs well beaten, two grated nutmegs, one teaspoonful of ground cinnamon, one-half a teaspoonful of ground cloves, and some bread crumbs.

DIRECTIONS.—Beat the butter and sugar together to a cream ; the bread crumbs should be dried thoroughly and passed through a sieve, beat all well together before adding the bread crumbs, then add enough of them to give proper consistency ; put the pudding into a tin mould, not quite filling it, and boil four hours, and serve with the following sauce :

The Sauce.—Use equal quantities of butter and sugar ; cream the butter, then add the sugar, beating them both until

Y

very light; add then the beaten yolk of an egg and a little grated nutmeg; heat on the fire a large wineglassful of sherry wine, diluted with the same quantity of water, and when just beginning to boil, stir it into the butter and sugar.

1046. Transparent Pudding.

Rub one-half a pound of butter with one pound of sugar, add one teaspoonful of rose water and half a grated nutmeg, beat the yolks of eight eggs with the butter and sugar, whisk the whites to a dry froth, butter a baking dish, cover the bottom with slices of sponge cake, spread with marmalade or sweetmeats, pour in the mixture and bake in a moderate oven; make a *meringue* of the whites of four eggs beaten stiff and four tablespoonfuls of sugar, flavor with bitter almond, spread it over the pudding, and leave it in a quick oven for a moment to brown slightly; a few sweet almonds blanched and finely shredded may be added to the *meringue*.

1047. Bread Pudding. *(Mrs. D.)*

Soak some stale bread in boiling milk, using as much milk as the bread will absorb, make it fine, add two or three eggs well beaten, sugar, and flavoring to taste; for a two-quart pudding add a piece of butter the size of an egg, and one-half a pound of raisins, and bake fifteen minutes in a hot oven; it may be frosted or not as desired, and serve with sweetened cream or the same sauce given for suet pudding, see recipe No. 1037.

1048. Cabinet Pudding.

Butter a mould well, line the bottom with raisins and citron cut into fancy shapes, cover this with pieces of cake, then more raisins and citron alternating with the cake until the mould is full to within an inch and a half of the top; mix in a bowl three tablespoonfuls of sugar, and the yolks of three eggs until they are a cream, then mix in slowly one pint of milk just brought to the boiling point, and pour this over the cake, etc.

in the mould, put it into a pan of cold water so that the water covers one-third of the mould, set it over the fire until the water boils, then put the whole into the oven to bake one hour, and serve with wine sauce.

1049. Queen of Puddings. *(Mrs. E. B. Jr.)*

ARTICLES.—One pint of crumbed bread, one quart of sweet milk, the grated rind of one lemon, one cupful of sugar, a piece of butter the size of an egg, and the yolks of five eggs, the whites of five eggs, the juice of one lemon, four tablespoonfuls of powdered sugar, and some jelly and marmalade.

DIRECTIONS.—Mix all together as is usual for puddings, except the whites of the eggs, the juice of the lemon, the powdered sugar, and jelly or marmalade, and bake in a quick oven, while baking beat the whites of the eggs to which add the juice of a lemon and the powdered sugar; when the pudding is baked spread a layer of jelly or marmalade over the top, and then the frosting, put back into the oven to brown. The pudding is to be eaten cold, with sweetened cream.

1050. Easy Dessert.

DIRECTIONS.—One tumbler full of rich cream, whip stiff and add pulverized sugar to sweeten; flavor with vanilla, and pour over lady fingers or sponge cake laid in a dish.

1051. Snow Pudding.

DIRECTIONS.—Dissolve half a box of gelatine in one pint of boiling water, stir into it two cups of sugar with the juice of two lemons, let come to a boil; put in a cold place, and when nearly cold stir into it the beaten whites of three eggs; beat twenty minutes and put in a cold place, either in forms or not.

Sauce for Same.—Beat one cup of sugar into yolks of three eggs, stir into one pint or more of boiling milk, one tablespoon of cornstarch and the beaten eggs and sugar; keep constantly stirring so as not to scorch or burn; serve cold, and flavor with vanilla, or any other flavoring to the taste.

1052. Soft Custard.

ARTICLES.—One quart of milk, eight eggs, half a pound of sugar, one teaspoonful of almond extract.

DIRECTIONS.—Beat the sugar and eggs together, and turn the milk boiling hot on them, stirring it all the time; then add the flavoring to taste; strain into a kettle or pitcher and place in boiling water; stir constantly till it thickens, for if it curdles it is spoiled; turn it into custard glasses. It is better to continue to stir it till nearly cool before placing in glasses, and serve with sponge cake.

1053. Lemon Pie.

ARTICLES.—Three-fourths of a cupful of sugar, the yolks of two eggs, three tablespoonfuls of flour, one lemon grated, two cupfuls of milk, boiled, and the whites of two eggs.

DIRECTIONS.—Mix the yolks of the two eggs and sugar together, next the grated lemon, and then the flour; add the milk gradually, continually stirring; this is for one pie; fill and bake; when baked, take the whites of the two eggs and beat to a stiff froth, add four tablespoonfuls of powdered sugar and beat all well together, spread it lightly on the fire and put back in the oven until it assumes a light brown color.

1054. Lemon Pies. *(Mrs. W.)* [TIME.—ONE HOUR.]

ARTICLES.—One-half cup of sugar, yolks of two eggs, one lemon, juice and rind, one tablespoonful of good corn starch dissolved in a little milk, and milk enough to fill pan.

DIRECTIONS.—Make a puff paste; bake with bottom crust, fill with the above custard; when done, beat the whites with two tablespoonfuls of sugar to an egg, pour over the top and bake a nice brown.

1055. Vol-au-Vent Crust.

Roll puff paste three-fourths to one inch thick and about the size desired; lay it on a baking tin, and if a small *vol-au-vent* is desired cut it round; if large, oval; for cutting round, use a sauce pan cover; trace with a knife, dipped in water to prevent sticking, a smaller inner circle, for the cover, leaving an edge about one inch broad, and making the knife penetrate to nearly half the thickness of the paste, or a smaller tin cover may be laid on the paste, and pressed in gently, to mark the inner circle, bake, and when well risen and of a nice, light brown, take out; lift the cover immediately, being careful not to make any openings in the lower part; this is called one of the nicest operations in cookery, lay the cover aside and if the inner part does not seem thoroughly baked, return to the oven for a short time, if an oval shape is desired, the paste may be cut with an oval basin, or marked with a vegetable dish, and cut with a knife.

1056. Blanc Mange of Corn Starch.

ARTICLES —Two large cupfuls of milk, two heaping tablespoonfuls of corn starch, one egg, sugar and vanilla to taste.

DIRECTIONS.—Set the milk to boil, dissolve the cornstarch in a little cold milk, when the milk commences boiling, stir in the dissolved cornstarch, stirring rapidly till smooth and thick; remove from the fire, add the egg well beaten, then the sugar and flavor; pour it into a flat glass dish, when cold, turn it out on a plate and garnish with any kind of preserve; or it may be poured into small individual moulds to cool; if in tin moulds, they must be buttered; if in stoneware moulds, such as egg cups, etc., dip them first in cold water, glass requires no preparation.

1057. Blanc Mange of Arrow Root.

ARTICLES.—One quart of milk, two large spoonfuls of arrow root, one teaspoonful of salt, and half a cupful of sugar.

DIRECTIONS.—Boil the milk; dissolve the arrow in a little cold milk, then add to the boiling milk, stir rapidly about five minutes, then add the salt, then the sugar, stirring continually, strain it and fill your moulds, and serve cold with any preserve or alone.

1058 Floating Island.

ARTICLES.—One quart of milk, two eggs, one heaping teaspoonful of cornstarch, sugar, vanilla, and flavor to taste.

DIRECTIONS.—Boil the milk, dissolve the cornstarch in a little cold milk, then add to the boiling milk, stir until it thickens a little, remove from the fire, stir in the yolks of the two eggs, and then add the sugar and flavoring; pour into a glass dish, have a pan of boiling water on the stove, beat the whites of the two eggs to a stiff froth, then take a large silver spoon, dip into the hot water, and then cut out a piece of the stiff egg, drop into the boiling water, and let it cook about two minutes, take out with a skimmer and place the pieces on the top of the custard, and serve cold.

1059. Charlotte Russe.

ARTICLES.—Three eggs, teacupful of flour, one-half teacupful of granulated sugar, one heaping teaspoonful of baking powder.

DIRECTIONS.—Beat the eggs and sugar well together, add the baking powder to the flour and mix all well-together; bake in a long, low, tin pan, cut into lady fingers and line a glass dish with the cake.

Cream for Same.—Beat one quart of sweet cream to a stiff froth, add powdered sugar and vanilla to taste; the cream should be kept cool while being beaten; if not thick enough, add two teaspoonfuls of gelatine dissolved in a little heated cream. If gelatine is added, let it stand half an hour before pouring into the dish lined with the six lady fingers, otherwise the beaten cream can be put into the dish at once.

1060. Bavarian Cream.

Whip one pint of cream to a stiff froth, laying it on a sieve; boil another pint of cream or rich milk, with a vanilla bean and two tablespoonfuls of sugar, until it is well flavored, then take it off the fire and add half a box of Cox's or Chalmer's gelatine soaked for an hour in half a cupful of water, in a warm place near the stove; when slightly cool stir in the yolks of four eggs well beaten; when it has become quite cold, and begins to thicken, stir it without ceasing, a few minutes until it is very smooth, then stir in the whipped cream lightly until it is well mixed, put it into a mould or moulds and set it on ice or in a cool place.

1061. Bavarian Cream with Chocolate

Is made as above, adding two sticks of chocolate soaked and smoothed, to the yolks of the eggs.

1062. Bavarian Cream with Strawberries.

Pick two and one-half pounds of strawberries, squeeze them through a colander and add six ounces of sugar to the juice; when the sugar is dissolved, add half a box of gelatine, soaked as before described, place it on the ice, stir it smooth; when it begins to set, then stir in a pint of cream whipped, put it in a mould or moulds and serve with fresh strawberries around it.

SAUCES FOR PUDDINGS.

1063. Fairy Butter. [Time.—Twenty minutes.]

ARTICLES.—Four ounces of butter, five ounces of powdered sugar, the grated rind and juice of half a lemon.

DIRECTIONS.—Cream the butter thoroughly and add the sugar gradually, beating hard and fast, until it is very light; add the lemon and beat three minutes more. To be served *piled*, as it falls from the spoon.

1064. Wine Sauce. [Time.—Fifteen minutes.]

ARTICLES.—One pint of sugar, half a pint of softened butter, two gills of wine, one gill of water, one gill of sweet cream, and nutmeg to taste.

DIRECTIONS.—Beat the butter and sugar to a froth, boil the wine and water together and pour them on the sugar and butter, stirring fast; next add the cream, and last the nutmeg.

1065. Almond Sauce. [TIME.—FIVE MINUTES.]

ARTICLES.—Blanch and pound one and one-half ounces of sweet almonds, four bitter almonds, half a pint of cream, one and one-quarter ounces of sugar, and the yolks of two eggs well beaten.

DIRECTIONS —Put the almonds, sugar and cream in a double boiler, then add the eggs and let cook five minutes.

1066. Lemon Sauce.

Cream two ounces of butter, and stir in half a pint of powdered sugar, the juice and grated rind of half a lemon, a tablespoonful of flour and one egg; beat all well together until very light, then add a gill of boiling water. If not as thick as liked, it may be stirred over the fire for a short time.

CAKES FOR BREAKFAST, DESSERT, AND TEA.

1067. Green Corn Fritters.

ARTICLES.—Green corn, one cupful, one egg, one tablespoonful of milk, a little salt and butter, flour to thicken, and two teaspoonfuls of baking powder.

DIRECTIONS.—Grate the corn and allow to every cupful one egg, a tablespoonful of milk, and a little salt and butter; stir all together and thicken with a little flour with the baking powder. They may be fried in hot lard, or cooked on a griddle the same as batter cakes.

1068. Quick Muffins. (*Mrs. W.*) [TIME.—ONE-HALF AN HOUR.]

ARTICLES.—Two eggs, two tablespoonfuls of lard or butter, one teaspoonful of salt, two teaspoonfuls of baking powder, one quart of sweet milk, and flour.

DIRECTIONS.—Beat the eggs well, add the melted lard or butter, one teaspoonful of salt, one quart of milk, two teaspoonfuls of baking powder, and flour to make a moderately stiff batter, and bake immediately in muffin rings.

1069. Sally Lunns. [TIME.—ONE HOUR.]

ARTICLES.—One quart of flour, four eggs, one cup of milk, one cup of lard and butter mixed, a teaspoonful and a half of baking powder, and one teaspoonful of salt.

DIRECTIONS.—Beat the eggs very light, yolks and whites separately, melt the shortening, sift the baking powder into the flour, and add the whites the last thing; bake steadily three-quarters of an hour, or until a straw thrust into it comes up clear, and eat while hot.

1070. German Puffs. *(Mrs. W.)* [TIME.—ONE-HALF AN HOUR.]

ARTICLES.—Three cups of flour, three cups of milk, three eggs, three tablespoonfuls of melted butter, and a little salt.

DIRECTIONS.—Three cups each of flour and milk, three eggs, whites and yolks beaten separately, and *very light*, three tablespoonfuls of melted butter, and a little salt; pour in well-buttered muffin rings, bake a nice brown, and eat hot with hard or plain pudding sauce.

N. B.—Be very careful in opening the oven door, lest they fall.

1071. Pop Overs for Breakfast. [TIME.—ONE-HALF HOUR.]

ARTICLES.—One pint of flour, one pint of milk, one egg.

DIRECTIONS.—Stir the milk into the flour, beat the egg very light, add it, stirring it well in; meanwhile have a set of gem pans well buttered, heating in the oven; put in the dough, (the material is enough for one dozen puffs) bake for one-half an hour in very hot oven. This is one of the simplest but most delicate breakfast cakes made; ignorant cooks generally spoil several batches by persisting in putting in baking powder or soda, as they cannot believe that the puffs will rise without it.

1072. Coffee Cake. (*Kittie Meyers.*) [TIME.—ONE HOUR AND A QUARTER.]

ARTICLES.—One cup brown sugar, one cup molasses, one cup butter, one cup cold coffee, four cups flour, one pound raisins chopped fine, one pound currants, four teaspoonfuls baking powder, and spice to taste.

DIRECTIONS.—Mix sugar, butter, then coffee, then molasses, then spices, then raisins and currants, then flour and baking powder, and bake in two loaves about one hour and a quarter.

1073. Spice Cake. (*Mrs. W.*) [TIME.—THIRTY MINUTES.]

ARTICLES.—One cupful of butter, two cupfuls of brown sugar, three and one-half cupfuls of flour, one cupful of cold water, three eggs, three teaspoonfuls of baking powder, one teaspoonful of cinnamon, one-half teaspoonful of cloves, and one-half a nutmeg.

DIRECTIONS.—Beat the butter and sugar well together, then add the eggs and one cupful of cold water, then the spices, and lastly the flour and baking powder well sifted.

1074. Spice Cake.

ARTICLES.—One cup butter, two cups brown sugar, one cup molasses, one cup sweet milk, the yolks of three eggs, four cupfuls of flour, and three teaspoonfuls of baking powder.

DIRECTIONS.—Mix the butter and sugar, then the eggs, next the molasses, then the milk, lastly the flour with the baking powder, and bake in one loaf.

1075. Marble Cake. [TIME.—ABOUT ONE HOUR TO BAKE.]

ARTICLES.—For the *white* part. One cup of butter, three cupfuls of sugar, eight eggs, one cupful of sweet milk, one teaspoonful of cream of tartar, one-half teaspoonful of soda, and three cupfuls of flour.

For the *dark* part. One cupful of butter, two cupfuls of

brown sugar, one cupful of molasses, one cupful of milk, four cupfuls of flour, the yolks of three eggs, one-half a teaspoonful of soda, and one teaspoonful of cream of tartar.

DIRECTIONS.—Make the doughs separate and when ready to put in the baking pan put in alternately spoonfuls of each kind of dough, to give it a marble-like appearance, and bake in one loaf in a moderate oven.

1076. Marble Cake. (*Kittie Meyers.*) [TIME.—ABOUT ONE HOUR.]

ARTICLES.—One-half a cupful of butter, one cupful of sugar, one-half a cupful of water, one and one-half cupfuls of flour, one teaspoonful of baking powder, and the whites of five eggs beaten to a froth.

DIRECTIONS.—Cream the butter and sugar, add the water, then half the flour, then half of the eggs, and then the rest of the flour and eggs, mix lightly, take three tablespoonfuls of the dough, mix red sugar with it to color it, and when you place the dough in the pan, add the red dough in spots through the cake and bake about an hour in a medium oven.

1077. Silver Cake. [TIME.—ABOUT ONE HOUR AND A QUARTER.]

ARTICLES.—One and one-half cupfuls of sugar, one-half a cupful of butter, three-quarters of a cupful of milk, three cupfuls of flour, three teaspoonfuls of baking powder, almond flavor, and the whites of eight eggs beaten to a froth.

DIRECTIONS—Mix the butter and sugar to a cream, add the milk, then half of the flour and half of the beaten eggs, then the other half of the flour and eggs ; the baking powder, which has been well mixed with the flour, and should always be sifted ; flavor to taste with almond flavor, make in one loaf, and bake in a medium oven about one hour and ten minutes.

1078. Gold Cake. [TIME.—ABOUT ONE HOUR AND A HALF.]

ARTICLES.—One and one-half cups of sugar, three-quarters of a cup of butter, one-half cup of milk, the yolks of eight eggs, three cups of flour, and three teaspoonfuls of baking powder.

DIRECTIONS.—Mix the sugar and butter to a cream, add the eggs, then the milk, and lastly the flour in which the baking powder has been well mixed; this cake must be well stirred; bake in one cake, in a medium oven about one hour.

1079. Loaf Cake.

ARTICLES.—Three-quarters of a cupful of butter, one cupful of sugar, three eggs, three-quarters of a cupful of milk, three teaspoonfuls of baking powder, flour to thicken, and flavor to taste.

DIRECTIONS.—Mix and bake in one loaf.

1080. Cup Cake. *(Millie Lantz.)*

ARTICLES.—Three-fourths of a cupful of butter, one cupful of sugar, four eggs, one-half a cupful of sweet milk, three cupfuls of flour, and three teaspoonfuls of baking powder.

1081. Stirred Cake.

ARTICLES.—One cupful of butter, one cupful of sugar, one cupful of sweet milk, three eggs, four cupfuls of flour, three teaspoonfuls of baking powder, and flavoring to taste.

DIRECTIONS.—Mix the butter and sugar, add the eggs, next the milk, then the flour in which the baking powder has previously been well mixed, stir well and bake in one loaf in a medium oven.

1082. Lemon Cake. [TIME.—ABOUT ONE HOUR.]

ARTICLES.—One cupful of butter, two cupfuls of powdered sugar, five eggs, one-half a cupful of milk, one lemon, four cupfuls of flour, three teaspoonfuls of baking powder.

DIRECTIONS.—Mix the butter and sugar to a smooth cream, then add the eggs and milk, then the lemon grated, and then the flour and baking powder, and bake in one loaf, one hour.

1083. Tip Top Cake.

ARTICLES.—Half a cupful of butter, one and one-half cupfuls of sugar, one cupful of milk, two eggs, three cupfuls of flour, three teaspoonfuls of baking powder.

DIRECTIONS.—Mix and bake in one loaf.

1084. Fruit Cake. (*Eliza Kimball.*) [TIME.—FOUR TO FIVE HOURS.]

ARTICLES.—One pound of dark sugar, three-quarters of a pound of butter, two pounds of raisins, two pounds of currants, one pound of citron, one pound of figs, one pound of flour, nine eggs, one-half gill of brandy, one-half gill of essence of lemon, cloves, cinnamon and nutmeg to taste, and baking powder.

1085. Fruit Cake. (*Mrs. D.*)

ARTICLES.—Two cupfuls of butter, three cupfuls of sugar, one cupful of syrup, one cupful of sweet milk, eight eggs, two nutmegs, eight cupfuls of flour, four pounds of seeded raisins, four pounds of currants, one-half pound of citron, one glassful of brandy, spice to taste, three teaspoonfuls of cream of tartar, and two of soda.

DIRECTIONS.—Beat the butter and sugar to a cream, add the eggs, then the milk, flour, soda, tartar, spice, and last of all the fruit.

1086. Fruit Cake. (*Mrs. G.*)

ARTICLES.—Two pounds of flour, two pounds of sugar, one and one-half pounds of butter, four pounds of seeded raisins, four pounds of currants, two pounds of citron, one pound of almonds, one ounce of mace, two teaspoonfuls of rose water, two wineglassfuls of brandy, two of wine, and ten eggs.

DIRECTIONS.—Beat the sugar and butter to a cream, then add the whites and yolks of the eggs beaten separately.

1087. Almond Cake. (*K. M.*) [TIME.—ABOUT AN HOUR.]

ARTICLES.—One cupful of butter, two cupfuls of sugar, one

cupful of water, whites of eight eggs beaten to a froth, two cupfuls of flour, one cupful of corn starch, two teaspoonfuls of baking powder, two ounces of shelled bitter almonds.

DIRECTIONS.—Blanch the almonds, chop fine and soak in a small quantity of rose water; mix with the dough made in the usual manner, and bake in one loaf.

1088. Walnut Cake. [TIME.—ABOUT ONE HOUR.]

ARTICLES.—Three-fourths of a pound of butter, one pound of sugar, six eggs, one wineglassful of sherry wine, one nutmeg, one and one-half pounds of raisins, one pound of flour, three teaspoonfuls of baking powder, and two quarts of nuts in the shell.

DIRECTIONS.—Mix the butter and sugar, add the eggs, next the wine, grate the nutmeg, and add, then the raisins, the meats of the nuts, stirring them in well; then add the flour with which the baking powder has previously been well mixed, and bake in one loaf in a quick oven.

1089. Nut Cake.

ARTICLES.—One-half of a pound of butter, one pound of sugar, four eggs, one cupful of sweet milk, one-half pint of chopped hickory nuts, three teaspoonfuls of baking powder, and flour to thicken.

DIRECTIONS.—Mix the butter and sugar, then the eggs, then the milk, next the hickory nuts, and then the flour with which the baking powder has been mixed.

1090. Cocoanut Cake. (*Mrs. K.*)

ARTICLES.—Half a cupful of butter, three-quarters of a pound of sugar, two eggs, one cupful of flour, and one cocoanut grated fine and mixed with the dough.

DIRECTIONS.—Mix the butter and sugar, then the eggs and cocoanut, then the flour. and bake in one loaf.

1091. Pound Cake. (*Sister Mary.* [Time.—About one hour.]

Articles.—Nine eggs, one pound of powdered sugar, half a wineglassful of sherry wine, half a wineglassful of rose water, one pound of butter, one quart of flour, one grated nutmeg, and one-half a wineglassful of brandy.

Directions.—Break the nine eggs into the sugar, while beating well, add the wine and rose water; work the butter to a cream with one pint of the flour, add the brandy and grated nutmeg, sift the other pint of flour, and warm it by the fire; when the oven is ready for the cake, throw the warmed flour into the eggs, then the butter, work all together as quickly as possible, make in one loaf and bake immediately in a hot oven.

1092. Pound Cake. [Time.—One hour and a quarter.]

Articles.—One pound of sugar, one pound of flour, three-quarters of a pound of butter, one-quarter of a pound of almonds, eight eggs, one nutmeg, and one teaspoonful of baking powder.

Directions.—Stir the butter and sugar to a cream, beat the whites and yolks of the eggs separately to a froth, add both to the butter and sugar, next the almonds and spice, and then the flour with the baking powder; put in a pan and bake in a medium oven one hour and a quarter.

1093. Pound Cake. [Time.—One hour and one-quarter.]

Articles.—Three-quarters of a pound of butter, one pound of powdered sugar, eight eggs, to be beaten separately, one-half of a wineglassful of brandy, and one pound of flour, and raisins if desired.

Directions.—Mix the butter, sugar and yolks of eggs well together, then add the brandy; next add one-half of the whites of the eggs beaten to a froth, then one-half of the flour, then the other one-half of the eggs, and then the remainder of the flour, and bake one hour and one-quarter in a medium oven.

1094. Winchester Biscuit. *(Mrs. Geo. Dorr.)* [Time.—Twenty minutes.]

Articles.—One pint of milk, one pint of rye or graham flour, three eggs, one teaspoonful of sugar, and one saltspoonful of salt.

Directions.—Beat the eggs separately, stir the flour into the milk, add the sugar, salt, and the yolks of eggs, stir well, putting the whites in last, bake in tin muffin pans, and serve as soon as they are taken from the oven.

1095. Soft Ginger Bread. *(Mrs. Geo. Dorr.)* [Time.—Twenty minutes.]

Articles.—One cupful of butter, one cupful of sugar, two cupfuls of molasses, one cupful of sour milk, four cupfuls of flour, two eggs, one teaspoonful of soda, and one tablespoonful of ginger.

Directions.—Stir the sugar and butter to a cream, beat the eggs together, add with one cupful of flour, then molasses and the remainder of the flour; dissolve the soda in the milk, add ginger, beat well and bake in a dripping or biscuit tin.

1096. Tea Cake. [Time.—Twenty minutes.]

Articles.—One cup of sugar, four eggs, four tablespoonfuls of flour, and two teaspoonfuls of baking powder.

Directions.—Mix the sugar and eggs well together, then the flour and baking powder, and bake in muffin rings in a quick oven about twenty minutes.

1097. Strawberry Dumplings.]Time.—Half an hour.]

Articles.—Three pints of flour, one-half of a cupful of butter, one pint of milk, and three tablespoonfuls of baking powder.

Directions.—Mix the flour, butter and baking powder well together, roll about one-half of an inch thick, put one gill of berries and one tablespoonful of sugar in each dumpling, and bake or boil for one-half hour.

SPRING BEDS, MATTRESSES AND STEAM CARPET BEATING.

ALLAN & BARNARD
148, 150 & 152 NIAGARA ST.

— MANUFACTURERS OF —

SPRING BEDS AND MATTRESSES,
FOWLER'S PATENT METALLIC
ROLL-UP CHAIN TOP-SPRING BED,
KREIGHOFF'S PATENT METALLIC SPRING BED,
THE BOSTON SPRING BED,
ALLAN'S UPHOLSTERED SPRING MATTRESSES,
HAIR MATTRESSES,
JAPANESE HAIR MATTRESSES,
FIBRE OR PALM LEAF MATTRESSES,
HUSK MATTRESSES,
SEA GRASS MATTRESSES.

OLD HAIR MATTRESSES,
THOROUGHLY STEAMED, PICKED, AND MADE OVER EQUAL TO NEW.

PRIME LIVE GEESE FEATHERS.

FEATHER PILLOWS.　　　**OLD FEATHERS RENOVATED.**

Prices very Reasonable.　　"Send for Price List."

—OUR—
STEAM CARPET BEATING & RENOVATING WORKS,
Are acknowledged to be unsurpassed in the country, and we can guarantee satisfaction.

148 to 152 Niagara Street, - **BUFFALO, N. Y.**

USE PINCKNEY'S CELEBRATED SPICES.

GUARANTEED
ABSOLUTELY PURE
AND NET WEIGHT.

H. A. PINCKNEY & CO.,
PHILADELPHIA AND LONDON, Eng.

FOR SALE BY ALL THE
PROMINENT GROCERS IN THE UNITED STATES AND CANADA.

A FULL LINE CAN BE HAD OF
DINGENS BROS.,
BUFFALO, N. Y.

1098. Strawberry Short Cake. [TIME.—TWENTY MINUTES.]

ARTICLES.—Three pints of flour, one-half a cupful of butter, one pint of milk, three teaspoonfuls of baking powder, and a little salt.

DIRECTIONS.—Mix the butter, flour, salt, and baking powder well together, then add the milk, roll one-half an inch thick, put small pieces of butter all over it, lay another layer of dough one-half an inch thick on top, put into a shallow pan, and bake twenty minutes in a hot oven, (the addition of the pieces of butter between the two layers of dough makes it cut open easy after it is done,) after it is baked cut it open and put a layer of strawberries with sugar sprinkled over between the layers, then cover with the other crust and add another layer of strawberries with sugar sprinkled over them, and serve with cream.

1099. Little Plum Cakes.

ARTICLES.—One-half of a cupful of butter beaten to a cream, one small cupful of sugar, three eggs, one-half of a pound of currants, one pound of flour, three teaspoonfuls of baking powder, two teaspoonfuls of ground cinnamon.

DIRECTIONS.—Beat the butter to a cream, then add the sugar, next the eggs and cinnamon, then the currants, and then the flour and baking powder, drop in small hillocks on buttered tins, and bake in a quick oven.

1100. Pednuns. (*Madame Grimard.*) [TIME.—THIRTY MINUTES.]

ARTICLES.—One teacupful of water, one teacupful of sugar, butter the size of an egg, three eggs, and lard to fry the cakes.

DIRECTIONS.—Place the butter, sugar and water in a saucepan on the stove, let it come to a boil, then add sufficient flour, stirring very fast till the dough does not cling to the sides of the pan, take the pan off the fire and add three eggs well beaten, stir well. Fry the same as doughnuts; first dip your spoon in the hot lard, then take up a spoonful of the dough and drop it in the pan of hot lard—this prevents the dough from sticking to the spoon. Sprinkle with powdered sugar and serve hot.

1101. Ricka's Drop Cakes. [TIME.—TWENTY MINUTES.]

ARTICLES.—One cupful of butter, one cupful of milk, two cupfuls of sugar, one quart of flour, three teaspoonfuls of baking powder, and three eggs.

DIRECTIONS.—Mix the butter and sugar, add eggs, then milk, then flour, to which you have previously added the baking powder, and mix well. Bake in patty pans, hot oven, ten minutes, and serve warm.

1102. Snow Balls.

ARTICLES.—Two cupfuls of sugar, four eggs, eight tablespoonfuls of milk, enough flour to make a soft dough, as soft as can be rolled, and baking powder; proportion in all cases when it is used, three teaspoonfuls to one quart of flour.

DIRECTIONS.—Mix the butter and sugar well together, then add the milk, and then the flour, roll the dough about one inch thick, cut in small pieces, and fry in hot lard; when done sift powdered sugar over them.

1103. Cookies.

ARTICLES.—Two cupfuls of sugar, one cupful of butter, three-quarters of a cupful of milk, three eggs, two quarts of flour, six teaspoonfuls of baking powder, and one-half a teaspoonful of salt.

DIRECTIONS.—Mix well, roll very thin, and bake in a quick oven.

1104. Hard Fried Cakes.

ARTICLES.—Six eggs, one cupful of sugar, one teaspoonful of salt, and flour enough to make a very stiff dough.

DIRECTIONS.—Mix the eggs and sugar well together, then add the flour, in which the salt has been mixed, roll the dough thin and cut in pieces four inches square, make four slits in each piece about two and one-half inches long, pick up the two outside and the center piece, and pinch them together, then drop in hot lard and fry a light brown, when done sprinkle sifted sugar over them.

1105. Fried Cakes.

ARTICLES.—One cupful of sugar, one cupful of sweet milk, three tablespoonfuls of butter, two teaspoonfuls of baking powder, two eggs, and one quart of flour.

DIRECTIONS.—Take the quantity of flour and baking powder, add the sugar and rub the butter in well, then the eggs and a little salt, also flavor it with the nutmeg and lastly the milk ; cut in shape and fry in hot lard.

1106. Fried Doughnuts. (*Mrs. Gates.*) [TIME.—ABOUT FORTY-FIVE MINUTES.]

ARTICLES.—Two eggs, one cupful of sugar, two-thirds of a cupful of sweet milk, two tablespoonfuls of melted butter, two teaspoonfuls of baking powder, a little nutmeg, and flour enough to make a soft dough.

DIRECTIONS.—Beat the eggs and mix with the sugar, add the butter, then the milk, and then the nutmeg, mix the baking powder in a little flour, which add, then add enough more flour to make a soft dough ; roll out thin, cut in strips, twist and drop in hot lard.

1107. French Fried Cakes. (*Mrs. W.*) [TIME.—ONE HOUR.]

ARTICLES.—Six eggs, one cup of sugar, two teaspoonfuls of baking powder, flour, and three tablespoonfuls of rose water.

DIRECTIONS.—Beat the eggs and sugar one-half an hour, add the rose water, flour to thicken, also the baking powder, roll very thin, cut in fancy shapes with a jigger, and fry a light brown in hot lard, and when done sprinkle pulverized sugar over.

1108. Chocolate Eclairs.

ARTICLES.—Four eggs, the weight of the eggs in sugar, half their weight in flour, one-quarter of a teaspoonful of soda, one-half of a teaspoonful of cream of tartar sifted well with the flour.

DIRECTIONS.—Mix as usual, put a spoonful of batter in each tin and bake in a steady oven; when nearly cold, cover the top with chocolate iceing.

1109. Cocoanut Drops.

ARTICLES.—Ten ounces of sugar, twelve ounces of grated cocoanut, and the whites of three eggs.

DIRECTIONS.—Beat the eggs to a stiff froth, mix all well together, drop on tin plates in small pieces the size of a very small egg, and bake in a quick oven.

1110. Macaronies.

ARTICLES.—Six eggs, two cupfuls of sugar, one-half a pound of almonds, one-half a pound of citron, two teaspoonfuls of cinnamon, one of allspice, one-half of cloves, one-half of pepper, one-half of salt, flour enough to roll thin, and baking powder in proportion to the flour used.

DIRECTIONS—Mix the eggs and sugar together, then the almonds which have been peeled and chopped fine, then the citron chopped fine, then the cloves, pepper and salt, then the flour, roll thin and bake in a quick oven.

1111. Maccaroons.

ARTICLES.—One-half of a pound of almonds, some rose water, the whites of three eggs beaten to a stiff froth, and one-half of a pound of sugar, powdered.

DIRECTIONS.—Mix the eggs and sugar together, then add the almonds, which have been blanched and pounded into a mortar, with enough rose water to make a smooth paste mixed with the almonds; stir well, drop with a spoon on a buttered plate or paper, sift sugar over them and bake in a slow oven.

1112. Lemon Snaps.

ARTICLES.—Nine cupfuls of flour, eight cupfuls of sugar, one and one-half cupfuls of butter, one and one-half pounds of almonds blanched and chopped fine, three lemons grated, and eighteen eggs.

DIRECTIONS.—Mix the butter and sugar to a cream, next the eggs, then the almonds, then the lemon, and then the flour; roll thin, cut in any shape, and bake on tins which have been buttered, in a quick oven.

1113. Seed Cookies. [TIME.—ONE HOUR.]

ARTICLES.—Two small cups of sugar, one cup of butter, one-half of a cupful of sweet milk, one egg, three teaspoonfuls of baking powder, caraway seed, and flour to thicken.

DIRECTIONS—Mix the butter and sugar to a cream, add one-half of a cupful of sweet milk, one egg, also caraway seed, (if liked), mix very soft, roll out and cut in shapes; sprinkle sugar over the top and bake.

1114. Boston Cream Cakes.

ARTICLES.—One-half of a pound of butter, three-quarters of a pound of flour, eight eggs, and one pint of water.

DIRECTIONS.—Stir the butter into the water, which should be warm, set it over the fire, and slowly bring it to a boil, stirring it often, when it boils, stir in the flour, let it boil one minute, stirring all the time, take it from the fire, turn it into a deep dish and let it cool, beat the eggs very light, and whip into the cooling paste, first the yolks and then the whites, drop in great spoonfuls on buttered paper on the top of which are placed muffin rings, and bake ten minutes in a quick oven.

1115. Cream for the Filling.

ARTICLES.—One quart of milk, four tablespoonfuls of corn-starch, two eggs, sugar to taste, and vanilla to flavor

DIRECTIONS.—Put the milk in a basin to boil; when boiling, add the cornstarch which has been dissolved in a little milk, stir very rapidly for two minutes to prevent its becoming lumpy, remove it from the fire, add the eggs which have already been beaten, then the sugar and then the vanilla, stir until cool, then drop it into the cakes, which must be opened at one side and serve cold.

1116. Almond Snaps.

ARTICLES.—One pound of flour, one-quarter of a pound of almonds, blanched and chopped fine; four eggs and one-half of a cup of sugar.

DIRECTIONS.—Beat the eggs and sugar together, then add the almonds, and then the flour; roll thin, cut with a cookie cutter, and bake in quick oven.

1117. Cinnamon Snaps.

ARTICLES.—One pound of flour, one pound of sugar, one pound of butter, three tablespoonfuls of ground cinnamon, and one glassful of brandy.

DIRECTIONS.—Mix the butter and sugar, then add brandy, then the cinnamon, and next the flour; roll thin, cut in small squares, and bake on buttered tins, in quick oven.

1118. Ice Cream Cake.

ARTICLES.—Whites of four eggs, two cupfuls of flour, one cupful of sweet milk, one-half of a cupful of butter, two teaspoonfuls of baking powder, and bake in four layers.

Frosting to put between layers.—Three cupfuls of granulated sugar, one-half of a pint of boiling water, boil hard until clear and candied; then pour the boiling hot sugar on the whites of three eggs, well beaten, and stir it all the time till it is stiff and creamy, and flavor with lemon juice or extract of vanilla; when cake and frosting are both cold, spread frosting between the layers.

1119. Ice Cream Cake.

ARTICLES.—The whites of eight eggs, one cupful of butter, two cupfuls of sugar, one cupful of sweet milk, two cupfuls of flour, one cupful of cornstarch, and two teaspoonfuls of baking powder.

DIRECTIONS.—Cream the butter and sugar, add the milk, next the flour with which the baking powder has been well mixed, then the cornstarch, next the whites of the eggs beaten very lightly, and bake in layers one inch thick.

Icing for between the layers.—The whites of four eggs beaten very light, four cupfuls of sugar; pour one-half of a pint of boiling water over the sugar and boil until it is clear and will candy in water; pour the boiling syrup over the beaten eggs, and beat hard until the mixture is cold and has become a stiff cream; before it is quite cold, add one-quarter teaspoonful of pulverized citric acid, and two teaspoonfuls of vanilla flavor, and then spread between the layers of cake.

1120. Delicate Cake. (*Jennie.*) [TIME.—ABOUT ONE HOUR.]

ARTICLES.—One cup butter, two cupfuls of sugar, one cupful of sweet milk, three cupfuls of flour, three teaspoonfuls of baking powder, and the whites of six eggs beaten to a froth.

DIRECTIONS.—Mix the butter and sugar, add the milk, then half the flour, and half the beaten eggs, and then the rest of the flour and the rest of the eggs; the baking powder should always be well mixed with the flour sifted, made in one loaf, and baked in pretty hot oven.

1121. Delicate Cake.

ARTICLES.—One pound of sugar, seven ounces of butter, one pound of flour, and the whites of sixteen eggs.

DIRECTIONS.—Beat the sugar and butter to a cream, add gradually the flour; beat the eggs to a stiff froth, add to the flour, etc., and bake in one loaf.

1122. White Cake. [TIME.—THREE QUARTERS OF AN HOUR.]

ARTICLES.—Six ounces of butter, one pound of sugar, the whites of fourteen eggs, three teaspoonfuls of baking powder, and three-quarters of a pound of flour.

DIRECTIONS.—Mix the butter and sugar, next half of the flour, next half of the eggs, which have been beaten to a stiff froth, then the other half of the flour, and the balance of the eggs; mix the baking powder well with the flour, make into one loaf and bake in a quick oven.

1123. White Sponge Cake. (*Mrs. Gates.*) [TIME.—ONE HOUR.]

ARTICLES.—Two-thirds of a cupful of sugar, the whites of five eggs, half a cupful of flour, two teaspoonfuls of baking powder, and one teaspoonful of essence of lemon.

DIRECTIONS.—Beat the whites of the eggs to a stiff froth, add the sugar, stir lightly, add next the flavoring, then the flour well sifted, and in which the baking powder has been well mixed, and bake in a slow oven about forty-five minutes.

1124. White Sponge Cake. [TIME.—THREE-QUARTERS OF AN HOUR.]

ARTICLES.—The whites of eight eggs, one cupful of powdered sugar, one-half a cupful of cornstarch, one-half a cupful of flour, and one teaspoonful of baking powder.

DIRECTIONS.—Mix the whites of the eggs beaten to a stiff froth, with the sugar, then add the cornstarch and flour with the baking powder, and bake in a rather quick oven.

1125. Angel's Food. [TIME.—FORTY MINUTES.]

ARTICLES.—The whites of eleven eggs, one and one-half tumblerfuls of granulated sugar, one tumblerful of flour, one teaspoonful of vanilla, and one teaspoonful of cream of tartar.

DIRECTIONS.—Sift the flour four times, then add the cream of tartar, and sift again, but have the right measure before putting in the cream of tartar; sift the sugar and measure it, beat the eggs to a stiff froth on a large platter; on the same platter add the sugar lightly, then the flour very gently, and then the vanilla, do not stop beating until you put it in the pan to bake; bake forty minutes in a very moderate oven, try with a straw, and if too soft let it remain in the oven a few minutes longer; turn the pan upside down to cool, and when cold, take out by loosening around with a knife. The tumbler for measuring holds two and one-quarter gills.

1126. Mother's Sponge Cake. (*M.F.F.*) [TIME.—ABOUT AN HOUR.]

ARTICLES.—Two dozen eggs, four cupfuls of sugar, five cupfuls of flour, and one lemon.

DIRECTIONS.—Beat the yolks and sugar together, then add the juice and rind of the lemon, next half of the flour, then the whites of the eggs previously beaten to a froth, next the remainder of the flour, and bake in a medium oven.

1127. Sponge Cake. (*Mrs. K.*)

ARTICLES.—Three eggs, one cupful of sugar, two teaspoonfuls of sweet milk, one cupful of flour, one teaspoonful of baking powder.

DIRECTIONS.—Beat the yolks of the eggs with the sugar, add the milk, beat the whites of the eggs to a froth and mix with the above; then add the flour with the baking powder; stir altogether, and bake in one loaf.

1128. Chocolate Cake. [TIME.—ONE HOUR.]

ARTICLES.—Two cupfuls of sugar, one cupful of butter, the yolks of five eggs, and the whites of two, one cupful of milk, three and a half cupfuls of flour, and three teaspoonfuls of baking powder.

DIRECTIONS.—Beat the butter and sugar well together, add the eggs, then the milk, and lastly the flour and baking powder.

Mixture for Filling.—Whites of three eggs, one and a half cupfuls of sugar, three tablespoonfuls of grated chocolate, one teaspoonful of extract of vanilla, beat well together, and spread between the layers and on top of the cake.

1129. Dolly Varden Cake. (*Mdme. Riton.*)

ARTICLES.—One-half of a cupful of butter, one cupful of sugar, two eggs, three-quarters of a cupful of milk, two teaspoonfuls of baking powder, raisins, currants, citron and spices.

DIRECTIONS.—Make into a dough, leaving out the raisins, currants, citron and spices; divide into three parts; bake two layers of the plain dough, mix the raisins, chopped fine, the currants, citron and spices with the remaining third of the dough, and bake; put the layers together with frosting between, and the dark layer in the centre.

1130. Minnehaha Cake.

ARTICLES.—RED PART.—Yolks of two eggs, one-half of a cupful of butter, one-half a cupful of red sugar, and enough white sugar to make the cup two-thirds full, four tablespoonfuls of milk, one heaping cupful of flour, one teaspoonful of baking powder, and flavor to taste.

ARTICLES.—WHITE PART.—Whites of three eggs, two-thirds of a cupful of white sugar, one-half of a cupful of butter, four tablespoonfuls of milk, and two tablespoonfuls of cornstarch in a cup filled up with flour, one teaspoonful of baking powder, and vanilla to flavor.

DIRECTIONS.—RED PART.—Two eggs, one-half of a cupful of butter, one-half of a cupful of red sugar, and enough white sugar to make the cup two-thirds full, four tablespoonfuls of sweet milk, one heaping cupful of flour, one teaspoonful of baking powder and flavor to taste.

DIRECTIONS.—WHITE PART.—Whites of three eggs, two-thirds of a cupful of white sugar, one-half of a cupful of butter, four tablespoonfuls of milk, two tablespoonfuls of cornstarch in a cup filled up with flour, one teaspoonful of baking powder, and flavor with vanilla.

Icing.—ARTICLES.—One cupful of granulated sugar, and water enough to dissolve it, raisins and figs.

DIRECTIONS.—One cupful of granulated sugar, water enough to dissolve it ; boil until a little thick, then add whites of two eggs well beaten, spread between layers of cake, having pink cake in center, and split figs and whole raisins spread on top.

1131. Roll Jelly Cake.

ARTICLES.—Three eggs, one cupful of powdered sugar, one tablespoonful of water, one cupful of flour, and one-half a teaspoonful of baking powder.

DIRECTIONS.—Bake in thin layers ; when baked, spread with jelly and roll.

1132. Jelly Cake. *(Mrs. K.)* [TIME.—ABOUT THIRTY MINUTES.]

ARTICLES.—One cupful of butter, two cupfuls of sugar, one cupful of sweet milk, four eggs, three cupfuls of flour, four teaspoonfuls of baking powder.

DIRECTIONS.—Mix, bake in layers and spread jelly between.

1133. Layer Cake. *(Kittie Meyers.)* [TIME.—ABOUT HALF AN HOUR.]

ARTICLES.—Six eggs, (whites and yolks beaten separately) one and one-half cupfuls of sugar, half a cupful of water, two and one-half cupfuls of flour, two and one-half teaspoonfuls of baking powder.

DIRECTIONS.—Mix the sugar and the yolks, add the water, next the flour in which the baking powder has been well mixed, then the whites of the eggs ; bake in three layers in a hot oven about fifteen minutes ; put any kind of jelly or jam between the layers, and the top may be frosted if desired.

1134. Cream Cake. *(Mrs. Gates.)*

ARTICLES.—One cupful of sugar, butter the size of an egg, three eggs, four tablespoonfuls of milk, one and one-half cupfuls of flour, and two teaspoonfuls of baking powder.

FOR THE CREAM.—One cupful of milk, two eggs, half a cupful of sugar, two teaspoonfuls cornstarch, and flavor with vanilla.

DIRECTIONS.—Mix the butter and sugar to a cream, add the eggs well beaten, next the milk, then the flour well sifted, and to which the baking powder has been added, and bake in three jelly pans, in a hot oven.

FOR THE CREAM.—Put the milk over to boil; when it comes to a boil, add the cornstarch previously mixed to a paste with a little milk, next the sugar; let it cook one minute, take it off the stove, add the eggs well beaten, then the flavoring, and then spread warm between the layers of cake.

1135. Cream Cake. (*Mrs. Hedge.*) [TIME.—TWENTY MINUTES.

ARTICLES.—Three eggs, one cupful of sugar, one-half of a cupful of boiling water, two cupfuls of flour, two teaspoonfuls of baking powder, and lemon to flavor.

DIRECTIONS.—Beat the sugar and eggs well together, then add the boiling water, and then the flour, to which has been added the baking powder; bake in three layers for about twenty minutes.

CREAM FOR FILLING.—One tablespoonful of cornstarch wet in a little milk, one cupful of milk, one egg, sugar to taste, and vanilla to flavor. Put the milk in a basin to boil; as soon as it boils, pour in the cornstarch which has been dissolved in a little milk, let it boil about two minutes; then remove it from the stove, sweeten to taste with sugar, and flavor with vanilla.

1136. Cream Cake. (*Mdme. Riton.*) [TIME.—ABOUT FORTY-FIVE MINUTES.]

ARTICLES.—One-half cupful of butter, two cupfuls of sugar, one cupful of milk, three eggs, four cupfuls of flour and four teaspoonfuls of baking powder.

DIRECTIONS.—To be baked in layers and spread with cream,

made as follows :—One cupful of sweet milk, when boiling, thicken with a tablespoonful of cornstarch, stir in the yolk of one egg, sweeten to taste, and flavor with vanilla.

1137. Sponge Lemon Layer Cake.

ARTICLES.—One and one-half cupfuls of sugar, five eggs, one-half of a cupful of water, a pinch of salt, three cupfuls of flour, and three teaspoonfuls of baking powder.

DIRECTIONS.—Save the whites of two eggs, to make a frosting for between the layers.

1138. Nut Layer Cake. [TIME.—TWENTY MINUTES.]

ARTICLES.—Six eggs beaten separately, two cupfuls of sugar, one cupful of water, two and one-half cupfuls of flour, and two and one-half teaspoonfuls of baking powder.

DIRECTIONS.—Mix the eggs and sugar together, then add the water, then the flour and baking powder, and bake in layers about twenty minutes.

BETWEEN THE LAYERS.—Put over one-half of a cupful of milk with two cupfuls of powdered sugar, let it boil slowly for twenty minutes, then add one cupful of chopped hickory nuts ; flavor with vanilla, spread between layers and on top of cake.

1139. Chocolate Cake. [TIME.—ONE HALF AN HOUR.]

ARTICLES.—Yolks of eight eggs, one cupful of sugar, three-quarters of a cupful of butter, one-half of a cupful of milk, two cupfuls of flour, two teaspoonfuls of baking powder.

DIRECTIONS.—Stir butter and sugar well together, then add eggs, then milk, and then flour and baking powder, and bake in three layers about one-half an hour.

FROSTING FOR CAKE.—One and one-half pounds of sugar, one-half a pint of milk, a piece of butter the size of a nutmeg, two tablespoonfuls of plain chocolate mixed to a paste in boiling water, and vanilla to flavor. Boil milk, sugar and butter eight minutes, put into a bowl, stir until a little cool, add chocolate which has been dissolved, then vanilla, and stir until thick enough to put on cake ; place in a cool place for about three hours before cutting.

1140. Cocoanut Cake. [Time.—About one-half hour.]

Articles.—One and one-half cupfuls of sugar, one-half of a cupful of butter, three-quarters of a cupful of milk, two and one-half cupfuls of flour, two teaspoonfuls of baking powder, almond flavor, whites of eight eggs, and beaten to a froth.

Directions.—Mix the butter and sugar to a smooth cream, add the milk, then one-half of the flour with the baking powder, one-half of the beaten eggs, the remainder of the flour, the other one-half of the eggs, and bake in three layers.

Frosting for Cake.—[Time.—About fifteen minutes.] One and one-half pounds of sugar, one-half a pint of sweet milk, one-half a pound of dessicated cocoanut, a piece of butter the size of a nutmeg. Boil the sugar, milk and butter seven minutes, remove from the stove, place in a bowl, stir until a little cool, then add one-half a cocoanut spread on the cake, and sprinkle the other one-half of the cocoanut on the top of the cake ; if the frosting becomes too hard, stir in a little boiling water.

1141. Chocolate Frosting for Cakes.

Articles.—One and one-half pounds of sugar, half a pint of milk, a piece of butter the size of a nutmeg, two tablespoonfuls of plain chocolate, scraped and mixed to a paste with boiling water.

Directions.—Boil the sugar, milk and butter seven minutes, then place in a bowl, add the chocolate paste, stir until the mixture becomes thick, then spread on same as the cocoanut frosting ; should it become too hard to spread smoothly, do as stated in cocoanut frosting.

Remarks.—The above can be used for layer cake, and is sufficient for three layers.

1142. Sugar Frosting for Cakes.

ARTICLES.—One and one-half pounds of powdered sugar, half a pint of water, a piece of butter the size of a nutmeg, and flavor to taste.

DIRECTIONS.—Put the sugar, water and butter in a pan, boil eight minutes, take off the stove, put it in a bowl, add flavoring, stir it till it thickens, then spread on the cake; this frosting can be used instead of cream for layer cake.

1143. Egg Frosting for Cakes. [TIME.—ABOUT HALF AN HOUR.]

ARTICLES.—Whites of six eggs, powdered sugar, and vanilla flavor.

DIRECTIONS.—Beat the eggs to a stiff froth, stir in sugar, then add half a teaspoonful of vanilla flavor, spread upon the cake and set it in a hot oven about one minute, or until the frosting hardens, and then lay it away in a cool place.

REMARKS.—The above can be used for layer cake, and is sufficient for three layers.

1144. Cocoanut Frosting for Cakes. (*Eugenie.*) [TIME.—ABOUT FIFTEEN MINUTES.]

ARTICLES.—One and one-half pounds of sugar, half a pint of milk, half a pound of dessicated cocoanut, and a piece of butter the size of a nutmeg.

DIRECTIONS.—Boil the sugar, milk and butter for seven minutes, then place in a bowl, stir until it cools a little, put in half of the cocoanut and stir till it thickens; spread on your cake and sprinkle the top with the remainder of the cocoanut; should the frosting become too hard to spread over the cake smoothly, place the bowl in a pan of hot water; take a broad knife, dip in the hot water, spread and smoothen the frosting on the cake.

REMARKS.—The above can be used for layer cake, and is sufficient for three layers.

FANCY BEVERAGES.

1145. Punch.

To make punch of any sort in perfection the ambrosial essence of the lemon must be extracted by rubbing lumps of sugar on the rind, which breaks the delicate little vessels that contain the essence, and at the same time absorbs it. This, and making the mixture sweet and strong, using tea instead of water, and thoroughly amalgamating all the compounds, so that the taste of neither the bitter, the sweet, the spirit, nor the element, shall be perceptible one over the other, is the grand secret, only to be acquired by practice.

In making hot toddy, or hot punch, you must put in the spirits before the water; in cold punch, grog, etc., the other way.

The precise portions of spirit and water, or even of the acidity and sweetness, can have no general rule, as scarcely two persons make punch alike.

1146. Brandy Punch.
(Use large glass.)

One tablespoonful of raspberry syrup, two tablespoonfuls of white sugar, one wineglassful of water, one and one-half wine-glassfuls of brandy, one-half of a small-sized lemon, two slices of orange, and one piece of pine-apple.

Fill the tumbler with shaved ice, shake well, and dress the top with berries in season; sip through a straw.

1147. Brandy Punch.
(For a party of twenty.)

One gallon of water, three quarts of brandy, one-half of a pint of Jamaica rum, two pounds of sugar, the juice of six lemons, three oranges sliced, one pine-apple, pared and cut up, one gill of Curaçoa, two gills of raspberry syrup, ice, and add berries in season.

Mix the materials well together in a large bowl, and you have a splendid punch.

MEN'S FURNISHING GOODS.

HUMBURCH & HODGE,
— IMPORTERS OF —
ENGLISH WALKING AND DRIVING GLOVES
HOUSE JACKETS, ROBES,
STEAMER AND CARRIAGE RUGS,

329 MAIN STREET, - BUFFALO, N. Y.

HOSIERS.   GLOVERS.   SHIRT MAKERS., &c.

JAMES CHALMERS' SONS,
GELATINE.

CHALMERS' GELATINE

—IS SPECIALLY PREPARED FOR—

FAMILY USE,

And is acknowledged to be an article of the

HIGHEST STANDARD OF EXCELLENCE.

—THIS—

GELATINE

Is manufactured under the personal supervision of the manufacturer, thereby ensuring perfection in all the various processes of manufacture.

UNIFORM WEIGHT AND QUALITY GUARANTEED.

—AND WHEN MADE UP FOR—

JELLIES, ETC.,

— WILL BE FOUND —

VERY PURE AND HANDSOME,

—AND IS A—

FIRST-CLASS GELATINE

IN EVERY RESPECT.

1148. Mississippi Punch.
(Use large glass.)

One wineglassful of brandy, one-half a wineglassful of Jamaica rum, one-half a wineglassful of Bourbon whiskey, one-half a wineglassful of water, one and one-half tablespoonfuls of powdered white sugar, one-quarter of a large lemon, and fill a tumbler with shaved ice.

The above must be well shaken, and to those who like their draughts "like linked sweetness long drawn out," let them use a glass tube or straw to sip the nectar through. The top of this punch should be ornamented with small pieces of orange, and berries in season.

1149. Hot Brandy and Rum Punch.
(For a party of fifteen.)

One quart of Jamaica rum, one quart of Cognac brandy, one pound of white loaf sugar, four lemons, three quarts of boiling water, and one teaspoonful of nutmeg.

Rub the sugar over the lemons until it has absorbed all the yellow part of the skins, then put the sugar into a punch-bowl; add the ingredients well together, pour over them the boiling water, stir well together, add the rum, brandy and nutmeg; mix thoroughly, and the punch will be ready to serve. As we have before said, it is very important, in making good punch, that all the ingredients are thoroughly incorporated, and, to insure success, the process of mixing must be diligently attended to. Allow a quart for four persons, but this information must be taken *cum grano salis*, for the capacities of persons for this kind of beverage are generally supposed to vary considerably.

1150. Irish Whiskey Punch.

This is the genuine Irish beverage. It is generally made one-third pure whiskey and two-thirds boiling water, in which the sugar has been dissolved. If lemon punch, the rind is rubbed on the sugar, and a small proportion of juice added before the whiskey is poured in.

1151. Whiskey Punch.

One wineglassful of whiskey (Irish or Scotch), two wineglassfuls of boiling water, and sugar to taste.

Dissolve the sugar well with one wineglassful of the water, then pour in the whiskey, and add the balance of the water, sweeten to taste, and ut in a small piece of lemon rind, or a thin slice of lemon.

1152. Gin Punch.
(Use large glass.)

One tablespoonful of raspberry syrup, two tablespoonfuls of white sugar, one wineglassful of water, one and one-half wineglassfuls of gin, one-half of a small-sized lemon, two slices of orange, one piece of pine-apple, and fill the tumbler with shaved ice.

Shake well, and ornament the top with berries in season. Sip through a glass tube or straw.

1153. Sherry Punch.
(Use large glass.)

Two wineglassfuls of sherry, one tablespoonful of sugar, two or three slices of orange, and two or three slices of lemon.

Fill the tumbler with shaved ice, shake well, and ornament with berries in season. Sip through a straw.

1154. Claret Punch.
(Use large glass.)

One and one-half tablespoonfuls of sugar, one slice of lemon, and two or three slices of orange.

Fill the tumbler with shaved ice, and then pour in your claret, shake well, and ornament with berries in season. Place a straw in the glass. To make a quantity of claret punch, see "*Imperial Punch,*" No. 1163.

1155. Port Wine Punch.
(Use large glass.)

The same as claret punch, using port wine instead of claret, and ornament with berries in season.

1156. Pine-Apple Punch.
(For a party of ten.)

Four bottles of champagne, one pint of Jamaica rum, one pint of brandy, one gill of Curaçoa, juice of four lemons, four pine-apples sliced, and sweeten to taste with pulverized white sugar.

Put the pine-apple with one pound of sugar in a glass bowl, and let them stand until the sugar is well soaked in the pine-apple, then add all the other ingredients, except the champagne. Let this mixture stand in ice for about an hour, then add the champagne. Place a large block of ice in the center of the bowl, and ornament it with loaf sugar, sliced orange, and other fruits in season. Serve in champagne glasses. Pine-apple punch is sometimes made by adding sliced pine-apple to brandy punch.

1157. Curaçoa Punch.
(Use large glass.)

One tablespoonful of sugar, one wineglassful of brandy, one-half of a wineglassful of Jamaica rum, one wineglassful of water, one-half of a pony glassful of Curaçoa, and the juice of half a lemon.

Fill the tumbler with shaved ice, shake well, and ornament with fruits of the season, sip the nectar through a straw.

1158. Roman Punch.
(Use large glass.)

One tablespoonful of sugar, one tablespoonful of raspberry syrup, one teaspoonful of Curaçoa, one wineglassful of Jamaica rum, one-half of a wineglassful of brandy, and the juice of half a lemon.

Fill with shaved ice, shake well, dash with port wine, and ornament with fruits in season. Imbibe through a straw.

1159. Milk Punch.
(Use large glass.)

One tablespoonful of fine white sugar, two tablespoonfuls of water, one wineglassful of Cognac brandy, one-half of a wineglassful of Santa Cruz rum, one-third of a tumblerful of shaved ice.

Fill with milk, shake the ingredients well together, and grate a little nutmeg on top.

1160. Hot Milk Punch.
(Use large glass.)

This punch is made the same as the above, with the exception that hot milk is used, and no ice.

1161. English Milk Punch.

Put the following ingredients into a very clean pitcher, viz.: The juice of six lemons, the rind of two lemons, one pound of sugar, one pine-apple, peeled, sliced and pounded, six cloves, twenty coriander seeds, one small stick of cinnamon, one pint of brandy, one pint of rum, one gill of arrack, one cup of strong green tea, and one quart of boiling water.

The boiling water to be added last; cork this down to prevent evaporation, and allow these ingredients to steep for at least six hours; then add a quart of hot milk and the juice of two lemons; mix, and filter through a jelly bag; and when the punch has passed bright, put it away in tight-corked bottles. This punch is intended to be iced for drinking.

1162. Regent's Punch
(For a party of twenty.)

The ingredients for this renowned punch are:—Three bottles of champagne, one bottle of Rhine wine, one bottle of Curaçoa, one bottle of Cognac, one-half of a bottle of Jamaica rum, two bottles of Madeira, two bottles of seltzer, or plain soda-water, and four pounds of raisins.

To which add oranges, lemons, rock candy, and instead of water, green tea to taste. Refrigerate with all the icy power of the Arctic.

1163. Imperial Punch.

One bottle of claret, one bottle of soda-water, four table

spoonfuls of powdered white sugar, one-quarter of a teaspoonful of grated nutmeg, one liqueur glass of maraschino, about one-half of a pound of ice, and three or four slices of cucumber rind.

Put all the ingredients into a bowl or pitcher and mix well.

1164. Rocky Mountain Punch.
(For a mixed party of twenty.)

This delicious punch is compounded as follows : Five bottles of champagne, one quart of Jamaica rum, one pint of maraschino, six lemons, sliced, and sugar to taste.

Mix the above ingredients in a large punch-bowl, then place in the center of the bowl a large square block of ice, ornamented on top with rock candy, loaf-sugar, sliced lemons or oranges, and fruits in season. This is a splendid punch for New Year's Day.

1165. Tip-Top Punch.
(For a party of five.)

One bottle of champagne, two bottles of soda-water, one liqueur glassful of Curaçoa, two tablespoonfuls of powdered sugar, and one slice of pine-apple, cut up.

Put all the ingredients together in a small punch-bowl, mix well, and serve in champagne goblets.

1166. Royal Punch.

One pint of hot green tea, one-half a pint of brandy, one-half a pint of Jamaica rum, one wineglassful of Curaçoa, one wineglassful of arrack, juice of two limes, a thin slice of lemon, white sugar to taste, and one gill of warm calves-foot jelly, to be drunk as hot as possible.

This is a composition worthy of a king, and the materials are admirably blended ; the inebriating effects of the spirits being deadened by the tea, whilst the jelly softens the mixture, and destroys the acrimony of the acid and sugar. The whites of a couple of eggs well beaten up to a froth, may be substituted for the jelly where that is not at hand. If the punch is too strong, add more green tea to taste.

1167. Gothic Punch.
(For a party of ten.)

Four bottles of still Catawba, one bottle of claret, three oranges, or one pine-apple, and ten tablespoonfuls of sugar. Let this mixture stand in a very cold place, or in ice, for one hour or more, and then add one bottle of champagne.

1168. Audubon Club Punch.
(For a party of twenty to twenty-five.)

Two quart bottles of champagne, one quart bottle of sherry wine, one quart bottle of Cognac, one quart bottle of St. Cruz rum, one quart bottle of Sauterne wine, one quart bottle of claret wine, six quart bottles of lemon soda, one pine-apple, sliced, four lemons, sliced, and one-half of a pound of powdered sugar.

Let the sliced pine-apple and lemon soak in the Cognac an hour or more, half a day is better, pour the sherry and Sauterne wine over the sugar, let it dissolve, place a large lump of ice in your punch-bowl, pour in the sweetened sherry and Sauterne, then your Cognac and pine-apple, next the rum and claret, then the lemon soda, and last the champagne, just before serving. Garnish the bowl with clusters of grapes, or the top of the block of ice with same, or berries in season.

1169. Egg Nogg.

Egg nogg is a beverage of American origin, but it has a popularity that is cosmopolitan. At the South it is almost indispensable at Christmas time, and at the North it is a favorite at all seasons. In Scotland they call egg nogg, *"auld man's milk."*

1170. Egg Nogg.
(Use large glass.)

One tablespoonful of fine sugar, dissolved with one table. spoonful of cold water, one egg, one wineglassful of Cognac brandy, one-half of a wineglassful of Santa Cruz rum, and one-third of a tumblerful of milk.

Fill the tumbler one-quarter full with shaved ice, shake the ingredients until they are *thoroughly mixed together*, and grate a little nutmeg on top.

1171. Egg Nogg.
(For a party of forty.)

One dozen eggs, two quarts of brandy, one pint of Santa Cruz rum, two gallons of milk, and one and one-half pounds of white sugar.

Separate the whites of the eggs from the yolks, beat them separately with an egg-beater until the yolks are well cut up, and the whites assume a light fleecy appearance. Mix all the ingredients (except the whites of the eggs) in a large punch-bowl, then let the whites float on top, and ornament with colored sugars. Cool in a tub of ice, and serve.

1172. Sherry Egg Nogg.

One tablespoonful of white sugar, one egg, and two wine-glassfuls of sherry.

Dissolve the sugar with a little water, break the yolk of the egg in a large glass, put in one-quarter of a tumblerful of broken ice, fill with milk, and shake up until the egg is thoroughly mixed with the other ingredients, then grate a little nutmeg on top, and quaff the nectar cup.

1173. Mint Julep.
(Use large glass.)

One tablespoonful of white pulverized sugar, two and one-half tablespoonfuls of water, and mix well with a spoon.

Take three or four sprigs of fresh mint, and press them well in the sugar and water, until the flavor of the mint is extracted, add one and a half wineglassfuls of Cognac brandy, and fill the glass with fine shaved ice, then draw out the sprigs of mint and insert them in the ice with the stems downward, so that the leaves will be above, in the shape of a bouquet. arrange berries, and small pieces of sliced orange on top in a tasty manner, dash with Jamaica rum, and sprinkle white sugar on top. Place a straw across the top, and you have a julep that is fit for an emperor.

1174. Brandy Smash.
(Use small glass.)

One-half of a tablespoonful of white sugar, one tablespoonful of water, and one wineglassful of brandy.

Fill two-thirds full of shaved ice, use two sprigs of mint, the same as in the recipe for mint julep. Lay two small pieces of orange on top, and ornament with berries in season. For gin or whiskey smash, take whiskey or gin.

1175. Sherry Cobbler.
(Use large glass.)

Two wineglassfuls of sherry, one tablespoonful of sugar, and two or three slices of orange.

Fill a tumbler with shaved ice, shake well, and ornament with berries in season. Imbibe through straw or glass tubes.

1176. Champagne Cobbler.
(One bottle of wine to four large glasses.)

One tablespoonful of sugar, one piece each of orange and lemon peel.

Fill the tumbler one-third full with shaved ice, and fill balance with wine, ornament in a tasty manner with berries in season. This beverage should be sipped through a straw.

1177. Whiskey Cobbler.
(Use large glass.)

Two wineglassfuls of whiskey, one tablespoonful of sugar, and two or three slices of orange.

Fill the tumbler with ice, and shake well. Imbibe through a straw.

1178. Brandy Cocktail.
(Use small glass.)

Three or four dashes of gum syrup, two dashes of bitters, one wineglassful of brandy, and one or two dashes of Curaçoa.

Squeeze lemon peel; fill one-third full of ice, and stir with a spoon.

1179. Mulled Wine with Eggs.

One quart of wine, one pint of water, one tablespoonful of allspice, and nutmeg to taste; boil them together a few minutes; beat up six eggs with sugar to your taste; pour the boiling wine *on the eggs*, stirring it all the time. Be careful not to *pour the eggs into the wine*, or they will curdle.

1180. Port Wine Sangaree.
(Use small glass)

One and a half wineglassfuls of port wine, one teaspoonful of sugar, fill the tumbler two-thirds with ice, shake well and grate nutmeg on top.

1181. Egg Flip.

Put a quart of ale in a tinned saucepan on the fire to boil; in the mean time, beat up the yolks of four, with the whites of two eggs, adding four tablespoonfuls of brown sugar and a little nutmeg, pour on the ale by degrees, beating up, so as to prevent the mixture from curdling, then pour back and forward repeatedly from vessel to vessel, raising the hand to as great a height as possible—which process produces the smoothness and frothing essential to the good quality of the flip. This is excellent for a cold, and, from its fleecy appearance,, is sometimes designated "a yard of flannel."

1182. Crimean Cup, a la Marmora.
(From a recipe by the celebrated Soyer)
(For a party of thirty)

One quart of syrup of orgeat, one pint of Cognac brandy, one-half of a pint of maraschino, one-half of a pint of Jamaica rum, two bottles of champagne, two bottles of soda-water, six ounces of sugar, and four middling-sized lemons.

Thinly peel the lemons, and place the rind in a bowl with the sugar, macerate them well for a minute or two, in order to extract the flavor from the lemon. Next squeeze the juice of the lemons upon this, add two bottles of soda-water, and stir well till the sugar is dissolved; pour in the syrup of orgeat, and whip the mixture well with an egg-whisk, in order to whiten the composition. Then add the brandy, rum and maraschino, strain the whole into the punch-bowl, and just before serving add the champagne, which should be well iced. While adding the champagne, stir well with the ladle; this will render the cup creamy and mellow.

1183. Tom and Jerry.
(Use punch-bowl for the mixture.)

Five pounds of sugar, twelve eggs, one-half of a small glassful of Jamaica rum, one and one-half teaspoonfuls of ground cinnamon, one-half of a teaspoonful of ground cloves, and one-half of a teaspoonful of ground allspice.

Beat the whites of the eggs to a stiff froth, and the yolks until they are as thin as water, then mix together and add the spice and rum, thicken with sugar until the mixture attains the consistence of a light batter.

To deal out Tom and Jerry.—Take a small bar glass, and to one tablespoonful of the above mixture, add one wineglassful of brandy, and fill the glass with boiling water, and grate a little nutmeg on top. Adepts in serving Tom and Jerry, sometimes adopt a mixture of one-half brandy, one-quarter Jamaica rum, and one-quarter Santa Cruz rum, instead of brandy plain. This compound is usually mixed and kept in a bottle, and a wineglassful is used to each tumbler of Tom and Jerry.

N. B.—A teaspoonful of cream of tartar, or about as much carbonate of soda as you can get on a dime, will prevent the sugar from settling to the bottom of the mixture. This drink is sometimes called Copenhagen, and sometimes *Jerry Thomas*.

1184. TO PREPARE COMPANY DINNERS.

It is very simple to prepare a dinner served *a la Russe*, as it matters little how many courses there may be. If it were necessary to prepare many dishes, and to have them all hot, and in perfection at the same minute, and then be obliged to serve them nearly all together, the task might be considered rather formidable and confusing. But with one or two assistants, and with time between each course to prepare the succeeding one, after a very little practice it becomes a mere amusement.

The soup, or the stock for the soup, and the dessert, should be made the day before the dinner.

A bill of fare should be written, and pinned up in the kitchen. Everything should be prepared that is possible in the early part of the day, then, after the fish, chickens, birds, etc., are dressed and larded (if necessary), they should be put aside, near the ice. If sweet-breads are to be served, they should be larded, parboiled, and put away also. The salad (if lettuce) should be sprinkled with water (not placed *in* water), and put in a cool, dark place in a basket, not to be touched until the last three minutes.

The plates and platters for each course should be counted, examined, and placed on a table by themselves.

After this, the kitchen should be put in order, and the tables cleared of all unnecessary things. Then everything needed for the courses to be cooked should be placed in separate groups at the back of a large table, so that there may be no confusion or loss of anything at the last minute. If there are sweetbreads, have them egged and bread-crumbed; if peas are to be served with them, place them in a basin at their side, properly seasoned. If there is macaroni with cheese, have the proper quantity desired already broken on a dish, with a plate of grated cheese and a tin cup, with the necessary amount of butter to be melted, side by side. If there is a fillet of beef to be baked and served with a mushroom sauce, have the fillet in the baking pan already larded, the mushrooms in the basin in which they are to be cooked, at the side; also the piece of lemon and the spoonful of flour ready. The stock will be in the kettle at the back of the stove. By-the-way, in giving a fine dinner, there should always be an extra stock-pot, separate from the soup, at the back of the stove, as it is excellent for boiling the sweetbreads or the macaroni, and making the sauces, etc.

If a simple salad of lettuce is to be served, have the oil, vinegar, pepper and salt, and the spoonful of finely chopped onion, in a group all ready. If a *Mayonnaise* dressing is to be served, that should be made in the morning.

Look at the clock in the kitchen, and calculate the time it will take each dish to cook, and put it to the fire, so that it will be finished "to a turn" just at the proper minute.

During dinner, one person should attend to placing out of the way all the dishes brought from the dining room, and, if necessary, should wash any spoons, platters, etc., which may be needed a second time. She should know beforehand, however, just what she is to wash, as every one must know exactly her own business, so that no questions need be asked at the last moment. The cook can attend to nothing but the cooking, at the risk of neglecting this most important part.

As the course just before the salad is sent into the dining room, begin to make the salad, having everything all ready. First, pick over the lettuce leaves, wash and leave them to drain, while you prepare the dressing. It should *just* be ready when its turn comes to be sent to the table.

If the dinner company is very large, and there are many dishes, the cooking of them may be distributed between two persons, and perhaps the second cook may use the laundry stove; but with a little practice and the one or two assistants, *one* cook can easily prepare the most elaborate dinner, if it is only properly managed before the time of cooking. She should, of course, never attempt any dish she has not made before. A *bain-marie* is very convenient for preserving cooked dishes, if there is some delay in serving the dinner.

Of all things, never on any occasion serve a large joint or large article of any kind on a little platter, as nothing looks so awkward. Let the platter always be at least a third larger than the size of its contents.

We give several bills of fare which are long enough and good enough for any dinner party. Guests do not care for better or more, if these are only properly cooked. They can be easily prepared in one's own house, and this is always more elegant than to have a list of a hundred dishes from a restaurant.

1185. BILLS OF FARE, OR MENUS.

Winter Dinner.

Oysters on the half shell,
Ox tail soup,
Baked Haddock, Anchovy Sauce,
Sweet Breads, Tomato Sauce,
Roast Beef, garnished with Roast Potatoes,
Stewed Ducks with Turnips,
Salad, Lettuce,
Cheese, Cold water Wafers,
Charlotte Russe with French bottled Strawberries around it,
Chocolate Ice Cream,
Fruit,
Coffee.

This bill of fare is common at dinner parties. It is not difficult to prepare, as there are only four of the courses which are necessarily prepared at dinner time. The oyster course is very simple, and may be placed on the table before the guests enter the dining room. The soup may be made the day before, and only requires heating at the time of serving. The *charlotte russe* can be purchased, if desired, at the confectioner's, or the cake for it may be made the day before. So, after the meats are ready, the cook has nothing more to do but to make the salad, which is an affair of three minutes, and the coffee, for which she has a long time (the coffee having been ground and in readiness in the coffee pot two or three hours before dinner). The four last courses before the coffee are easily purchased outside. The cheese may be a Cheddar or a Roquefort. The fruit may be on the table during the dinner as one of the decorations.

Dinner Bill of Fare.

Mock Turtle Soup,
(It can be purchased canned, if you do not wish to prepare it,)
Oyster Patties,
Yellow Pike (*au gratin*),
Chicken Croquettes, with French Peas,
Saddle of Venison, with Potatoes *a la Neige*,
Broiled Pigeons,
Shrimp Salad,
Rum Omelet,
Pine Apple Bavarian Cream,
Vanilla Ice Cream,
Fruits,
Cake,
Coffee.

Dinner for Spring.

White Soup with Almonds,
Baked Pickerel, (*Sauce Hollandaise*),
Lamb Croquettes, with Spinach,
Spring Chicken baked, new Potatoes,
Roast Leg of Veal—stuffed, new Peas,
New Lettuce,
Omelet with Mushrooms,
Lemon Ice Cream,
Cheese,
Fruit,
Cake,
Coffee.

Dinner.

Menu.

Oysters served on a block of ice,*
Soup, Julienne, (can be purchased in cans if desired),

---

* Take a block of clear ice nine or ten inches square, and with a heated flatiron make a cavity in the top to hold the oysters; previous to laying the oysters in the cavity, sprinkle a little salt in same and place the oysters therein, set it in a cool place until dinner is ready, then lay a napkin on a platter and let the block of ice rest on the napkin; the effect is very pleasing by gaslight.

Soft Shell Crabs,
Calves' Head *a la Maitre d' Hotel*,
French canned String Beans, stewed,
Scollops of Quails with Truffles,
Beef *a la Mode* with Roast Potatoes,
Macaroni with Cheese,
Plum Pudding with Rum,
Raspberry Ice Cream,
Cake and Fruit,
Coffee.

Menu.

Soup—French Oyster Soup,
Stewed Duck with Turnips,
Roast Turkey, Chestnut Filling, Cranberry Sauce,
Potatoes *a la Neige*,
Shrimp Salad,
Lemon Pie,
Omelet with Rum,
Ice Cream,
Fruit, Nuts, Cake,
Coffee.

Dinner.

Menu.

Soup—Noodle,
Fish—Yellow Pike, baked, *Sauce Espagnol*,
Roast Lamb, Mint Sauce,
Stewed Tomatoes,
Roast New Potatoes,
Chicken Croquettes,
Salad, Lettuce.
Sago Pudding,
Cake, Nuts,
Coffee.

1186. SERVING OF WINES.

At dinners of great pretension, from eight to twelve different kinds of wines are sometimes served. This is rather ostentatious than elegant. In my judgment, neither elegance nor good taste is displayed in such excess. Four different kinds of wine are quite enough for the grandest occasions imaginable, if they are only of the choicest selection. Indeed, for most occasions, a single wine—a choice claret—is quite sufficient. In fact, let no one hesitate about giving dinners without any wine at all. Proper respect for conscientious scruples about serving wine would forbid a criticism as to the propriety of serving any dinner without it. Such dinners are in quite as good taste, and will be just as well appreciated by sensible people; and it makes very little difference whether people *who are not sensible* are pleased or not.

1187. Menus with Wines.

If three wines are served let it be a fine Sauterne with the fish, a claret with the roast, and a champagne with the fruit and dessert, and if a fourth is desired let it be a Chateau Yquem with an *entree*. The following arrangement of a MENU where wines are served, is decidedly original, showing the guest at a glance the wines he may expect, and thereby enabling him to regulate the consumption thereof; it may be varied to suit the host.

Dinner.

Menu.

Wines.	Menu.
	Oysters—On the half shell,
	SOUP—Mullagatawny,
Sauterne	FISH—Baked White Fish, *sauce Hollandaise*,
	Sweet Breads, Tomato Sauce,
Claret	Roast Beef with Roast Potatoes,
	Shrimp Salad,
	Asparagus, Cream Dressing,
	Plum Pudding with Rum,
Champagne . . .	Almonds, Cold water Wafers, Cake,
	Fruit,
	Coffee, *au Cognac*.

Dinner.

In honor of _____

April_____188__

Wines.	*Menu.*
	Oysters on block of ice (see page 382.)
A small glass of sherry	
	SOUP—Mock Turtle,
Sauterne	FISH—Baked Haddock,
	Chicken Croquettes, Tomato Sauce,
	Broiled Snipe on Toast, Potatoes *a la Parisienne.*
Claret	Roast Leg of Veal, stuffed,

C. W. MILLER'S
COACH AND BAGGAGE EXPRESS

General Coach, Ticket and Baggage Office,
469 MAIN STREET.
STABLES:—202, 204 and 206 Pearl Street.

The largest, finest and most complete assortment of Coaches, Coupes, Cabriolets and Coupelets in Western New York, can be found at the above stables, at reasonable prices.

FOR CALLING, SHOPPING, FUNERALS AND WEDDING PARTIES.

Careful drivers in livery with stylish turnouts furnished at a moment's notice.

Moving made easy and comfortable by the use of my large and commodious

Covered Moving Vans and Carts,
WITH REQUISITE HELP IF REQUIRED.

☞ **RAILROAD TICKETS SOLD TO ALL POINTS.** ☜

Baggage called for and Checked from Hotels or Private Residences to destination.

```
GENERAL OFFICE,           -    -    -         469 Main Street
BRANCH OFFICE (Stables)   -    -    202, 204, 206 Pearl Street
     "         "          -    -    -         Tupper, cor. Pearl
     "         "          -    -    -         169 Allen, cor. Park
     "         "          -    -    836 Niagara, cor. Rhode Island
```

OFFICE OPEN DAY AND NIGHT.
TELEPHONE COMMUNICATION AT STABLE.

All orders carefully and promptly executed.

C. W. MILLER, Proprietor.

BUFFALO, N.Y.

45 Swan St., Cor. Ellicott, - BUFFALO, N. Y.

— I MAKE A SPECIALTY OF —

FINE BINDING,

— SUCH AS —

SERIAL WORKS, MAGAZINES, MUSIC, Etc.

Chateau Yquem Champagne . . (*Piper Heidsieck*)	Lamb Chops *a la Royal*, with Spinach, Salad of Lettuce, Omelette Souffle, Lemon Pie, Hickory Nut Cake, Cold Water Wafers, Sponge Cake, Almonds, Raisins, Figs, Coffee, *au Rum*, Cigars.

Thanksgiving Dinner.

Wines.	*Menu.*
A small glass of sherry	Oysters on the half shell,
Sauterne, . , . . (*Cruse Fils and Freres*)	Soup—Vermicelli. Fish—Yellow Pike, *au gratin*, Scollops of Quails with Truffles,
Claret—St Julien, . (*Cruse Fils and Freres*)	French Peas, Roast Turkey, Oyster and Chestnut Stuffing,
.	Saratoga Potatoes, Oysters and Macaroni, Lobster Salad,
Chateau Yquem, . . . (*Cruse Fils and Freres*)	Rum Omelet, Ice Cream, Chocolate Layer Cake,
Champagne, ... *Mumm's Extra Dry*	Angel's Food, Cold Water Wafers, Edam Cheese, Figs, Raisins, Nuts, Coffee *au Cognac*, Cigars, (*Henry Clay, Regalia Conchas.*)

By consulting the article on "Suitable Combination of Dishes" No. 1188, Page 386, a variety of Menus can be prepared to suit any taste, and be regulated as to expense, in the selection, or by the addition or omission of dishes to each course.

1189. Proper Temperature in which Wines Should be Served.

Sherry should be served thoroughly chilled.

Madeira should be neither warm nor cold, but of about the same temperature as the room.

Claret should be served at the same temperature as Madeira, never with ice; pure wines most generally will form a deposit in the bottles, and many condemn the wine as being impure, while the contrary is the rule; wines having a deposit in the bottle should be allowed to stand in a cool (not cold) place till settled, and either be carefully decanted, or served with a table wine basket.

Champagne should either be kept on ice for several hours previous to serving, or it should be half frozen; it is then called *Champagne frappe*. It is frozen with some difficulty. The ice should be pounded quite fine, then an *equal* amount of salt mixed with it. A quart bottle of champagne well surrounded by this mixture should be frozen in two hours, or, rather, frozen to the degree when it may be poured from the bottle

1189. SUITABLE COMBINATION OF DISHES.

There are dishes which seem especially adapted to be served together. This should be a matter of some study. Of course, very few would serve cheese with fish, yet general combinations are often very carelessly considered.

Soup.

Soup is generally served alone; however, pickles and crackers are a pleasant accompaniment for oyster soup, and many serve grated cheese with macaroni and vermicelli soups. A pea or bean soup (without bread *croutons*) at one end of the table, with a neat, square piece of boiled pork on a platter at the other end, is sometimes seen. When a ladleful of the soup is put in the soup plate by the hostess, the butler passes it to the host, who cuts off a thin wafer-slice of the pork, and places it in the soup. The thin pork can be cut with the spoon. Hot boiled rice is served with gumbo soup. Well-boiled rice, with each grain distinct, is served in a dish by the side of the soup tureen. The hostess first puts a ladleful of soup into the soup plate, then a spoonful of the rice in the center. This is much better than cooking the rice with the soup.

Sometimes little squares (two inches square) of thin slices of brown bread (buttered) are served with soup at handsome dinners. It is a French custom. Cold slaw may be served at the same time with soup, and eaten with the soup or just after the soup plates are removed.

Fish.

The only vegetable to be served with fish is the plain boiled potato. It may be cut into little round balls an inch in diameter, and served in little piles as a garnish around the fish, or it may be the flaky, full-sized potato, served in another dish. Some stuff a fish with seasoned mashed potatoes, then serve around it little cakes of mashed potatoes, rolled in egg and bread crumbs, and fried. Cucumbers, and sometimes noodles, are served with fish.

Beef.

Almost any vegetable may be served with beef. If potato is not served with fish, it generally accompanies the beef, either as a bed of smooth mashed potatoes around the beef, or *a la neige*, or as fried potato balls *(a la Parisienne)*, or, in fact, cooked in any of the myriad different ways. At dinner companies, beef is generally served with a mushroom sauce. However, as any and all vegetables are suitable for beef, it is only a matter of convenience which to choose. Horse-radish is a favorite beef accompaniment.

Corned Beef

should be served with carrots, turnips, parsnips, cabbage, or pickles around it.

Turkeys.

Cranberry sauce, or some acid jelly, such as currant or plum jelly, should be served with turkey. Many garnish a turkey with sausages made of pork or beef. Any vegetable may be served with a turkey; perhaps onions, cold slaw, turnips, tomatoes, and potatoes are the ones oftenest selected.

Chickens.

Fried chickens with cream dressing are good served with cauliflower on the same dish, with the same sauce poured over both. A boiled chicken is generally served in a bed of boiled rice. A row of baked tomatoes is a pretty garnish around a roast chicken. It is fashionable to serve salads with chickens.

Lamb

Is especially nice served with green peas or with spinach; cauliflowers and asparagus are also favorite accompaniments.

Pork.

The unquestionable combination for pork is fried apples, apple sauce, sweet potatoes, tomatoes, or Irish potatoes. Pork sausages should invariably be served with apple sauce or fried apples. Thin slices of breakfast bacon make a savory garnish for beefsteak. Thin slices of pork, egged and bread-crumbed, fried, and placed on slices of fried mush, make a nice breakfast dish; or it may garnish fried chickens, beefsteak, or breaded chops.

Mutton.

The same vegetables mentioned as suitable for lamb are appropriate for mutton. The English often serve salad with mutton.

Veal.

Any vegetable may be served as well with veal as with beef. We would select, however, tomatoes, parsnips, or oyster plant.

Roast Goose,

Apple sauce, and turnips especially.

Game.

Game should invariably be served with an acid jelly, such as a currant or a plum jelly. Saratoga potatoes, potatoes *a la Parisienne*, spinach, tomatoes, and salads, are especially suitable for game.

Cheese

Is served just before the dessert. It is English to serve celery or cucumbers with it. Thin milk crackers or wafer biscuits (put into the oven just a moment before serving, to make them crisp) should be served with cheese; butter also for spreading the crackers, this being the only time that it is usually allowed for dinner. Macaroni with cheese, Welsh rare-bits, cheese omelets, or little cheese cakes, are good substitutes for a cheese course.

Sweetbreads.

Sweetbreads and peas—this is the combination seen at almost every dinner company. They are as nice, however, with tomatoes, cauliflowers, macaroni mixed with tomato sauce or cheese. or with asparagus or succotash

ADDITIONAL RECIPES.

1190. Toad in a Hole.

A VERY DELICATE AND DAINTY TID BIT.

Take half a dozen of select oysters of uniform size, sprinkle with bread crumbs or cracker dust, cut half a dozen rashers of smoked bacon very thin, wrap one rasher around every oyster, securing the oyster in the bacon by means of a small wooden pin, lay them in a dish and put into a moderately hot oven ten minutes; toast a slice of bread, and well butter it, place the oysters, when done, upon the buttered toast, and pour over the whole the juice, and serve hot.

1191. Pate or Meat Pie. *(Mdme. Grimard.)* [TIME.— TO BAKE, ONE AND ONE-FOURTH HOURS.]

ARTICLES.— our pounds of lean fresh pork, one medium sized onion, or four shallots, one tablespoonful of chopped parsley, three cloves of garlic, and salt and pepper to taste.

DIRECTIONS.—Chop the onion or shallot and garlic fine and mix with the chopped parsley; cut the meat into squares of about one inch, place at the bottom of a crockery bowl, a sprinkling of the chopped herbs, and salt and pepper, next a layer of meat, then repeat the sprinkling of herbs, and salt and pepper till the meat is all in, and then put a sprinkling of the herbs on top, cover the dish and let it stand twenty-four hours; make a paste similar to pie paste, (not too rich), line a pan with the crust about one-quarter inch thick, fill the crust with the meat evenly distributed, about one and one-half inches thick, cover with the crust about the same thickness as the bottom, and bake in a medium oven about one hour and a quarter, then take out the pie, have two small eggs beaten up with one-half of a cup of cream, cut a small hole in the top of the crust, pour in the cream and eggs, replace in the oven for about ten minutes, and serve warm. The garlic may be omitted if desired, although the pate is much finer with it.

1192. White Bread.
FOR USE IN THE MORNING —MAKES FOUR LOAVES.

Dissolve thoroughly one cake of Gaff, Fleischmann & Co.'s compressed yeast in a pint of lukewarm water, and stir in sifted flour until the mixture is a little thicker than griddle cake batter. Set it in a warm place, free from draft, until it rises and begins to go back. Your sponge is now complete. Add to the sponge one quart of lukewarm water, one tablespoonful of salt, two of sugar, same of butter, add sifted flour enough to make a dough as soft as can be handled. Knead well. When thoroughly light, knead, make into loaves, place in well-greased pans for final rising. This last kneading should be very thorough. When light, bake, remembering that it will "spring" still more in the oven. When baked, lean it against something, throw a cloth over it, and cool by contact with the air on all sides. We advise all to use the morning directions at first, as this yeast is quicker than any other known.

1193. White Bread, Old Method.
TO MAKE OVER NIGHT.

Dissolve one cake of Gaff, Fleischmann & Co.'s yeast in two quarts of water. Add two tablespoonfuls, each, of salt, butter, and sugar; also sifted flour enough to make a moderately stiff dough. Knead thoroughly. In the morning, when thoroughly light, make into four loaves and let stand about one hour, or till light, then bake. Keep dough moderately warm, in winter, in warm weather, cool.

1194. White Bread, Quick Method.
MAKES FOUR LOAVES.

Dissolve thoroughly one cake of Gaff, Fleischmann & Co.'s compressed yeast in one pint of lukewarm water. Add one tablespoonful each of salt, sugar and butter; also sufficient flour to make dough as soft as can be handled. Set in a warm place to rise. When light, make into loaves.

1195. Parker House Rolls.
MAKES THIRTY ROLLS.

Two quarts of flour, measure after sifting; mix with it one tablespoonful of sugar, one teaspoonful of salt, rub in one tablespoonful of lard or butter. Boil one pint of milk and cool it; when lukewarm, add one-half of a cake of Gaff, Fleischmann & Co.'s compressed yeast, dissolved in one-half of a cup of lukewarm water or milk. Make a hole in the flour and pour in the milk and yeast, stirring in just flour enough to make a thin batter. Cover and let rise over night, and in the morning stir in the rest of the flour and knead for twenty minutes, using no more flour. The dough should be very stiff. Let it rise again; when light, roll out one-half an inch thick and cut with a round or oval cutter. Fold the edges together; rise again, well covered, until very light. Bake ten or fifteen minutes in a very hot oven. If not mixed over night, use a whole cake of yeast.

1196. Buckwheat Cakes.

Dissolve one cake of Gaff, Fleischmann & Co.'s compressed yeast in one and one-half quarts of water or milk; add one teaspoonful of salt, two tablespoonfuls of molasses or sugar, two tablespoonfuls of wheat flour, and sufficient buckwheat (about two quarts) flour to make a batter. Let it rise over night; in the morning thin if necessary and fry on a griddle. If wanted quick, use double quantity of yeast.

1197. Excellent Buns.

Dissolve one-half a cake of Gaff, Fleischmann & Co.'s compressed yeast in two cups of milk which has been boiled and cooled; add one-half of a teaspoonful of salt, one tablespoonful of sugar, and flour to make a stiff batter. Let it rise over night; in the morning add one cupful of sugar, one-half of a cupful of melted or softened butter, and flour to make it stiff enough to knead. Let it rise again until light, then shape into small biscuit and rise again. Bake in a hot oven until brown, then rub over tops with milk and sugar, and let stand in oven a few minutes longer. Makes two dozen.

1198. Muffins, *(Mrs. Coulson.)*

ARTICLES.—Twelve heaping tablespoonfuls of flour, two heaping teaspoonfuls of baking powder, a piece of butter half the size of an egg, half of a teaspoonful of salt, one egg, sufficient milk to make a batter, a little thicker than pancake batter.

DIRECTIONS.—Mix the flour and baking powder together; then add the salt, next milk enough to produce a smooth paste, melt the butter and add it, then the egg well beaten, if the batter is not thin enough, add more milk. Bake in muffin rings in a quick oven.

1199. Hints for Housekeepers.

Boiling water will remove tea stains and many fruit stains; pour the water through the stain, and thus prevent it from spreading through the fabric. Ripe tomatoes will remove ink and other stains from white cloth; also from the hands. A teaspoonful of turpentine boiled with white clothes will aid the whitening process. Boiled starch is improved by the addition of a little spermaceti, or salt, or both, or gum arabic dissolved. Beeswax and salt will make flat-irons as smooth as glass; tie a lump of wax in a cloth, and keep it for that purpose, when the irons are hot rub them with the wax rag, then scour with a paper or rag sprinkled with salt. Kerosene will soften boots or shoes hardened by water, and render them as pliable as when new. Kerosene will make the kettles as bright as new; saturate a woolen rag and rub with it; it will also remove stains from varnished furniture. If a shirt-bosom or any other article has been scorched in ironing, lay it where bright sun will fall directly on it; it will take it entirely out. Fish may be scaled much easier by dipping them in boiling water for a minute. Cool rain water and soda will remove machine grease from washable goods. Half a dozen onions planted in the cellar where they can get a little light, will do much towards absorbing and correcting the atmospheric impurities that are apt to lurk in such places.

1200. Value of Food.

AND TIME REQUIRED FOR DIGESTION.

	Per cent. of nutriment.	Time of digestion. h m		Per cent. of nutriment.	Time of digestion. h m
Apples	17	1.30	Milk	7	2.15
Barley	92	2.00	Mutton	30	3.15
Beans	87	2.30	Oatmeal	74	3.30
Beef	33	2.30	Peas	93	3.30
Bread	80	3.30	Peaches	25	2.00
Butter	85	3.00	Pears	16	3.30
Cabbage	8	4.30	Plums	29	2.30
Carrots	14	3.30	Pork	21	5.15
Cherries	25	2.00	Potatoes	20	2.30
Chickens	27	2.45	Rice	88	1.00
Codfish	21	2.00	Soup, Barley	20	1.30
Cucumbers	2	3.30	Strawberries	12	2.00
Eggs	23	1.30	Turnips	8	3.50
Grapes	27	2.30	Veal	25	4.30
Gooseberries	19	2.30	Venison	22	1.30
Melons	3	2.00			

INDEX TO PART I.

A

Apples .... Page 217
" to choose,.... Recipe 731
" how to keep,........ 732
" specked, to save.... 733
" dumplings, boiled... 734
" dumplings, baked... 735
" custard pies........ 736
" dried, pies......... 737
" dried, sauce........ 738
" fritters, Sadies'.... 739
" and crumb pudding.. 740
" marmalade, Italian.. 741
" jelly, clear......... 742
" ginger, Chinese..... 743
" jelly, Ida's......... 744
" mould and cream.... 745
" meringue, French... 746
" mince meat......... 747
" and almond pudding. 748
" sauce 749
" souffle, French...... 750
" tart and custard..... 751
" for dessert.......... 752
" trifle, Grace's...... 753
" suet pudding........ 754
" pudding, French.... 755
" pie, green.......... 756
Apothecaries fluid measure.. 828
   do   weight 831
Avoirdupois weight......... 832

B

Beans and Peas........Page 66
Beans, to improve,...Recipe 198
" baked, New Eng style 199
" baked, New York style 200
" dried, boiled pudding. 201
" dried, baked pudding. 202
" dried whole, French style 203
" dried, stewed........ 204
" and bacon, English
   style............... 205
" and meat........... 206
" a la creme.......... 207
" soup 208
" succotash in winter.. 209
" "   in summer. 210

Bedbug exterminator........ 818
Biscuits, etc 500
Bleeding of the nose, remedy 809
Book trade, table for........ 835
Breakfast table, the..... Page 9
Brains, animals'............ 85
" ox, to prepare, Recipe 286
" calves, hogs and sheep
   to prepare........... 287
" boiled, French style 288
" and tongue........... 289
" made of mock oysters 290
" fried, French style.. 291
" baked 292
" au beurre noir 293
" boiled 294
" stewed in wine...... 295
" a la matelote........ 296
" croquettes of....... 297
" a la Worcestershire. 298
Bread, Biscuit, Rolls__Page 145
" Yeast, to make excel-
      lent, Recipe 500
" with soda and cream
   of tartar............. 505
" or biscuit of cornmeal 507
" of rye or wheat flour
   with yeast........... 508
" of graham flour...... 509
" of graham and white 510
" of flour and potatoes. 511
" of rice.............. 512
" unleavened 528
" without yeast or soda 513
" stale, uses for....... 534
Breakfast biscuit............ 522
Biscuits, velvet............. 519
" of sponge flour..... 520
" of rye and wheat
   flour for tea........ 521
" of milk............. 523
" of sour milk........ 524
" graham 531
Crackers of rye or wheat
   flour............... 525
Crisps of wheat meal...... 532
Diamonds of graham flour 530
Drop cakes of rye or wheat 526
Gems, of graham flour.... 529

INDEX TO PART I.

Rolls, bakers' 517
" English............. 516
" French 514
" Irish 515
Twists, bakers' 518
Burns, remedy for............ 805

C

Cakes ....Page 121
" chocolate......Recipe 416
" delicate............. 423
" hunting nut......... 418
" jelly 425
" lemon 421
" plum 422
" pound 420
" rock 413
" snow 415
" strawberry short..... 414
" sponge,............. 419
" silver or bride's..... 426
" white cup........... 427
Camphor lard................ 808
Cheese ....Page 54
" custard and macaroni
                    Recipe 145
" fingers 146
" macaroni and fish.... 149
" improved Welsh rarebit 141
" and macaroni, French 144
" and macaroni........ 148
" mock crab, sailor
    fashion.............. 150
" pastry remakins..... 147
" sandwich............ 143
" stewed.............. 142
Chocolate 4
Chocolate, French............ 5
Classification .... Page 6
Cocoa ....Recipe 4
Cocoanuts ....Page 30
" bread pudding
                    Recipe 38
" cake................ 47
" custard............. 42
" and corn starch
    pudding........... 40
" ginger bread....... 45
" pound cake........ 46
" pie 43
" pie, rich.......... 44

Cocoanut pudding and pies,
    plain 39
" pudding, very rich 41
Coffee, French............... 8
Color, for ices, creams, ices,
    custard and jellies, Page 37
Brown............Recipe 65
Purple...................... 61
Pink 64
Red 60
White 63
Yellow 62
Cornstarch ....Page 43
" apple souffle, Recipe 99
" cake 105
" cocoanut jelly..... 103
" and cocoanut pies_ 112
" and condensed
    milk 114
" coffee 102
" color for creams... 110
" charlotte russe.... 116
" creams, general recipes for.......... 106
" custards, general
    recipes for........ 108
" thin custard 97
" cup pudding...... 100
" fruit blanc mange_ 101
" jellies, general recipes for.......... 107
" milk or cream, in_ 113
" muffled cake..... 98
" omelets........... 104
" puddings, general
    recipes for........ 109
" sauces............ 111
" snow 115
Counting.................... 833
Cream, mock................ 15
" real 13
" toast 14
Croquettes of rice........... 610
Curds....................... 18
Custard chocolate........... 24
" of condensed milk.. 22
" English 20
" French 21
" fruit............... 23
" frozen 55
" ices 57
" plain 19

INDEX TO PART I. 397

D

Dinner table .... Page 10
Distances from Buffalo to the principal points of the globe .... Recipe 836
Doughnuts, raised 593
" yeast 594
" fine 595
" plain cheap 596
Dry measure 829
Duties, maid of all work, Page 12
Dishes for dessert .... Page 189
   A cake trifle .... Recipe 639
   Apple hedgehog 644
   Apple de par 643
   Apple snow 642
   Custard with jelly 637
   Gateau de pomme 646
   Gooseberry fool 645
   Iced fruits 648
   Orange sponge 641
   Rice and pears 640
   Stewed plums 649
   " pears 650
   " fruit a compote 647
   Tipsey cake 638
Diarrhœa mixture 803
Dysentery or cholera infantum remedy ... Recipe 811

E

Eau sedatif .... Recipe 807
Ear-ache remedy 813
Eggs .... Page 49
" baked .... Recipe 122
" boiled 123
" dropped 124
" fried 125
" fricassee 127
" omelet with ham, herbs or meat 129
" poached 121
" plain omelet 128
" scrambled 126
" to preserve 117
" " with lime 120
" " mucilage 118
" to preserve with mutton fat 119

F

Farina .... Page 29
" baked pudding .... Recipe 36

Farina, boiled, plain 33
" boiled plum pudding 35
" ice pudding 34
Fish, salt .... Page 57
" best way to soak .... Recipe 151
" best way to cook 152
" balls 155
" chowder 568
" croquettes 156
" down east dinner 154
" East India style 166
" English baked 163
" French stew 164
" fritters 157
" fricasseed 162
" Italian style 167
" lobster 159
" oyster 160
" Parisian style 165
" sauce 153
" spiced, soused 158
" stewed 161
Flour, bread, etc .... Page 144
Foreign money, value, Recipe 820
Fried pastry, etc .... Page 177
   To fry pastry .... Recipe 592
Fried crullers 597
" crackers 598
" nonesuch 615
" Yankee marvels 616
" wonders 599
" Spanish puffs 600
" lemon turnovers 601
Fritters, fruit 606
" orange 607
" batter of all kinds 608
" bread 609
Freezing creams, etc 87
Fruit creams, ices, etc 57

G

Gelatine and Isinglass Page 33
Gingerbread 184
" rich .... Recipe 621
" cheap 622
" common 424
" cakes 623
" loaf 624
" honey comb 625
" cocoanut or almond 626
" orange 627
" nuts 628

Gingerbread, sugar crisps	629
" snaps	417
" molasses crisps	630
" fruit cake	631
" soft	632
" spice	633
" puffs	634
" pudding	635
Guarantee _____ Page	21
Grease spots, to remove	815

H

Hashes and entrees of cold meat _____ Recipe	373
" to make very good	374
Hominy _____ Page	61
" bread _____ Recipe	171
" cakes	170
" cakes	175
" fried	169
" gruel	174
" muffins	172
" plain boiled	168
" samp, boiled	173
Household remedies ___ Page	234
Household recipes	237

I

Ice creams _____ Page	35
" to make __ Recipe	54
" apple	73
" blackberry	68
" cherry	77
" cinnamon	83
" clove and allspice	85
" ginger	81
" gooseberry	70
" grape	78
" lemon	80
" nutmeg	82
" orange	79
" pear	74
" peach	76
" pine apple	72
" quince	75
" red currant	71
" raspberry	67
" strawberry	66
" vanilla	84
" whortleberry	69
" freezers	86
" spice	58
" with essences	59

Ice creams of jellies ____ Page	207
" " __ Recipe	691
" " light	692
" to improve	693
" of jelly, gold	694
" " silver	695
" " gold and silver	696
" of jelly, tapioca	697
" " manioca	698
" " cassava	699
" " arrow root	700
" " sago	701
" " rice	702
" " farina	703
" " maizena	704
" " cornstarch	705
" " calves' feet	706
" " cocoanut	707
" " grape	708
" " banana	709
" " wine, for invalids	710
" of jelly, very cheap	711
" " Irish moss	712
Ices, fruit	57
Ice cream, rich _____ Page	212
" "almond, Recipe	727
" " burnt	721
" " Bohemian	718
" " Chester	719
" " chocolate	713
" " coffee	714
" " German	726
" " housewife's	730
" " imperial	722
" " noyeau	724
" " pistachio	723
" " ratafia	717
" Sicilian	728
" Spanish,	720
" snow	729
" spring	725
" tea	715
" velvet	716
Indian meal, mush, bread, cake, puddings, etc. _____ Page	132
" and hogshead cheese __ Recipe	454
" and broth mush	455
" plain	456
" fried	457

INDEX TO PART I. 399

Indian Meal, corn bread
" (*Mrs Prudence's*) 458
" brown bread.. 459
" brown bread, New England.. 460
" brown bread with soda..... 461
" Washington's bread......... 462
" bread with yeast 463
" bread, togus... 464
" bread with suet 465
" mush bread... 466
" and wheat flour bread......... 467
" and wheat bread 468
" Johnny bread.. 469
" bread, grandmother's...... 470
" pone or biscuit 471
" batter biscuit Blot's......... 472
" and rye biscuit mother's...... 473
" and egg biscuit 474
" biscuit........ 475
" muffins....... 476
" wafers........ 477
" and wheat crumpets.......... 478
" fadge......... 479
" griddle cakes.. 480
" griddle cakes of all kinds...... 481
" drop nuts...... 482
" omelets....... 483
" pound cake, rich 484
" molasses cake. 485
" pudding without eggs.......... 286
" fruit and coffee cake.......... 487
" suet pudding... 488
" baked pudding. 489
" baked English pudding....... 490
" New England pudding....... 491
" French baked pudding...... 492
" steamed plum pudding........ 493
" and cheese boiled pudding. 494

Indian Meal, and pork boiled pudding....... 495
" and fruit boiled pudding........ 496
" and dried apple boiled pudding. 497
" and apple dowdy 498
" freedman's hoe cake......... 499

J

Jellies................Page 33
Jelly stock, plain....Recipe 48
" " to clarify...... 49
" lemon................. 50
" orange 51
" French................. 52
" twenty kinds.......... 53
" ice creams............ 691

K

Kid glove cleaning fluid, Recipe 816

L

Laws of business....Recipe 821
Lait de poule................ 806
Liquid measure.............. 827
Linear or long measure..... 823
Lobsters..............Page 168
" boiled plain, Recipe 571
" to boil............... 570
" broiled............. 576
" buttered............ 577
" balls 587
" croquettes 591
" curry of............. 581
" curry of, French.... 580
" cutlets fried in batter 584
" cutlets, plain....... 585
" cutlets, East India style 586
" to choose............ 569
" to dress............. 572
" fricasseed........... 582
" minced.............. 589
" mutton of........... 579
" pie.................. 588
" roasted 583
" salad 573
" scolloped 574
" scolloped, English way................. 575

Lobster soup		590
" stew		578

M

Maizena		Page	41
"	blanc mange, Recipe		89
"	cream cake		94
"	custard		88
"	floating island		93
"	pudding, baked		92
"	" lemon		90
"	" plain		91
"	sponge cake		96
Manioca		Page	205
"	blanc mange, Recipe		688
"	caudle for invalids		689
"	pudding		686
"	pudding, apple		687
"	soup		690
Measures of weight		Page	243
Meats			76
"	general recipes for cooking		107
"	baking	Recipe	366
"	boiling		367
"	broiling		368
"	cold		375
"	entrees of cold		376
"	frying		369
"	" semi		370
"	" covered		371
"	" with tomatoes		372
"	force		377
"	roasting		365
"	beef hearts	Page	76
"	" roasted, Recipe		245
"	" baked, stuffed		246
"	" boiled, stuffed		247
"	" stewed, whole		248
"	" sliced, stewed		249
"	" broiled		250
"	" fried		251
"	" soup		252
"	" corned		253
"	" hash		254
"	" pie meat		255
"	beef palates	Page	79
"	" to prepare, Recipe		264
"	" to stew		265
"	" to broil		266
"	" to fry		267

Meats, beef palates, au friture			268
"	" potted like venison		358
"	" pressed		359
"	beef rolled to eat like hare		356
"	calves' heads, and feet, Page		97
"	" a la maitre d'hotel Recipe		336
"	" boiled		334
"	" colored		337
"	" cheese		333
"	" fricassee		338
"	" hashed		339
"	" mock turtle		332
"	" stewed		335
"	hams, shoulders and bacon		Page 102
"	hams, shoulders and bacon, to prepare, Recipe		349
"	hams, shoulders and bacon, to steam		350
"	hams, shoulders and bacon, to boil		351
"	hams, shoulders and bacon, to bake		352
"	hams, shoulders and bacon, to bake, boil, etc.		353
"	haslets	Page	92
"	" to broil	Recipe	313
"	" to fry		312
"	" to stew		314
"	" and milk		315
"	hogs' heads and feet, Page		82
"	hogs' heads and feet, baked	Recipe	276
"	hogs' heads and feet cheese		272
"	hogs' heads and feet, corned		279
"	hogs' heads and feet, haslets and kidneys, stewed		277
"	hogs' heads and feet cheese improved		273
"	hogs' heads and feet, soused		274
"	hogs' heads and feet, stuffed		275
"	kidneys	Page	90

INDEX TO PART I.   401

Meats kidneys to prepare,
          Recipe 302
"   "   baked 308
"   "   beef, stewed.. 304
"   "   broiled 307
"   "   fried 306
"   "   gravy 310
"   "   rissoles of.... 305
"   "   roast 311
"   "   saute au vin... 309
"   "   stews......... 303
"   lambs' head and pluck. 340
"   liver............ Page 100
"   " to prepare, Recipe 341
"   " a la mode,(French) 348
"   " and bacon........ 344
"   " baked 345
"   " broiled 342
"   " fried 343
"   " saute 346
"   " stewed - 347
"   lights and lungs, Page 89
"   "   " to pre-
               pare,
               Recipe 299
"   "   "   fried .. 300
"   "   "   stewed 301
"   marrow bones, boiled,
      on toast............... 360
"   mutton, loin of, to eat
      like venison........... 361
"   mutton, shoulder of,
      spiced................. 362
"   ox heads........ Page 84
"   oxcheek cheese(Ameri-
      can style)..... Recipe 280
"   ox cheek, corned..... 283
"   "   "   hash......... 284
"   "   "   pies 285
"   "   "   stewed(Ger-
               man style). 281
"   "   "   stewed(French
               style)....... 282
"   ox heels......... Page 93
"   "   "   to clean and
              prepare, Recipe 316
"   "   "   boiled 317
"   "   "   fried 319
"   "   "   soup 320
"   "   "   stewed 318
"   ox tail soup............ 354
"   pigs' feet .... Page 94
"   "   broiled, Recipe 324
"   "   fried.......... 322

"   "   fried in butter 325
"   "   fricasseed 326
"   "   mock brawn.. 329
"   "   pettitoes 330
"   "   picked........ 323
"   "   pickled 327
"   "   stewed 321
"   "   with onions... 331
"   "   to cook thirty
              other ways... 328
"   pigs' cheek........... 278
"   sheeps' head, French. 271
"   "   trotters, boiled. 269
"   "   "   270
"   tongues............... 355
"   "   ox, potted..... 357
Mistress of the house... Page 6
Milk....................... 22
"   boiled.......... Recipe 1
"   and bread............. 12
"   coffee 7
"   porridge.............. 16
"   to preserve........... 2
"   rice 6
"   suet 11
"   tea................... 9
Mosquito ointment.......... 802
Mush................... Page 133
"   of graham flour, Recipe 527
"   of oatmeal............. 533

N

Nursery recipes........ Page 236

O

Oysters .... Page 158
"   baked........ Recipe 541
"   boiled 542
"   broiled 543
"   catsup 566
"   chowder boiled..... 550
"   "   "   baked..... 551
"   cracker salad....... 567
"   devilled 559
"   fried 544
"   fritters, French style. 554
"   "   557
"   Indian curried...... 556
"   marinade........... 555
"   meat................ 558
"   minced.............. 553
"   omelet 560
"   patties, plain........ 561
"   pie 562

INDEX TO PART I.

Oysters pickled 563
  "   raw 538
  "   roast in the shell.... 540
  "   scolloped 564
  "   "   French style   565
  "   steamed, Washington
         style 539
  "   stewed, plain 545
  "   "   with milk 546
  "   "   " cream ... 547
  "   "   " eggs 548
  "   "   " wine, ..
         ....French style 549
  "   to feed 535
  "   to keep alive and good 536
  "   to open 537

P

Pancakes, batter .....Recipe 603
  "   Irish 605
  "   rye flour 604
  "   snow 602
Paper trade, table for 834
Pastry and pies ....Page 27
  Housefat, how to clarify,
         Recipe 428
Pies, apple, sweet 433
  "   "   sour 434
  "   "   mock green 435
  "   "   mock 436
  "   "   and pie-plant .. 437
  "   blackberry 445
  "   cherry 443
  "   cranberry 447
  "   currant 450
  "   custard 442
  "   gooseberry 451
  "   imitation mince 453
  "   mince meat for 452
  "   peach 448
  "   pie-plant 438
  "   plum 449
  "   pumpkin 439
  "   raspberry 444
  "   squash 440
  "   sweet potato 441
  "   whortleberry 446
Paste, French puff 431
  "   other 432
  "   hygienic 429
  "   plain pie crust 430
Patties and pies 618
  "   "   " 619
  "   of bread 620

Patty paste fried 617
Peas, baked 215
  "   boiled 212
  "   green, in summer 213
  "   "   in winter 211
  "   pudding, boiled 214
  "   "   " 216
  "   soup 217
  "   "   in winter 218
Pickling, vegetables and fruit
                        Page 200
  "   the vinegar, Recipe 668
  "   "   vegetables and
             fruit 669
  "   "   cooking utensils 670
  "   "   bottles, jars or
             vessels 671
  "   from July to October 672
  "   beets 680
  "   barberries 684
Potatoes ....Page 62
Pickling, cabbage 685
  "   cauliflower 681
  "   East India piccalilly 674
  "   Indian pickle to
         keep ten years 673
  "   onions 672
  "   plums like olives 676
  "   peaches 677
  "   peppers 683
  "   tomatoes, whole 679
  "   "   green pic-
                  calilly 678
  "   vegetables, any 675
  "   a la maitre d'hotel,
             Recipe 192
  "   a la Parisienne 197
  "   baked, chopped 184
  "   to bake 179
  "   boiled 189
  "   to boil old 177
  "   to boil new 178
  "   browned, mashed 181
  "   to brown with meat 194
  "   cakes 182
  "   fried cold 185
  "   fried raw 186
  "   fry light brown or
         swelled 188
  "   hashed 195
  "   mashed 180
  "   puffs 191
  "   ribbons 187
  "   rissoles 190

INDEX TO PART I. 403

Pickling, souffle	196
" stuffed	193
" stewed	183
" steamed	186
Poisoning, advice in cases of	810
Postage, rates of	819
Preserves, jams, jellies, etc., Page	195
" the fruit Recipe	651
" " sugar	652
" " preserving kettles	653
" " proportion of fruit and sugar	654
" to keep good	655
" damson cheese	656
" fruit preserved without cooking	665
" fruit jam	666
" " ginger	667
" green gooseberry jam	657
" green gooseberry jelly	658
" peach, without boiling	664
" plum	661
" rhubarb marmalade	662
" " and orange	663
" strawberry jam	659
" " jelly	660
Pudding Page	115
" arrowroot, baked, Recipe	399
" " boiled	398
" best cheap, (Mrs. B.)	636
" condensed milk, baked	409
" " " boiled	408
" farina	410
" macaroni, baked	404
" " boiled	402
" pork	412
" sago, baked	401
" " boiled	400
" Spanish	411
" tapioca, baked	407
" " boiled	406
" vermicelli, baked	405
" " boiled	403

R

Rice Page	27
" and apples Recipe	31
" boiled	27
" " whole	30
Rice, fritters	32
" for children	28
" gruel	26
" pudding	29
" water	25

S

Sauces for meat Page	71
Sauce, butter Recipe	221
" caper	228
" celery	225
" egg	226
" mint	219
" maitre d'hotel	229
" New England egg	224
" onion	220
" oyster	227
" potato	223
" salad	230
" tomato	222
" for puddings, pies, etc. Page	73
" banana Recipe	239
" cold brandy	236
" " butter	237
" condensed milk, hard	240
" custard for tarts, puddings, etc.	231
" dried apple, French style	235
" dried fruit sauce of any kind	244
" egg, for pudding	232
" fruit	233
" hot milk	242
" orange, hard	238
" transparent	241
" water	243
" wine	234
Scurf, for taking away	812
Sick room, the Page	225
" hints to attendants	225
" cookery, arrowroot gruel, Recipe	782
" cookery, apple water	785
" cookery, alum whey	793
" cookery, beef tea	769
" " barley coffee	763
" cookery, boiled flour	786
" cookery, cooling drinks for fever	774

INDEX TO PART I.

Sick room, cookery, chicken broth 790
" cookery, calves' feet jelly 795
" cookery, chicken panada 800
" cookery, egg brandy 765
" cookery, egg nog 767
" " flax seed tea 762
" cookery, fruit drinks for invalids 771
" cookery, gum arabic mixture.. 776
" cookery, gruel... 759
" " Irish moss jelly 781
" cookery, isinglass jelly 784
" cookery, milk punch 766
" cookery, milk porridge 783
" cookery, mucilage of elm bark. 779
" cookery, mutton tea 788
" cookery, mutton broth 789
" cookery, mustard whey 794
" cookery, oatmeal coffee 764
" cookery, orange whey 796
" cookery, panada. 777
" " porridge French 801
" cookery, quince wine 775
" cookery, refreshing drinks for fevers 770
" cookery, rice water 769
" cookery, rice gruel 773
" " rennet whey 791
" " sago tea... 768
" " " gruel... 778
" " sweet whey 797
" " sippets 799
" " tea 757
" " toast 758

Sick room cookery, toast water 761
" " tapioca jelly 780
" " vegetable soup 787
" cookery, vinegar whey 792
" cookery, water gruel 772
" cookery, wine whey 798
" cookery, soups.. 363
" " stews . 364
Scurf cure 812
Square measure.. 825
Stings of hornets, wasps and bees 814
Surveyors' long measure.... 824

T

Table, the .... Page 7
Tea table, the 11
Tea .... Recipe 10
Tomatoes .... Page 52
" baked .... Recipe 133
" " whole 132
" boiled 135
" figs 140
" fritters 134
" leather 137
" paste 136
" preserved 139
" raw 130
" sauce 138
" stewed 131
Tooth powder 804
Troy weight 830
Tripe .... Page 78
" baked .... Recipe 259
" broiled 258
" fried plain 256
" " in butter 257
" fricasseed 263
" soused 260
" stewed plain 261
" " with onions.. 262

V

Vegetables .... Page 110
" carrots, fried Recipe 382
" " Flemishway 383
" " mashed 385
" " stewed 384

Vegetables, celery, fried	392
" " with cream	391
" " with milk	390
" cucumbers, to dress	396
" " a la poulette	397
" cucumbers, to roast	395
" " to stew	393
" " to stuff and boil	394
" onions, a la creme	388
" " baked	387
" " to stew brown	386
" onions, to stuff	389
" succotash in summer	210
" succotash in winter	209
" turnips, fried	380
" " mashed with onions	379
" turnips, plain boiled	378
" " puree	381

W

Waffles Recipe	612
" of eggs	614
" of yeast	613
Wafers	611
Washing fluid	817
Water ices	56
Weight of bushel, legal	822
Weights and measures Page	240
Wheaten grits Recipe	37
Wheys, recipes for	17
Widow Prudence's story, Page	18
Wood measure Recipe	826

Y

Yeast, bakers', how to make, Recipe	502
" cakes, how to make	501
" hop " " "	504
" potato " " "	503
" powder " " "	506

INDEX TO PART II.

A

Additional Recipes ___Page 390

B

Bavarian Cream____Recipe 1060
" with chocolate 1061
" strawberries 1062
Beverages, fancy_____Page 368
brandy cocktails, Recipe 1178
" smash_____ 1174
champagne cobbler____ 1176
Crimean cup a la Mar-
mora 1182
egg nog_____ 1169
" _____ 1170
" _____ 1171
" with sherry____ 1172
egg flip _____ 1181
mint julep_____ 1173
mulled wine with eggs 1179
port wine sangaree____ 1180
punch _____ 1145
" Audubon Club__ 1168
" brandy_____ 1146
" " _____ 1147
" brandy&rum,hot 1149
" claret_____ 1154
" curacoa_____ 1157
" Gothic_____ 1167
" gin_____ 1152
" imperial _____ 1163
" Irish whiskey___ 1150
" Mississippi_____ 1148
" milk_____ 1159
" milk, English __ 1161
" milk, hot_____ 1160
" pine apple _____ 1156
" port wine _____ 1155
" regent's_____ 1162
" Roman _____ 1158
" Rocky Mountain 1164
" royal _____ 1166
" sherry _____ 1153
" tip top_____ 1165
" whiskey _____ 1151
sherry cobbler_____ 1175
Tom and Jerry _____ 1183
whiskey cobbler _____ 1177

Bills of fare_____ 1185
Blanc mange of corn starch 1056
" " arrow root 1057
Bouillon for lunches_____ 869
Buckwheat cakes _____ 1196
Buns _____ 1197
Bread, white __ _____ 1192
" old method___ 1193
" quick method 1194

C

Cakes for breakfast, dessert,
tea, etc____Page 344
almond snaps ____Recipe 1116
" cake_____ 1087
angel's food_____ 1125
cinnamon _____ 1117
charlotte russe_____ 1059
chocolate _____ 1128
" layer _____ 1139
coffee_____ 1072
cocoanut _____ 1090
" layer _____ 1140
chocolate eclaires_____ 1108
cocoanut drops_____ 1109
cookies _____ 1103
cookies, seed_____ 1113
cream, Boston_____ 1114
" layer _____ 1134
" " _____ 1135
" " _____ 1136
cup _____ 1080
delicate_____ 1120
" _____ 1121
dolly varden_____ 1129
doughnuts_____ 1106
drop, Ricka's _____ 1101
dumplings, strawberry__ 1097
fruit_____ 1084
" _____ 1085
" _____ 1086
fried hard_____ 1104
" _____ 1105
" French _____ 1107
frosting, chocolate _____ 1141
" cocoanut_____ 1144
" egg _____ 1143
" sugar_____ 1142
fritters, green corn_____ 1067

INDEX TO PART II.

Cakes, gingerbread, soft	1095
gold	1078
ice cream	1118
"	1119
jelly, roll	1131
"	1132
" layer	1133
lemon	1082
loaf	1079
marble	1075
"	1076
macaronies	1110
maccaroons	1111
minnehaha	1130
muffins, quick	1068
nut	1089
" layer	1138
pednuns	1100
plum, little	1059
pop-overs	1071
pound cake	1091
"	1092
"	1093
puffs, German	1070
Sally Lunns	1069
silver	1077
spice	1073
"	1074
sponge	1127
" mother's	1126
" white	1123
" "	1124
" lemon layer	1137
stirred	1081
short cake, strawberry	1098
snow balls	1102
snaps, lemon	1112
tea	1096
tip top	1083
walnut	1088
Winchester biscuit	1094
white	1122
Carving ____ Page	297
Catsup, tomato ____ Recipe	998
Chickens ____ Page	300
spring, how to improve Recipe	931
" baked	932
broiled	933
broiled and roasted	934
croquettes	936
fricasseed	935
Clams ____ Page	293
Combination of dishes ____ Recipe	1189

Crabs, lobsters, etc ____ Page	294
Custard, soft ____ Recipe	1052

D

Dinners for company, to prepare	1184
Ducks, geese & game birds Page	302
roasted ____ Recipe	937
stewed	939
wild	938

F

Fish ____ Page	279
to select ____ Recipe	882
cod, salt to boil	889
" " with cream	890
baked	883
" with wine	884
boiled	885
broiled	886
bread stuffing for	904
chowder	893
au gratin	894
a la creme	895
fried	887
haddock, baked	902
halibut steak	898
potted	892
stewed, en matelote	888
spiced	891
mackerel, fresh to broil	896
" salt "	897
meat stuffing for	905
sturgeon, baked	901
" steak	900
" stewed	899
turbot	903
Floating island	1058
Frogs, fried	921
" fricasseed	920
Frosting for cakes, chocolate	1141
" " cocoanut	1144
" " egg	1143
" " sugar	1142

G

Game ____ Page	302
Goose, roast ____ Recipe	940
" stuffing	941
Grouse	945

H

Hints for housekeepers	1199

L

Lobsters ....Page 294

M

Meats ....Page 308
  beef a la mode ...Recipe 958
  " roast 957
  beefsteak to broil 959
  "   "   960
  "   for extra company 962
  "   smothered in
         onions 961
  beef croquettes 964
  " roll 963
  lamb ....Page 316
  " chops a la royal ....
             Recipe 981
  " croquettes 982
  mutton ....Page 313
    " broiled leg, Recipe 974
    " cutlets 976
    " haricot 980
    " Irish stew.......... 979
    " stew 977
    " stew, English 978
    " stuffed leg of..... 975
  veal ....Page 310
  " brochette, liver and
        pork ....Recipe 973
  " cutlets 967
  " fourchette........... 972
  " fricatelle 966
  " roast of.............. 965
  " sweet breads 968
  " " fried........... 969
  " " with tomatoes... 970
  " " bread and oyster
        vol-au-vent .. 971
Meat pie 1191
Menus 1185
  " with wines.......... 1187
Muffins, Mrs Coulson...... 1198

N

Noodles, boiled ....Recipe 859
  " plain............. 858

O

Omelets ....Page 323
  " with mushrooms...
            Recipe 1010
  " " oysters........ 1012

Omelets with rum 1014
  " " shrimps...... 1011
  " " souffle 1015
  " sweet for dessert .. 1013
Oysters ....Page 291

P

Partridge...........Recipe 945
Pie, lemon................ 1053
  " " 1054
Pigeons, broiled.......... 944
  " roasted........... 943
  " stewed in broth .. 942
Plover.................... 951
Poultry ....Page 297
  stuffing for ......Recipe 925
  turkey, boiled 928
  " galantine or boned 929
  " or chicken boned
      (a simple way) 930
  " roast 924
Prairie chicken............ 945
Punches 1145
Puddings, etc ....Page 333
  Albany ....Recipe 1041
  bread.................. 1047
  cabinet 1048
  cottage 1039
  easy dessert 1050
  Eve's.................. 1038
  Jink's 1040
  minute................. 1044
  plum 1045
  " with rum or brandy 1034
  queen of............... 1049
  roly poly.............. 1036
  suet 1037
  snow 1043
  " 1051
  tapioca cream 1042
  transparent............ 1046

Q

Quail, parboiled and baked 946
  roasted 947
  scallops of, with truffles 949

R

Rabbits, baked............ 955
  " hasenpfeffer 956
  " stewed 956
Rolls, Parker House 1195

S

Sauces for meats, etc., Page 316
- anchovy ....Recipe 987
- bechamel 992
- bread, for game........ 948
- boiled egg............ 986
- caper 984
- Chili 997
- drawn butter 983
- Espagnol............. 993
- fines herbes 991
- Hollandaise 989
- Mayonnaise 1016
- mushroom 990
- noodle............... 996
- pickle 985
- piquante 995
- poivrade 994
- red Mayonnaise........ 1017
- roux................. 983
- shrimp............... 988
- tomato catsup......... 998

Sauces for puddings ..Page 343
- almond........Recipe 1065
- fairy butter........... 1063
- German.............. 1035
- lemon 1066
- wine 1064

Salads................Page 324
- a la filley......Recipe 1029
- combination .....Page 327
- cold slaw......Recipe 1021
- chicken.............. 1026
- " 1027
- French dressing for ... 1018
- dressing 1032
- lettuce 1019
- lobster............... 1033
- Mayonnaise of cauliflower.. 1023
- " salmon. 1028
- potato 1031
- " 1020
- shrimp............... 1030
- string beans 1025
- tomatoes, a la Mayonnaise 1024
- vegetable 1022

Shell fish............Page 291
- clams, with cream 913
- " chowder, No. 1. 914
- " " No. 2. 915
- " fritters........... 906

Shell fish, crabs, a la Russe. 917
- " soft shell........ 916
- " devilled......... 918
- lobster patties 919
- oyster fritters.......... 906
- " pie or patties... 907
- " omelet 908
- " and macaroni .. 909
- " " tripe........ 911
- " " chestnuts .. 912
- " vol-au-vent 910
- " stuffing 927

Snipe, fried 950
Stuffing for poultry......... 925
- " " chestnut 926
- " " oyster.. 927

Soups ....Page 260
- from stock 262
- not made from stock.. 266
- asparagus....Recipe.. 842
- bean, turtle, No. 1.... 875
- " " No. 2.... 876
- beef with vegetables.... 838
- " kidney 866
- chicken, plain.......... 850
- clam 855
- " No. 2............ 856
- crab................. 864
- cream 868
- crouton or bread dice for 880
- eel 862
- egg balls for.......... 881
- force meat balls for.... 878
- " " " 879
- flour, to brown 877
- Julienne 839
- kidney, beef........... 866
- lobster............... 863
- leek, Scotch........... 844
- macaroni............. 846
- mock turtle... 852
- mullagatawny 840
- Nantucket............. 857
- noodle............... 860
- " with beef or veal.. 861
- oyster 853
- " French 854
- ox-tail 851
- pea, green 870
- " dried, split........ 871
- potato 872
- puree of carrots, French 845
- sago and tomato 841
- sorrel, French......... 843

INDEX TO PART II.

Soup, stock _____ 83
    tomato, summer _____ 873
    " winter _____ 874
    turtle, green _____ 865
    " mock _____ 852
    veal with macaroni ____ 867
    venison _____ 849
    vermicelli _____ 847
    white with almonds ___ 848

T

Terrapins, turtles and tortoises ___Page 296
Terrapins _____Recipe 922
Turtle or tortoise roasted __ 923
Toad in a hole _____ 1190

V

Value of food _____Recipe 1200
Vegetables _____Page 320
    asparagus on toast, Recipe 1003
Vegetables, artichokes ____ 1008
    beets _____ 1007
    cauliflower with white sauce _____ 1005
    cranberries to cook _____ 1009
    oyster plant, stewed _____ 1004
    potatoes, Lyonnaise _____ 999
    " a la neige _____ 1000
    " Saratoga _____ 1001
    spinach _____ 1006
    tomatoes, baked _____ 1002
Venison, broiled _____ 953
    " stewed _____ 954
    " roast saddle of ___ 952
Vol-au-vent _____ 971
    " crust _____ 1055

W

Wines, serving of _____ 1186
    their proper temperature 1188
Woodcock, fried _____ 950

ADDITIONAL RECIPES.

ADDITIONAL RECIPES.

ADDITIONAL RECIPES.

ADDITIONAL RECIPES.

ADDITIONAL RECIPES.

ADDITIONAL RECIPES.

ADDITIONAL RECIPES.

ADDITIONAL RECIPES.

ADDITIONAL RECIPES.

ADDITIONAL RECIPES.

ADDITIONAL RECIPES.

ADDITIONAL RECIPES.

ADDITIONAL RECIPES.

ADDITIONAL RECIPES.

ADDITIONAL RECIPES.

ADDITIONAL RECIPES.

ADDITIONAL RECIPES.

ADDITIONAL RECIPES.

ADDITIONAL RECIPES.

ADDITIONAL RECIPES.

ADDITIONAL RECIPES.

ADDITIONAL RECIPES.

ADDITIONAL RECIPES.

ADDITIONAL RECIPES.

ADDITIONAL RECIPES.

ADDITIONAL RECIPES.

ADDITIONAL RECIPES.

ADDITIONAL RECIPES.

ADDITIONAL RECIPES.

ADDITIONAL RECIPES.

ADDITIONAL RECIPES.

ADDITIONAL RECIPES.

CPSIA information can be obtained
at www.ICGtesting.com
Printed in the USA
LVHW081415200522
719344LV00003B/52